THE CAMBRIDGE SOCIAL HISTORY
OF BRITAIN 1750–1950

VOLUME 2

People and their environment

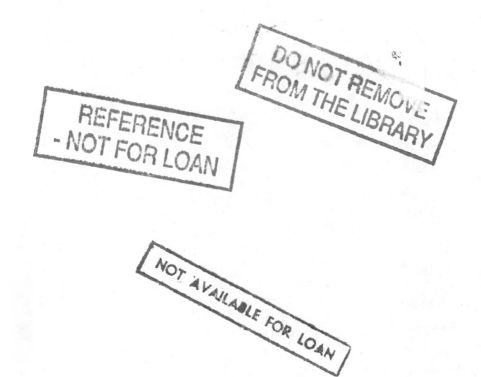

THE CAMBRIDGE SOCIAL HISTORY OF BRITAIN 1750–1950

VOLUME 2
People and their environment

Edited by

F. M. L. THOMPSON
Director of the Institute of Historical Research
and Professor of History, University of London

CAMBRIDGE
UNIVERSITY PRESS

Published by the Press Syndicate of the University of Cambridge
The Pitt Building, Trumpington Street, Cambridge CB2 1RP
40 West 20th Street, New York, NY 10011, USA
10 Stamford Road, Oakleigh, Melbourne 3166, Australia

© Cambridge University Press 1990

First published 1990

Printed in Great Britain at The Bath Press, Avon

British Library cataloguing in publication data

The Cambridge social history of Britain 1750–1950.
Vol. 2. People and their environment.
1. Great Britain. Social conditions, 1714–
I. Thompson, F. M. L. (Francis Michael Longstreth)
941.07

Library of Congress cataloguing in publication data

The Cambridge social history of Britain 1750–1950.
Includes bibliographies and indexes.
Contents: v. 1. Regions and communities –
v. 2. People and their environment – v. 3 Social
agencies and institutions.
1. Great Britain – Social conditions. 2. Social
structure – Great Britain – History. 3. Social
institutions – Great Britain – History. I. Thompson,
F. M. L. (Francis Michael Longstreth).
HN385.C14 1990   306'.0941   89–9840
ISBN 0 521 25788 3 (v. 1)
ISBN 0 521 25789 1 (v. 2)
ISBN 0 521 25790 5 (v. 3)

ISBN 0 521 25789 1 hardback
ISBN 0 521 43815 2 paperback

First paperback edition 1993

Contents

Figures

Tables

Contributors

MICHAEL ANDERSON is Professor of Economic History at the University of Edinburgh. He has made many contributions to the history of family structure, including *Family Structure in Nineteenth-Century Lancashire* (1971), *Approaches to the History of the Western Family, 1500–1914* (1980), and *Population Change in North-Western Europe, 1750–1850* (1987).

H. CUNNINGHAM is Senior Lecturer in History at the University of Kent at Canterbury. His work on the history of leisure and popular culture includes *Leisure in the Industrial Revolution, c. 1780–c. 1880* (1980).

M. J. DAUNTON is Professor of Modern History at University College London. He works chiefly in the field of urban and housing history, with books on *Coal Metropolis: Cardiff, 1870–1914* (1977), *House and Home in the Victorian City: Working-Class Housing, 1850–1914* (1983), and *A Property-Owning Democracy? Housing in Britain* (1987).

LEONORE DAVIDOFF is Research Professor in Social History at the University of Essex. Her work on the family, domesticity, and the separate spheres of women and men includes *The Best Circles: Society, Etiquette and the Season* (1973), and, with Catherine Hall, *Family Fortunes: Men and Women of the English Middle Class, 1780–1850* (1987).

PATRICK JOYCE is Lecturer in Modern History at the University of Manchester. Deeply interested in the social history of work, he has published *Work, Society and Politics: The Culture of the Factory in Later Victorian England* (1980), and edited *The Historical Meanings of Work* (1987).

D. J. ODDY is Professor of Economic History at the Polytechnic of Central London. He has written many articles on the history of diet and nutrition in the nineteenth century, and edited, with Derek Miller, *Diet and Health in Modern Britain* (1985).

Editorial preface

The historian's job is to find out about the past and make it intelligible and accessible to the present. Such an apparently straightforward task is by no means as simple as it may sound. Finding out what happened and interpreting it in patterns and designs which make sense of the past are complicated and demanding processes, requiring scholarship and expertise of a high order, but their value remains limited unless the results are communicated in a language and form which reach beyond the restricted circle of fellow-specialists. Communication is particularly important for social history, a field whose contours and boundaries have altered out of all recognition in the last generation, a subject which is bubbling with the vitality of an outpouring of monographs and journal articles, and a young discipline which lacks the settled framework of a conventional orthodoxy or a received interpretation within which or against which new departures or open rebellions can be placed or assessed. The old stand-bys – constitutional history, political history, diplomatic history, ecclesiastical history, for example – all have these established frameworks which define their subject matters and enshrine explanations of the course of history. These are widely familiar, although often misleading or mistaken; this means that the terms of debate are well understood, that revisions are easily recognised as revisions, and that the iconoclasm of overturning entrenched views does not go unnoticed. Economic history, while much younger than these other subjects, has nevertheless established its rules of enquiry, its methodologies, and its canons of debate, even if it has never succeeded in staking out a territory with sharply defined and stable boundaries. Some might say that it has dug a groove for itself which succeeds in shutting out adequate consideration of factors of central importance, for example the nature and operation of demand and of consumption, in which social history can be illuminating and supportive.

Social history derives its appeal and fascination in no small measure from its open-endedness, its freedom from the constraints of a formal tradition, its eclectic habits, and stands in no need of being rendered into an authorised version. This is just as well, for orthodoxies are not created by editorial decree and if perchance they are fashioned by bands of disciples then the three volumes of this series are in little danger of becoming a Cambridge gospel, for the authors do not belong to any one single camp and do not have a common axe to grind. That is not to say that they are a particularly disputatious or dogmatic bunch, but simply that they are a team of individualists each of whom has been invited to bring their own scholarly judgment to bear on the task in hand. That task is to communicate the fruits of recent writing and the most recent research in social history to the wider audience of students who are curious to know what the specialists have been doing and how their work fits into a general picture of the whole process of social change and development. There are two ways of producing a synthesis: single-handed combat, in which one author takes on the whole field and produces a digest and interpretation of a large slice of history; or a team effort, in which the field is sliced up among contributors according to their expertise and the overview is a co-ordinated package of separate authoritative elements. As with individual sports and team games, tennis and cricket or golf and football, each approach has its own attractions and disadvantages, for players and spectators alike, and each has its partisans. There are several examples of solo syntheses on offer in the field of modern social history, notably from Penguin, Fontana-Collins, and Hutchinson. As the author of one of these it is not my purpose to decry their merits. No doubt their main strength comes from the coherence and unity which a picture of an entire landscape may have when seen through one pair of eyes and painted by one hand, and their main weakness from the inability of a single pair of eyes to see everything or to be well educated and well informed about the structure and meaning of all the features in that landscape.

Such virtues and vices are neatly balanced by the collaborative synthesis, in which each major feature is given critical appraisal by a leading specialist, while the landscape as a whole is left to look after itself in the expectation that an impression will form in the mind of the beholder. It would be unwise to try to compensate for this by raising an overarching superstructure over the individual contributions in these volumes, for that would come close to courting a disaster akin to those which customarily visit university buildings designed in committee. The design of this, the first enterprise to marshal the resources of the multi-author technique to view the entire sweep of modern British social history, does, however, call for explanatory comment and description.

In the last generation or so social historians have been casting their nets wider and wider, into waters previously unnoticed and unexplored by historians as well as into those formerly fished with the conventional equipment of the political, administrative, or trade-union historian. So far has this gone that it is sometimes said that all history which is not concerned with the technicalities of high politics, diplomacy, or econometrics has become a kind of social history. This social history has moved a long way, in its intellectual approach as well as in its subject matter, from the 'history with the politics left out' which still served as a definition of social history in the 1940s. There may not be a 'new' social history in the same way that there is a 'new' economic history as a school of thought applying econometrics and models drawn from economic theory to the understanding of historical economic phenomena; but social historians draw widely on concepts from historical demography, social anthropology, sociology, social geography, and political science, as well as from economics, and are well aware of the importance of quantification. Social historians operating in this conceptually eclectic and experimental fashion do not have the methodological certainty, unity, or rigidity of 'new' economic history, and deal in conclusions which are probable and plausible rather than directly verifiable.

This social history has generated many vigorous controversies and debates on topics within the period covered by this series: on the standard of living, class formation, the labour aristocracy, or social control, for example, and more recently on gender roles and women's emancipation. These issues have not been picked out for separate treatment in these volumes. The debates are best followed in the original exchanges, or in the several admirable surveys which are available, and references can be found in the bibliographies here. The issues, moreover, are best understood when placed within the framework of the conditions, customs, and institutions that shaped the way in which the people lived. Hence questions of class, social relationships, gender differences and roles, and social conflict are discussed in the context of a series of particular themes which constitute the main elements in that framework. The thematic structure means that much matter of interest is left out, because it chances to fall into one of the oubliettes between themes; but while there is no attempt at a literally complete coverage, taken together the chapters add up to a comprehensive and balanced account of the complexity, and diversity, of the interactions between continuity and change which have determined the development of British society in the two centuries since 1750.

The series, indeed, provides three social histories of these two centuries, each one complete in itself at a level of partial coverage. That is to say, the volumes themselves are not divided chronologically, but into three broad thematic clusters: regional communities; social environment; and social institutions. Much of the recent pioneering work in social history has advanced through intensive study of particular localities and communities, and Volume 1, *Regions and Communities*, draws on this approach by presenting a series of chapters on the social histories of distinctive regions. This is not an attempt to parcel up the whole of Britain into a number of regions, which could run the risk of reducing social history to a sub-branch of local history. It is, rather, a collection of studies of regions – if Scotland and Wales can forgive the label – whose separate identity is clearly established by their distinctive national, institutional, legal, and administrative histories, and of those of undisputed significance as examples of immense social and economic change (the north-west), concentration of power and wealth (the metropolis), and violent changes in fortune (the north-east). The obvious geographical gaps in this disposition are bridged by two chapters, on the countryside and on the city, whose 'regions' are not localities with fixed boundaries but shifting social territories defined by environmental, occupational, and cultural criteria. Regional communities, their social cohesion, disintegration, and reformation, are strongly influenced by regional economies, and this volume, therefore, is more directly concerned than the following two with the links between economic history and social history, and with explicit confrontation of the interaction of economy and society.

Where questions of social structure and class relations are raised in the setting of specific localities in Volume 1, in Volume 2, *People and their Environment*, they are approached, using national data and national patterns, through a collection of studies of the living and working environment. The family and household, the social implications of demographic change, domesticity and the separation of home and workplace, housing and the changing meaning of the home, the working environment and employer–worker relationships, nutrition and patterns of food and drink consumption, and leisure and popular culture are the themes of this volume. Together they show how the social order was shaped, reproduced, and changed through the processes of getting, spending, and staying alive, through family, marriage, home, work, consumption, and leisure. These agencies both generated and mediated social tensions, but the more explicit, institutionalised, efforts to protect the social order, to control or suppress conflicts, to influence attitudes and behaviour, and to manipulate social conditions are reserved for Volume 3, *Social Agencies and Institutions.* Much of the running was made by those in power and authority, and the chapters on government and society which explain the changing impact of government on people's lives and the changes in popular expectations of what government could and should provide, as well as the chapter on crime and policing, are central to this theme. Most socialisation, however, took place through voluntary and non-official institutions that were largely generated from within a social group and not imposed upon it. These are the subject of chapters on philanthropy and voluntary associations; while education, religion, and health were in a half-way position, partly the province of official and often coercive action, partly a sphere of voluntaryism, self-help, and self-determination.

Each volume is self-contained, with its own set of bibliographies, and with each chapter carrying its own chronology of the 200 years. Together the three volumes, with their three different and complementary angles of approach, are designed to offer an integrated and well-rounded social history that is exciting and challenging, as well as being as up-to-date as the contributors, who have written at different times within the last five years, can make it.

F. M. L. THOMPSON

CHAPTER 1

The social implications of demographic change

MICHAEL ANDERSON

This chapter does not provide a comprehensive survey of demographic change in Britain between 1750 and 1950.[1] Its main purpose is to identify the principal changes in demographic behaviour which, in one way or another, set a context for, raised opportunities for, or constrained other aspects of social life in the 200 years covered by this volume.

I POPULATION, ITS DISTRIBUTION AND MOVEMENT

In 1750, the population of England was about 5.75 million. Scotland had 1.25 million people, and Wales 0.5 million. A century later, in 1851, the numbers had more than doubled, to 16.7 million, 2.9 million and 1.2 million respectively; by 1951 they had reached 41.6 million, 5.1 million and 2.2 million.[2]

In general, as is clear from Figure 1.1, Scotland's population grew more slowly than that of England and Wales, but in both countries the rate of growth, rapid in the mid-eighteenth century in comparison with the past, peaked in the early nineteenth century, remained high until the end of the century and subsequently declined. At its highest rate, in the years 1811–21, England added 18 per cent to its population in a decade and Scotland nearly 16 per cent. At its absolute peak, in the last decade of the nineteenth century, Great Britain's population grew by almost 4 million: in just one decade there were 4 million more people to be fed, employed, amused and housed. In a long-term

---

[1] For broader general surveys see N. L. Tranter, *Population and Society, 1750–1940* (1985); M. Anderson, *Population Change in North-Western Europe, 1750–1850* (1988); R. Mitchison, *British Population Change since 1860* (1977); M. Flinn, ed., *Scottish Population History from the Seventeenth Century to the 1930s* (Cambridge, 1977).

[2] B. R. Mitchell and P. Deane, *Abstract of British Historical Statistics* (Cambridge, 1962), pp. 5, 6, 20–2; E. A. Wrigley and R. S. Schofield, *The Population History of England, 1541–1871: A Reconstruction* (1981), pp. 208–9.

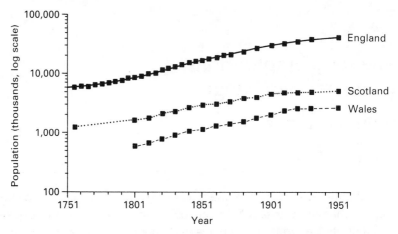

Figure 1.1 Population: countries of Great Britain, 1751–1951
Sources: See n. 1.

historical perspective, the most remarkable feature of demographic change in our period was the ability of the British society and economy to cope so well with this massive and unprecedented rise in population.

Not merely did numbers rise, they also became more concentrated, particularly in the areas of expanding trade and industry. In Scotland, what became the industrial and commercial central belt,[3] though it covered only 14 per cent of the land area, had 37 per cent of the country's 1755 population; this area of Scotland had 47 per cent of the population by 1821, 68 per cent by 1911 and peaked in 1931 at 75 per cent, falling back to 70 per cent by the end of the period. By contrast, the counties to the north, with nearly three-quarters of the land area and just over half of the population in 1755, had only one fifth by 1951. In England, the old agricultural counties lying predominantly to the south and east of a line between the Severn and the Wash (and excluding London, Surrey and Middlesex), contained 44 per cent of the population in 1801. By 1881, this figure had fallen to 29 per cent and remained there until after 1931, rising to 31 per cent by 1951. At the same dates, the shares of London and its two satellite counties had risen from 14 per cent to 19 per cent

[3] This area is defined as including the counties of Ayrshire, Dumbartonshire, Lanarkshire, Renfrewshire, Clackmannanshire, Stirlingshire, Fife and the Lothians, together with the city of Dundee. The 1755 figures are from T. C. Smout, *A History of the Scottish People, 1560–1830* (1969), p. 261. The later figures are from Mitchell and Deane, *Abstract*, pp. 21, 23.

of the population, and then fallen back after 1931 to 17 per cent. The share of counties to the north and west of the Severn–Wash line had grown from 45 per cent in 1801 to 53 per cent in 1881 and declined only slightly by 1951. In Wales, the population of one county, Glamorgan, had increased, as a percentage of the Welsh population, from 13 per cent in 1801 to 38 per cent in 1881 and to 55 per cent in 1911, where it roughly remained until 1951.[4]

These changes were associated with rapid growth in certain counties. In 1911, for example, there were more than six times as many people in Lancashire as there had been in 1801, and the population had reached 4.76 million. But, in proportional growth terms, Lancashire was surpassed in England and Wales by Surrey, Monmouthshire and Durham, as well as by Middlesex and Glamorgan which each grew by nearly fifteen times. In Scotland, the highest levels of both absolute and relative growth between 1801 and 1911 were in Lanarkshire, with an increase of over 1.25 million people (nearly nine times).

These concentrations in the manufacturing and trade centres of the country were not immediately accompanied by massive rural depopulation. In England, no county experienced a decadal loss of population before 1841–51, and only Herefordshire, Hertfordshire and Rutland (plus London between 1931 and 1951) had falls in our period of more than 10 per cent below their peaks. Wales and Scotland saw more and earlier decline but it was not dramatic except in a few areas. In Wales, all but one of the counties experienced some inter-censal population loss at some time (in all but Montgomeryshire beginning in the second half of the nineteenth century – and in Glamorgan and Pembrokeshire being confined to the interwar period). Half of the Welsh counties experienced losses of more than 10 per cent of their peaks, and four of more than 20 per cent, the most marked being Montgomeryshire where the population in 1951 was only two-thirds of the 1841 level. Yet, of all the Welsh counties, only Montgomeryshire had a smaller population in 1951 than in 1801, and then only just.

In Scotland (with the exception, by the 1830s or 1840s, of the highland counties and of Peebles in the Borders), there were no significant absolute population losses at county level before 1851. By 1911, however, only seven counties (Aberdeenshire, Fife, Lanarkshire, Midlothian, Renfrewshire, Stirlingshire and West Lothian) had not experienced some population decline. After 1911, rural population

---

[4] The county growth figures here and in the next paragraphs are calculated from Mitchell and Deane, *Abstract*, pp. 20, 22.

loss was widespread and even Aberdeenshire, Fife, Renfrewshire and West Lothian had falling populations in the interwar period. All in all, at some time in our period, over two-fifths of Scottish counties lost more than 10 per cent of their peak populations, and over a quarter lost more than 25 per cent; at the extreme, Sutherland and Shetland had, in 1951, only 54 per cent and 59 per cent respectively of their highest nineteenth-century populations. Five counties had lower populations in 1951 than in 1801; the most significant losers were Argyllshire (down 36 per cent) and Sutherland (down 39 per cent).

At parish level, the picture is very different, and a clear basis for major social dislocation can be seen in some areas. Detailed research remains to be done on a national level for England and Wales, but in Scotland the population of some individual parishes was already declining before 1800.[5] Thereafter, excluding the burghs of 1801, about one parish in seven had lost more than half its 1801 population by 1951, and almost one third of all parishes had 1951 populations less than half the level of their nineteenth-century peaks. Three parishes in every five had lost more than 10 per cent of their 1801 populations and four-fifths were more than 10 per cent below their nineteenth-century peaks. On the other hand, one fifth of all non-burghal parishes had more than twice their 1801 populations in 1951, but almost all of these were parishes either on the coasts or in the Central Belt. In the Borders and the Highlands and Islands, by contrast, three-quarters of parishes were more than 10 per cent below their 1801 sizes and well over two-fifths had populations less than half the level of their nineteenth-century peak. Moreover, the remaining populations of the extensive Highlands and Islands parishes were also far more concentrated onto the larger settlements and coastal fringes as a consequence of two centuries of both voluntary and involuntary displacement of the population.[6]

These movements at parish level are in part a reflection of another significant shift in population distribution in our period, an increasing concentration of population in the towns, with all the social consequences of urban living and, in the larger towns, all the mortality and other problems associated historically with high population

[5] Flinn, ed., *Scottish Population*, p. 307.
[6] The figures on parish population change in Scotland have been calculated from the respective county reports of the *1951 Census of Scotland, I*, Table 3; a partial survey of the English situation can be found in J. Saville, *Rural Depopulation in England and Wales, 1851–1951* (1957), chap. 2; E. Richards, *A History of the Highland Clearances*, 2 vols. (1982, 1985).

density. Already, by 1750, one in every nine of the population of England and Wales lived in London, a European colossus with a population of about 675,000; roughly another 340,000 (or 5.5 per cent) lived in places with populations of over 10,000. London continued to expand over the nineteenth century, reaching 1 million (about 10 per cent of the national population) in 1811, over 2 million by 1851, passing 3 million in the 1860s and 4 million in the 1880s; by then it contained its peak share of the population of almost 15 per cent. In 1901 its population was 4.5 million, but thereafter it fell, first slowly, and then rapidly during and after the Second World War. By 1951 the population was only 3.3 million (about 7.5 per cent of the national population) though its suburbs were still growing. No other English town had a population of more than 100,000 until the 1811 census (when only 7 per cent of Englishmen lived in places of between 20,000 and 100,000 people). Thereafter urban growth was rapid. Including London, 23 per cent of the population of England and Wales lived in cities of 100,000 or over in 1851 and 35 per cent in places of 20,000 or more. By 1911, 35 per cent lived in places of 100,000 and over, a figure which remained constant until the Second World War and then declined a little, largely because of the fall in the population of London.[7]

In 1750, Scots were even less likely than their southern neighbours to be living in large centres of population. Edinburgh (plus its suburbs), with a population of perhaps 57,000, Glasgow and its suburbs (about 32,000), Aberdeen (around 16,000) and Dundee (about 12,000) were the only towns in 1755 with populations larger than 10,000 and only four other towns are likely to have mustered over 5,000 people; these places together contained fewer than one Scot in eight. The remaining people were scattered widely over the countryside, a few per cent in the large number of small burghs, many with no more than a few hundred inhabitants, most of the rest still in tiny settlements, often of only half a dozen families.[8] By the census of 1801 things had changed but little; Scotland still had no town of 100,000 inhabitants, though Edinburgh and Glasgow both exceeded 80,000, and about one in five of the population lived in towns of over 5,000 people. By 1851, when the census authorities believed that in England

---

[7] P. J. Corfield, *The Impact of English Towns, 1700–1800* (Oxford, 1982), pp. 8–9; A. F. Weber, *The Growth of Cities in the Nineteenth Century* (1899; reprinted 1967), pp. 46–7; Mitchell and Deane, *Abstract*, pp. 24–7.

[8] Smout, *History*, p. 261; B. Lenman, *Integration, Enlightenment and Industrialisation: Scotland 1746–1832* (1981), p. 5.

almost exactly half of the population lived in urban areas, in Scotland the figure was 52 per cent. By now, the big towns had begun significantly to grow. The cities of over 100,000 people contained 17 per cent of the population, and centres over 5,000 had 26 per cent. Even so, much of Scotland's 'urban' population was still concentrated in small places. By 1911, 36 per cent of the population lived in places in the 100,000 and over category (and only 38 per cent in 1951). In 1911, 59 per cent were in places of 5,000 and over, and the growth of the smaller places continued so that, by 1951, nine Scots out of every ten lived in places with populations exceeding 10,000.[9]

These patterns of national and local population growth and decline were associated with enormous population movements through internal migration, immigration and emigration. First, there were great tides of immigration, producing a society in which some cities – and especially London – were always characterised by substantial and clearly identifiable immigrant communities. Right from the eighteenth century there was a significant Irish component in the British population and by the time this can first be measured accurately at the 1841 census (and probably including some temporary seasonal migrants), there were some 125,000 Irish-born persons in Scotland, and 290,000 in England and Wales.[10] Following the failure of the potato crop in Ireland in the 1840s, a major influx occurred, running in Glasgow in 1848 at 1,000 per week.[11] This flow continued at a slower rate even after 1870 (and expanded again after the Second World War). Nationally, at the recorded proportional peak in 1861, 602,000 persons in England and Wales, and 204,000 in Scotland, were of Irish birth (about 7 per cent of the population of Scotland and 3 per cent of the population of England and Wales).[12] Locally, the effect could be even more significant. There were substantial Irish-born concentrations even in rural areas in south-west Scotland, while Paisley, Glasgow, Kilmarnock and Dundee all had over 10 per cent of their populations Irish-born (Dundee was the highest at nearly 19 per cent). In England, outside Liverpool (with 22 per cent of its 1851 population born in Ireland), and Manchester and Salford (with 13 per cent), the concentrations were considerably lower though still significant;

---

[9] Weber, *Growth of Cities*, pp. 58–9; Mitchell and Deane, *Abstract*, pp. 24–7.
[10] *1841 Census of Great Britain, Enumeration Abstract*, PP 1843, XXII, Preface, pp. 14–17.
[11] Flinn, ed., *Scottish Population*, pp. 456–7.
[12] Compare the coloured population of Britain in 1981 at about 4 per cent, of whom about half were first generation migrants (*General Household Survey* (1981), Table 2.21).

Bradford, for example, had 9 per cent of its population Irish-born and London 5 per cent. While the national percentage born in Ireland fell after 1851 (to less than 2 per cent by 1911), the descendants of this Irish influx continued to be a major social and economic force within many urban centres in Britain, and in some areas formed a focus for major tensions and outbreaks of public disorder.[13]

A second major source of immigrants was the Continent of Europe. Relatively insignificant and of widely spread origins in the mid-nineteenth century, continental immigrants rose rapidly in numbers between 1870 and 1914, the most important group being Eastern European Jews fleeing from Tsarist persecution. In all perhaps 120,000 arrived in this period and especially between 1882 and 1905. At the 1911 peak there were about 285,000 'aliens' living in England and Wales and 25,000 in Scotland. The largest proportions by far were of Russian, Polish and German origin, but significant numbers also came from France and Italy.[14] Again the major social impact was a local one with heavy concentrations of Russian Jews in certain areas of Leeds, Manchester and the East End of London, and with other immigrant communities settled in very tightly circumscribed areas of the capital, areas which sometimes became the focus of short-lived disturbances.

Finally, in addition to a significant white colonial and East-Indies-born population (about 71,000 in 1871, mainly the children of administrators and soldiers), a small and probably slowly declining black community existed, particularly in seaport towns, right back to the eighteenth century. After the First World War, and especially after 1948, the non-white population began to grow but even in 1950 the total numbers in the whole of Britain were probably less than 50,000.[15]

The scale of immigration was thus high in our period and its social consequences at times considerable. The rate of outflow, however, was even higher though its social consequences have been much less explored. In Scotland, few individual parishes in the Highlands absorbed all their natural increase (the gap between births and deaths) at any time within this period, and the same was increasingly true

[13] M. A. G. O'Tuathaigh, 'The Irish in Britain: A Problem of Integration', *Transactions of the Royal Historical Society*, 31 (1981), pp. 149–73.
[14] C. Holmes, 'The Promised Land? Immigration into Britain 1870–1980', in D. A. Coleman, *Demography of Immigrants and Minority Groups in the United Kingdom* (1982), pp. 1–21.
[15] J. Walvin, *Black and White: The Negro in English Society, 1555–1945* (1973); Holmes, 'The Promised Land?'; C. Peach, 'The Growth and Distribution of the Black Population in Britain, 1945–1980', in Coleman, *Demography*, pp. 23–42.

of most of rural Britain where, as we have seen, many populations eventually went into absolute decline even though births exceeded deaths by ten or more per thousand per annum.[16] However, this problem was not just a rural one; many towns were also producing more people than they could retain. In Scotland, where the evidence is clearest, in no decade after 1870 did all four of the great cities of Edinburgh, Glasgow, Aberdeen and Dundee absorb all of their natural increase.[17] The consequence, for rural and urban areas alike, was massive emigration.

Taken as a whole, there was probably net emigration from Britain in every decade in our period prior to the 1930s, when substantial net inflow, mainly in the form of returning emigrants, occurred. Precise estimates are difficult to make because there are no comprehensive statistics before 1853 and even these have serious shortcomings until 1877 and significant difficulties until 1912. Overall, however, it seems that in excess of 10 million English-born persons, and approaching 2.5 million Scots, left Britain for overseas destinations between 1750 and 1939. Before 1850 the majority of this outflow was of a 'settler' type, most intending permanent emigration and going to a great extent in family groups. After the mid-nineteenth century, however, and particularly from the 1880s, a higher proportion of departures was of young single males, many of whom either went expecting to return, or who did so as the relative fortunes of the British and North American economies fluctuated over time. Overall, net emigration of English-born persons between 1750 and 1939 was probably well in excess of 5.5 million; around 1.75 million Scots also left permanently for overseas.[18]

The outflows varied significantly in intensity at different periods. Before 1801 we have for England only very rough residual figures computed by Wrigley and Schofield;[19] these suggest that net emigration in the second half of the eighteenth century was running at between 3,000 and 7,000 per annum, falling from a little over 1 per cent of the population per decade in the 1750s to around 0.5 per cent

[16] Flinn, ed., *Scottish Population*, p. 308.   [17] *Ibid.*, p. 312.

[18] Most of the figures in this and the next three paragraphs are computed from N. H. Carrier and J. R. Jeffery, 'External Migration: A Study of the Available Statistics', *Studies of Medical and Population Subjects*, 6 (1953), modified where appropriate by reference to the important and more detailed discussions of D. Baines, *Migration in a Mature Economy: Emigration and Internal Migration in England and Wales, 1861–1900* (Cambridge, 1985).

[19] Wrigley and Schofield, *Population History*, pp. 528–9.

by 1800.[20] Between 1815 and 1850 there seem to have been around 0.5 million (net) English and Welsh emigrants in total, and another 100,000 Scots, and even in this period total native-born emigrants almost certainly exceeded the very large inflow of Irish and other overseas-born immigrants. Between 1850 and 1869, with numbers returning still relatively low, emigration rose markedly to exceed 1 million English-born, and over 0.25 million Scots (for comparison, the population of England and Wales in 1851 was just under 18 million and the population of Scotland just under 3 million).

Thereafter emigration continued at a high rate until 1914, but with particularly high levels in the 1880s (over 800,000 net English and Welsh emigrants – around 4 per cent of the mean population) and in the ten years up to 1914 (when England and Wales lost 1.3 million from their native populations and Scotland some 380,000); in each of the years 1910–13 Scotland lost more than 1 per cent of its population, and in all four years emigration more than exceeded natural increases. After the First World War (with the sole exception of 1920) emigration fell away in England and Wales, but Scottish emigration continued at a high level, with, net, around 350,000 people moving overseas (7 per cent of the mean population). As we have seen above, for both England and Wales and Scotland, some of this outflow was replaced by immigrants from Ireland and from overseas. Nevertheless, net population loss through migration was around 2.7 million from England and Wales between 1841 and 1930, and 1.4 million from Scotland between 1861 and 1930; the Scottish figures include the substantial emigration to England and Wales, but even if this is excluded Scotland lost a higher proportion of her natural increase through emigration between 1881 and 1930 than any other Western European country except Norway and Ireland.[21]

With emigration at this level, almost every family (especially in Scotland) from all parts of the social scale lost at least one member overseas

---

[20] For Scotland and Wales we have no precise figures for this period but we know that significant highland emigration was under way from the 1760s. The overall figure for Scotland between 1763 and 1775 was probably the equivalent of well over 1 per cent of the population (computed from figures cited in Flinn, ed., *Scottish Population*, p. 443).

[21] Norway lost 40 per cent of her natural increase between 1835 and 1938. Scottish net emigration was 43 per cent of natural increase in 1881–90, 47 per cent in 1901–10, 57 per cent in 1911–20, and 104 per cent in 1921–30 (Baines, *Migration*, pp. 61–2). In Ireland the population fell steadily from more than 8 million in 1841 to just over 4 million in 1926–7, in spite of strongly positive natural increases throughout the period.

in the last hundred years of our period. No part of the country escaped entirely, though in England and Wales losses were especially high in Cornwall and in other parts of the south-west and in South Wales, while in Scotland it seems likely that the Highlands and Islands experienced the most severe emigration. Young single males formed a high proportion of the emigrants, especially towards the end of the period; almost two-thirds of English and Welsh emigrants in the years 1871–1900 were males, while the net losses of males through emigration between 1900 and 1913 were more than double the numbers killed during the First World War.[22]

One important side-effect of this pattern of emigration was to skew the sex ratio of the native population strongly in favour of women. In England, after the outflow of the 1850s, the sex ratio among the 25–9 age group (men per thousand women) fell from 906 (1851) to 879 (1861); in Scotland, the comparable figures were 828 to 769, the lower Scottish figures being a reflection of the long-standing higher rates of emigration from that country.[23] The emigration surges of the 1880s and, in Scotland, of the 1900s, produced similar effects. Together with mortality differentials (see below), emigration produced what came to be seen as a significant 'spinster problem' in the second half of the nineteenth century.[24]

But these long-distance movements were not the only migration-induced disruptions of social relationships and local community life. Right back into the medieval period it is clear that the English (and probably also the Welsh and Scots) had been migratory peoples. The relative (compared with continental Europe) insignificance of a land-holding peasantry had by 1750 produced an agricultural system characterised by a wage labour force. Over the course of our period this wage labour sector increasingly ceased to consist of individuals working part time or as a passing phase of the early life course, and became instead more and more dependent on life-time wage labour employment. At the same time rising urbanisation increased the centuries-old flow of surplus rural population to the towns (as well as the equally significant, though smaller, counter-flows from town to countryside).

[22] Winter estimates the total of war-related deaths for Great Britain and Ireland as about 610,000 (J. M. Winter, 'Some Demographic Consequences of the First World War in Britain', *Population Studies*, 30 (1976), pp. 539–52).

[23] Mitchell and Deane, *Abstract*, pp. 12–13.

[24] For a review of this problem and some evidence of how it was met at mid-century see M. Anderson, 'The Social Position of the Spinster in Mid-Victorian Britain', *Journal of Family History*, 9 (1984).

Even in the seventeenth and early eighteenth centuries the rural population had never been static. Around 70 per cent of the rural witnesses at English diocesan courts analysed by Clark for the period 1660–1730 had moved at least once; about one in seven had moved between counties.[25] Comparison of population listings for the English village of Clayworth between 1676 and 1688 shows that 61 per cent of the population had disappeared over a twelve-year period (only about two in every five of these disappearers are known to have died).[26] Farm servants were particularly mobile[27] but even apparently established farming families moved around to some degree. Most of the rural movement was relatively short-distance, and short-distance movement was also observed in the movement to the towns, though some longer distance migration (especially to London and the larger cities) was also to be found.[28]

From the mid-nineteenth century we are able to measure these patterns more precisely. Preliminary figures from the National Sample from the 1851 census[29] show that about 54 per cent of the population were recorded as not living within 2 kilometres of their stated place of birth. The figure for towns (including Londoners who recorded their place of birth simply as 'London') was 56 per cent, but perhaps more surprising at first glance is the fact that 52 per cent of the rural

[25] P. Clark, 'Migration in England during the Late Seventeenth and Early Eighteenth Centuries', *Past & Present*, 83 (1979), pp. 64–71.

[26] T. P. R. Laslett, *Family Life and Illicit Love in Earlier Generations* (Cambridge, 1977), chap. 2.

[27] A. Kussmaul, 'The Ambiguous Mobility of Farm Servants', *Economic History Review*, 2nd ser., 34 (1981), pp. 222–35.

[28] Clark, 'Migration', pp. 64–71, 76–7; E. J. Buckatzsch, 'Places of Origin of a Group of Immigrants into Sheffield, 1624–1799', *Economic History Review*, 2nd ser., 2 (1949–50), pp. 303–6. There were also very high levels of mainly short-distance migration in pre-industrial rural Scotland: see R. A. Houston, 'Mobility in Scotland 1652–1811: The Evidence of Testimonials', *Journal of Historical Geography*, 11 (1985), pp. 379–94.

[29] The National Sample from the enumerators' books of the 1851 census of Great Britain has been developed at the University of Edinburgh over the past fifteen years with assistance from the Economic and Social Reserch Council. The entire sample contains around 400,000 individuals, but the material used in this chapter is drawn from a number of sub-samples of the data. Individual level data are based on the weighted aggregates of three systematic one in forty sub-samples from the entire data set for smaller rural settlements, plus six such samples from the rest of the country; the total size of this sub-sample, before weighting, is 50,406 though the numbers given in the tables are based on weighted figures (the weighted total is 29,939). The family and aggregate household level data are derived from the preliminary version of a SIR database, which contained at the time of writing only data from one of the one in forty sub-samples (containing 9,828 persons in private households). Some of the household data sub-divided by occupation is from an earlier weighted sub-sample where sixty-five entire sampling clusters, containing 27,920 individuals in all (23,300 after weighting), were included.

population were also life-time migrants when measured in this way. Closer inspection of the data reveals that rural areas with high migrant populations were not just confined to expanding industrial villages, but were spread extensively through the agricultural areas of the country as well. If attention is confined to the major industrial towns in the sample the figure for immigrants still only just reaches 60 per cent.

Much of this migration was short-distance so that the impact on social relationships through separation between kin may have been less significant than first impressions might suggest. This was especially true of rural migrants, over two-thirds of whom moved less than 25 kilometres. The equivalent figure for short-distance urban migrants, on the other hand, was under two-fifths (and for migrants to London under one fifth).[30] Nevertheless, while continuity of close rural social relationships seems at least to have been possible, considerably greater efforts were required for many urban dwellers if they wished to remain in contact with their places of birth.

Immigration when measured in this way is obviously heavily skewed by age, but we can use this effect to throw some light on the timing of first migration. When this is done it is clear that in all areas the rate accelerates rapidly during the teenage years and in the early twenties, the proportion who were migrants being 45 per cent in urban areas at ages 10–14 (43 per cent in rural areas), 55 per cent (49 per cent) at ages 15–19 and 67 per cent (58 per cent) at ages 20–4. Even among very young children considerable movement may be observed. While some of this may be a function of mothers temporarily moving away from home for childbirth, and a small amount may be a result of measurement error in the methods used, the figures are of some interest. Already among children in their second year of life over a quarter in both urban and rural areas were recorded in 1851 at more than 2 kilometres from their place of birth. This suggests that there existed in nineteenth-century society a considerable degree of transiency among at least some sectors of the population.[31]

---

[30] Note, however, that these figures can only be approximate until further research is done on that segment of the population who only recorded a county of birth.

[31] For some elaboration of these points, on the basis of an earlier data set, see M. Anderson, 'Urban Migration in Victorian Britain: Problems of Assimilation?', in E. François, ed., *Immigration et société urbaine en Europe occidentale: XVIe–XXe siècles*, Editions Recherches sur les Civilisations (Paris, 1985).

This transiency is also revealed more locally among urban residents by the rapid rates of population turnover within towns. One study of thirty streets in Liverpool, for example, has revealed that only 18 per cent of the population remained at the same address for ten years, with 40 per cent moving within one year. Even of those born in Liverpool, 35 per cent moved in this period.[32] Other studies confirm that this high rate of movement was widespread in towns though much was confined within a few hundred yards.[33] Contemporary comment suggests that the insecurities of nineteenth-century life, the commonly small margin between income and subsistence needs, and a minutely variegated rented housing market, all contributed to unstable urban residence patterns. Certainly, as living standards rose over the late nineteenth century, population turnover within towns seems to have declined and the arrival of rented council housing, plus slow expansion of the previously small owner-occupied sector, meant that, by the mid-twentieth century, house moving had become a much more infrequent affair for the mass of the population.[34]

II DEATHS, BIRTHS AND MARRIAGE

For most of our 200-year period, almost the whole country experienced natural increase in its population – in other words, on average, births in each year exceeded deaths. This section explores some of the socially significant aspects of this historically unique demographic period.

As a start to the discussion, Figure 1.2 presents the available reasonably reliable estimates of the birth and death rates of England and Wales and of Scotland in our period.

For Scotland, we do not have – and almost certainly will never have – continuous series of birth and death rates such as those estimated by Wrigley and Schofield for England. Estimates for 1755 which suggested a crude birth rate of over forty-one and a crude death rate of around thirty-eight per thousand (figures which are both far higher

---

[32] R. Lawton and C. G. Pooley, *The Social Geography of Merseyside in the Nineteenth Century*, Final Report to SSRC (1976).

[33] *Fourth Report from SC on Settlement and Poor Removal*, PP 1847, XI (1847), pp. 51–2; C. Booth, *Life and Labour of the People of London*, 1st ser., *Poverty*, vol. 3 (1889), pp. 61, 81; M. Anderson, *Family Structure in Nineteenth-Century Lancashire* (Cambridge, 1971), pp. 41–2; R. M. Pritchard, *Housing and the Spatial Structure of the City* (Cambridge, 1976); R. Dennis, 'Intercensal Mobility in a Victorian City', *Transactions of the Institute of British Geographers*, new ser., 2 (1977), pp. 349–63; C. G. Pooley, 'Residential Mobility in the Victorian City', *Transactions of the Institute of British Geographers*, new ser., 4 (1979), pp. 258–77.

[34] Pritchard, *Housing*, chaps. 4–6.

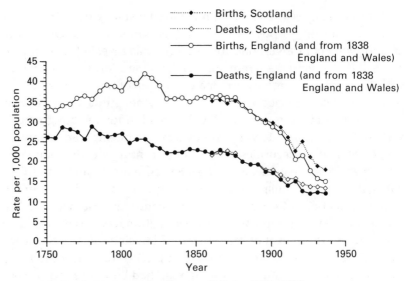

Figure 1.2 Crude birth and death rates, Britain, 1751–1939
Sources: Wrigley and Schofield, *Population History*, pp. 528–9; Mitchell and Deane, *Abstract*, pp. 29–32, 36–7.

than England's) are almost certainly too high.[35] Thereafter, until the late 1850s (when the figures for Scotland are very much like those for England and Wales), no data are available, with the exception of some rough estimates for the 1790s which suggest significant regional variations and a national death rate around the level of England's (though a lower birth rate).[36] It seems, nevertheless, almost certain that Scotland had higher mortality than England well into the nineteenth century. There was near famine in parts of Scotland in 1782 and serious epidemics of infectious disease – particularly in the towns – in 1808, 1831, 1836–7 and 1846–9; the last of these has been described by one group of scholars as 'a period of quite exceptionally lethal character more redolent of the seventeenth than of the nineteenth century'.[37] There is thus a real possibility that Scotland (and especially its highland areas) experienced a demographic regime in the eighteenth century something like that of France, and had, during the classic 'industrial revolution' period, a quite different

---

[35] Rosalind Mitchison has recently reworked the bases of the calculations reported in Flinn, ed., *Scottish Population*, p. 59. See her 'Webster Revisited: A Re-Examination of the 1755 "Census" of Scotland', in T. Devine, ed., *Themes in Scottish Social History* (Edinburgh, 1989).
[36] Flinn, ed., *Scottish Population*, p. 259.   [37] *Ibid.*, pp. 372–3.

demographic transition from that experienced by England and Wales.[38]

Turning to the figures for England in Figure 1.2, for the period 1751 to 1851 three points merit particular attention. First, compared with some other parts of Europe and especially with France, both the birth rate and the death rate were low in eighteenth-century England, which had what Wrigley and Schofield call a 'low pressure' demographic regime.[39] Secondly, the high level of fertility between the 1780s and the 1820s is of importance, though its interpretation is subject to dispute.[40] The third point to note is the rapid fall in the death rate in the first thirty years of the nineteenth century for which the most likely explanation is some combination of an improvement in the standard of living and a fall in smallpox mortality following the introduction of vaccination.[41]

For the period since 1861, the birth and death rates for Scotland are very similar to those for England and Wales, confirmation of the fact that it was differences in net migration which were responsible for the different growth rates of the two countries in this period. In both countries also, the birth rate began a steady decline in the 1870s, with Scotland trailing a little behind England and Wales. And in both countries the death rate shows some fall in the 1880s and then a more rapid fall from the late 1890s, with Scotland again lagging behind.

The social significance of changes of this size in the level of mortality was clearly considerable, resulting as they did in an increase in the expectation of life (the average number of years lived) in England from around 36 in the second half of the eighteenth century to around 40 in the central years of the nineteenth century, and then, for England

[38] For a neat comparison of French and English demography in the eighteenth century, see Wrigley and Schofield, *Population History*, pp. 246–7.

[39] *Ibid.*, p. 247. Some doubts have been raised about the reliability of Wrigley and Schofield's findings for this period but it seems inconceivable that the effects that they observe are entirely artefacts of the undoubted poor quality of the English data of this period. The problems are reviewed in Anderson, *Population Change*, chaps. 2 and 6.

[40] For a review of this controversy see Anderson, *Population Change*; also the broad interpretations offered by R. S. Schofield, 'English Marriage Patterns Revisited', *Journal of Family History*, 10 (1985), pp. 2–20, and by D. Levine, *Reproducing Families* (Cambridge, 1987).

[41] Over this period of time the data assembled by P. H. Lindert and J. G. Williamson, in 'English Workers' Living Standards during the Industrial Revolution', *Economic History Review*, 2nd ser., 36 (1983), pp. 1–25, seem to me conclusive enough for present purposes. For a wider review of mortality change in this period see Anderson, *Population Change*, chap. 7. The role of smallpox is vigorously asserted by A. J. Mercer, 'Smallpox and Epidemiological–Demographic Change in Europe: The Role of Vaccination', *Population Studies*, 39 (1985), pp. 287–308.

and Wales, to 52 for males and 55 for females for 1911–12, and to 66 and 72 respectively for 1950–2.[42] The Scottish trends thereafter were roughly in parallel with those for England and Wales though the improvement was in general just a little delayed.[43]

Such average figures are, however, misleading for they fail to take account of the changes in the age distribution of mortality, and of the different experiences of different occupational groups and of people living in different parts of the country (and especially in the towns compared with the rural areas). Figure 1.3 shows the quinquennial average age-specific mortality rates for England and Wales between 1841 and 1955. No detailed figures are available on a national English basis for earlier in the period,[44] though Wrigley and Schofield[45] have published infant mortality rates for thirteen parishes for the second half of the eighteenth century which, when adjusted for probable levels of under-registration, range between 70 for rural Hartland

[42] The life table data used here and in later calculations in this chapter are drawn before 1838–54 from tables developed by Wrigley and Schofield for *Population History*; the authors kindly provided me with the more detailed life tables used in the calculations of their published figures and these are used later in the chapter when cohorted figures are required. For the period up to 1871 I have also used these life tables, except when reference is needed to sex-specific data when I have used the data published in the Third English Life Table. Thereafter, I have used the figures provided by successive English life tables as published in the *Decennial Supplements* to the *Annual Reports of the Registrar General of Births, Deaths and Marriages for England and Wales* (published, like the Annual Reports, as Parliamentary Papers until 1920) and to the *Registrar General's Statistical Reviews for England and Wales* published by the General Register Office. Scottish life tables can be obtained from the decennial supplements to the *Annual Reports of the Registrar General of Births, Deaths and Marriages for Scotland*; the first decennial supplement appears in PP 1895, XXIV, and includes data on occupational mortality but no life tables; the first life tables appear in the *Supplement to the 48th Detailed Annual Report of the Registrar General of Births, Deaths and Marriages for Scotland*, PP 1906, XXI; this report contains life tables for each decade from 1861–70 to 1891–1900.

[43] For example, expectation of life for women for 1871–80 was 44.62 for England and Wales and 43.80 for Scotland; for 1881–90 the figures were 47.18 and 46.33 respectively (*Supplement to the 55th Annual Report of the Registrar General of Births, Deaths and Marriages in England and Wales*, PP 1895, XXIII, Pt I, p. xviii; *Supplement to the 48th Detailed Annual Report*, PP 1906, XXI, pp. cxviii–ix.

[44] The figures used in the calculation of survival rates below are derived from the application of the model mortality schedule devised by the Cambridge Group for their work for Wrigley and Schofield, *Population History*, to the estimated level of mortality in any quinquennium. The results cannot be used to show changes in age-specific mortality. The assumption that the mortality schedule remained constant, while perhaps more questionable for the period before 1750, seems more valid thereafter, with scarlatina to a great extent replacing smallpox as a major killer in early life (Roger Schofield in a personal communication).

[45] E. A. Wrigley and R. S. Schofield, 'English Population History from Family Reconstitution: Summary Results 1600–1799', *Population Studies*, 37 (1983), pp. 157–84; these are approximate figures adjusted for under-registration by amending the rates from p. 179 of Wrigley and Schofield's paper by the factors suggested on p. 178.

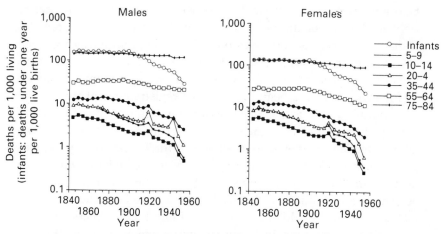

Figure 1.3 Changing age-specific mortality, England and Wales, 1841–1960
Sources: Annual Reports of the Registrar General for England and Wales.

and around 250 for the towns of Gainsborough and Banbury. The average death rate for the thirteen parishes (166 per thousand) is below the national average; the overall mortality of these parishes was more favourable than that of England as a whole and no London parishes or parishes for any other major city were included. If the shape of the mortality schedule remained unchanged from the later eighteenth to the mid-nineteenth centuries, then extrapolation from Wrigley and Schofield's national aggregate reconstruction data for the second half of the eighteenth century[46] would suggest that eighteen babies out of every hundred born would have failed to reach their first birthday; this is clearly a figure compatible with the parish family reconstruction data when its bias is taken into account.

It thus seems likely that infant mortality fell somewhat between the later eighteenth and the mid-nineteenth centuries. Thereafter, however, as Figure 1.3 shows, it fell little, if at all, until the early twentieth century. By contrast, child mortality (deaths between ages 1 and 15), having possibly fallen by rather less than infant mortality around the turn of the century, went into a steady decline from the 1870s, and was accompanied or followed shortly afterwards by a reduction in deaths among young adults. At the other end of the life course little change in the death rates of those aged 55–64 is visible

---

[46] Wrigley and Schofield, *Population History*, pp. 529, 714.

before the twentieth century. For the over-74s there was little change right to the end of the period. In general, the patterns for females were similar to those of males but with falling mortality of women of any age group preceding that of men by a few years. Also, as is the case in Britain today, female mortality was below that of males.

However, from the beginning of civil registration right up to the First World War, this was not true for some groups of children and young adults.[47] As late as the 1911–12 English life table, female mortality exceeded that for men at all ages from 9 to 15; the excess was particularly marked in rural areas where it covered the whole age range from 12 to 19. Ten years earlier female mortality nationally had been higher than that for males at all ages from 3 to 14; in the quinquennial data from the Third English Life Table for the years 1838–54, the higher female rates included the entire age span from 10 to 39; this higher adult female mortality, extending often at least up to age 35 and not confined to areas with high rates of mortality associated with childbirth, continued in certain parts of rural England and in many mining areas right up to 1914.[48]

Excess female mortality at ages where modern life tables show considerable female advantage is found widely in Western Europe at this period but it has until recently attracted little serious research, in spite of its possible significance in providing clues to differences between the two sexes in social, nutritional and environmental conditions.[49] Some of the female excess mortality was childbirth-related; Schofield has estimated maternal mortality for England at 7.7 per thousand live births in the later eighteenth century,[50] while for most of the nineteenth century it was nationally at a level of about five per

[47] *Decennial Supplement to the 75th Annual Report of the Registrar General of Births, Deaths and Marriages in England and Wales*, Pt I, PP 1914, XIV.

[48] Abridged life tables for types of areas and for each county are given in the *Decennial Supplement to the 75th Report*, Pt II, PP 1920, X.

[49] D. Tabutin, 'La Surmortalité féminine en Europe avant 1940', *Population*, 33 (1978), pp. 121–48. A wide-ranging though very inconclusive discussion of the issue, including some useful points of clarification by Richard Wall, appears in a special section of *Annales de Démographie Historique* (1981); see also S. R. Johansson, 'Sex and Death in Victorian England: An Examination of Age- and Sex-Specific Death Rates', in M. Vicinus, ed., *A Widening Sphere: Changing Roles of Victorian Women* (1977), pp. 163–81.

[50] R. S. Schofield, 'Did Mothers Really Die? Three Centuries of Maternal Mortality in "The World We Have Lost"', in L. Bonfield *et al.*, eds., *The World We Have Gained* (Oxford, 1986). Flinn, ed., *Scottish Population*, pp. 296–7, arrives at a figure of over 6 per cent for eighteenth-century Scotland while suggesting that Edinburgh in the 1750s may have had a rate of between 14 and 18 per 1,000 live births.

thousand, though with significant local variations.[51] Maternal mortality then fell steeply to only 0.5 per thousand births in 1952 (compare
0.1 per thousand births in 1978).[52]

However, since female children under the age of 15 also showed
excess mortality over males, and went on doing so for so long, other
factors than maternal mortality must have been involved. Much of
the excess, particularly in rural areas, was due to high levels of respiratory tuberculosis, and the pattern on a registration district and county
basis reveals that poor agricultural areas, and districts with large
unskilled working-class populations, were especially affected. This
in turn suggests that part of the responsibility lies with low levels
of nutrition, particularly during the adolescent growth spurt, a by-
product of a contemporary insistence on trying to keep the male
'breadwinner' well fed even during hard times; it is noticeable in
this context that other areas with high excess rates were mining districts where the same culturally maintained bias in food allocation
seems to have been present. Women and girls in these areas may
also have had less access to other household resources, including
washing facilities and changes of clothing. Additional factors in the
female excess were probably that women and girls spent more time
indoors in a poorly ventilated (and often, given contemporary dress
and cooking techniques, dangerous) environment, and the fact that
it would have been largely to women and girls that the task of nursing
the sick would have been delegated, thus compounding the risk of
infection, notably from diseases like tuberculosis.[53]

Available evidence on urban–rural, on other inter-community and
on occupational differences in mortality before the mid-nineteenth
century is scarce, but it is clear that variation in mortality between
different areas (and even between different rural areas) was very significant. As we have already seen, in the second half of the eighteenth
century, infant mortality in the market town of Gainsborough was
three and a half times that of the remote and scattered coastal parish

---

[51] The rate seems to have risen in Scotland in the first third of the twentieth century
parallel with the increased hospitalisation of births (Flinn, ed., *Scottish Population*,
p. 297).

[52] *Report on Confidential Enquiries into Maternal Deaths in England and Wales, 1976–1978*,
DHSS Report on Health and Social Subjects, No. 26 (1982), p. 1.

[53] A similar pattern may be observed in Scotland though nationally only for the 10–14
age group for the period 1861–70 (*Supplement to the 48th Detailed Annual Report*, PP
1906, XXI, pp. xciii–xciv); however, reference to the successive *Detailed Annual Reports*
suggests that this still unresearched phenomenon remains visible, at least in rural
areas, for most of the nineteenth century.

of Hartland;[54] in London infant deaths were clearly higher still.[55] At the same period similar if slightly smaller differences can be seen at the other childhood age groups.[56]

For the nineteenth century we are on surer ground once the Registrars General began to produce regional and occupational statistics. Woods[57] has calculated that a male baby born in Liverpool in 1861 could expect on average to live for twenty-six years. A similar baby born in Okehampton could expect to live for fifty-seven years; Bristol, Birmingham, Leicester, Derby, Manchester, Sheffield, Hull, Newcastle and parts of industrial Lancashire had mortality rates about as high as Liverpool while there were many rural areas at least as favourable as Okehampton. However, high mortality was not just a function of urban living. Some rural parishes, and especially those around the Wash and on the north Norfolk coast, had infant mortality levels as bad as, or worse than, all but the most insanitary areas of London, and had male life expectancy at birth of well below 45. Some non-urban areas like the Cornish mining districts had a very high level of adult male mortality. Woods comments correctly that 'There was . . . as great a range of mortality experience in England and Wales in the 1860s as there was between that of England and Wales as a whole in the 1840s and the 1960s, namely some 30 years.'[58] Similarly large differences can be observed for Scotland where the Registrars General very conveniently distinguished cities, towns and rural areas in their statistics. In 1861 the crude death rate in the four Scottish cities was 28.1, while in the other towns it was 23.4; in the rural areas taken as a whole it was only 17.9. In the counties of Caithness, Orkney and Shetland the figure was only 15.5.[59]

In England and Scotland the mortality differences between areas fell over the second half of the nineteenth century, largely as a result of a fall in urban rates at a time when rural rates showed only hesitant improvement in many areas. In Scotland, for example, the rural death

[54] Wrigley and Schofield, 'English Population', p. 179.
[55] Wrigley and Schofield, Population History, p. 253.
[56] Maternal mortality was also much higher in the parishes with high infant death rates (Wrigley and Schofield, 'English Population', p. 181).
[57] R. I. Woods, 'The Structure of Mortality in Mid-Nineteenth Century England and Wales', Journal of Historical Geography, 8 (1982), pp. 373–94.
[58] Ibid., p. 376.
[59] The figures here and in the next paragraph are from Flinn, ed., Scottish Population, p. 382; it may be noted that the rural death rate was actually higher in 1890–2 than it had been in 1860–2. For more detail see M. Anderson and D. J. Morse, 'The People', in W. H. Fraser and R. J. Morris, eds., People and Society in Scotland, vol. 2 (Edinburgh, 1989).

rate was 64 per cent of that for the cities in 1861, 83 per cent in 1891 and 91 per cent in the 1930s. Even by the post-Second World War period, however, considerable differences remained between different parts of the country. In England and Wales, for 1949–53, the male rural standardised mortality rate (the rate, that is, controlled for differences in the age structures of different areas) was only 79 per cent of that for conurbations; the rural rate for women was 91 per cent of that for conurbations. For the Tyneside conurbation the male rate was 45 per cent above the rural average and that for females was 40 per cent higher.[60]

Even at their worst, however, these urban–rural and regional differences were small compared with differentials between occupational groups. The first even roughly reliable national figures on occupational mortality became available only for the 1860s and 1870s (and then only for England and Wales). By then some of the worst sources of high mortality in such occupations as mining and seafaring had already been removed. In almost all records for the nineteenth century the healthiest group was the clergy, combining as they did a middle-class life style with a high propensity to live in the countryside. If we take the clergy as our standard and restrict ourselves to the age groups 25–44 (the group where the social consequences of high mortality were at their worst) we obtain the figures on occupational differentials shown in Table 1.1.

In examining this table two preliminary points may be noted. First, the worst occupations were not in general factory employments; instead the high-risk jobs involved, in the main, old, often heavy manual, technology. Second, when comparing 1900–2 with 1860, 1861 and 1871 it should be remembered that overall mortality fell markedly between the two periods, from 11.3 per thousand for all males at the earlier dates to 8.4 per thousand at the later. All the occupations shown in the table saw some improvement in their mortality between the two dates, though, bearing in mind that the later data are for all occupied males while the earlier are for all males, the improvement for innkeepers hardly represents much real amelioration.

Perhaps the most remarkable feature of Table 1.1 is the fact that the occupational differences in general widened over time. At the end of the nineteenth century, thirty years after the problems had

[60] Registrar General's *Decennial Supplement for England and Wales, 1951, Occupational Mortality*, Pt II, vol. I, *Commentary* (1958), p. 86.

Table 1.1 *Death rates per thousand living, and standardised mortality ratios compared with clergy, 25–44 age group, England and Wales, 1860, 1861, 1871 and 1900–2*

	1860, 1861, 1871		1900–2	
Occupational group	DR per 1,000	SMR	DR per 1,000	SMR
Clergy	6.0	100	3.4	100
Farmers and sons	7.7	128	4.8	141
Corn miller	9.3	155	6.9	182
Carpenter/joiner	9.4	157	6.2	182
Barrister/solicitor	10.0	166	6.0	176
Cotton manufacture	10.7	178	7.2	212
Fisherman	11.3	188	9.5	279
Potter/earthenware manufacture	12.6	210	9.0	265
Tailor	12.9	215	7.5	220
Printer	13.0	217	7.9	232
Glass manufacture	13.2	220	9.3	274
Innkeeper	18.0	233	17.9	526
Barger/lighter/waterman	15.0	250	11.0	324
File maker	16.3	272	13.4	394
Chimney sweep/soot merchant	17.5	292	12.0	353
All occupied males	–	–	7.8	229
All males	11.3	188	8.4	–

Sources: See n. 42.

first been identified by the Registrar General, file makers were still dying in large numbers from respiratory disease from flying grit and from lead poisoning from the moulds used to hold the files; chimney sweeps remained at the top of the cancer mortality list; potters and tin miners were still succumbing to tubercular conditions exacerbated by dust; seamen, fishermen, bargees and lightermen, dock labourers and coalminers, railway labourers and shunters were still high on the accident list – fifteen times or more likely to die an accidental death than were the clergy; innkeepers and inn servants died in their hundreds from the effects of excess alcohol consumption and from tuberculosis. A few improvements could be observed; fewer match girls were dying of phossy jaw, though legislation to ban white phosphorus match production had to wait until 1910. Improved ventilation significantly improved conditions in cotton mills. On the other hand, technological developments also brought new hazards in their wake, like mule spinners' cancer, attributable to a change to mineral oils for lubrication of the machinery.

Overall, the twentieth century, against a background of rapidly falling mortality, saw a very gradual narrowing of occupational differences, though in some areas they widened still further.[61] By 1951 the few remaining tin miners showed a standardised mortality ratio (SMR) against all occupations of 617 compared with 141 in 1890-2. Seamen were up from 135 in 1890-2 to 233 in 1949-53, and dockers from 188 to 233. Tool grinders still had mortality 50 per cent above average. Mine workers' chances of dying in an accident outside the home but not in a vehicle remained eleven times those of clerical workers, and for railway platelayers the excess probability was over sixteen times. New problems emerged among groups like medical radiographers, while car and coach proprietors had an SMR of 427 in 1949-53. But elsewhere much was greatly improved. Pottery workers saw their SMR fall from 171 in 1890-2 to 133 in 1949-53; the figures for textile workers were down from 114 to 103. Looking, as we can in the twentieth century, from the point of view of Social Classes, we can see a clear amelioration for the unskilled worker. In 1921-3 Registrar General Class 5 workers aged twenty to sixty-four had mortality 52 per cent above that of Class 1. By 1930-2 the differential had fallen to 23 per cent. By 1949-53, using 1931 Social Class definitions, it was down to 18 per cent.

However, just as some urban–rural and regional differences are attributable in great part to occupational differences, so much of the occupational difference was only indirectly connected to work conditions. As many seamen and more dock labourers died around 1900 of respiratory TB than died in accidents. More significantly, perhaps, the wives and children of many men in high mortality occupations also had high death rates. In 1949-53 the wives of coal hewers and getters had an SMR of 146 compared with their husbands' 153, while

---

[61] These figures and those in the next two paragraphs are calculated from the successive *Decennial Supplements* to the *Reports of the Registrar General of Births, Deaths and Marriages in England and Wales* (see also n. 42 above). The first *Report* to give detailed discussion of the mortality of married women by husbands' occupation is that for 1930-2; infant mortality is first discussed in the *Report* for 1910-12 and in more detail in the *Report* for 1920-2; a considerable amount of retrospective information is presented in the *Report* for 1949-53 (see n. 60 above). Some of the difficulties of assessing the precise patterns of change in the twentieth century (and particularly of changes between 1930-2 and 1949-53) are discussed in E. R. Pamuk, 'Social Class Inequality in Mortality from 1921 to 1972 in England and Wales', *Population Studies*, 39 (1985), pp. 17-31.

fishermen's wives, with an SMR of 126, were actually worse placed in the league table of mortality than were their husbands. At the Social Class level the same was true, though over time some narrowing took place. In 1930–2 the wives of men in Class 5 had mortality chances 40 per cent higher than those in Class 1; by 1949–53 the differential was down to 15 per cent.

Nevertheless, in certain areas very significant differences remained. As mortality from respiratory tuberculosis fell after the First World War the Class differences in mortality from the disease widened; for Class 5, wives' mortality was three times that of Class 1 in 1949–53, compared with two and a half times in 1930–2. Maternal death rates for Class 5 wives remained almost 50 per cent above that of wives of Class 1 even though other Class differences narrowed significantly. Differential mortality among children aged between four weeks and one year fell hardly at all between 1921 and 1949–53: Class 5 figures were 403 per cent of Class 1 in 1921 and 381 per cent in 1949–53. Compared even with Class 2, infants in Class 5 in 1951 were more than three times as likely to die of a whole range of conditions, including whooping cough, meningitis, pneumonia, suffocation by food and accidental suffocation in bed or cradle. For gastroenteritis the excess was 311 per cent, a significant relative deterioration on the 140 per cent excess of 1921; though Class 5 gastroenteritis mortality had fallen 84 per cent in the intervening period, for Class 1 the fall had been 88 per cent and for Class 2 it was 91 per cent.

In sum, the rapid fall in mortality in the last 100 years of our period was not primarily a process whereby those with the highest mortality caught up with those more favourably placed at the outset. Rather, in general, all classes benefited roughly equally, not a surprising conclusion perhaps if we remember that it was a fall in infectious diseases which provided almost all the improvement overall and that, while in most cases the lower classes had had higher death rates from these diseases, the higher classes had also succumbed in large numbers (and the children of the lower classes remained to the end predominantly those who continued to suffer the most).

Nevertheless, overall, mortality fell dramatically over our period and the overall effects of these changes can most easily be appreciated if we examine the survival chances of a number of cohorts born in England or England and Wales at roughly thirty-year intervals between 1681 and 1946. The experience of these different groups is charted in Figures 1.4 and 1.5; Table 1.2 gives a more detailed

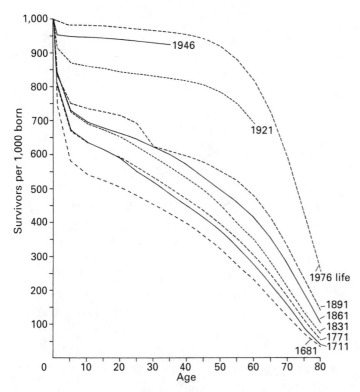

Figure 1.4 Survivors by birth cohort (males), England and Wales, 1681–1946
Notes and sources: See n. 42 and the appendix to Anderson, 'What Is New';
the figures relate to England until the mid-nineteenth century, and to
England and Wales thereafter.

breakdown of the figures and compares them with the non-cohorted
1975-7 English life table.[62] The graphs show the slow improvement
in survival over the first 150 years of our period and the dramatic
improvements of the twentieth century. The impact of the First World

---

[62] The figures for 1741 and 1801 are excluded from the graphs for clarity of presentation;
they fall roughly midway between 1681 and 1711, and between 1771 and 1831 respectively. The figures were calculated by applying to each cohort separately, for each
five-year period of life (single years below age 5), the life table survival experience
nearest in time to the date at which the cohort would have passed through any
particular age. Thus, for example, for the 1861 birth cohort, survival for the period
1886-90 was calculated by taking survival from ages 25 to 29 from the 1881–90 life
table, while survival between 30 and 34 and 35 and 39 was taken from the 1891–1900
life table. For the period after 1841 the results were checked against R. A. M. Cash
et al., *The Chester-Beatty Research Institute Serial Abridged Life Tables, England and Wales,
1841–1960*, 2nd edn (1983), but allowance was made for war deaths using data from
Winter, 'Some Demographic Consequences'.

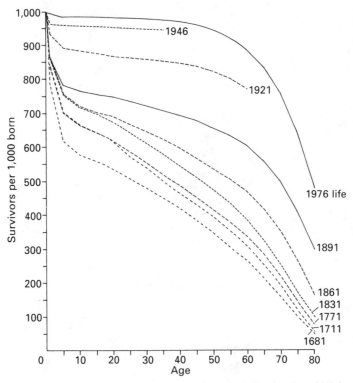

Figure 1.5 Survivors by birth cohort (females), England and Wales, 1681–1946
Notes and sources: As Figure 1.4.

War is clearly evident; even for this cohort of men aged 23 in 1914, about one in eleven would have died as a direct result of the war; had we taken the cohort aged 18 in 1914 the figure would have been one in eight. The postwar influenza epidemic took a further heavy toll in the same age groups. Few families and almost no communities escaped the impact of these sudden demographic and personal shocks, equal in many ways in their impact on the adult males of local populations only to some of the major epidemics of the early modern period.

In 1711, the median age at death was about 32 for males (35 for females); by the 1771 cohort it had reached just 35 (37), for the 1831 cohort 44 (46), for the 1861 cohort 49 (56) and for the 1891 cohort, heavily depleted as it was in its youth by the First World War, 57 (69). The same percentage of the 1921 male cohort has survived to be

Table 1.2 *Percentages of males and females dying in different age spans, by birth cohort, 1681–1946, and according to the 1975–7 life table*

	Year of birth										Life table
	1681	1711	1741	1771	1801	1831	1861	1891	1921	1946	1975–7
MALES											
Percentage dead by											
1	26	20	23	20	20	16	16	17	9	3	1
5	42	33	38	33	33	28	27	25	13	5	2
25	52	45	48	44	43	38	36	31	16	7	3
65	82	78	79	75	74	72	65	59	–	–	28
Percentage dying between											
5–25	17	18	18	16	15	18	12	8	4	1	1
25–65	63	60	59	56	54	52	45	40	–	–	16
Median age at death	20	32	28	35	37	44	50	58	–	–	73
FEMALES											
Percentage dead by											
1	21	16	19	16	16	14	15	15	7	3	1
5	39	30	34	30	30	25	24	22	11	4	1
25	49	43	45	41	41	36	33	26	14	5	2
65	79	75	75	72	70	68	58	44	–	–	17
Percentage dying between											
5–25	18	19	17	16	15	18	12	6	3	1	1
25–65	58	56	55	52	50	47	38	24	–	–	15
Median age at death	26	35	32	38	41	47	57	70	–	–	79

Sources: See n. 42; the 1975–7 life table is from *Annual Abstract of Statistics* (1983).

65 as survived to be 5 in the 1711 and 1771 groups. Of the 1946 cohort of males, 94 per cent survived to be 10. As recently as the 1921 cohort this figure was only 87 per cent, while for the 1891 and 1711 cohorts the figures were 73 per cent and 63 per cent respectively (the figure for the 1978–80 English life table is over 98 per cent).[63] No matter from what angle one approaches the figures, the twentieth century clearly reveals the sharpest improvements in life-chances. Equally important, it is only well into the twentieth century that mortality reached a sufficiently low level that its possibility of occurrence in any year could more or less be ruled out of the forward thinking of anyone aged between one and late middle age. The possible consequences of this change for a wide range of attitudes and behaviour (images of children, prospects of inheritance, investment and career

[63] *Annual Abstract of Statistics*, 119 (1983), Table 2.31.

planning, willingness to undertake risky ventures like emigration or military service) still remain largely unexplored.[64]

III BIRTHS, MARRIAGES AND THEIR IMPLICATIONS

Figure 1.2 has already demonstrated the overall trend of the birth rate in our period for England and Wales: a peak around 1800, stability until the 1870s, followed by a decline to very low levels in the 1930s (with 1933 as a low point), and then a sudden if temporary recovery after the Second World War. The crude birth rate is susceptible to arbitrary fluctuation if the age structure of the population changes over time. However, similar patterns can also be seen in the gross reproduction rate (GRR); this provides an estimate, for a girl born in any year, of the number of female children that she would bear by the end of her childbearing period, if age-specific fertility rates remain unchanged.

Since the GRR is not affected by population age structure it is clear that there were major and genuine variations in fertility in the period under review. These variations must have been due to some combination of changes in marriage patterns, changes in illegitimacy and changes in the numbers of children born to married women. Each of these are now examined in turn.

Taking first the proportions of the population never married, no national evidence is available for Scotland before the mid-nineteenth century. In England and Wales the proportion of women never married seems to have fluctuated between 9 and 12 per cent in the eighteenth and early nineteenth centuries; it reached rather over 10 per cent by the mid-nineteenth century and more than 14 per cent in the first third of the twentieth; thereafter, the fall to the historically low level of the 1970s began in the late 1930s.[65] The problem of how nineteenth-century society found appropriate social roles for the large numbers of single middle aged and older people of both sexes remains to be fully explored, but we already know that lodgings for men, living with kin in old age for women, posts as domestic servants and governesses, and annuities given to spinster daughters by their fathers' wills, all form parts of the answer.[66]

---

[64] For a first attempt, see M. Anderson, 'The Emergence of the Modern Life Cycle in Britain', *Social History*, 10 (1985), pp. 69–87.

[65] Schofield, 'English Marriage Patterns'; Mitchell and Deane, *Abstract*, pp. 15–18.

[66] For an amplified discussion see Anderson, 'Social Position of the Spinster'.

The celibacy rates for Scotland have, since records began, been somewhat higher than those for England/England and Wales, a phenomenon due in part to low rates of nuptiality in the more remote and sparsely populated rural areas. It is hard to avoid the conclusion, however, that the particularly high celibacy figures for Scotland (with around one fifth of women remaining unmarried right up to the Second World War) were in part a reflection of a society where emigration meant that at no prewar census were there ever more than ninety-two men aged 25–9 for every hundred women in that age group; in 1861 the figure was as low as seventy-seven. Against this background of high emigration it is worth noting that in 1921, in both England and Wales and in Scotland, a larger percentage of both men *and* women were married in the 20–4 and 25–9 age groups than had been in 1911; whatever else the First World War had done, it had not, as is sometimes alleged, removed so many men as to leave a whole generation of women condemned to spinsterhood.

So far, attention has been concentrated on the men and women who never married, but socially just as important were the widowed. As might be expected, the high rates of mortality noted earlier produced high rates of marital break-up through death. Some approximate estimates can be made by using published distributions of the combined ages of husbands and wives at marriage, linked to cohort life tables for the median age at marriage group, and with the simplifying assumption that deaths of husbands and wives were statistically independent. On this basis it can be estimated that about 24 per cent of marriages of couples marrying in the later 1730s would have had their marriages terminated by death within ten years, while around 56 per cent of marriages would not have lasted twenty-five years; only 15 per cent would have lasted for forty years or more. Improvement thereafter was only gradual for a century or more. For the cohort marrying in the 1850s, about 19 per cent of marriages would not have lasted ten years, and around 47 per cent twenty-five; for the 1880s cohort the figures are 13 per cent and 37 per cent respectively. The experiences of many of those marrying in the early years of the twentieth century were drastically curtailed by the slaughter in the trenches in the First World War, but for the rest the improvement in adult mortality produced a marked reduction in the early termination of marriages through death. On the assumptions used here, 91 per cent of their marriages lasted at least ten years, and 74 per cent twenty-five; 44 per cent lasted for forty years or more. If we again ignore the (much smaller) war losses of the Second World War, just 5 per cent of marriages of the late 1930s were ended by death within ten years; 85 per cent of couples who had not divorced (79 per cent of all couples) reached their Silver Wedding Day. Thereafter, divorce rather than death became the great disrupter of marriages, producing in the 1980s total disruption rates very similar, when duration is controlled, to those by death alone for the 1820s.[67]

One immediately important effect of the high rates of marital disruption through death, right up to the twentieth century, was a high incidence of living widowed persons. There are no good estimates available before the mid-nineteenth century but in the second half of that century at any one time around 2 per cent of men aged 25–34 (3 per cent of women) were widowed, around 4 per cent of men aged 35–44 (8 per cent of women), 7 per cent of men aged 45–54 (16 per cent of women), and 14 per cent of men aged 55–64 (30 per cent of women). These figures fell slowly over the nineteenth century (they actually rose for a time for the 55–64 age group), then fell faster in the twentieth century. However, even by 1951 some 7 per cent of men aged 55–64, and 22 per cent of women in this age group were widowed. Given, as we shall see, a longer period of childbearing, one side-effect of these high nineteenth-century levels of widowhood was a very significant number of children in single parent, and especially in female headed, households. Another consequence was the presence in the society in old age of a very large surplus of widowed women, most of whom were dependent on other than earned income for their support.

One other source of marital dissolution should also be mentioned briefly here: disruption of marriages through separation and divorce. Separation is almost impossible to quantify, there being only scanty and unsystematic legal provision before 1895 (and therefore no reliable documentation). By the early twentieth century, however, about

---

[67] M. Anderson, 'What Is New about the Modern Family: An Historical Perspective', Office of Population Censuses and Surveys (hereafter OPCS), *Occasional Papers*, no. 31 (1983). The figures used in this paragraph differ slightly from those employed in the 1983 paper, which employed a further simplifying assumption that all couples married at the median age at marriage for their cohorts. The new estimates published here are derived from work undertaken in collaboration with Frances Proven and Geoff Cohen, and incorporate bivariate age at marriage distributions from Wrigley and Schofield, 'English Population', and from the *Annual Reports* of the Registrar General for England and Wales; in practice, the difference in results produced by the two methods are fairly small until the most recent birth cohorts.

10,000 mainly working-class women were obtaining orders for maintenance in England and Wales each year; this figure reached nearly
20,000 by the late 1940s. By contrast, divorce was statistically fairly
unimportant until right at the end of our period; nevertheless, successive stages of liberalisation of legislation (in England and Wales in
1857, 1923 and 1937; in Scotland in 1939) caused much stir at the
time and were accompanied by, though probably did no more than
marginally cause, upward steps in the divorce rate. In England and
Wales (the trend in Scotland was similar) the number of decrees of
divorce and annulment rose from only about 330 in the whole period
between 1700 and 1857 to an annual average of about 150 in the 1850s,
275 in the late 1870s and over 600 immediately before the First World
War. In the early 1930s the annual figure passed 4,000 and by the
late 1940s was over 30,000 having risen dramatically during and after
the war. Petitions per 10,000 marriages were 1.38 in 1911, 3.86 in
1921, 6.34 in 1937 and 26.98 in 1950.[68]

One factor which somewhat mitigated these effects, however, was
the high incidence of remarriage. Wrigley and Schofield have noted[69]
that in the sixteenth century 'Perhaps as many as 30 per cent of all
those marrying were widows or widowers' and it seems likely from
the scattered available evidence that in the second half of the eighteenth century in England and Wales the figure was still between
15 per cent and 20 per cent. By the mid-nineteenth century about
14 per cent of males and 9 per cent of women who married were
widowed. The figures fell slowly for the rest of the century, reaching
8.9 per cent and 6.6 per cent respectively in the early 1900s, 7.3 per
cent and 4.6 per cent in the early 1930s and 6.4 per cent and 5.4
per cent in the early 1950s.[70]

So far this section has focussed primarily on the fairly dramatic
long-term changes in the proportions of the population who entered,

---

[68] O. R. McGregor *et al.*, *Separated Spouses: A Study of the Matrimonial Jurisdiction of
Magistrates Courts* (1970), pp. 15–16, 32–5. O. R. McGregor, *Divorce in England* (1957),
chaps. 1, 2. The annual figures for England and Wales and for Scotland are usefully
collected in B. R. Mitchell and H. G. Jones, *Second Abstract of British Historical Statistics*
(Cambridge, 1971), pp. 31–2; a more analytical review, including data on changes
by 'Social Class' can be found in G. Rowntree and N. H. Carrier, 'The Resort
to Divorce in England and Wales, 1858–1957', *Population Studies*, 11 (1958), pp. 188–
233.

[69] Wrigley and Schofield, *Population History*, p. 258.

[70] The full series of statistics can be found for the period since 1900 in OPCS, *Marriage
and Divorce Statistics* (1982), Ser. FM2, no. 7, Table 3.2; earlier series are in the *Annual
Reports of the Registrar General*.

re-entered, and remained in, the marital state. Compared with these aspects, changes in the age at which marriage occurred were much less significant. Before the second half of the nineteenth century precise data are difficult to obtain since even in the early years of civil registration in England and Wales age information was only patchily recorded, and there was wide variation between different areas. Schofield, modifying his earlier estimates based on family reconstitutions, has suggested that mean marriage ages for women fell sharply in the later eighteenth century. Women born around 1716 had mean first marriage ages of 25.3, while those born around 1791 married on average at about 22.6 years of age; the falls were particularly due to rising proportions of women marrying at very young ages.[71] Thereafter, it seems that mean and median marriage ages increased sharply, with the 1816 birth cohort having a mean marriage age of around 25.3, a figure consistent with national figures for the late 1850s when we can compute approximate median ages of 24.4 for men and 22.9 for women, rising to 26.7 and 24.4 in the late 1910s and falling to 25.2 and 22.4 by 1951.[72]

For Scotland, the evidence is thinner, though the nineteenth-century evidence is compatible with England. Flinn and his colleagues are rightly sceptical of contemporary comment which suggests very low marriage ages in eighteenth-century Scotland[73] (though the possibility of quite low marriage ages in the Islands and the coastal fringes of the Highlands cannot be ruled out). The estimated median female marriage age for Kilmarnock in the mid-eighteenth century of 23.5 is comparable with English figures but more interesting is the finding that 'urban' wives had a median marriage age which was over six years younger than women from the rural sector, a discovery which certainly matches the suggestions of scholars who believe that in eighteenth-century England marriage ages were particularly low in areas and among groups exposed to more commercialised production

[71] Schofield, 'English Marriage Patterns'; the importance of changes in the age distribution of marriage is discussed in J. A. Goldstone, 'The Demographic Revolution in England: A Re-Examination', *Population Studies*, 40 (1986), pp. 5–34.

[72] Figures back to 1901–5 are given in OPCS, *Marriage and Divorce Statistics*, Table 3.5 (though the figures for 1906–10 and earlier appear inconsistent with those previously published in the 1938 *Registrar General's Statistical Review*, Table K, which go back to 1896); earlier figures are in the *59th Annual Report of the Registrar General, England and Wales*, PP 1897, XXI, pp. xiii–xiv.

[73] The Scottish material cited in this paragraph is drawn from Flinn, ed., *Scottish Population*, pp. 274–9.

whether through certain kinds of capitalist agriculture, other day-labour, or through proto-industry.[74]

In the later nineteenth and early twentieth centuries there is clear evidence of regional and occupational differences in the age at first marriage. Using an indirect method computed from the percentages single at the 1861 census, the range in the estimated mean ages at marriage in the registration districts of England and Wales can be estimated as 9.7 years for males and 9.0 years for females.[75] One extreme district, Auckland in County Durham, had 59 per cent of its female population aged 20–4 married; another, Hampstead in London, had only 12 per cent. In Dudley in Staffordshire 96 per cent of the female population aged 45–9 were married while in Fylde in Lancashire the figure was only 68 per cent. Further analysis suggests that marriage was especially delayed in the relatively few areas still characterised by small family farms and where the non-familial labour supply in the area consisted largely of living-in farm servants. Marriage was also delayed for both sexes in areas (mainly with high middle-class populations) characterised by high incidences of domestic servants. The age at marriage for both sexes was significantly linked to local sex ratios, reflecting imbalances of in- and out-migration in areas with highly gender-skewed labour markets. To a limited extent, high concentrations of local employment in agriculture pulled down the marriage age somewhat, but neither high levels of female employment nor high levels of employment in coal mining, textiles, metals and engineering had much independent effect on marriage patterns at the registration district level.

At the individual level the most reliable evidence on marriage ages for any part of our period was computed by staff of the English Registrar General's office for 1884–5 and is reproduced in Table 1.3; the median figures have been computed from the published quinquennial distributions of the age of the population at marriage and are therefore only approximate. Clear discrepancies arise between the marriage patterns of the professional classes and of farmers on the one hand, and of mining and textile workers on the other.

At other points in the hundred years before 1950 only indirect indi-

---

[74] Goldstone, 'Demographic Revolution'; D. Levine, *Family Formation in an Age of Nascent Capitalism* (1977); see also his review of Wrigley and Schofield's *Population History* in *Social History*, 8 (1983), pp. 148–59.

[75] For more detail see M. Anderson, 'Marriage Patterns in Victorian Britain: An Analysis Based on Registration District Data for England and Wales', *Journal of Family History*, 1 (1976), pp. 55–78.

Table 1.3 *Mean and median ages at marriage, England and Wales, 1884–5*

Occupational group	Bachelors		Spinsters	
	Mean	Median	Mean	Median
Miner	24.1	23.5	22.5	21.6
Textiles	24.3	23.6	23.4	22.5
Shoemaker, tailor	24.9	23.8	24.3	23.2
Artisan	25.4	24.2	23.7	22.9
Labourer	25.6	24.3	23.7	22.8
Commercial clerk	26.3	25.5	24.4	23.4
Shopkeeper/shopman	26.7	25.5	24.2	23.7
Farmers and relatives	29.3	28.1	26.9	24.9
Professional/independent	31.2	29.6	26.4	24.7
All	26.1	24.6	24.6	23.3

Source: W. Ogle, 'On Marriage Rates and Marriage Ages...', *Journal of the Royal Statistical Society*, 53 (1890), pp. 253–80.

cators of marriage ages can be obtained,[76] but they suggest relatively little change in the overall patterns. At all times, except perhaps in the interwar period, miners married young and married wives on average a year or more younger than the general population. Textile workers, together with other semi-skilled factory workers, also showed some tendency to younger marriage, particularly in the nineteenth century. At the other extreme, throughout the period, farmers and the professional and higher administrative classes typically married at least two years older than the average and had wives at least one year older, though still substantially younger than themselves (over four years for farmers and nearly four for professional workers in 1851). There is some evidence, however, to suggest that professionals were particularly likely to delay marriage in the second half of the nineteenth century, and that, subsequently, some shift towards the average pattern for the population as a whole may have occurred.

These changes in marriage patterns were of major importance in

[76] The following sources and methods were used to obtain these extremely approximate results: the 1851 National Sample data on proportions married at different ages; T. H. C. Stevenson, 'The Fertility of Various Social Classes in England and Wales from the Middle of the Nineteenth Century to 1911', *Journal of the Royal Statistical Society*, 83 (1920), p. 426 (for marriage durations of 0–5 years only); W. A. B. Hopkin and J. Hajnal, 'Analysis of the Births in England and Wales, 1939, by Father's Occupation', *Population Studies*, 1 (1947–8), p. 197; *1951 Census of England and Wales, Fertility Report*, age distribution data for women of marital duration of one year (Table B2).

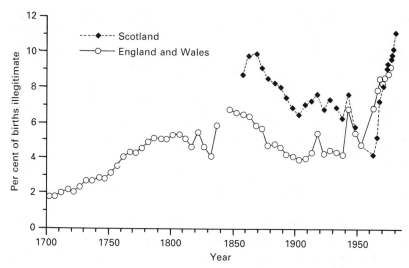

Figure 1.6 Illegitimate births per 100 live births, Britain, 1700–1980
Sources: Laslett *et al.*, eds., *Bastardy*, pp. 14–15, 17; Flinn, ed., *Scottish Population*, pp. 350–1; *Annual Reports of the Registrar General of Births, Deaths and Marriages for Scotland.*

altering the birth rate in our period; indeed, marriage-related changes were the most important single set of factors for the population rise of the eighteenth and early nineteenth centuries. Thereafter, their impact was less (but never without significance for fertility) but from the 1870s onwards it was the number of births per woman, rather than the proportion of women married, which became the crucial determinant of population growth.[77]

We can conveniently deal first with illegitimate and premaritally conceived births. Changes in this aspect of behaviour are now one of the best charted areas in historical demography, though the social significance of the trends is a topic of unresolved debate.[78] The figures for England and Wales are charted in Figure 1.6. Further analysis of some of the background to these figures reveals several points of interest. First, there was a close *positive* relationship between illegitimacy and prenuptial pregnancy; fluctuations in illegitimacy were not simply a result of variations in pressure to enter 'shotgun marriages'. Secondly, there was a close and continuing relationship between illegitimate and legitimate fertility, particularly in the nineteenth century;

[77] Wrigley and Schofield, *Population History*, chap. 7.
[78] For a summary of the controversy and a short bibliography, see M. Anderson, *Approaches to the History of the Western Family, 1500–1914* (1980), pp. 54–9, 89–90.

this is arguably of interest in attempts to understand the legitimate fertility decline as well as the illegitimate. Thirdly, there was an apparent inverse relationship between illegitimacy and the age at marriage. These parallelisms suggest that very similar factors were influencing a range of fertility-related behaviour; this view is further supported both by the general closeness in age of those bearing first children in and out of wedlock (the latter being on average only about a year younger in most studies),[79] and by the very high incidence of premarital conception. Indeed, premarital sex was a normal (though perhaps more or less normal at different points in time) part of the courtship process for very large sections of the population throughout our period.[80]

By the early nineteenth century something approaching 20 per cent of first births were illegitimate and over half of all first births were probably conceived outside marriage.[81] By 1938, when official figures for England and Wales become available, 13.4 per cent of all births occurred outside of, or within eight and a half months of, marriage; of all premaritally conceived births, about 70 per cent were legitimated by the marriage of the parents before the birth of the child – comparable figures for 1951 were 12.3 per cent and 60 per cent. At this latter date, however (and almost certainly earlier), by no means all of these extra-maritally conceived maternities were first births; a rough estimate suggests that both in 1938 and in 1950 less than one quarter of first births were extra-maritally conceived.[82] This pattern whereby the interwar period (and to a lesser extent the immediate postwar period) had particularly high incidences of at least outwardly stable conventional Christian family morality is notable in other areas also; its causes merit more attention than they have so far received.

At a more local level there were great, and largely unexplained, differences in illegitimacy. Rural illegitimacy was usually well above urban right through to the 1930s (though from then on the cities tended to top the list). Different community studies reveal large differences between places in the late eighteenth century (for example Colyton between 1741 and 1790 had 7.8 per cent of its births illegitimate,

[79] The evidence is usefully summarised by E. A. Wrigley, 'Marriage, Fertility and Population Growth in Eighteenth Century England', in R. B. Outhwaite, ed., *Marriage and Society: Studies in the Social History of Marriage* (1981), pp. 137–86; and T. P. R. Laslett *et al.*, eds., *Bastardy and its Comparative History* (1980), chap. 1.

[80] Laslett *et al.*, eds., *Bastardy*; Levine, *Family Formation*, chap. 9.

[81] Laslett *et al.*, eds., *Bastardy*, pp. 54–5.

[82] *Registrar General's Statistical Review for England and Wales for the Year 1970, Part II, Tables, Population* (1972) Table UU, p. 195.

Gainsborough at the same dates only 3.5 per cent).[83] In the nineteenth century, at the county level, equally large differences can be observed,[84] and these seem in many cases to persist over long periods of time (possibly reflecting a local variation in tolerance towards illegitimacy). Interestingly, these variations in illegitimacy are often paralleled by variations in legitimate fertility.[85]

The limited evidence for Scotland suggests that a considerable rise in illegitimacy must have taken place between the mid-eighteenth and mid-nineteenth centuries;[86] thereafter the rates roughly paralleled the English, though the turning points were slightly different.[87] What is of particular interest in the Scottish context, however, are the very marked nineteenth-century regional disparities – high in the north-east and south-west, low in the north and north-west; these differences broadly persisted from the time that they were first observable in 1855 right through to the end of our period. While rural–urban differences were fairly small (with rural areas as a whole somewhat above urban and even above the four cities), differences within the predominantly agricultural counties were enormous. In 1855, 'A teenage girl in Banff was more than 20 times as likely to have a bastard as one in Ross and even for girls in their twenties, the likelihood of becoming an unmarried mother was between four and six times greater in Banff than in Ross.'[88] In general, areas with high illegitimacy tended to have earlier marriage and higher overall fertility – and some connection clearly exists also with high premarital pregnancy. But illegitimacy also seems to have been closely related to family and community structure and to women's positions within a family and local economy. In rural areas illegitimacy was high among those groups of the population where parental and community control

---

[83] Laslett *et al.*, eds., *Bastardy*, pp. 96–7.

[84] *Ibid.*, chap. 1; Cumberland in 1870–2 had an illegitimate fertility ratio of 29.2 and Shropshire 28.2; at the other extremes Hampshire had a figure of only 13.6 and Somerset of 13.3; Middlesex was the lowest county with a ratio of 9.4 (*ibid.*, pp. 34–5).

[85] *Ibid.*, pp. 32ff.

[86] L. Leneman and R. Mitchison, 'Scottish Illegitimacy Ratios in the Early Modern Period', *Economic History Review*, 2nd ser., 40 (1987), pp. 41–63.

[87] These parallelisms, indeed, go beyond Britain – see, e.g., E. Shorter *et al.*, 'The Decline in Non-Marital Fertility in Europe 1880–1940', *Population Studies*, 25 (1971), pp. 375–93.

[88] Flinn, *ed.*, *Scottish Population*, p. 353; summary statistics by county and urban/rural divisions from 1861 to 1931/9 can be found on pp. 350–3. Detailed maps of illegitimacy in the late nineteenth century at parish level are currently being prepared by Donald Morse of the University of Edinburgh.

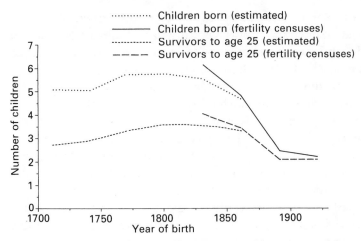

Figure 1.7 Completed family size and survivors, England and Wales, 1710–1930

Notes and sources: See text and n. 92; the illegitimacy corrections use data referenced in the sources to Figure 1.6; data on percentage never married from Wrigley and Schofield, *Population History*, p. 360, and from censuses of population; life tables as for Figure 1.4.

over courtship was relatively low and where women who bore illegitimate children could, if necessary, support themselves relatively easily; in the 'peasant economy' areas where these conditions did not apply illegitimacy was at its lowest. Further exploration of English illegitimacy in these terms – and especially in the context of the age and socio-economic position of the mothers – is clearly called for, but awaits the availability to scholars of the nineteenth-century registration returns.[89]

Finally in this section we turn to marital fertility and especially to completed family size. Figure 1.7 shows estimates of mean completed family size, and of survivorship, for England and Wales (England before the 1831 birth cohort). In the upper pair of lines, the dotted line is derived from an indirect estimating technique based on the gross reproduction rate and originally employed by Wrigley and Schofield to compare the results of family reconstitution with those from aggregative analysis.[90] The solid line gives the Registrar

[89] For Scotland, see T. C. Smout, 'Sexual Behaviour in Nineteenth Century Scotland', in Laslett *et al.*, eds., *Bastardy*, chap. 7. For an interesting recent demonstration of this point for one English settlement, see J. Robin, 'Illegitimacy in Colyton, 1851–1881', *Continuity and Change*, 2 (1987), p. 324.

[90] Wrigley and Schofield, 'English Population', Table 12.

General's estimates derived from the two fertility censuses of 1911 and 1951 supplemented by the family census of 1946. The patterns are clear, with a peak of between 5.7 and 6.2 children per married woman being reached for those born between 1771 and 1831 and a steady fall in fertility occurring from the 1870s. Those born in the 1880s had only half as many children to care for, entertain, clothe and feed as their parents had had; their own children had only two-thirds as many as they did. In two generations – and across almost the whole population – the average number of children born per married woman fell from around six to only a little over two.[91]

In this context, however, the lower pair of lines in Figure 1.7 is also of importance, showing estimates of the average number of children per family surviving to age 25.[92] When compared with the early eighteenth century, by the early nineteenth almost one extra child per family was reaching adulthood; this was the result of higher fertility combining with falling mortality to boost survival. Thereafter, further falls in mortality in the later nineteenth century to a great extent offset the fall in fertility; as a result, although the number of children born to each family fell steadily from the 1870s, it was only those marrying in the early twentieth century who managed to reduce the number of their children surviving to adulthood even to the eighteenth-century level. While women born after the First World War had about one third of the number of children of women born in the late eighteenth and early nineteenth centuries, the number of children surviving to adulthood fell by only some 40 per cent. The benefits to families of falling family sizes can thus be exaggerated – and this may be especially true for lower-class families where earlier child mortality would have been highest.[93] Nevertheless, it remains the case that the standards of living, accommodation, travel and education which developed in the interwar and especially in the post-Second World War periods would have been much more difficult

---

[91] For a very effective discussion of the possible significance of the very rapid and widespread initial stages of the decline in fertility, see R. I. Woods, 'The Fertility Transition in Victorian England', *Population Studies*, 41 (1987), pp. 283–311; this paper also provides an excellent review of a number of different interpretations of the fertility decline in England and Wales.

[92] These estimates are calculated by applying the life table data described in n. 62 above to the birth data described in the text.

[93] In social welfare terms, the benefits were, of course, even smaller since the period of the fertility decline corresponds with a reduction in the earnings opportunities for children both through a contraction of labour demand and limitations on supply imposed by the extensions of compulsory education.

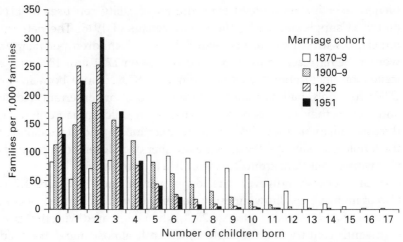

Figure 1.8 Completed family sizes, by marriage cohort, England and Wales, 1870–9 to 1951
Notes and sources: 1911 Census of England and Wales, Fertility Report; papers of the *Royal Commission on Population, VI*; OPCS, *Birth Statistics*, Ser. FM1, Table 10.5; the more recent published data exclude information on numbers of children in very large families; the plotted data are rough estimates only, but relate to small numbers of families only.

if not impossible to attain with an average of even an extra two children per family.

From a rather different perspective, the social consequences of these shifts were even more significant. Over the eighteenth century, England and Wales had to produce about one third of an additional economic and social 'slot' per person per generation. In the early and mid-nineteenth centuries, by contrast, between three-quarters and one such extra 'slots' per generation had to be found. The implication of this for a whole range of phenomena, from housing to welfare expenditure, from emigration to the expansion of domestic service, are clearly considerable.

The subsequent contraction in family size was accompanied by two other changes in childbearing behaviour which are arguably of even greater social significance. First, not merely did average family size fall but very small families became, eventually, normative. Figure 1.8 shows estimates of the distribution of family sizes for a number of different marriage cohorts. A clear pattern emerges of an increasing concentration onto small families. For the 1870s the most marked fea-

ture is the wide dispersal of family sizes; no one size category contained more than 10 per cent of families; more than 5 per cent fell
into all sizes from zero to ten. More than one in ten of all families
were of eleven children or more, and these families actually included
more than a quarter of all children born. In the late nineteenth century,
therefore, the family experience both of parents and of children was
very diverse, and not merely in terms of the numbers of persons
who had to share living space and parental care and affection; given
the clear relationship between family size and standard of living,
experiences would also have differed markedly even within socio-
economic groups in opportunities for diversity of diet and access to
'luxuries' like toys, books, trips and education. The other curves in
Figure 1.8 show the way in which, from the 1870s to the 1950s, a
predominance developed not merely onto the small family but onto
the two-child family. This brought with it a steady homogenisation
for the mass of the population of many features of growing up. It
allowed, for the first time, for example, most children to spend at
least part of their childhood in a room of their own, as well as making
possible such new goods as the small family car.

Secondly, these smaller numbers of children per woman tended
increasingly to be concentrated into the earlier years of married life.
As early as 1874, Ansell[94] found in his study of upper middle and
upper class families that, where only one child was born, childbearing
had ceased on average by age 31 and, where family size was two
or three, the average age at the end of childbearing was only 34.
As the fertility decline got under way, similar patterns seem also
to have been adopted by the population as a whole; as a result falling
family size was accompanied by a marked shift towards an earlier
end to childbearing for the majority of couples.[95] Among the implications were significant changes in the processes of socialisation for
adult roles, producing by the 1940s, for example, whole generations
of women who had never been used to dealing with the needs of
a small baby.

---

[94] C. Ansell, *On the Rate of Mortality at Early Periods of Life*, National Life Assurance
Society (1874), p. 69; the full distribution is given in Table XIII, p. 89.

[95] For evidence from family reconstitutions for later nineteenth-century Scotland, see
A. Gilloran, 'Family Formation in Victorian Scotland' (unpublished PhD thesis, Edin-
burgh University, 1985); S. P. Walker, 'Occupational Expansion, Fertility Decline
and Recruitment to the Professions in Scotland, 1850–1914' (unpublished PhD thesis,
Edinburgh University, 1986); and the work in progress by D. Kemmer; see also
Woods, 'Fertility Transition', p. 291.

While overall marital fertility levels before the fertility decline were far from maximal,[96] no substantial evidence has yet appeared to suggest widespread deliberate birth control within marriage before the mid-nineteenth century.[97] The substantial fertility differences which did occur between areas (at the 1851 extremes, married women in Cornwall were around 28 per cent more fertile than married women in London) seem most likely to have reflected differences in infant and foetal mortality, maternal health and nutrition, and infant feeding patterns, though this is not to deny the possibility that some small groups may have been deliberately limiting family size as early as the eighteenth century.[98] What is more certain is that the nineteenth-century fall in family size did not take place equally across all socio-economic groups. Recent research has questioned the older view that the middle classes were the first to practice widespread fertility limitation, arguing that there was some general downward movement of the indicators for all social groups from at least the 1860s and that the 'social classes' employed by the Registrar General and reproduced in Table 1.4 are too insensitive to capture the full complexity of the onset of fertility decline.[99] These arguments cannot be ignored, though it is still clear that the largest nineteenth-century falls in fertility took place among certain sections of the middle classes, and among some groups closely associated with them.

Banks has used the detailed tabulations of the 1911 fertility census to try to identify 'pioneers' within the middle classes (and especially

---

[96] Using as a standard the fertility of the Hutterite community of the 1930s (a group where marriage was early and no contraception was employed), the combination of delayed marriage and non-marriage by a substantial number of women reduced fertility in England and Wales to 48 per cent of the standard level. Even within marriage the level of fertility in the 1850s was only some 67 per cent of the Hutterite Standard (A. J. Coale and S. C. Watkins, *The Decline of Fertility in Europe* (Princeton, 1986), chap. 2).

[97] A. McLaren, *Birth Control in Nineteenth-Century England* (1978), chap. 1.

[98] Such is one possible interpretation of the data produced by E. A. Wrigley, 'Family Limitation in Preindustrial England', *Economic History Review*, 2nd ser., 19 (1966), pp. 82–109; see also Levine, *Family Formation*, chap. 5. Data on fertility by county for England and Wales and for Scotland are conveniently summarised in Coale and Watkins, *Decline of Fertility*, chap. 2; an extended though not wholly satisfactory discussion is in M. S. Teitelbaum, *The British Fertility Decline* (Princeton, 1984). Data at parish level for Scotland are currently being analysed by Donald Morse.

[99] Woods, 'Fertility Transition'. There are, however, as Woods recognises, major problems of interpretation of the data for this period caused by the fact that the 1911 fertility census data is based for the middle years of the century on a tiny number of survivors whose ages at marriage are certainly not representative of the population from which they were drawn, and whose fertility histories may also be biased if a connection exists between fertility levels and longevity.

Table 1.4 *Children born and surviving to 1911, per 100 families, by date of marriage and 'Social Class', 1851–91*

'Social Class'	Date of marriage				
	1851–60	1861–70	1871–80	1881–5	1886–91
Children born					
1 Upper and middle	642	592	480	396	340
2 Intermediate 1–3	731	663	558	468	409
3 Skilled	758	711	629	556	491
4 Intermediate 3–5	744	700	624	557	496
5 Unskilled	781	737	672	614	558
6 Textile workers	736	671	584	510	441
7 Miners	823	827	776	723	655
8 Agricultural labs.	794	728	670	617	545
All occupied	747	700	618	547	487
All	728	679	605	539	482
Children surviving					
1 Upper and middle	445	440	381	325	286
2 Intermediate 1–3	511	489	432	374	333
3 Skilled	502	503	470	430	388
4 Intermediate 3–5	501	501	469	431	390
5 Unskilled	509	507	483	455	421
6 Textile workers	473	451	418	378	334
7 Miners	500	550	544	525	486
8 Agricultural labs.	568	555	536	509	457
All occupied	507	501	464	423	383
All	489	484	454	416	378

Source: Stevenson, 'Fertility of Various Social Classes', pp. 401–32.

has suggested an important role for certain professions and persons in occupations with a clearly laid out career structure). His data for the earliest years are based, however, on very small numbers of marriages and the differences, which are much less apparent when age at marriage is controlled, appear to be in great part an artefact of the different combinations of ages at marriage of the tiny minority of survivors who married in the 1860s and still survived to 1911.[100]

[100] J. A. Banks, *Victorian Values: Secularism and the Size of Families* (1981), esp. chaps. 4 and 8. I am grateful to Debbie Kemmer for sharing with me her results and thoughts on Banks's work and on the difficulties of interpreting possible changes in fertility in the period before 1870.

By the marriages of the early 1880s, however, when the data have become robust enough to merit detailed examination, the gap between the least fertile (represented in Table 1.4 by Registrar General's Class 1) and the highly fertile miners (Class 7) was at its historic widest (over three children; it remained at around two even after child mortality is taken into account). For this group of marriages, even among wives marrying as early as ages 20–4, men in such occupations as barristers (average 3.16 children), physicians, surgeons and general practitioners (3.48), solicitors (3.52), bank officials (3.62), civil and mining engineers (3.71) and persons in scientific pursuits (3.85) all had families of fewer than four children; by contrast, miners with wives in the same age group at marriage had on average 7.36. In view of their intense public opposition to artificial family limitation, the fact that the wives of clergymen of the Church of England in this age-at-marriage group had only 4.01 children is perhaps also of some interest.[101]

One effect of these differential shifts in fertility was to produce in the early twentieth century very clear differences not only in average family size but also in the distribution of numbers of children across families of different occupational groups. In Stevenson's table (Table 1.4), the spread between the group with the lowest number of children per family and the group with the highest number was, for the marriages of the 1850s, only from 14 per cent below to 10 per cent above the average for the population as a whole. With the marriages of the late 1880s, however, this spread was from 30 per cent below to 36 per cent above the average. Figure 1.9, based on the only surviving occupational data for Scotland from the 1911 census, is confined to marriages where the wife was aged 22–6 at marriage and the marriages had lasted at least fifteen years. While for some of the upper middle-class groups the trend towards the normative two-child family of the twentieth century is already apparent, in other groups (including but not exclusively those where family labour had a crucial part to play in the family economy)[102] a pattern of almost unrestricted fertility remains.

[101] The data in this paragraph are calculated from the *1911 Census of England and Wales, Fertility Report*, Pt. II, Table 35.
[102] Crofters would be a group particularly likely to retain high fertility for longest according to the model proposed by R. Lesthaeghe and C. Wilson, 'Modes of Production, Secularization and the Pace of the Fertility Decline in Western Europe 1870–1930', in Coale and Watkins, *Decline of Fertility*, chap. 6; the special conditions affecting the fertility of heavy industry and mining areas are well reviewed in M. R. Haines, *Fertility and Occupation: Population Patterns in Industrialization* (1979).

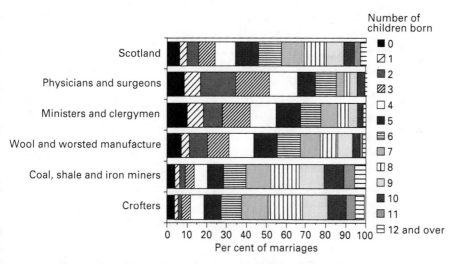

Figure 1.9 Number of children born by occupation of husband, Scotland, 1911 (wives aged 22–6 at marriage, and marriage duration at least 15 years) *Source: 1911 Census of Scotland*, III, PP 1914, XLIV, Table XLVII.

The 1946 family census data[103] suggest that for marriages of the first third of the twentieth century occupational differentials changed very little. Even among women aged 45–9 in 1951 (most of whom would have married in the late 1920s), the differential between unskilled manual workers (at 132 per cent of the average) and professional and higher administrative workers (at 76 per cent) remained large; by this date (and probably earlier) there is some evidence that patterns of female employment and types of community involvement had begun significantly to influence family size differentials within the working class.[104] In general, however, only among marriages of the 1930s did the occupational differentials begin to fall, and this was in large part due to a continued slow fall in fertility among lower manual workers at a time when the fertility of the rest of the population was beginning to rise again.

[103] A useful summary of the relevant data is given in the *Report of the Royal Commission on Population* (Cmd 7695, 1949), pp. 24ff; the fuller data are presented in D. V. Glass and E. Grebenik, 'The Trend and Pattern of Fertility in Great Britain', *Papers of the Royal Commission on Population*, 6 (1954).

[104] *1951 Census of England and Wales, Fertility Report*, pp. xlivff. D. Gittins, *Fair Sex: Family Size and Structure, 1900–39* (1982), chaps. 3–5.

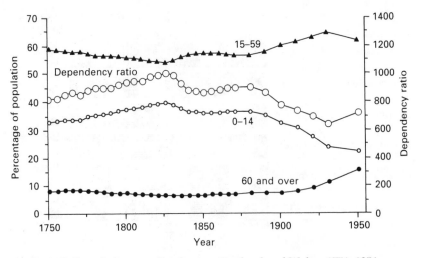

Figure 1.10 Population age distribution, England and Wales, 1751–1951
Notes and sources: Wrigley and Schofield, *Population History*, pp. 447, 528–9;
later figures computed from censuses of population by Wrigley and
Schofield's method. The figures relate to England until the mid-nineteenth
century and to England and Wales thereafter.

IV STRUCTURAL IMPLICATIONS OF DEMOGRAPHIC CHANGE

The previous sections have shown the significant changes which
occurred in each of the different demographic phenomena in the 200
years of our period. When the interactions between these elements
are explored, some further points of importance emerge.

Turning first to the age structure of the population of England/
England and Wales, Figure 1.10, based on Wrigley and Schofield's
figures to 1871 and on censuses thereafter, shows changes in the proportion of the population in the three broad age bands 0–14, 15–59
and 60 and over. The most striking change in proportional terms
clearly occurred in the 60 and over age group. In 1766 rather less
than one person in every twelve was in this age group and by 1826
the ratio had fallen to one in fifteen. Thereafter the proportion of
old people rose steadily over the nineteenth century, to reach over
one in thirteen by 1911, nearly one in eight by 1931 and almost one
in six by 1951. Within these figures the proportion of very old people
– for example of 75 and over – remained fairly stable over the nineteenth century (1.04 per cent were 75 or over in 1801, 1.03 per cent
in 1826 and 1.07 per cent in 1851) but then rose slowly (to one person
in sixty-nine aged 75 or over in 1911) and then rapidly so that by

1951 one person in twenty-eight was aged 75 or over. Undoubtedly, the mid-twentieth-century aged population (and certainly those in their late 60s and early 70s) was on average healthier and fitter in some 'objective' sense than that of earlier centuries (though man-days lost through ill-health actually rose); nevertheless, rising numbers against a background of falling employment, and in the context of an increasingly formalised right to income maintenance through public and private pension provision associated with a fixed idea of a 'retirement age', were bound to appear to create significant public problems of economic support for the aged.[105]

However, as Figure 1.10 also shows, this rise in the aged element in the population took place against a background where, in the twentieth century, the 'dependency ratio' (calculated here as the numbers 0–14 plus 60 and over divided by the numbers 15–59) reached an all-time low. The main cause of this rapid reduction in the dependency ratio in the late nineteenth century was the fall in the birth rate, but the effect was startling. In 1826 nearly two persons in every five in the population were aged under 15. By 1911 this figure had fallen to three in ten and by 1951 to only just over one in five. The absolute number of 5–14 year olds in 1951 was almost exactly the same as it had been in 1881 (while the population as a whole was 41 per cent larger) and the figure was 17 per cent below that for 1911. The implications of shifts of this magnitude both for public services like education and social welfare and for the occupational structure have not been given the attention that they deserve.

Looking, finally, from the point of view of 'adults' (those between 15 and 59 were the main producer group even of eighteenth-century society), two particular points merit comment. First, as Wrigley and Schofield have pointed out, the period 1750–1825, often seen as a crucial phase of the 'industrial revolution', took place against a background of steadily (if slowly) *deteriorating* producer/consumer balance.[106] Secondly, more dramatically and perhaps of potentially

---

[105] In practice, however, there is some suggestion that as early as the eighteenth century most old people were in fact heavily dependent on poor relief – see D. Thomson, 'I Am Not My Father's Keeper: Families and the Elderly in Nineteenth Century England', *Law and History Review*, 2 (1984), pp. 265–86; and R. M. Smith, 'The Structured Dependence of The Elderly as a Recent Development: Some Skeptical Historical Thoughts', *Ageing and Society*, 4 (1984), pp. 413–15. On the spread of the formal practice of retirement, see Anderson, 'Emergence'; and L. Hannah, *Inventing Retirement: The Development of Occupational Pensions in Britain* (Cambridge, 1986).

[106] Wrigley and Schofield, *Population History*, p. 449.

real social and economic significance, the interwar depression coincided with a peak in the proportion of the population in the principal employed age groups. In spite of war losses, in 1931 the proportion of the population aged 15–59 in England and Wales (the figures for Scotland are a little lower) was 15 per cent (8.2 percentage points) higher than it had been in 1871 and 5 per cent (3.2 percentage points) higher than it had been in 1911. Put at its most stark, the 1931 excess of population in the economically active age groups compared with 1911 was over 1.5 million people, at a time when officially recorded unemployment at its worst did not quite reach 3 million.

In addition, over the same period, the population of prime working age was steadily aging. Whereas in the mid-nineteenth century there were nearly two adults aged 20–39 for every one aged 40–59, in the twentieth century the ratio changed rapidly; by 1951 the two groups were more or less evenly matched. The dynamism and flexibility introduced into the labour force by large and growing successive cohorts of young new entrants was steadily disappearing at the very same time that major and much more rapid shifts in employment patterns were coming to be required.

These demographic changes also had a major impact in a quite different area: the family and the kinship group. First, the high rates of mortality of the eighteenth and nineteenth centuries, together with the long periods of childbearing of the pre-fertility decline period, meant that very large numbers of children lived through much of their childhood having lost at least one parent through death; they were thus genuinely 'single parent families' (rather than simply 'single parent *households*'). Precise estimation of the proportion of children affected is difficult because ages of parents at childbearing varied widely (especially in the pre-twentieth-century period). Table 1.5, however, provides some insight into this problem. It traces the experience of cohorts of what we may consider as 'typical' children. These children are all assumed to have been born when their mothers were aged 30 (26 for the 1946 group) and to have had fathers who were older than their mothers by the average number of years for their cohort. The table shows the proportion of such children who could have expected to lose parents by ages 10, 15 and 25, and also the median age of losing these parents, on the assumption that the death of the father was independent of the death of the mother. These figures are somewhat lower than those for all children (particularly for age at losing fathers), since the distributions of parents' ages at marriage

Table 1.5 *Estimated percentage of 'typical' children losing parents by certain ages, by children's birth cohort, 1741–1946*

| Cohort born | Percentage losing parent(s) | | | | | | | | | Median age at losing | |
| | By age 10 | | | By age 15 | | | By age 25 | | | | |
	Father	Mother	Both	Father	Mother	Both	Father	Mother	Both	Father	Mother
1741	14	14	2	20	20	4	36	34	12	31	33
1771	12	12	2	20	19	4	35	33	12	32	34
1801	12	12	2	19	19	3	34	32	11	33	35
1831	11	11	1	17	17	3	32	30	10	34	36
1861	11	11	1	17	17	3	33	29	10	35	36
1891	9	8	1	14	12	2	26	22	6	37	41
1921	5	4	0	8	6	0	16	12	2	41	47
1946	2	1	0	3	3	0	10	7	1	45	53

Source: Derived from the life tables (see n. 42) and based on children born when their mothers were 30 (25 for 1946), assuming that parents married at the median age for their cohort and that spouse mortality was independent; for qualifications to the figures see text.

are upwardly skewed, as is the probability that a parent will die for children of higher birth orders. Laslett, using Coale and Demeny model life tables with a male expectation of life at birth of 35 as a reasonable approximation to early eighteenth-century conditions, estimates that 46 per cent of girls might have lost their fathers by the age of 25; this compares with around 40 per cent on the present estimates.[107] Nevertheless, because they provide figures on a consistent basis over time, the data of Table 1.5 remain of considerable interest, particularly in establishing the timing of the main changes.

Another perspective on this issue – which also takes some account of separation on the one hand and remarriage on the other – could be gathered if we were able to investigate the percentage, of all households containing children, which had only one parent present; precise evidence on this point is, however, scrappy at all periods. For nineteen English community listings from various dates between 1599 and 1811, Laslett has shown that about 16 per cent of unmarried persons listed as 'children' of the head of household were recorded as living with a widowed parent who had not remarried; of these, two-thirds were living with mothers, one third with fathers. In addition, 5 per cent of children were recorded as living with a remarried parent and residing therefore in that ambiguous and often problematical status of 'step-child'.[108]

At only two other points in our period do we have any further evidence on this topic. For 1851 we can make use of some preliminary tabulations from the National Sample from the 1851 census of Great Britain. Including cases where relationships were inferred from surnames, marital status and position in the household, about 14 per cent of those children who were living with parent(s) were living with a widowed parent who had not remarried, 2 per cent with an unmarried parent and 4 per cent with a parent whose spouse was absent from the home on census night. Of all children under the age of 15, 77 per cent were explicitly stated as living with two married or cohabiting parents (79 per cent if reasonable inferences about relationships are allowed). Depending on the criteria used, between 6 and 7 per cent of such children lived with a widowed parent (widows

---

[107]   Laslett, *Illicit Love*, p. 162n. In the 1946 birth cohort of the National Survey of Health and Development, 7.2 per cent of girls had lost one or both parents by age 15, compared with 6 per cent as estimated by the technique used here (K. Kiernan, 'Teenage Marriage and Marital Breakdown: A Longitudinal Study', *Population Studies*, 40 (1986), pp. 35–54).

[108]   Calculated from Laslett, *Illicit Love*, Table 4.2.

outnumbering widowers by three to one), about 4 per cent with a temporarily or permanently separated parent, and 1 per cent lived with a never-married parent; up to 2 per cent seem to have lived without any parent but in a group of brothers and sisters. At least 6 per cent of children in this 0–14 age group lived separated from any close relatives at all. This last figure was around 4 per cent even for the 0–9 year age group, nearly 5 per cent of whom lived with a widowed parent. Of all family groups, only around three-quarters had two parents present on census night, and 15 per cent were headed by a widowed parent.

Finally, for 1921, the Registrars General calculated that just under 6 per cent of 0–9 year olds had lost fathers and rather over 2 per cent mothers; in all, including cases where the sex of the parent was unknown and where both parents had died (this latter group being less than 0.5 per cent of all children), nearly 9 per cent of 0–9 year olds (and about 11.3 per cent of 0–14 year olds) had lost at least one parent.[109] Today less than 1 per cent of first marriages end in death within ten years and only 3 per cent within twenty years duration.[110]

Clearly, then, very many children in the eighteenth and nineteenth centuries experienced the death of at least one parent and suffered the emotional, economic and residential consequences. Only well into the twentieth century did a major amelioration of this problem emerge; the end of our period, by chance, coincides with the period of the historically greatest stability in the growing-up experiences of children.

The postwar period also, however, saw other major changes. Figure 1.11 plots some of the more significant of the results of analysing the interrelationships between mortality, nuptiality and fertility as they impacted on the life courses of women. For simplicity of computation the calculations relate to women who themselves and whose families experienced all life course transitions at the estimated median age for the cohort. The graph is thus a simplification of the complexities of reality, since the distributions of events around some of these medians were in the past very large. Nevertheless, as a single indicator of 'typical' experience, the plots show the broad parameters of change very adequately.

---

[109] The figures are presented in the *Reports* of the *1921 Census of England and Wales*, and of the *1951 Census of Scotland*.

[110] R. Haskey, 'The Proportion of Marriages Ending in Divorce', *Population Trends*, 27 (1982).

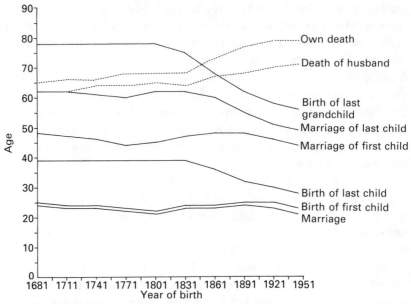

Figure 1.11 Life courses of women by birth cohort, England and Wales, 1681–1946

Notes and sources: The data are for England until the mid-nineteenth century and for England and Wales thereafter; for marriage age data see nn. 70–2; age at birth of first child data are approximate, derived from various family reconstitution studies and from fertility data in the *Annual Reports* of the Registrar General for England and Wales; age at birth of last child data for the eighteenth century are estimated from Wrigley and Schofield, 'English Population', and thereafter from various sources including Ansell, *Rate of Mortality*, and M. Britton's 'Birth Intervals and Family Building', *Population Trends*, 18 (1980), pp. 8–16; survival is estimated from life table data (see source to Figure 1.4).

A number of points may be noted. The decline from the mid-nineteenth century in family size, and the clustering of children into the early years of marriage (plus some smaller changes in the age of marriage), led to a fall in the age of a 'typical' woman at the birth of her last child of around eleven years between the 1831 and the 1946 birth cohorts; there was also a fall of about thirteen years in her age at the marriage of her last child, and a fall in her age at the birth of her last grandchild of about twenty-two years. Almost all of these reductions occurred in the twentieth century. By contrast, and more gradually over time, a 'median woman's' age at the death of her husband rose by about twelve years and her age at her own death by about fourteen. Thus, while in the 1681 birth cohort such a woman's last child married in the same year that her husband died and she herself died thirteen years before the birth of her last grandchild, women in the 1861 cohort who followed our 'typical' path could expect their husbands to live around seven years after the marriage of their last child, and the women themselves five years beyond the birth of their last grandchild. The 1861 birth cohort, the grandparents of the interwar period, was the first where a woman experiencing a 'median' life-cycle would have known all her grandchildren. Subsequent events were equally dramatic. For example, men born in the 1891 cohort who were entering old age right at the end of our period could expect to live some six years after the birth of their last grandchild and their wives could expect to live another fifteen.[111] Mid-twentieth-century levels of life expectancy gave a woman around twenty-two years of life after the marriage of her last child, compared with just three for the 1681 birth cohort and six for the cohort born in the early 1830s.

The implications of these estimates for the likelihood of knowing and relating to particular kin are considerable, but, more speculatively, they may also have other implications. At 1980s mortality levels, a 'typical' woman will have some seventeen years between the birth of her last child and the birth of her first grandchild, years in which she is likely to seek to follow the increasing postwar trend (no doubt itself aided by the greater certainties of modern demographic behaviour) of returning to the labour force once the family is established. By contrast, a similar woman born in the 1860s had only thirteen years between the births of her last child and of her first grandchild, and a woman born in 1831 had only nine. In earlier generations it was easy to conceive of spending one's whole adult life caring first for one's own children and then helping with the care of one's grandchildren. This, it may be noted, was the pattern found by sociologists in the 1950s in 'traditional working-class communities',[112] areas where the older demographic patterns continued for somewhat longer than elsewhere and where low geographical mobility meant that children's children were more frequently accessible.

Women growing old in the later nineteenth and earlier twentieth centuries did so at a period of life during which their own children

---

[111] Survival rates of the 1980s would give men another fourteen years of life and women another twenty-three.

[112] For a summary of this literature and a bibliography, see R. Frankenburg, *Communities in Britain* (1966), esp. chaps. 5, 7.

were themselves childbearing. Under these circumstances it was easy for a pattern of reciprocity (grandchild-care by grandparents, parent-care by children) to occur. As late as the 1861 cohort, for these 'typical' families, the last grandchild reached the age of five in the same year that his or her maternal grandfather died. The demographic changes of the twentieth century transformed the situation – though it was the 1960s and 1970s before the pattern fully had worked itself out.[113]

However, this pattern, associated as it often has been with 'traditional' working-class communities, had in fact been a relatively short-lived phenomenon. On the figures used here, in the 1861 grand-maternal cohort the last grandchild reached the age of five in the year that his or her grandmother died. In the 1681 cohort the grandmother would have died thirteen years *before* her last grandchild was born, a pattern which changed relatively little for grandmothers born well into the first half of the nineteenth century. Before the late nineteenth century, therefore, the possibility of – and indeed the need for – a three-generational system of child and grandmaternal care was much less evident.

Another point to note in this connection is that twentieth-century changes in some ways significantly increased 'the burden of the aged'. One side-effect of the fact that, by the 1950s, the aged were a larger proportion of the population is that they had on average fewer children to look after them in a period when, perversely, they themselves were likely to live somewhat longer. Thus the 2.3 children who reached age 25 from the 1891 cohort of mothers could expect their mothers to live on average twelve years past age 65. This gives an admittedly crude but still interesting statistic: the ratio of survival years past 65 to children alive; for the 1891 birth cohort the value is somewhat over five. By contrast, the 3.6 children reaching age 25 from the 1801 cohort of mothers had mothers who on average would die only three years past 65, giving a ratio of less than one. Not merely, towards the end of our period, did the demographic basis of the relationship between the generations change in terms of potential reciprocity, but the average burden in terms of years of old age falling on each child markedly increased.

The implication of demographic changes for changes in the possibility of relationships with other kin over the life-cycle are more difficult

---

[113] This point is amplified in Anderson, 'What Is New'.

to estimate meaningfully by the kinds of techniques used so far. While each individual has only one parent of each sex, the number of siblings which any given individual is likely to have alive at any particular age will depend on his or her birth order as well as on numbers of siblings born and dying by that age – and, as we have already seen, both numbers born and the numbers dying had, before the twentieth century, a wide dispersal about the median. Put into human terms, this meant that different individuals alive at the same time had very different numbers of surviving relatives – and in this case it is probably what happened to the dispersal rather than the 'typical' which was the more interesting change over time. At one, extremely unlikely, extreme, an individual, both of whose parents had seven siblings each of whom married and had eight children all of which survived, would have had, at age 25, one hundred and twenty-eight first cousins and twenty-eight uncles and aunts. By contrast, a person born in 1831 whose relatives all followed the median experience for their generation would have had only 2.6 adult uncles/aunts on each side; allowing for non-marriage of these uncles and aunts, and assuming that those who married had an average number of children surviving to age 25, only sixteen cousins would have actually lived to adulthood. Even this is a significant figure compared with the median person born in 1921 who, with just 1.3 uncles/aunts on each side, each having on average a mere 2.1 children, was lucky to have just five first cousins alive. However, as already noted, these are median figures based on simplified assumptions which ignore distributions; in practice many adults in the real 1831 birth cohort had fewer living cousins even than five, while others had many more.

Moreover, in either case, the 1831 cousins would have been born over a period of more than thirty years, compared typically with only about ten years for the 1921 cohort. The realistic 'normal' size of the close kin peer groups, therefore, may not have been all that different over time, though the greater homogeneity of experience of the twentieth-century cohorts remains. All this anyway assumes that contact between first cousins and with uncles and aunts was maintained – and this is clearly less likely before the twentieth century, in periods of high rates of emigration and significant long-distance internal migration, and in the absence of modern means of rapid communications. Moreover, we should not necessarily assume that people wanted to and did maintain contact even where this was possible. While there are references in the published literature to cousins claiming privileges of kinship after long lapses of time,[114] there is rather little evidence that, outside the commercial and professional middle classes,[115] functional contact with more remote kin was ever of any great importance. Certainly very few individuals named as 'cousin' appear in households listed at the 1851 census.[116]

V THE HOUSEHOLD

The second main theme to be covered in this chapter is the household. By contrast with demography, the household has not been a subject of official concern over most of our period. As a result, the level of information available is much sparser. Nevertheless, it is now well established that throughout our period mean household size in typical communities (certainly throughout England and lowland Scotland) seldom exceeded six persons and was typically rather under five. Figures published by Wall give a mean size for the period 1750–1821 for England of 4.81,[117] and provisional estimates from the 1851 census sample for Great Britain suggest a figure of around 4.75. For the 1911 census the figure was about 4.4, while for 1947 a survey by Gray cited by Wall gives a mean size of 3.67; the 1951 census figure was 3.18.[118] Attempts to chart more precisely the timing of the decline are bedevilled by changes in census definitions but it seems fairly evident that a steady fall took place from the 1890s and that this was primarily influenced right to the end of our period by falling family size – though the figures for the immediate post-Second World War

---

[114] For a late 1950s case, see C. Rosser and C. C. Harris, *The Family and Social Change: A Study of Family and Kinship in a South Wales Town* (1965), p. 229; a literary reference is T. Hardy, *Tess of the d'Urbervilles* (1925 edn), p. 40.

[115] D. Crozier, 'Kinship and Occupational Succession', *Sociological Review*, new ser., 13 (1965), pp. 15–43.

[116] Though it seems likely that a proportion of those listed as 'servants' and perhaps also as 'lodgers' and 'visitors' were in fact relatives of the head of household.

[117] R. Wall, *Family Forms in Historic Europe* (Cambridge, 1983), p. 497.

[118] *Ibid.*, the survey was one of a number conducted by the Government Social Survey in the postwar period to investigate housing conditions; for the 1851 census data see n. 29 above, and M. Anderson, 'Households, Families and Individuals: Some Preliminary Results from the National Sample from the 1851 Census', *Continuity and Change*, 3 (1988), pp. 421–38; *1951 Census of England and Wales, Housing Report*, p. xxxi.

period may be somewhat inflated by house sharing as a result of wartime damage and dislocation (see below).[119]

Mean household size can, however, be a misleading concept because, within a fairly constant size, changes can occur in household composition. Also, the mean tends to aggregate the experiences of different groups and to conceal shifts over the life course. In addition, because the size distribution is skewed upwards, most people have always lived in households significantly larger than the mean.[120] Taking the latter point first, for the 100 'English standard' communities for 1574–1821, we can calculate a mean 'experienced household size' of 6.1;[121] this can be compared with estimates of 6.2 for the 1851 census sample, 5.5 for the 1911 census and 4.7 for the 1951 census. While in 1951 8 per cent of households (comprising 11 per cent of individuals) contained six or more individuals, in 1911, 27 per cent of households (comprising 45 per cent of individuals) fell into this size range. Comparable figures for 1851 are 34 per cent of households (55 per cent of individuals), and in the Cambridge Group's 100 communities a remarkably similar 33 per cent of households (54 per cent of individuals).[122] Though the average size of household was relatively small, a majority of persons right to the end of the nineteenth century lived in households which were, by modern standards, large.[123]

Again, by modern standards at least, households were also very overcrowded. In the eighteenth and early nineteenth centuries there

---

[119] This at least must presumably be much of the cause of the high rates of sharing of accommodation by newly married couples in the late 1940s and early 1950s (though the data are also unfortunately somewhat skewed as a result of the method of data collection); see A. Holmans, 'Housing Careers of Recently Married Couples', *Population Trends*, 24 (1981), pp. 10–14.

[120] For a summary of the problems, see Anderson, *Approaches*, pp. 22–8.

[121] Calculated from T. P. R. Laslett and R. Wall, eds., *Household and Family in Past Time* (Cambridge, 1972), Table 4.6; the 'mean experienced household size' is mean household size weighted by the number of persons in each household and is neatly given intuitive meaning by Laslett as 'a single measure of all the answers which would be given if every member of a community were asked, what size of household do you live in?' (p. 40).

[122] Published census figures are usefully assembled in *ibid.*, pp. 138–43.

[123] There were, of course, major variations over the life course and by socio-economic group. In 1851, children, born on average into households of 6.4 persons, were by age 10 living in households averaging 7.4. People in their late 20s and early 30s lived only on average 5.7 to a household, and after some rise in middle age household size fell to 3.6 for women and 4.2 for men for the 75 and over age group. In the 65 and over age group, 2 per cent of men and 6 per cent of women lived alone. In general, members of higher socio-economic groups lived in rather larger households, largely because of the number of servants which they maintained; agricultural labourers and clerks lived in relatively small households, largely because they had, for rather different reasons, the fewest children living at home.

were frequent complaints from social investigators about gross over-crowding, particularly in the hovels which were frequently the only homes of many agricultural workers and their families.[124] Even in 1911, when the first complete figures become available, 75 per cent of the population of England still lived in a one or two roomed dwelling, and 9 per cent of the population lived more than two to a room.[125] In certain areas the problem was much worse, with the proportion of the population living more than two to a room being 35 per cent in Stepney, 37 per cent in Shoreditch, 40 per cent in Finsbury (compared with 8 per cent for London as a whole). In several mining areas of Durham and Northumberland the figure was well over 40 per cent; for these counties as a whole it was 29 per cent. Improvement was small at the time of the 1931 census, but by 1951 falling family size, massive urban building and rebuilding programmes, and wartime bombing had left only 2 per cent of the English and Welsh populations living more than two to a room. Concern was now being expressed officially at occupation levels of above one to a room, the lot in 1951 of 26 per cent of the population as a whole (but, for example, of 42 per cent of the population of the Tyneside conurbation).

If things were bad in England, however, the problem was much worse in Scotland (though the average size of room in Scottish towns was always well above the English). Nevertheless, enormous privacy problems clearly emerged in a situation where, in 1861, 26 per cent of the whole Scottish population lived in single room dwellings (and 39 per cent in two room dwellings).[126] At that date 57 per cent of the population lived more than two to a room and 19 per cent more than four to a room. By 1911 things had improved only slightly. There were still areas like Kilsyth, Wishaw and Armadale where more than 20 per cent lived in single roomed houses and nationally almost 50 per cent still lived in one or two roomed property, with 45 per cent living at two or more to a room. Locally this latter problem was even worse, with more than 70 per cent of the population of a town like Coatbridge living more than two to a room and almost 35 per cent

[124] A useful summary of the evidence here is G. E. Fussell and C. Goodman, 'The Housing of the Rural Population in the Eighteenth Century', *Economic History*, 2 (1930), pp. 63–90.

[125] *1911 Census of England and Wales*, III, PP 1913, LXXVII, pp. x, xv, xvii, Table 2; *1951 Census of England and Wales, Housing Report*, Table 8B.

[126] The figures are calculated or obtained from the following: *1861 Census of Scotland, Population Tables and Report*, PP 1862, L, Table IX; *1911 Census of Scotland, Report*, PP 1913, LXXX, Tables XLIV, XLV; *1951 Census of Scotland*, III, Tables 48, 49, 56.

of the population of Wishaw living four or more to a room. As in England it was only in the years around the Second World War that a marked improvement emerged. Even in 1951 over a quarter of the Scottish population still lived in one or two roomed dwellings and a quarter of the people of Glasgow lived more than two to a room.

This reduction in the numbers of people sharing the same living space was accompanied by a steady reduction in the presence of members from outside the conjugal family of the household head. These people in the past were of three main kinds: relatives outside the conjugal family, 'servants' and lodgers.

Relatives were never numerically of great significance overall (though sharing with relatives could be very important for certain groups of the population at certain times in their lives).[127] The numbers of kin resident in typical households in Britain may, in fact, have been larger at the end of our period than at any previous date, though it seems likely that this was in large part due to a combination of a rising marriage rate and a housing shortage which had been much exacerbated by the Second World War. Wall's evidence, based on a rather small and almost certainly unrepresentative sample of population listings, suggests that about 5 per cent of the population lived as relatives in someone else's house in the period 1750–1821. For 1851, the preliminary estimate for the non-institutionalised population is 6.3 per cent. A survey conducted in 1947, cited by Wall, suggests a figure as high as 11.5 per cent, but it is hard to believe that comparable figures for the interwar period would have even begun to approach this level.[128]

Co-residing relatives were drawn throughout our period from a narrow band of close kin.[129] Over time, however, the balance between different kinds of relatives shifted considerably. On the one hand, compared with the eighteenth century and probably even with the nineteenth, a much larger proportion of married couples, many with children of their own, were at the end of our period sharing with their own parents or parents-in-law, many of whom were in turn still married. By contrast, in the early modern period it was very rare

---

[127] This was especially true in old age, especially for spinsters (Anderson, 'Social Position of the Spinster').
[128] Wall, *Family Forms*, p. 497.
[129] In 1851 under 3 per cent fell outside the narrow band of direct antecedents or descendants of the head of household, or of his siblings and their spouses and children.

indeed to find households containing two lineally related married couples; only 7 per cent of households examined by Wall for the period 1750–1821 contained persons of three successive generations.[130] Indeed, Laslett has suggested that it was probably a basic principle of early modern society that a newly married couple established a household of their own and that even widowed parents would only be taken into the households of their married children if considerable hardship would otherwise have resulted.[131]

By the mid-nineteenth century, households containing lineally related ever married persons of two successive generations were somewhat more common, and this was particularly so among certain groups of the population such as small farmers,[132] and in certain areas such as the cotton manufacturing districts, where grandmothers were employed in taking care of children while their mothers worked in the textile factories.[133] By this period nationally, 6 per cent of households contained two lineally related ever married persons and 10 per cent of households contained related persons spanning three or more generations. Unfortunately, after 1851 we have no national or other representative data available until 1947, when the presence of very large numbers of parents and married children of the household heads suggests that sharing had become a very common practice indeed, a view strengthened by a retrospective survey conducted in the late 1970s which suggests (though on the basis of a rather inadequate sample design) that over half of couples marrying in the years before 1955 began marriage sharing accommodation (mostly with kin); by the late 1960s, however, this pattern was changing fast, though whether this was a new form of behaviour or whether it represented a reversion to a prewar pattern is unclear.[134]

The second large group of relatives present in households in the early modern period were what we may call 'parentless kin', that is siblings, nieces and nephews and grandchildren, all living apart

---

[130] R. Wall, 'Regional and Temporal Variations in English Household Structure from 1650', in J. Hobcraft and P. Rees, eds., *Regional Demographic Development* (1977), pp. 94, 98.

[131] In K. W. Wachter *et al.*, *Statistical Studies of Historical Social Structure* (1978), pp. 81, 104.

[132] Of family labour farm households, 13 per cent had one or more married children plus at least one parent living in the same household, a condition which can be compared with just 7 per cent of households as a whole.

[133] Anderson, *Family Structure*, esp. chap. 10.   [134] Holmans, 'Housing Careers'.

from their own parents. Siblings, nieces and nephews and grandchildren together comprise about two-thirds of all co-resident kin for the period 1750–1821 and three-quarters at the time of the 1851 census.[135] In 1851, two-thirds of this group had no parents living with them in their households. The reasons for their presence in such numbers (more than 1 per cent of the entire population, for example, were living as nieces/nephews in 1851) are difficult to establish in detail but several factors seem relevant. Many were clearly orphans (or children who had lost one parent and whose surviving parent had remarried) and the numbers were thus a consequence of the high rates of mortality referred to above. The fact that many appear as young employed workers in highly migrant communities suggests that some were either young people left behind when the rest of the family moved away in search of work, or were adolescents who had followed a long-standing pattern of teenage migration in search of work and had been provided with homes at their destinations by close relatives. Some, and particularly some of the grandchildren, were the children of unmarried mothers, while many others were probably being farmed out, to relieve overcrowding, or to provide companionship for elderly relatives, or both.[136]

In addition, some were directly employed in a more productive manner by the relatives with whom they shared. Preliminary analysis of the 1851 census sample suggests that non-conjugal family kin were particularly clustered in small employer households, the households of the self-employed and in the households of farmers. Their presence in over a fifth of professionals' households presumably relates more to sponsorship and/or companionship functions and will be a topic meriting further research.

The second large group of non-family members to be found in households in the early modern period and also in the nineteenth century is 'servants', though the functions associated with the title 'servant' were subject to considerable change between the early eighteenth and the late nineteenth centuries.[137] In the 1650–1749 listings analysed by Wall 'servants' made up nearly 14 per cent of the entire popula-

---

[135] Wall, *Family Forms*, p. 500.

[136] Anderson, *Family Structure*, chaps. 6, 9–11; on farming of children in the twentieth century, see, e.g., M. Young and P. Willmott, *Family and Kinship in East London* (1957). For an interesting recent demonstration of the use of grandparents to care for illegitimate children in one particular settlement, see Robin, 'Illegitimacy'. Some important new findings on this point are emerging from work currently in progress by Rory Paddock of the University of Edinburgh.

[137] A. Kussmaul, *Servants in Husbandry in Early Modern England* (Cambridge, 1981).

tion.[138] Nationally at this time the largest proportion of servants would probably have been 'servants in husbandry' (living-in servants of both sexes whose prime, though not exclusive, tasks were to provide the core farm labour of the period). Significant numbers of the remainder would have been 'trade servants' of one kind or another.

Over the course of the eighteenth century the substitution of hired day-labourers for living-in servants became increasingly common both in agriculture and in manufacturing, and much new manufacturing activity never used labour resident in the homes of the employers. Some fall in numbers is already apparent in Wall's figures for the period 1750–1821, when 'servants' still comprised 10.7 per cent of the population. Even in 1851, indeed, some 9 per cent of all boys aged 15–19 were still recorded at the census as living-in farm servants.

Traditionally, the literature has tended to portray this decline in the older forms of service as associated with the rise of a largely new class of 'domestic servant', presented stereotypically as made up of young girls performing basic cleaning and ceremonial functions for the household, often as part of a small team.[139] Certainly the number of 'domestic servants' expanded steadily in the nineteenth century, peaking at over 1.5 million at the 1891 census. And certainly young girls were especially involved; in 1851, 27 per cent of single girls of 21 and more than 20 per cent of unmarried women in the whole age group 18–27 were employed as domestic servants, a pattern which changed only a little as late as 1911.[140]

However, if we look at the situation of servants as a whole in the various files of the 1851 census sample we can estimate that 16 per cent of households in 1851 had servants or living-in apprentices; almost exactly two-thirds of these servants were women. The men were predominantly farm servants (at least 47 per cent of all male servants) and only 7 per cent of males at most were domestic servants, with another 5 per cent being outdoor servants (such as grooms and gardeners); 1 per cent were bar/hotel servants, 9 per cent apprentices and 7 per cent living-in trade assistants. Of the women, over 90 per cent were domestic or hotel servants, with less than 4 per cent being given titles which suggest agricultural employment (though many of the substantial number of domestic servants employed by farmers

---

[138]   Wall, *Family Forms*, p. 498.
[139]   T. McBride, *The Domestic Revolution* (1976); for a more balanced view, see L. Davidoff, 'Mastered for Life: Servant and Wife in Victorian and Edwardian Britain', *Journal of Social History*, 7 (1974), pp. 406–28.
[140]   1851 National Sample; McBride, *Domestic Revolution*, p. 112.

no doubt spent much of their time on agricultural work). Of the female domestic servants, most were described simply as 'domestic' or 'general' or 'house' servants (53 per cent). Of the rest, 'housemaid' (6 per cent) and 'housekeeper'/'housework' (5 per cent) were the commonest occupational titles.

The employers of these 'servants' covered a very wide range of occupational groups. Of all females living as servants at the 1851 census, only around one fifth were in the households of professionals, of employers of more than twenty-five workers and of clerical and related workers. Nearly a quarter worked for farmers, and more than another fifth for members of the 'petite bourgeoisie' (mostly for people who were self-employed or employers of no more than two workers). About one tenth worked for people who had no current occupation, mostly annuitants and others living off capital or land. Over half of all domestic servants worked in households in which they were the only resident female servant, and only 8 per cent in households with more than one other resident female servant. From the point of view of servants, the multi-servant upper middle-class household was the home only of a small minority.

If, however, we look at servants from the point of view of the household heads, while servants were widely spread across socio-economic groups, certain groups did have a much enhanced likelihood to have living-in domestic servants. At one extreme were professional households, where almost four-fifths kept at least one domestic servant and about one fifth more than two. Among other groups, three-fifths of small employers and the unambiguously self-employed, and over a quarter of lower non-manual workers, had at least one living-in servant – though very few had more than one. The other large group to have servants was farmers. Of those farmers who also employed day-labour, over two-thirds had one or more living-in female servants. So did about one third of farmers who otherwise used only family labour. At the other extreme, about 2 per cent of the working classes had a living-in servant – though these figures are perhaps significant even so. One other point also merits comment. In general, the same groups which took in servants also had in their households many young unmarried children, nieces and nephews and grandchildren. Often, clearly, kin performed a similar role to servants, though in professional households companionship rather than more menial domestic services was normally the more important motive.

Domestic servants were an important, perhaps even an essential, part of nineteenth-century society. Their numbers, however, fell after 1891 as wages rose, as new social attitudes and relatively smaller rural populations reduced the supply of girls coming forward, and, latterly, as smaller and more easily managed houses reduced the willingness of the middle classes to employ them. A temporary rise in the interwar period still left the number of servants proportionately well down on the nineteenth-century figures; the Second World War brought a rapid collapse in service, so that by the 1947 survey their numbers were down to a mere 0.5 per cent of the population.[141]

The final group, lodgers, are the shadowiest of all, their numbers being very dependent on changing definitions of 'the household' both by contemporaries and by modern analysts. The most recent research of the Cambridge Group suggests that lodgers may have formed a significant component of eighteenth-century society, particularly in the towns, comprising, perhaps, 5 per cent of many urban popula- tions.[142] By the nineteenth century they had become a very important feature indeed, especially among recent urban migrants and above all among the Irish immigrants. In 1851, lodgers were present in 12 per cent of all households (11 per cent of male headed, 18 per cent of female headed). Such households were heavily concentrated into certain socio-economic groups, lodgers being found in one in nine of skilled workers' households, nearly one fifth of those of semi-skilled workers, and one in seven of the households of non-agricultural labourers; hardly any lived in the households of the professional and clerical middle classes or in the households of farmers. Almost one third of Irish-born males aged 20–44 lived as lodgers.

Nineteenth-century social investigators tended to focus attention on the problems of the large urban lodging-houses but in 1851 only one fifth of all lodgers lived in groups of more than five; 28 per cent lived in a household in which they were the only lodger and 24 per cent in households in which there were just two. The typical lodger was a young single or childless married person (72 per cent of all lodgers were single and another 10 per cent were married but aged under 35; of all lodgers 67 per cent were male), living with a private family, and often eating with them and either sharing a room with some of them or occupying just one room in a house.

The subsequent history of lodging is even more obscure than that

[141] Wall, *Family Forms*, p. 498.
[142] Laslett and Wall, eds., *Household*, p. 220, editors' note to Table 7.3.

of other aspects of household structure. There is an impression that in the interwar period in the London area 'going into digs' was still a common feature for certain sections of the population but it was already being eroded by improved transportation and shorter working hours. Other important factors were a steady fall in orphanhood and in population mobility, two factors high levels of which had tended to support it in the past. In the 1947 survey the numbers were down to only 2.3 per cent of the population, a figure which may itself have been somewhat inflated by the after-effects of the war.[143]

Summarising the household composition picture for the mid-nineteenth century and earlier, it is clear that very large, very complex households were relatively rare but, equally, that simple households consisting of a conjugal family alone were also very much a minority, a position in marked contrast to that of the mid-twentieth century. In all, in 1851 just 36 per cent of households contained a married couple, at least one child, and no other person; 21 per cent of households lacked either a wife or at least one child and had no other person present; 44 per cent of households, equally split between the conjugal family and non-conjugal family headed, contained at least one extra person as lodger, servant or living-in employee, visitor or relative. For some socio-economic groups the home was even less a private conjugal family place. Only 10 per cent of professional households (none where there was a conjugal family of the head present) had no extra members present. Among the other groups the same was true for 42 per cent (30 per cent) of farming households and half (72 per cent) of households where the head was in a clerical or other white-collar occupation. Even the skilled, semi-skilled and unskilled manual workers groups had large numbers of outsiders present. This was the case in between one third and two-fifths (depending on the group) of all non-agricultural manual workers' households; it was the case in between one quarter and two-thirds of all such households with a conjugal family present. The same pattern can be seen in about a quarter of households headed by agricultural labourers. No comparable data appear to have been published on this topic, either in aggregate or in part, for any other part of our period.

---

[143] Wall, *Family Forms*, p. 498.

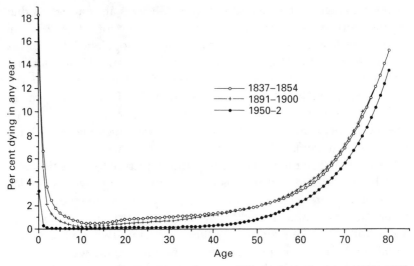

Figure 1.12 Percentage dying in each year of life (males), England, 1837–1952
Notes and sources: Figures from the Third, Sixth and Eleventh English Life
Tables (see n. 42); the Third Life Table data are believed to underestimate
mortality at the older age groups (Wrigley and Schofield, *Population History*,
p. 709).

VI CONCLUSION: THE GROWING HOMOGENEITY OF SOCIAL EXPERIENCE

We have already seen a number of ways in which the life course
experience of different sectors of the population became increasingly
similar over the last hundred years of our period. Class differences
in mortality and fertility, having widened in the later nineteenth century, narrowed, especially during and after the interwar period. Class
differences in the age at marriage and in household size and composition were also reduced. A rising proportion of the population shared
the experiences of marriage and of running their own households.

These trends ran parallel with a rise in homogeneity of experience
along another dimension, an increasing similarity across the population in the ages at which major life-cycle transitions occurred. As
Figure 1.12 shows, changes in the patterns of mortality concentrated
death very largely into the period after age 55; as a result, by the
end of our period, early death of a close relative came to be seen
as a special tragedy, rather than, as it certainly was for the Victorians,
an expected if still highly disruptive feature of most people's exper-

iences of growing up.[144] At the same time, for most women, childbearing was increasingly restricted to a narrow age band early in marriage; children born outside this period were, by the 1950s, likely to be labelled by outsiders, often incorrectly, as 'accidents'.

So homogeneous, indeed, had the life experiences of the majority of the population become, that any significant deviation from what could by the 1950s clearly be called a 'normal' life course was likely to label the perpetrator as 'odd', 'unlucky' or worse. Indeed, in some communities, social roles were simply lacking for those who did not conform to the broad parameters of a 'normal' life-cycle.[145] The institutionalisation of 'retirement' in the late nineteenth and early twentieth centuries was a major feature of an increasingly age-graded end to the life course. Equally, entry into marriage, and shifts between household statuses, seem to have followed an increasingly age-graded course.

Taking marriage first, we have already noted that the median age at marriage changed relatively little over the period; the dispersion around the median changed, however, very significantly. We can use the 1851 census sample to get a rough indicator of this situation; Figure 1.13 plots the percentage of the female population never married by single years of age.[146] Both in 1851 and in the published census data for 1911 entry to marriage for a group of single women was a highly protracted affair (the trends for men are similar though the shifts are not quite so marked). If we deduce a distribution of marriage ages from the 1851 data and then rank the population from the youngest marriers to the oldest, the central 80 per cent of the distribution married over a period of about twenty years; for the 1911 data the spread was still seventeen years and as late as 1931 little change in the shape of the distribution can be observed. By 1951, however, a new pattern (which reached its peak in the 1970s) had clearly begun to emerge. For reasons that we do not fully understand, entry into marriage

---

[144] For elaboration of some of these points and of others made below, see Anderson, 'Emergence'.

[145] See, e.g., Young and Willmott, *Family and Kinship*.

[146] The calculations which follow are only approximate since they ignore any cohort effects which may have occurred over the thirty years before the censuses. In practice, in the periods discussed here any such effects are unlikely to have done more than slightly alter the conclusions drawn. More detail of the method used can be found in Anderson, 'What Is New'.

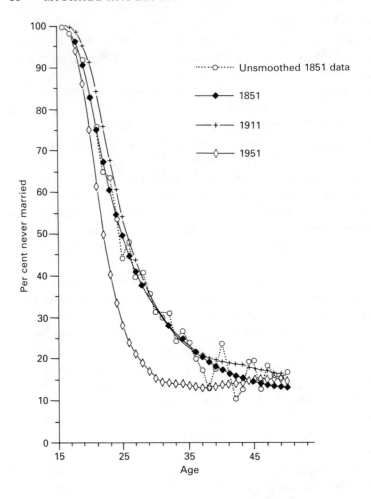

Figure 1.13 Percentage never married (females), England and Wales, 1851–1951

Notes and sources: The 1851 data are from a sub-sample from the National Sample from the 1851 census of Great Britain and, like the other data, relate to England and Wales; they differ slightly from those published in Anderson, 'What Is New' and 'Social Position of the Spinster', being based on the enlarged and more representative sub-samples of the data; the circles show the 1851 census results unsmoothed; the data fluctuate because of sampling error and also because the single at all earlier censuses had a marked propensity to round their ages to zero; the heavier solid line plots the data after processing through a smoothing programme; the 1911 data, from the *1911 Census of England and Wales*, VII, 1912–13, CXIII, Appendix Table 3, were smoothed before publication; 1951 data are from the *1951 Census of England and Wales, General Tables*, Table 17.

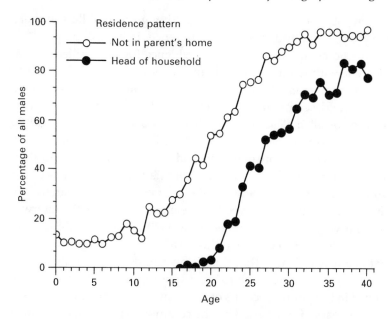

Figure 1.14 Residence patterns (males), England and Wales, 1851
Source: National Sample from the 1851 Census of Great Britain.

became much more age graded, with the central 80 per cent of the distribution covering only some eight years.[147]

Along with this shift went a marked fall in the number of years over which a cohort 'left home' and entered into the headship of its own households. As Figure 1.14 shows (and as we should expect from our earlier discussion of parentless kin), in the mid-nineteenth century a substantial proportion of children were not living with their parents at all ages from birth to early teens. Thereafter, the proportion who had 'left home' rose rapidly. By age 25 over three-quarters of boys were no longer at home but under half were household heads. At all ages between 17 and 27, 30 per cent or more of boys were neither 'children' nor heads of households. At the peak at age 20, 49 per cent of boys (and 46 per cent of girls) were in this 'intermediate' residential status. Even in their early 30s, under three-quarters of men were heading households of their own; indeed, not much more than

[147] The same method is used for 1951 as for 1851 data so as to maintain comparability. No figures earlier than 1851 are available since data classified by single years of age are required to obtain sufficient accuracy in the estimates. It seems likely, however, that entry to marriage in the eighteenth century was slightly less protracted than in the nineteenth.

80 per cent of men did so at any stage, though in middle age there were marked ethnic and social class differences in headship rates.[148]

We have no adequate quantitative evidence for any earlier or subsequent date within our period, but information is available for 1979.[149] At this date the age gap between leaving home and establishing one's own household seems to have averaged little more than one year; 80 per cent of all males left home between ages 17 and 27 and 80 per cent established their own households between the ages of 20 and 30. The evidence on marriage and on household composition in the later nineteenth and earlier twentieth centuries (discussed above) suggests a slow change in life course residential patterns in the nineteenth century, followed by accelerated change in the interwar period, and very clear beginnings of the 1970s pattern by 1951. More research is, however, required in this area.

What is already clear is that this rising homogeneity of life experience, associated as it was with rising disposable incomes among teenagers even in the poorer sections of the population, and aided perhaps in the final years of our period by the common experience of national service, paved the way for the emergence of a 'teenage culture' in the 1960s. It is also likely to have been significant in the growth of an advertising-led consumer society in the same period. The rising predictability of life, partly induced by economic stability and high levels of employment but supported by reduced death-chances for all but the old, is one further example, in the final years of our two centuries, of a dramatic transformation in life experiences in which demographic change played a vital contributory part.

[148] The same assumptions about cohort effects are to some extent required here as were noted for the marriage data in n. 146 above.
[149] The figures come from the *General Household Survey* data released by OPCS. Further information is in Anderson, 'What Is New'.

CHAPTER 2

The family in Britain

LEONORE DAVIDOFF

The historical study of the family has been fraught with difficulties, not least because many records are more informative of what people in the past thought the family should be, rather than giving us much information on how families were actually constituted or reporting the experience of family life. The fact, too, that everyone at some time lives in a family and that many of its features seem timeless, rooted in biology, makes it perplexing to grasp the great diversity of families over time.

Yet even the definition of who was part of the family has changed radically. At the beginning of the period, the family was often still conceived as a group of dependants: wife, children, lesser kin, servants and apprentices attached to the household of the masculine head, usually the master/husband/father. The male principal had only recently come to be regarded as part of that family unit. In political thought, theology and the common sense of daily life, this conception of the family was the template for most other organisations and was seen as the foundation of society.

Numerous recent studies have thrown some light on the many variations in the lived experience of individuals in families, kinship networks and households. The problem is, however, that, like a torch turned on particular items in a darkened but crowded room, such research can only illuminate what is caught in its beam, leaving the general picture still obscure.

It can also be misleading that often the only general information we have is in the form of censuses or listings which catch families and households as a snapshot. For a rounded picture, the cycle of individual lives as they form and disband families must be observed. Even with such care, however, it has to be recognised that, on the whole, the further back in time we go, the less we know about those who could not leave written records.

The first part of this chapter, for example, has more to say about the upper levels of British society than the mass of the population. And some groups, like children, whose experience can only be seen through the eyes of adults, will always remain in the shadows. Even where the outlines of a major change such as the late nineteenth-century decline in the number of children born to married couples is well documented, the explanation may lie with so many different factors, and be so subtle and so shrouded in the silence of personal decision, that it may never be fully known.

But the family, both as an idea and in its various institutional forms, has been of such historical significance that these obstacles should not stand in the way of an attempt to make at least tentative generalisations. In doing so, we must always remember that the intensely private small family of the late twentieth century which is now the predominant form, is only one way among many of organising personal relationships. Even up to the mid-nineteenth century, for example, the notion of *friendship* embraced patrons, peers and kin alike and was regarded as a potent source of both support and obligation. We also have to understand that the dualism of our own age, which so clearly demarcates family and privacy from work and public life, is of relatively recent origin.

Despite the gaps and weaknesses in the state of our knowledge, both the idea of the family and its lived experience must be understood as integral to the historical record, interwoven with the legal, economic, political and social institutions of British society at every level.

I 1750–1850

The aristocracy, gentry and middling ranks

Over this period, about one third of the British population had resources above a minimum based on subsistence gained solely through labour. The families in this group varied from the great landed aristocrat to the small shopkeeper. The aristocracy and gentry, although only 2–3 per cent of the total society, held undisputed political and social leadership. Their wealth flowed from agricultural rents although increasingly supplemented by urban ground rent, minerals and financial ventures. Their ownership of land, which had been made absolute with the Restoration, gave them a monopoly of political power and office. The aura of natural rights surrounding these privileges was based on the belief in Lordship, passing from God through King to the male head of each family. These rights derived from aristocratic rank; at the top by titles to the peerage, further down by untitled gentry status. For all, rank was legitimated by birth and heredity and it was the family name which ensured honorific position. The challenge to such a view in liberal doctrine was mitigated by the central place it gave to private property as well as its implicit assumptions that individuals would be placed in families.

From feudal times, family had been the central organising principle for the landed estate. As the aristocracy grew more literate in the eighteenth century, interest in their genealogies flourished. Family framed their political affairs at both national and local level. Their great houses and county seats were magnets for followers and clients, the Court being the greatest house of all. Claims to their friendship were made by rendering loyalty and deference in return for protection and access to place. Ultimately, birth and rank had to be supported by land. Land brought in wealth to support the lavish life style which justified leadership, land signified political rights and duties from Parliament to the local bench. But land, being a finite resource, had to be protected from fragmenting as it descended through the male line while supporting numerous family members. This tension, while never completely resolved, was controlled by the principles of impartible inheritance and primogeniture, that is inheritance of the main property by the eldest son, or kinsmen next in line. In special cases, daughters might inherit but only in default of male heirs.

Estates were held together by the legal mechanism of *entail* which restrained the incumbent's powers to sell or alienate land, making the heir a steward of the patrimony. Since the seventeenth century, these restraints had been strengthened, enhancing the aura of the aristocratic family beyond the present generation. Provisions from the property, however, had to be made for the widow, daughters and younger sons, even though often in the long run these were subordinate to keeping the property and title intact.

Women could own land through inheritance and the settlements made on them when they married. These could be protected from the common law right of husbands to their wives' property by special legal rules under equity, often in the form of a trust where the wife or daughter was nominal owner but the property was administered by male relatives or attornies. Under these conditions, and given women's customary exclusion from the political realm, it was extremely difficult for them to take on the rights and duties attached to land, even that which they did own. Only widows had formal opportunities for directing their property.

It was rather in their capacity as widowed mother of the heir, as dowager, that women could wield power behind the scenes, and the widow with her unmarried daughters usually moved into the Dower House on the estate giving precedence to the heir's young wife. The existing system of 'dower', that is the widow's right to one third of the property, was slowly being superseded by more individual discretion of fathers in drawing up financial arrangements at the time of marriage.

Inevitably there were disjunctions between title or name and the landed wealth to support them. Marriage was the easiest method of recouping these deficiencies or consolidating properties. The bridegroom marrying into a wealthy family might be required to forgo his own surname and adopt that of his in-laws to preserve the line but he gained wealth, status and political capacity by doing so. The eighteenth-century search for heiresses was brisk and on the increase. There had been a slow shift from marriages arranged solely to control property to a freer choice by young men and women or at least the right to veto to parents' or guardians' wishes.

In 1753, Lord Hardwicke's reforming act had attempted to control the runaway marriage of vulnerable heiresses. Such marriages which had resisted filial obedience in affairs of the heart are regarded by some historians as a forerunner of early nineteenth-century romantic ideas about courtship and marriage.

In an attempt to maintain suitable partners for the young, occasions where they might meet were multiplied. For the titled aristocracy, London, the Court and the Social Season remained paramount as a marriage market, supplemented by spas like Bath where affluent gentry also congregated. For the local squirearchy, mini-seasons in county towns sufficed. The wedding was a large public affair where tenants often renewed their loyalty to the great house. The bride, wearing her wedding dress, received guests at the family seat for a week or more and the newly wed couple would be presented at Court to mark formally their change in status. The following birth and majority of the heir were publicly marked with cannons firing and feasting by local followers.

Landed families were public institutions, their great houses which dominated the countryside had evolved from castles populated by throngs of male retainers and soldiers. Family events of marriage, birth and death were played out before these crowds. By the seventeenth century, a separation of the more immediate family had begun although there were still large halls where 'friends' and clients congregated.

After the Restoration, as long as a public image of family life was upheld, sexual and emotional entanglements were becoming people's own affair. Young men gathered in officers' messes and clubs, their central interests were sport, gambling and fashions, the 'Dandies' around Beau Brummel being only the best known. Their sexual encounters were with mistresses and high-class prostitutes or they might have friendships with clever, even learned women (married or not) who had created something like a salon culture in late eighteenth-century London. Homosexual fraternities flourished at least in the capital. Whatever their predilections, family life was eschewed along with business habits. In these metropolitan circles, once marriage alliances were settled and the birth of an heir assured, intrigue and lax morality continued. Nevertheless, the 'double standard' which condoned men's pre- and extra-marital affairs but took a stricter line with women, curtailed female sexual adventures and placed a premium on chastity before marriage.

In a reaction against Puritan republicanism, beliefs and morals alike had become latitudinarian and the Anglican establishment insisted on little above nominal church attendance. The aristocratic family and its entourage was oriented to public occasions: the assizes, quarter sessions, Parliament and Court diaries framed its comings and goings while Christmas and rent days were occasions for entertaining tenants. Lavish display and dispensing of food, drink and entertainment became the duties of sovereignty. Up to one quarter of gentry accommodated kin and visitors in their homes at any one time, and a wider circle depended on their bounty. The family seat was not only an administrative and judicial centre, but a show case in which to exhibit status and the spoils of wealth; an arena in which to make connections. Its rituals exuded glamour, mystery and power.

By the mid-eighteenth century, however, a section of the upper class began to adopt a more domesticated, orderly life style, to withdraw from the public world and encourage companionate relationships between husband and wife, parents and children, vaunting the pleasures of the home fireside. Much of the impetus for this change had come from wealthy merchants, lawyers and bankers, the 'urban gentry' who were related by birth and marriage to the landed estate. Ideas of simplicity and classical restraint merged into a secularised version of Puritanism to extol rural retreats even before the more thrusting message of the later eighteenth-century evangelical revival. A Suffolk squire, born in 1751, who was fond of hunting and gambling and busy with affairs of his estate, nevertheless subscribed to the Society for the Reformation of Manners. He copied verses from Dr Cotton's highly popular 'The Fireside' into his diary:

> From the gay world, we'll oft retire
> To our own Family and Fire
> Where Love our Hours employs
> No noisy neighbour enters here
> No intermeddling stranger near
> To spoil our heartfelt joys.

> Tho Fools spurn Hymen's gentle Power's
> We who improve his golden Hours,
> By sweet Experience Know
> That Marriage rightly understood
> Gives to the tender and the good
> A Paradise below.[1]

By the third quarter of the eighteenth century, the Great Hall with huge tables loaded with food where all sat down together had been modified: smaller rooms were in use for more private family life. Upper servants no longer were drawn from the gently born but were the children of tenant farmers or tradesmen, and were increasingly banished to the servants' hall or kitchen. Literacy and travel had raised expectations of refinement. Luxuries, exotic fruits and flowers and elegant furniture, were filling the sparsely furnished rooms. The desirability of country life rose with the cult for improving the estate, beautifying the house and landscaping the gardens. Civility in the form of handkerchiefs, silver forks, rugs, footstools, and other paraphernalia from the Continent, permeated even the houses of country squires. Better transport meant more opportunity for women to take part in entertainments. In towns, pleasure gardens and public meeting places allowed the informality of card playing, tea drinking, strolling and flirting. The balls, routs and musical parties in Assembly Rooms made huge private establishments less necessary.

By the mid-eighteenth century, more aristocratic children were being born and surviving amid growing pressure for mothers to breast

---

[1] George Betts, manuscript diary, Ipswich Record Office, HD79/AF2/2/1–3.

feed their own babies rather than using wet nurses. The advice of male doctors began to supersede women's control of infancy, breaking established customs such as swaddling. These children were brought up to carry the marks of nobility on their person, in their language and behaviour. Until the Civil War, particularly for boys, this had meant several years acting as upper servants in the castles and great houses of kinsmen or patrons, a service which included military training. Now they were being kept at home. While many were cared for by servants and taught by governesses and tutors, domesticated parents lavished more time and attention on the development of their offspring.

The belief grew that young children were innocent and delightful playthings. Toys and books especially for them began to appear in affluent homes. At about age 7 boys were removed from the leading strings and petticoats of infancy in the public ceremony of 'breeching'. They were sent to school or handed over to male tutors to mark their move to the superior masculine world. In a late eighteenth-century gentry family which produced several generations of admirals and generals, the widowed mother brought up numerous sons with the aid of a domestic tutor. It was remarked that 'her methods of managing her children are very excellent. They both fear and love her and are most obedient to her least intimation.'[2]

Despite the supreme power of the landed interest, doubts had been raised by Enlightenment ideas and the French Revolution about the humanity as well as utility of their rule. Simultaneously, the evangelical revival had particular appeal to gentry with few resources who claimed that the only true nobility was with those whose souls had been saved. By 1800, the essence of domination through the aristocratic family, the 'mysteries of blood and semen' were being radically questioned.[3] It was the loose alliance between squirearchy and the upper echelons of commercial and professional groups which had begun this shift in outlook.

Nevertheless, the form and function of the family among the middle ranks differed from the landed interest. The bulk of their property was in stock or tools, funds or trained skill which produced an income, rather than land. While the family of the lord or squire whose resources were based on solid wealth had a choice in the way they spent their time, the manufacturer, farmer or shopkeeper and professional had to produce goods and services for a market in order to survive.

[2] F. Hett, *The Memoirs of Susan Sibbald: 1783–1812* (1926), p. xxi.
[3] J. Powis, *Aristocracy* (Oxford, 1984), p. 91.

At the beginning of the period, most people in the middle ranks depended on an enterprise in which all members of the family plus servants, shopmen and others in the household contributed labour. Although a wife acted informally as partner, by tradition and the common law doctrine of 'coverture' (that is the wife's legal personality was absorbed in her husband), she could not make contracts or act in a commercial capacity. Partners for expanding businesses were sought among male kin: sons, brothers, nephews, brothers-in-law and sons-in-law. Kin were favoured since they could be trusted in a world where few public institutions, for example, viable banks, yet existed. *Family*, in a wide sense, was the most important commercial organisation. On the other hand, women's capital was vital to the family business and often contributed in the form of a trust where her maintenance would be assured from profits and interest but leaving the bulk available for investment.

Among this group, young men entered the business and professions in their mid-teens and were usually trained by working with their relatives. Girls helped in their own or other relatives' families. Unlike the aristocracy, marriage for this group was delayed, often to the late 20s. Only when a young man set up on his own, or went into partnership, might he marry. Often his sister might marry his partner and a minority cemented such ties by 'sibling marriages', that is where two brothers from one family married two sisters from another or brother and sister married sister and brother, while cousin marriages were also popular.

The late age at marriage meant up to ten years of celibacy during which brothers and sisters were often close, sharing everyday life with a common stake in the family patrimony. Unmarried sisters often acted as housekeepers to bachelor brothers. Despite late marriage, families were large, so that women were childbearing and breast feeding into their early 40s. Older children cared for and guided younger and later, as uncles and aunts to their siblings' offspring, were important sources of help and general education while having the use of youthful labour and company from their nieces and nephews in informal exchanges of children. The boundaries of these families were widely drawn. Friendship was a more egalitarian category than in the aristocracy, defined to cover both kin and others with a similar outlook, and friends could be as important as family as sources of succour.

At the heart of family life was motherhood, for among the

evangelically inspired homes children were first taught the religious message at home. The childhood home became a foretaste of the Heavenly Home which was their ultimate goal. The emphasis on motherhood echoed sentiments already present in the upper classes. Its elevation raised doubts about the total authority of husbands and fathers. These issues crystallised around the sensational legal battle of Caroline Norton to win the right to keep her young children after separation from her licentious and cruel husband and led to the Custody of Infants Act in 1839.

Most boys in the middle ranks went to day schools, private academies or local grammar schools where they learned useful subjects such as accounting and languages as well as a smattering of the upper-class standard fare of Greek and Latin. By the 1850s, more wealthy families had started to send sons away to public school. Girls more often were still taught at home by mothers, older sisters or aunts. They practised household skills and gained basic literacy while the better off might learn French, drawing and music. Even when they were sent to school for a year or two, these were small, with a deliberately family atmosphere.

For many, family life continued as part of the productive process. The finances of household and workshop, farm or professional practice often overlapped. Servants as well as family members turned their hand to serving in the shop, cooking the dinner or cleaning the parlour which also served as the bank or school house. Living quarters were above, behind or next door to the mill, shop or space for whatever business took place.

With such close association between home and work, women could oversee the household and help in the business. In any case they were responsible for feeding and caring for apprentices, shopmen, pupils and numerous visitors. Men spent much time managing the enterprise and at markets selling and buying goods. But they also were in and out of the 'house place' for meals, helping with the children, reading by the fire, seeing customers or clients in the parlour and taking part in the endless rounds of tea drinking and dropping in of relatives, friends and neighbours. Many men left active business in their 50s to make way for younger family members and spend more time at home.

To bring up the large numbers of children to a high standard of behaviour and literacy, these families emphasised order in daily life which accorded well with both their business commitments and religious principles. In many households, parents, children, servants and apprentices gathered for prayers morning and evening when the master/husband/father praised, blamed and prayed for each before the gathered household.

Mealtimes were becoming fixed, the children expected to behave properly at table. Reading secular as well as devotional literature aloud around the fireside was a favourite evening relaxation. All went to church or chapel as part of the community of like-minded and often related families. In addition to religious activities, families as well as individuals took up a variety of amateur enthusiasms such as botany, verse writing and philanthropy although men had a wider field of action than women in the burgeoning voluntary societies and clubs which were the hallmark of the emerging middle class.

Occasions such as birthdays, funerals, anniversaries and Christmas were marked by family gatherings with special food. For example, the family of a book engraver had seven surviving children so that, with the parents, there was ample opportunity for birthday celebrations. For winter birthdays they held 'Parnassian Evenings' with something extra for supper and mother reading a special book aloud. In summer these were varied with 'gypsy rambles' and supper in the open. In 1813 when the eldest son turned 21, the family walked to an inn in a nearby village where 'the day was passed as happily, perhaps, as if a host of tenants had been regaled in front of the ancestral hall'.[4] On such anniversaries, at the New Year or with the approach of old age, men and women 'cast up' their accounts with God of their own and their children's progress towards salvation.

Through the nineteenth century, the family was central to the economic, religious, social and emotional life of the middle class. However, families were large, interleaved by marriage with other families, blurring their boundaries with categories such as friend and cousin. The numbers of individuals involved provided choice as to which branches to cultivate. Both economic well being and moral imperatives encouraged people to keep in touch with widespread networks through letter writing, visiting and the exchange of gifts. Recognition of degrees of kinship was particularly marked by elaborate mourning, with special black clothes, and rituals of withdrawing from social contacts, especially for women.

The elevation of family life raised levels of housing, comfort and

[4]   A. Gilbert, *Autobiography and other Memorials of Mrs Gilbert*, ed. J. Gilbert, 2 vols. (1874), vol. 1, p. 157.

consumption, while maintaining these standards was reassuring evidence to the local community of the family's business soundness. By the early nineteenth century, in larger towns, enclaves of middle-class residences began to be built well away from manufacturing and commercial areas in the first large-scale suburban developments such as Edgbaston in Birmingham. The City of London merchant population had begun to move west to Bloomsbury, north to Islington and beyond. The supplying of items such as carpets, furniture, tableware, books, garden plants, kitchen equipment, clothing and increased services from doctors, writers and teachers laid foundations for many family fortunes. By the 1830s and 1840s, aspirations for a domesticated genteel life motivated the better off, even farmers, to exclude working people from their dining tables and sitting rooms. The more refined furnishing of the living place were now kept separate from housework as cooking became confined to kitchens and sitting places evolved into a separate parlour.

By mid-century, more young women were being retained purely as domestic servants, sleeping in separate quarters and taking on enlarged household routines of cleaning, polishing, cooking, serving and childcare. Wives and adult unmarried sisters or daughters ran these homes but were no longer responsible for basic processes such as weaving cloth, growing fruit and vegetables or caring for apprentices and others housed for a business. Their time and efforts were turned to the education and training of the children, who no longer helped around the business premises.

Women took the lead in a more formal social life now emerging in upper middle-class circles. Less well-off families and those in provincial towns or farmers in remote areas and all those on small and uncertain incomes could only practise fragments of this pattern. A vase of flowers on the table – a conceit introduced in the 1820s in the face of superstitious belief in bad luck caused by bringing living plants into the house – might be a considerable innovation. Some curtains at the windows, a piano in the stone-flagged kitchen, an upholstered chair before the still large open hearth where dogs slept, show the slow and uneven adoption of such refinements.[5]

Many of the changes in domestic surroundings had begun with the aristocracy and wealthy urban gentry. Innovations in water supplies and sanitation, such as pumps for wells, were often adapted

[5] RIBA, *Rooms Concise: Glimpses of the Small Domestic Interior*, Catalogue of RIBA Exhibition (1981).

from large public institutions, like barracks, hospitals and workhouses which were first built at this time. Large open chimneys were closed in and iron cooking stoves installed, colza oil lamps supplemented expensive wax candles to lengthen daylight. However, the unending supply of cheap servant labour allowed rising standards with little technological change. It was now possible to wash the body daily in the privacy of bedrooms with water carried up several flights of stairs (to the enrichment of bucket, washbasin and ewer manufacturers). Even aristocratic households were substituting young women for up to a half of the retinue of the thirty or so servants.

From the late eighteenth century, the fashionable dinner crept up from noon to mid-afternoon, and by 1800 to 4 or 5 p.m. with a light supper served at 10 p.m. By mid-century, dinner was 7.30 or 8 for the majority. Instead of two large courses where all was spread out in lavish display and the master carved at the head of the table, the continental system of serving courses sequentially handed round by servants began to be adopted, although such expenditure of servant power and household resources could not be rigorously followed by the more modest. Luncheon and tea had become ladies' affairs with men away at governing, sporting or business affairs where they dined in the masculine ambience of clubs and inns.

Formal dining became the centre of social life, possibly once a week for the aristocracy, once a month for those further down the scale. Elaborate dinner arrangements, the mixture of guests and correct organisation or precedence in the procession from drawing room to dining hall, were part of the upper-class hostess's preoccupations. Rich dark furnishings pronounced this room more masculine, where gentlemen stayed behind to drink port, smoke and talk of business, politics and topics unfit for feminine hearing. The ladies withdrew to the more delicately furnished drawing room with 'spindly guilt or rosewood, and silk or chintz'.[6] The largest houses had smoking and billiard rooms for men while women had their boudoirs.

The middle-class villa reflected this pattern much modified for lower incomes, aided by the fall in prices for luxury items in the second quarter of the nineteenth century. Here, too, servants were living apart and eating in the kitchen to be summoned by bells. Children were, where possible, now kept in rooms set aside as a nursery. In keeping with the home as an escape from the worldly cares and

[6] M. Girouard, *Life in the English Country House: A Social and Architectural History* (1978).

vulgarity of urban streets, middle-class villas were set in gardens. With the invention of plate glass (and the removal of the glass tax in the 1820s), large windows and glass doors increased the effect of making the garden an extension of the house. Both upper- and middle-class domesticity was replete with gardening enthusiasms from the great herbaceous beds and glass houses – aristocratic pineapples enjoyed central heating long before human beings – to the shrubs by the area railings and the ferns in a glass 'Ward case' on the parlour table of the urban terrace house.

By the middle years of the nineteenth century, lax aristocrats, hard-headed manufacturers and boorish farmers had all been affected by a new ethos. According to a contemporary, 'the toasts and coarse allusion of the last century [were] abolished even in gentlemen's society'.[7] As fortunes rose, often based on the grinding drudgery of the emerging working class, at least nominal charity became part of the upper- and middle-class code, along with gentility of manners. The aristocracy still based its claim to honour, power and leadership on land, name and rank, but the reforms of the 1830s and growing political power of the middle ranks in the 1840s meant that even great lords now followed more serious pursuits within a more formal social scene. The model of Queen Victoria and the sober Court devoted to domestic pastimes well illustrates the transformation from the dissolute style of Regency London.

Provincial and nonconformist backgrounds had barred many in the middling ranks from political and social power. For them, in particular, the family had become a vital resource. They indefatigably advocated familial forms for all institutions except those which were intended to punish, control or harden by their specifically non-familial structure: workhouses, hospitals, barracks and boys' public schools. In their doctrine, simply living a solid domestic existence became an act of patriotism and class reconciliation.

This conception blended with the aristocratic code to produce the peculiarly early nineteenth-century concept of *gentility*. With enough wealth and high rank, a variety of behaviours could be genteel, but below these exalted levels, a fairly strict code of speech, behaviour and, above all, commitment to the family was essential. *Gentlemen* were manly, strong and active in supporting and protecting their womenfolk and children, a view of masculinity heightened by the

[7] H. G. Mundy, ed., *The Journal of Mary Frampton from the Year 1779 until the Year 1846* (1885), p. 395.

cult of chivalry which arose with the publication of Scott's novels early in the nineteenth century.[8] It was increasingly a slur on manhood if wives, or even daughters, had to work for income, although it was always permissible to use women's capital. *Ladies* were not to be seen outside the protection of the domestic sphere except in carefully regulated places like the private Botanical Gardens, music festivals or balls and, of course, at church and chapel.

The feminine ideal was to be dependent, young, weak and childlike, encouraged by the widening age gap between spouses, for by midcentury, in the upper middle class, husbands were on average six years older than their wives. These strongly contrasted masculine and feminine identities were observed in clothes, colouring, objects of use, parts of the house.

Such marked gender identities fitted the revolution in ideas about sexuality which had begun in the mid-eighteenth century. For centuries, women, the daughters of Eve, had been seen as insatiable sexual beings dominated by their desires, who would drain men's vitality with their carnal demands. By the late eighteenth century, women's sexuality had been transcended into motherhood. Young girls had to be kept pure from sexual knowledge, however, as, once aroused, they would be more voracious than men. It was now men whose nature embodies the sexual drive. Middle-class habits of self-control and thrift were grimly set to minimise wasteful 'spending' of male sexual energy. The nineteenth-century middle-class home, now free from the pollution of sexual knowledge, spawned a twilight world of pornography and prostitution, encouraged by the late age at marriage. For many men, sexual attraction seemed hopelessly split between two realms, the pure angel at home and the woman of the streets, women who had 'fallen' out of the respectable world and forfeited social recognition. Yet family members, locked within a common inheritance, were preoccupied with themes of power and dependence and there are numerous hints of favourite forbidden themes: brother/sister and father/daughter incest.[9]

Over the period, the idea of the pure home and family associated with women was increasingly contrasted to the public, masculine world of economic, political and intellectual affairs with its sordid

[8] M. Girouard, *The Return to Camelot: Chivalry and the English Gentleman* (New Haven, 1981).

[9] L. Davidoff and C. Hall, *Family Fortunes: Men and Women of the English Middle Class, 1780–1850* (1987), chap. 7.

compromises and inevitable immorality. Gentlemen moved between the public and the private sphere but, as Hannah More had pronounced in 1809, ladies were circumscribed by a smaller but equally important circle.[10] Not all, of course, could aspire to the ideal being created and some did not wish to. Among the less well off, women continued to be active in helping in the family enterprise or even working for wages. Among a number of wealthy, often nonconformist radical provincial families, daughters were well educated and took an interest in public affairs. In the 1830s and 1840s some of these, such as Harriet Taylor (John Stuart Mill's collaborator and later wife), were uneasy about the supposed perfection of 'separate spheres'.

The lower ranks

In the mid-eighteenth century, the remaining two-thirds of the population was made up of those possessing little or no property: access to a bit of land, some tools and perhaps some skill but primarily depending on their labour for subsistence, the majority to be found in rural villages. However, the development of mines, textile mills, market and resort towns and the rapid growth of larger cities, particularly London, made for a great variety of living and working arrangements. Most people lived in households where productive work was continually going on. Small strips of fields were tilled, animals kept around the cottage or on the common, spinning and weaving or other crafts were done on the premises. Everyone had to take part in a work rhythm which followed the tasks to be done. Women and children, while regarded as supplementary contributors, were expected to earn their own keep. Conditions were harsh and the family economy was often unable to provide support.

The use of communal lands, co-operation over tools, animals, water and fuel, meant that others in the village played a part in family decisions. Public opinion overlooked behaviour through gossip and the reinforcement of values by repeated proverbs and maxims. There were also stronger sanctions such as 'rough music' where groups would gather outside the miscreant's house banging pots and pans, or effigies of the offending parties were carried in procession.

Favourite targets were second marriages where there was a large age discrepancy, not only regarded as unnatural but threatening the interest of previous children. Men whose wife-beating went beyond

[10]   H. More, *Coelebs in Search of a Wife* (1809).

the accepted norm, suspected incest cases, wives whose scolding or independent behaviour threatened to upset expected female subordination, or the husband who let himself be cuckolded, all might be subjected to rough music.

A sub-stratum of beliefs in supernatural forces, ghosts, and spirits, reinforced community controls and gave informal power to elders in the village through the mainly oral culture where children learned by listening and imitating. Wizards and wisewomen were regularly consulted on problems of courtship, marriage, sexuality and childbirth, as well as crops and animal welfare. Their powers were a more immediate part of village culture than the ultimate authority of church or magistrate's bench.

The induction of apprentices (complete with sexual initiation), courtship, death and inheritance were conducted in public. Much everyday life, too, often including cooking and eating, was carried on in the streets, fields, village greens and market squares where shopkeepers might sleep under their open stalls. The hiring fairs where young people chose and were chosen for the year's work, fairs for sales of goods and Holy Day celebrations of the ostensibly Christian calendar were still 'plaited with pagan good cheer'.[11] These were occasions where community norms could be re-established, pledges could be witnessed and values reaffirmed in mime or music.

The somewhat better-off households in these communities supplemented their working hands with servants and apprentices, often from outside their own area. This was especially the case for those who were childless, whose children were too young to work or had grown up and left home. More highly developed crafts in larger towns might be organised within guilds of livery companies which controlled entry and orchestrated a variant of community ritual vesting authority over families through the head, usually the master/husband/father but a minority of mistresses.

Boys and some girls were apprenticed, often to both master and mistress. Like living-in farm servants or children still at home, these young people also took part in childcare, housework, labour for subsistence and sale of products for the market. Where parents were too poor to keep a number of children, they were sent out to service, but even the better off chose this way to ensure training and opportunities for saving for their adolescent children. Poor law authorities

---

[11] R. Porter, *English Society in the 18th Century* (Harmondsworth, 1982), p. 167.

automatically sent orphans or destitute children into apprenticeships, often far from other family members.

Putting young people under the authority of master and mistress also avoided tension between parents and children and allayed the ever-present fear of masterless youths and maidens. Formal apprenticeship was from about age 14 to 20, usually with one master and mistress, and required a cash premium, while farm servants traditionally changed places annually. Girls tended to be placed in less formal situations but were also apprenticed in housewifery with less access to higher paid, more skilled crafts.

The ages 10 to 25 were a stage in life spent between a person's own family and setting up a family at marriage. The master and mistress were responsible politically, economically and socially for these young people. Master and mistress dictated the work to be done and decided the quality and quantity of food and comfort. They rewarded with praise and meted out punishments by restricting liberty, verbal or physical abuse. Both young people and life-time servants were part of their master's family, even taking their right to parish relief from him, not their parents, who they might see at most once a year and who were often known as 'friends'.

This subordinate status remained the probable fate of a substantial minority, for it is estimated that about one in six or even one in four never married. Men with some resources gained full adult status through becoming craftsmen, working a smallholding or becoming a day-labourer and by marriage. The latter involved a complicated process of courtship culminating in the Big Wedding complete with gifts from kin and peers.[12] Women moved from service to marriage for there was little place for a single woman on her own. As one commentator said, 'a Youth could be set afloat in the World as soon as he has got a Trade in his Head but a Girl is such a tender, ticklish Plant to rear, that there is no permitting her out of leading-strings til she is bound to a Husband'.[13]

Young children still at home helped doing small tasks and learned general skills; a minority picked up basic literacy possibly from attending a small dame school which was as much child-minding as teaching. Since so many families were broken by death (30 per cent of marriages were for the second time), many children were already living away

---

[12] J. Gillis, *For Better, For Worse: British Marriage 1600 to the Present* (Oxford, 1985).
[13] Quoted in J. M. Beattie, 'The Criminality of Women in 18th Century England', *Journal of Social History*, 8 (1974–5), p. 98.

from their parents with kin or others. When they became servants or apprentices, their general education and behaviour were taken over by master and mistress. They also undoubtedly learned much from older fellow-servants or the children of the house still at home. Relationships with peers coloured their working and free time. However, active sexuality was discouraged since youth was seen as a time to build up skills and savings, and the normal age of marriage was in the mid- to late 20s Elaborate betrothal rituals which prevented early pairing off of couples, and which were enforced by peers, sustained this pattern.

At the beginning of the period, when the social distance between servants and their employing family was narrower and the possibility of apprentices becoming masters (and mistresses) in their own right more common, some might complete the cycle by marrying the son or daughter of their master or mistress; occasionally an apprentice might marry his master's widow. It was common for a young man to marry a somewhat older woman who had the advantage of acquired property and skill as well as lower potential fertility.

The greatest single change for the family in this period was the decline in apprenticeship and service, which accelerated in the 1780s and 1790s. By the time the Statute of Artificers was repealed in 1814, the major form of labour had shifted to a mixture of outwork production for sale and day hire for wages. However, over more than half the country, in the north, the west, Wales and Scotland, smaller farms continued to use living-in servants. There were pockets of special arrangements such as the bondager system in the north-east where men were hired only if they brought the labour of their wives or another female with them. Skilled trades, too, continued to train through apprenticeship although this less often included living in the master's household. Nevertheless, the trend was for young people, as well as adults, to earn enough by day-labour for their own support.

These changes had a profound effect on the family, both at the level of society and as individual experience. Master and servant had been political and civil statuses with the servant subsumed under the headship of the household; payment in kind or money wages were immaterial to this relationship. The servant's status was, in these terms, identical to the wife and children, giving labour and deference in return for support, protection and representation by the household head. Female servants had to leave on marriage as they were then 'contracted' to their husbands. Male servants (or journeymen), if they had the resources, then moved on to become masters in their own right. Widows also became household heads. Now this pattern had been broken.

By the early nineteenth century, many families kept their young people at home as extra hands producing cloth or other goods for sale, pooling the proceeds, usually under the direction of the father/husband. However, it was now easier for young people to earn an income directly and many set up their own households. Similarly, where grain growing for profit flourished, as in the south and east, large numbers of day-labourers (mostly male) were now employed. But without the competition from nascent industry, wages were low and great distress followed. Those who would have been farm servants bitterly resented the pretensions of farmers which they blamed for the change. The late eighteenth-century Suffolk poet, Robert Blomfield, coming from an agricultural labouring family, wrote of 'the *separate* table and the costly bowl' which had 'violated the feelings of the poor':

> to leave them distanc'd in the madd'ning race,
> Where'er refinement shows its hated face.[14]

Boys now moved directly into the labour market, first at 'boys' rates' then climbing to a full wage at about age 20. Apprenticeships, such as they were, shortened, ending at 17 or 18. Predictably, the age at marriage started to fall; by the mid-nineteenth century it was about five and a half years lower for both men and women. The birth rate rose sharply so that early nineteenth-century Britain was a fast-growing and youthful society with almost three-quarters of the population under 30 and just under one half under 20. Much of the new factory and workshop employment demanded tractable nimble child labour, a development fuelled by the drain of large numbers of adult men in the Napoleonic War.

Courtship and marriage and the setting up of a household had always been important steps to full adult status despite the large numbers who remained celibate. Courtship rituals included much folk wisdom, often enforced by peers, while parents and neighbours, master and mistress overlooked young people's behaviour. Farm servants, for example, slept in well-separated quarters, the maids in a chamber with daughters of the family next to the master and mistress's room, the men in the loft or barn. Nevertheless, courting by visiting the

[14] R. Blomfield, 'Farmer's Boy', *Poems* (1845), p. 43.

girl's bedroom was common and in certain areas might include 'bundling' in bed together while fully clothed. Pledging a troth might be followed by sexual intercourse since any ensuing pregnancy was regularised by marriage, sanctioned by pressures from parents, masters, mistresses and peers as well as others in the community.

Marriage might or might not be solemnised in church. In the mid-eighteenth century, it is estimated that at least half of all unions were sealed in a simple folk ceremony; exchanging rings or in rituals such as jumping over a broomstick before a few witnesses. These were binding as contracts in the eyes of the couple and the local community. Yet if circumstances changed and a partner was not fulfilling his or her part the marriage could be undone by giving the ring back or jumping backwards over the broomstick. Such practices indicated the real strength of the position of married women at this level, despite their lack of civil status. Even the public handing over of a woman to another man, or 'wife sale' was often arranged beforehand with the wife's permission if not instigation.

The tighter control of marriage by the church and state as a result of Lord Hardwicke's Act of 1753 forced many of these practices underground so that large numbers of working people lived in consensual unions with no formal marriage or 'living tally' as it was known. Given these customs, when young men whose partners had become pregnant could not find work in the district, the couple might have to separate, even if a child was expected. The rising illegitimacy rate from the late eighteenth century onwards, which has been seen by some historians as evidence for a new sexual freedom for women, must be seen against this background.[15] And even as this sequence was changing, the strict bastardy clauses in the new Poor Law of 1834 put the onus of support squarely on the young woman or her parents. Such stringency, however, did not prevent women left on their own to bring up children, whether through widowhood or desertion, from being a major category dependent on state support through the poor law.[16]

The difficulty and expense of getting married was compounded by the shift to wage labour and volatile economic conditions which might

---

[15] This view has been given much public attention in a history of the family which posits progress from tradition to modernity. Its greatest publicist has been E. Shorter, *The Making of the Modern Family* (1977). An alternative view has been put forward by Gillis, *British Marriages*.

[16] P. Thane, 'Women and the Poor Law in Victorian and Edwardian England', *History Workshop Journal*, 6 (1978).

encourage immediate earning but also mobility in looking for work. There may have been less opportunity for community pressure to ensure completion of the cycle of courtship, intercourse and marriage. The 25 per cent of brides pregnant at marriage in the first half of the eighteenth century had risen to 38 per cent a century later.[17] As the birth rate rose, and opportunity for work was often limited, the poverty and unrest which followed provoked a flurry of reactions from Malthus's dour predictions of mass starvation to pressure for reform of the poor law.

In the eighteenth century as many as one in five had been recipients of poor relief at some time in their life. The right to community support to help couples marry, for the parentless young, the old and infirm or anyone in need, was a deeply held belief. But the new poor law concentrated on disciplining the able-bodied man. For the first time wives and children were defined solely as his dependants who he was to be forced to support by the threat of incarcerating the whole family in the new barrack-like workhouse rather than being allowed food or small sums as 'out relief' to tide them over in their own homes. Once inside the workhouse, husbands and wives, parents and older children were deliberately separated, a particularly hated part of the new regime.

Aid available for families from charities – the coal or shoe or blanket or loan club – was now more often run by upper- and middle-class patrons than the guilds and trades set up to take care of their own members. Patrons, too, held a similar view of the family, urging the breadwinners' total responsibility and trying to influence wives to reach unrealistic standards of cooking and housekeeping, given their limited resources. Evangelicals invoked a stricter moral code to suppress public display in games or among courting couples, to curb drinking, swearing and gambling, as when an early nineteenth-century Essex vicar castigated the local fair as an 'abode of moral darkness'.[18] Inns and taverns were stigmatised as unfit for women and children, seen as representing the opposite of family values.

Such views were by no means entirely imposed from above. The dislocation of village culture, the imposition of steady work rhythms in factory and workshop had made their mark. Those who had turned

---

[17] P. Laslett, 'Long-Term Trends in Bastardy in England', in *Family Life and Illicit Love in Earlier Generations* (Cambridge, 1977), p. 130.

[18] S. Golding, 'The Importance of Fairs in Essex, 1759–1850', *Essex Journal*, 10 (1975), p. 59.

to enthusiastic religion such as Methodism found a new structure to their days and new controls over behaviour. Concern with individual salvation was made manifest in cleanliness of body, clothes and house, learning to read and write, less time and money spent on drinking and the rejection of strong language and belief in superstitious forces. Sunday schools, philanthropic efforts and masses of cheap reading material poured out the message. A domestic setting was a necessity for this new way of life and even radicals who rejected the route of individual salvation adopted the benefits of an ideally more ordered life. The reality, except for the most highly skilled and fortunate, was much harder to sustain as numerous children swamped cramped quarters and stretched a meagre income.

Although many of these changes were gradual, by the mid-nineteenth century, the organisation and experience of life in working-class households had profoundly altered. Young men now 'clubbed out' rather than living as servants or they lodged, paying for board and room. They headed their own young families possibly even when lodging with others. The fast-growing population was on the move from rural areas to towns, from the south to the north and Midlands. The assumed sequence of going into service, saving and marrying late had been broken, yet the new poor law regulations forced people back to their parents' parish if they needed support. Nevertheless, even in times of dearth there was little return to the older pattern of delayed marriage.

Men with skills increasingly looked for work elsewhere, for example in the growing metal and building trades or on the railways. As 'tramping artisans' they had the advantage of access to lodgings vetted by their association. If married, these men would leave families behind and lodge wherever they worked. Often their host family was in the same trade, as when an 18 year old carpenter from Kent arrived in London in 1817. He lodged with several fellow-builders with a landlady who cooked and washed and treated him so that he felt 'quite at home'.[19] Gangs of navvies building railways and roads (many of them Irish), soldiers and sailors, agricultural labourers seeking harvest work made up bands of mobile men. They might establish semi-permanent liaisons with local women who were then in charge of any resulting children.

Many younger women drifted to towns and engaged in short-term

[19]   J. Burnett, *Useful Toil: Autobiographies of Working People from the 1820s to the 1920s* (1974), p. 284.

relationships or prostitution for a time before settling down into more permanent unions. Girls and young women, who now seldom worked in the fields except at sowing or harvest, stayed to help their parents if there was outwork in the area or went into workshops and factories where, at tasks labelled as women's work, their wages continued at about half those of men and made it almost impossible for them to survive on their own. Many more young women were going to do housework and childcare in the homes of the middle class, now seen as purely *domestic* servants. Whatever the rhetoric, these young women were no longer members of the employing family but in a twilight position between the older service relationship and waged work. By mid-century, by far the majority of living-in servants were young women.

Poorer people tried to survive the harsh conditions of the expanding cities by 'huddling' together in households made up of more than one family. In particular, the few elderly who survived, whether widowed parents or unrelated, might do light domestic tasks and child-minding while adults worked for wages. By the 1840s, deteriorating living conditions in industrial villages and manufacturing towns increased infant and child mortality so that completed family size did not rise and women continued to bear many children, still the best insurance against indigence and the workhouse in old age. By mid-century, however, in areas where women's waged work was widely available such as textile and pottery towns, some women seem to have been deliberately limiting the number of pregnancies, mainly by abortion. They relied on networks of information passed from woman to woman and the knowledge of 'handy' women who also acted as informal midwives and nurses, and who laid out the dead.

Those children who survived were, as before, starting work at an early age. Now, however, they might be in fields, workshops or factories with unbroken hours of toil and little opportunity to pick up general skills. Their fragile position was only guaranteed by membership of some family group, whether their own or by informal adoption. This was their only inheritance, 'a foothold in an occupation . . . some slight defence against the vicissitudes of adult life'. For a child without even this sense of identity, the outlook was indeed bleak.[20]

Many of the families in towns were new arrivals, more isolated than in the communities they had left or the 'urban villages' which

---

[20]   D. Vincent, *Bread, Knowledge and Freedom: A Study of 19th Century Working Class Autobiography* (1981), p. 71.

later emerged within cities. Young people living at home no longer had their closest ties with fellow-servants or the family of master and mistress. In both town and country, parents and siblings now lived together often in the enforced intimacy of wretched housing.

Conflict between family members over resources was endemic, particularly where adolescent children were restive over contributing earnings to the common pool, and women were often bitter about lack of support from their husband (or partner). Under these conditions, violence continued as part of personal relationships, inflamed by heavy drinking. It is possible that the incidence of incest increased, for whereas in the past, girls and young women had liaisons with fellow-servants or, possibly, the master, or son of the household, now fathers, uncles and brothers were their everyday companions and often had at least nominal control over them.

With more people spending their days in workshops or factories and living in urban areas, routines of daily living were changing. There was less time and opportunity to gather fuel and food from common lands, woods and hedges, which were, in any case, now enclosed, or to grow it in gardens. More was bought which required minimal preparation or was ready for eating. Paying for labour in wages rather than in kind threw the poor back on their own meagre resources or those of closer neighbours, among whom networks of mutual help remained. What cooking there was might be accomplished with much pooling and borrowing of equipment. For example, where beer was still brewed as a staple drink, few households owned the complete set of necessary mash and brewing tubs so that neighbours shared, as they did the yeast or as they might take turns baking the oat cakes of the north, going from house to house, 'taking their meal tubs and coal to heat the bakstone'.[21]

Water supplies were limited to a fetid village pond, unreliable public wells or what rainwater could be collected. What laundry that was done was often taken to brooks or rivers where groups of women would wash together. Free or cheap cleaning agents – urine, dung or lye soaked in water – were used as bleaching agents for clothes as well as for the infrequent body wash. Women organised and performed most of these tasks and provided clothing, the cloth now almost always bought or even ready-made second-hand garments.

Where women were employed in wage work, a variety of ways

---

[21] J. Lawson, *Letters to the Young on Progress in Pudsey during the Last 60 Years* (Stannenglen, 1887), pp. 8–9.

to fulfil these household duties was used: widowed parents, younger children of both sexes, neighbours or kin living near by and cooked-food shops, such as the novel fish and chips, flourished. Mothers might have their infants brought to the factory or shop for breast feeding. Adult men occasionally helped in the home but this was only regularised in areas like Lancashire where women had worked from the inception of the cotton mills. Here, one evening a week on 'Mary Ann night', the whole family joined in. On the whole, however, the trend was for a sharper division of labour between men, women and children.

This level of housekeeping presupposed a certain standard of living. For many others, homes were single roomed hovels or a mud-floored cottage with little furniture but a straw pallet to sleep on and hunger was never far off. Even the slightly more prosperous household gathered by a meagre fire in the evenings as home-made rush lights quickly burned away for even cheap tallow candles were beyond their means. A loom, last or other tools might still figure as the most prominent piece of furniture in the room. Meals were eaten whenever and wherever possible. Much enforced sharing between family members and other households was the only bulwark against total destitution and an important basis for rebuilding community bonds. For example, there are hints that women breast fed each others' children when necessary, helped each other through family illnesses or even took in others' children for short periods.

As the economy became more cash oriented, women's main housekeeping task shifted to budgeting the precarious income, making it stretch by casual washing, taking in lodgers, piecework, gleaning or whatever came to hand. There was wide variation in whether wives worked for wages even in the same areas. For example, in mid-nineteenth-century Leicester, 40 per cent of wives of hosiery workers did wage work compared to 20 per cent in other industries.[22] In this situation, a family's standing for *credit*, for services rendered, loans given and general financial and personal viability, became a critical resource. Women were at the centre of these credit networks whether obtaining tick from shopkeepers or giving and receiving services. These activities contrasted with the earlier part of the period when

[22]   N. Osterud, 'Gender Divisions and the Organization of Work in the Leicester Hosiery Industry', in Angela John, ed., *Unequal Opportunities: Women's Employment in England, 1800–1918* (Oxford, 1986).

women tried to protect family subsistence in times of dearth by publicly leading protests over the price of grain.

Many of these changes in work and family life brought anguished responses from literate workingmen as well as middle-class observers. Apprehension focussed on the related issues of men's traditional authority over their wives and the place of children, often expressed by a distrust of industry and the town which sprang up around it. In 1784, a commentator grieved to see: 'a Young well made fellow, or rather one who might have been, in a loom where a woman will generally earn as much, what a sight, what a perversion of masculine strength! Women can bear confinement and a domestic life much better than men.'[23]

The fear that the moral and political authority of men would be undermined by the new forms of labour and the ignominy of being supported by wife and children is a thread running from the conservative evangelicals through early radicals and on to the indictment of the capitalist system in the 1840s by Marx and Engels. Even employers who depended mainly on female and child labour eagerly supported a division of labour which disciplined men into wage work. They also welcomed the emphasis on domestic felicity which could be bought with increased consumption of cloth, pottery and other goods which they were producing. The toll of such daily toil on the health of working-class women fired humanitarian concern with fears for the future of a labour force while fears about their morals were even more widespread.

The disquiet about men's position in the family had been inflamed by the widespread use of child labour in the first half of the nineteenth century. Displaced handloom weavers saw their sons, or worse, their daughters, able to earn more in factories than they could scrape together despite their skills. In early workshops and factories these children's labour had often been organised by their fathers but technical change and demand soon outstripped these arrangements although parents continued to find jobs for their children where possible.

Men returning from the Napoleonic War to bleak conditions of unemployment echoed these anxieties. Late eighteenth-century friendly societies, formed and run as men's clubs, stressed the manliness of providing for self and dependants, an ethos which carried

---

[23] W. LaPorte, *Cursory Remarks on the Importance of Agriculture in its Connection with Manufacturing and Commerce* (1784), p. 40.

over into early trade unions. Significantly, the second wave industrialising processes were in metal manufacture and the railways which had evolved from male-dominated skills of blacksmiths, wheelwrights and joiners. They became the backbone of the articulate working-class movement. Skilled men, in particular, put this in terms of a natural division of labour. Tailors, fearing female competition, declared that the women had been 'unfairly driven from their proper sphere ... unfeelingly torn from the maternal duties of a parent and encouraged unjustly to compete with men in ruining the money value of labour'.[24]

There were few alternative visions to the way the family and its division of labour was interlocking with industrial capitalism. In the 1820s a small group of radical men and women, influenced by Robert Owen, had queried the separation of production from consumption and the allied sexual division of labour within the family. Their questioning of men's domination within marriage went deeper than any subsequent nineteenth-century ideas. But by the 1830s and 1840s, middle-class reformers had pushed through measures such as the factory acts which controlled the employment of women and children and in 1842 excluded them from underground mining, providing some protection from exploitation but also marking their dependent status.

Chartists, too, in this period rejected the more radical view of the Owenites and opted for power and rewards for men as family heads. One of the primary tasks of the mid-century trades unions became the reassertion of the adult man's authority in the face of threats to both his manhood and his family's survival.[25] The discussion of the 'Woman Question' and of family arrangements passed to more middle-class observers, both conservatives and early feminists who, on the whole, accepted the basic division between public and private spheres.

By mid-century, these forces consolidated in a deeply held belief that men had a life-time responsibility to work for a money wage to support a family through obtaining a marketable skill or the sale of their muscle power and ingenuity. The idea of a 'family wage' paid to the husband/father was becoming fused with middle-class imperatives. Women would care for children, provide food and clothing and what home comforts were possible by clever housewifery

[24]   B. Taylor, '"The Men Are as Bad as Their Masters...": Socialism, Feminism and Sexual Antagonism in the London Tailoring Trade in the 1830s', in J. Newton, M. Ryan and J. Walkowitz, eds., *Sex and Class in Women's History* (1983), p. 208.

[25]   S. Rose, '"Gender at Work": Sex, Class and Industrial Capitalism', *History Workshop Journal*, 21 (1986).

and budgeting as well as supplementing an inadequate income. Widowers left with numbers of young children quickly married again or found substitutes in female kin, housekeepers or landladies to 'do' for their domestic needs.

Not all groups accepted these norms. Those living at the edges of forests, in quarrying communities, the crofters and fishermen of coastal regions and others all had varying expectations for the division of labour within the family while casual labourers could never hope to earn enough to fulfil the terms of this model. The lingering on of the 'petty wedding' implying a limited commitment of men and women is evidence of alternative arrangements.

Certain categories of family member were particularly vulnerable to falling outside the provision of the ideal family form: mothers on their own, widows, women who never married, children from large families. Nevertheless, as productive work was increasingly separated from other aspects of life, this concept of the family became deeply rooted in British culture.

II 1850–1950

The upper and middle classes

Through the twentieth century, landed families, with the royal family at their head, continued to command homage. But the basis of their dominance had been shaken with a decisive shift to industry and commerce as the basis of wealth, the declining fortunes of agriculture and decimation of their sons in the Great War. Scions of aristocratic and gentry families mixed with upper middle-class boys at public schools, they entered the same professions and married their sisters as life styles merged.

For the middle ranks, the family's prospects were now further removed from the fortunes of the enterprise. The unit for accumulation and concentration of capital shifted into the public sphere, first as the private company and in the twentieth century as the public corporation run by a new generation of salaried senior management with fee-paid Boards of Directors. Further down the social pyramid, in small businesses, and particularly retail shops, the family remained directly vulnerable to trade cycles and creditors. The family business was rapidly being overtaken, however, by organisations spawning posts in lower management, clerical and salaried positions in business, state bureaucracies and education. The families in both these sectors were exceptionally conscious of status gradations and family resources were strained to upholding and enhancing their position.

For all these groups, marriage was gradually transformed from being partly a property contract to a concentration on consumption and companionship. It was becoming more important for married women, as primary consumers, to be able to contract debts. The Married Women's Property Acts of the 1870s and 1880s allowed women to keep control of their income, so satisfying creditors but also fulfilling demands of the early feminists. Discussions about the acts had brought out fears that the law would interfere in the family, that fathers' rights would be undermined or they would shirk their responsibilities. These arguments had been raised at the time of the first, very limited, divorce reform two decades before in 1857 and would be again in every attempt to shift the balance of power between husbands and wives through to the divorce reforms of the 1920s. For as participation in formal religion declined, the sacred quality of the home and women's moral place within it became even more a focus for moral stability and spirituality. Most measures of reform retained the basic family form of male control and protection. Income tax, for example, was framed as a duty of male household heads who were then given allowances for wives and children.

Paradoxically, it was upper-class circles, those who took part in national and regional 'Society', who continued to practise a family life of formal and public display. Appearing at the events of the Season, in London, the Scottish grouse moors or at country house balls, dinners and the local hunt, were central to a family's inclusion in the highest circles which, in turn, led to patronage and power. Women were automatically expected to become hostesses and run the establishment of their husbands' position. The wives of cathedral officials, public schoolmasters, university dons (who were allowed to marry in the 1870s), civil servants, the armed service ('the senior officer flings his mantle of rank over his better half') usually lived in housing which went with the appointment. A wife had her allotted role just as if she had 'married a country house'. If a man was unmarried, he had to find a sister or other female relative to fulfil these obligations.

Family rituals such as christenings, confirmations and marriages were integrated into formal Society events. In wealthy circles, daughters in their late teens were groomed for 'coming out' in Society, those at the top being presented at Court, thus marking them ready for the marriage market. Upper-class life required large retinues of servants and material plant for formal entertaining. All attended the Anglican Church regularly as a matter of convention, if not belief.

The rationale for the large houses and expensive displays was the leadership of gentility, duty based on proprietorship. These duties were primarily for family members to be seen at the right places and given social recognition by visiting and being visited, plus mild philanthropy preferably in the local area. Carrying out these rituals, particularly for women, was seen as part of setting the tone for those below and was used to justify the huge expenditures of time and money, sometimes inimical to the interests and inclinations of family members. It was almost impossible for a family to reject the embrace of Society even in small towns. The ostentatiously 'Bohemian' behaviour of the Bloomsbury group demonstrates the power of social dictates.[26] At all levels it was considered especially important to maintain a level of formality and display in front of the retinue of household servants. A reworking of paternalism was fostered not only by squires and wealthy farmers, but provincial manufacturers who deliberately created a family atmosphere by including their workforce in events such as the birth, marriage or coming of age of the eldest son of the family.[27]

At the highest levels, families moved amongst the often overlapping circles of kin and formal acquaintance. Grandparents retained considerable power through their control of resources and could insist on frequent visits from their offspring. In any case these families were peripatetic, moving from town house to country mansion, the homes of relatives and friends and rented holiday villas, a mobility made easier by the pattern of rental rather than ownership.

The upper middle class, in both London and the provinces, followed a modified version of this pattern. In their large suburban villas with a complement of two to four indoor servants and several gardeners, they entertained formally and patronised local events. Although they did not 'neighbour' except with the few at their social level, they were more securely rooted in the locality than the aristocracy and gentry. Their social round could include tennis, croquet and other activities in private homes or in clubs and church affairs. Aunts, uncles and cousins were important parts of their social landscape. All these

[26] L. Davidoff, *The Best Circles: Society, Etiquette and the Season* (1986)
[27] P. Joyce, *Work, Society and Politics: The Culture of the Factory in Later Victorian England* (Brighton, 1980).

establishments depended on large numbers of specialised servants, with the household divided between front premises for display and back stairs working areas. There were housemaids, kitchen maids and cooks and parlourmaids (who had replaced male servants by the 1890s) to wait on family members.

Childcare was largely turned over to nurserymaids and nannies. At the highest levels, where women's first duty was to Society and their husbands' position, mothers might see their children only at specified times. In the late afternoon, washed and dressed, the children would be brought down from the nursery to be read to and play quiet games. Fathers could be even more remote. Individual families varied but there was no question of parents, even mothers, being expected to spend the majority of time with their children: 'To me she was the perfect mother. I would not have liked her to dose me, bathe me, comfort me or hold my head when I was sick. These intimate functions were performed by Nanny ... I did not like mother even to see me in the bath.'[28]

Up to the First World War, many girls were educated at home by mothers, elder sisters or governesses. However, the mother's primary function was to train her daughters for social conventions of paying calls, appearing in company and preparing her for the marriage market. If through lack of funds, reclusive tendencies or ineptness a family did not go into local Society, girls were almost doomed to remain unmarried. Beatrix Potter, of Peter Rabbit fame, was the daughter of a second generation cotton magnate, and was held under a nursery regime into her 20s, only escaping after her parents' death.[29]

Boys were at school from about the age of 7, boarding and public school if possible. Here the regime was spartan, punishments severe and great emphasis placed on loyalty to the school, especially through sport. Emotional attachments between boys were frowned on but flourished in a hot-house atmosphere. When girls' public and grammar schools began from the 1870s, they imitated these features, although less academic and finishing schools continued to stress accomplishments and lady-like behaviour.

The divisively separate destinies of boys and girls separated siblings. They spent most of childhood and youth in single sex surroundings, only meeting at formal occasions such as dances. Marriage, quite aside from sexual ignorance, often brought the shock of reality. Young men,

[28]　M. Lutyens, *To Be Young: Some Chapters of Autobiography* (1959), p. 15.
[29]　M. Lane, *The Tale of Beatrix Potter* (1971).

whose emotional life had been bound up in their male companions, and whose heterosexual experience, if any, was confined to prostitutes, found flesh and blood women very different than the idealised cult of sacred womanhood encouraged by the chivalric ethos of the public school. Young women were so sheltered from worldly knowledge as to make the basic facts of economic as well as sexual life a mystery and many couples floundered on mutual incompatibility.

By the twentieth century, more families were able to take part in a more modest suburban middle-class life style. Social contacts were made through golf and cricket clubs, amateur dramatics, church and chapel. At this level, an absence of formal Society encouraged more family-centred activities like music making, garden and parlour games, small dinner parties and seaside holidays. These solid suburban dwellings, with their front and back entrances, staffed by one or two servants, redolent with an atmosphere of toast and wax polish, represented the acme of the ideal home.

In the ranks of the new salariat such as shop assistants, school-teachers, civil servants, a passion for the written word made enthusiastic followers of progressive and religious activists, from Bible reading groups to the socialist Clarion Club. In the 1890s, both young men and women took enthusiastically to bicycles as a way of extending their home-bound horizons. Girls with a little more education than their mothers (who may have been in service) were encouraged to take part, and the educational ladder was urged on children of both sexes. The somewhat more genteel were ambivalent about daughters working but tacitly recognised their economic contribution to the household. A not very successful Edwardian merchant living on the fringes of Hampstead fulminated against women working for wages, but he was not above borrowing small sums from his eldest daughter who had persisted in becoming a schoolteacher.[30]

The 'closed world of home' in late nineteenth- and early twentieth-century Britain may have been exceptionally claustrophobic because a small number of children had become the focus of all their parents' attention.[31] While more children were surviving there is strong evidence that the size of families had begun to fall around mid-century, starting with the aristocracy and gentry, and followed by prosperous business and professional families. Clergymen, expressing public

[30]   Anonymous manuscript diary, daughter of an East India merchant, born 1887, in author's collection.
[31]   R. Church, *Over the Bridge* (1958), p. 22.

outrage during famous trials of birth control propagandists in the 1880s, were nevertheless clearly limiting their own numbers of children. The motivation was complicated and is even now not fully understood. The age at marriage remained high as couples waited to amass resources to sustain the 'paraphernalia of gentility'.[32] It was the births in the later years of marriage which seem to have been curtailed in particular. Concern with the health of wives was one factor. The growing costs of running a middle-class household, with an increasing range of consumer durables that might include a private carriage or one of the early automobiles, was another, making it harder to afford large families. With the rise of corporate business there was less need for large numbers of sons and nephews who now required expensive schooling rather than informal apprenticeship in the family firm.

By the interwar period, the expanding salariat had also curtailed numbers of children to the point, where, in interwar Britain, clerks had the lowest birth rate of any occupational group. The proportion of childless couples at all levels grew and the one to three child family was becoming the norm even for the respectable working class. Contraception, which was patently being practised, must have included both abstinence and withdrawal (coitus interruptus). Intense concern with self-control as part of the 'character' which was the lynch-pin of middle-class respectability was closely connected to this prudent pattern.

The tangle of beliefs about heredity which assumed that morals as well as 'germs' of parents were directly inherited in the minds and bodies of their children added to the psychological burden of parenthood. This reinforced concern that childhood should be a period of innocence, untainted by the pollution of sexuality and the suppression of masturbation, continued to be an obsession in some middle-class families and schools.

Although for the most part there was still a thick mist of prudish silence and ignorance surrounding sexual topics, in the late nineteenth century, the feminist-inspired crusade against the Contagious Diseases Acts from the 1860s to 1880s – passed in an attempt to control venereal disease in the armed forces – brought the discussion of the double standard of licence for men and chastity for women into the open, indeed, as many lamented, onto the very breakfast tables of

[32] J. Banks, *Prosperity and Parenthood: A Study of Family Planning among the Victorian Middle Class* (1956).

respectable families. In this climate, some regarded birth control as interference with the wages of sin, and the handmaid of promiscuity. Conservative women joined with some feminists to advocate higher standards of chastity for men, a solution which appealed to the proponents of 'social purity'. The all-male, mainly lower middle-class White Cross Army of the early twentieth century pledged chastity in a pattern reminiscent of the temperance movement. For women, chastity remained the only safe option continually contrasted to higher class prostitutes, the demi-monde, who were outside Society and thus cut off from the benefits of respectable marriage.

The code of sexual respectability had been further emphasised in the 1880s by the consolidation of male homosexuality as a social identity, the term *homosexual* dating from this period. The subject received immense publicity with the Oscar Wilde trials under recent legislation which brought all forms of male homosexual activity within the criminal law.[33] Homosexual identity was further reinforced with the new breed of twentieth-century scientific 'sexologists' who shifted discussions of sexual behaviour into a medical mode. By the 1920s, close relationships between women also came under increasing suspicion, the term 'lesbian' coming into circulation in the 1920s with the sensational publication of Radclyffe Hall's *Well of Loneliness*.

The First World War, with its uncertainty and carnage, undermined some of the rigid conventions of the middle class who proportionally lost more young men. Many young people became restive under strict injunctions on personal behaviour. Although many of the freedoms that young women gained were temporary to the war, their wider experience did have an effect, symbolised in radical changes in costume, the bobbed hair and short skirts of the 1920s. Women who had taken no direct part in the feminist movement nevertheless began to demand more consideration of their needs, and the revelation that mortality in childbirth was actually rising in the 1930s was alarming. Marie Stopes's campaign for *married love*, birth control knowledge within marriage, struck a responsive chord although the church and many medical experts followed reluctantly. 'Family planning' was accepted mainly as part of a concern for maintaining the traditional form of the family and for the care of children, and not as a matter of women's rights over their own fertility. It was similar in intention to the 1920s legislation for children's welfare. Women's magazines

[33]   J. Weeks, *Sex, Politics and Society: The Regulation of Sexuality since 1800* (1981), pp. 102–5.

and radio programmes now stressed the physical and psychological responsibilities of mothers who, in any case, had fewer residential servants to help with childcare.

Nevertheless, from the mid-nineteenth century, there had been an undercurrent of restlessness among women subordinated within the domesticated role of the respectable middle-class family. The discussion around the first Divorce Act of 1857 was matched by the sensation novels of the 1860s with their themes of bigamy and familial murder which were avidly devoured by a female readership. The secret appeal at the heart of these novels centred on female independence and sexuality, the counterpart to the flourishing world of male pornography whose central theme was male power and childlike female submission.

Starting with the claim to control their own property, in the 1860s, women's independence from their secondary status within marriage grew. By the 1890s, husbands were no longer able to imprison or chastise their wives with impunity as pressure increased to incorporate women as individual citizens through the vote. Social freedoms such as smoking and leaving home unchaperoned erupted in discussions over the 'New Woman'. The renewed emphasis on masculine, military virtues and a sentimentalised view of women as domestic angels in the decades leading to the First World War may have been partly a backlash reaction to this challenge.

Despite the fears aroused by the feminist challenge, the structure of marriage endured, in no small part through men's dominance in the economy. Only upper-class women with property of their own could afford legal separation or divorce which reached a high point of almost a third of upper-class marriages in the Edwardian period. Women's greatest chance of economic and social survival was still through marriage despite the opening up of some professional and clerical positions. Their vulnerability is evident in the position of older spinsters. Few headed households, even fewer had capital to set up in business. A substantial proportion over 65 ended their days dependent on charity, significantly more than bachelors.[34] This is not to imply that all women wanted to marry; many chose to live more independent lives, freed from the subordinate status of marriage and the burden of childbearing and rearing.[35]

---

[34] M. Anderson, 'The Social Position of the Spinster in Mid-Victorian Britain', *Journal of Family History*, 9 (1984), p. 390.

[35] For an alternative view of attitudes to celibacy, see S. Jeffreys, *The Spinster and her Enemies: Feminism and Sexuality, 1880–1930* (1985).

Improvements in girls' education in the late nineteenth century and pressure for a more realistic alternative for those who did not marry led to the setting up of various residential positions: in sisterhoods, nursing, boarding schools, colleges and settlement houses. Often these institutions were set up along familial lines with the older women acting as motherly or elder sister figures, a strategy which sometimes set up tensions with their public activities.[36]

The working class

The middle-class view of the family not only framed its own practice but affected the working class. Legislation was cast and charity dispensed in the belief that such a family form was the basis of the social order. Great efforts were made to identify masculine pride with a man's financial support of the family as the key to keeping men steadily at work. Unease about the challenge to authority by gangs of urban youth, was countered by movements led by lower middle-class men, the Scouts and brotherhoods, who stressed the necessity of work, sober recreation and chivalry towards women.

Proposals for state or voluntary aid to families, such as maintenance for deserted wives, paid maternity leave for insured women workers or school meals, were opposed on the grounds that feckless, irresponsible men would defect from their supreme function of fatherhood.

As more men were included in the franchise and organised into the trade-union movement and later the Labour party, the assertion that men were responsible household heads was also part of the masculine claim for political recognition and furthered the division between respectable men and the stigmatised poor. This distinction was inadvertently strengthened by feminist agitation over married women's property which drew attention to the plight of vulnerable wives whose hard-won income belonged to their husbands and uncovered the widespread incidence of wife-beating which was assumed to be solely a working-class phenomenon.

Similar fears were raised by the growth of factory work for women and girls. The impersonal surroundings, mixing of the sexes, higher disposable income all gave an independence which was countered by urging and coercing girls into domestic service with its familial setting. Without exception, all residential institutions for women and

[36] M. Vicinus, *Independent Women: Work and Community for Single Women, 1850–1920* (1985).

girls prepared and sent girls into service. Girls' clubs and organisations emphasised domestic pursuits, even the Girl Guides only reluctantly allowed camping. The debate over raising the age of consent for girls' sexual relationships, the panic over revelations of the 'white slave trade' and later measures to police the morals of women in munitions factories during the First World War revealed the ambivalent attitude towards working-class girls, seen as innately innocent victims yet potentially sexually uncontrollable.

The married working-class woman, on the other hand, was assumed to be naturally more responsible, although often ignorant, and much effort was expended in teaching housewifely skills, for cleanliness was taken as a sign of care. In keeping with her expected role, a woman was urged that good management and saving would further the family's interests more than earning wages even when family resources were patently inadequate. From state agencies, charities and voluntary societies, more was being expected from mothers. Children now had to go to school, decently dressed, clean, healthy and well mannered, a heavy responsibility for most mothers and becoming an impossible burden for those with fewest resources. Throughout the period, the role of motherhood was elevated but with little thought given to the material context. For example, from the early twentieth century, 2 to 5 year olds were no longer taken into primary schools despite the fact that proposed nursery provisions never materialised.

The post-First World War feminist proposal for family allowances to be paid to the mother was opposed on the grounds that it would lead to dissension within the family and parental negligence. Even after Booth's late nineteenth-century survey showing that a third of London families depended on women's earnings for survival, married women's *unemployment* was never considered a problem. This view carried into early twentieth-century national insurance provisions, and structured interwar unemployment benefits. The principle of married women's dependence was inherited in the Beveridge Report of 1942 and subsequent welfare state legislation as it also was in voluntary schemes from friendly societies to life insurance.

At the turn of the century, the widening gap in completed family size between the classes, and the fears publicised by the eugenics movement that the wrong people were breeding, increased pressure for higher standards of motherhood. Yet the knowledge and means of reliable contraception continued to be withheld on the grounds of upholding morality and the sanctity of marriage, a position bitterly resented by many thoughtful working-class women. Ambivalence about whether working-class women should be workers or wives and mothers was epitomised by the attitude to widows who were at times objects of charity and at others punitively forced to work for the lowest wages or risk having their children taken away by poor law authorities or even private organisations.

In the mid-nineteenth century, a series of reforms created a category of juvenile crime, special children's poor law facilities, reformatories, industrial and ragged schools, and, together with church and chapel state-aided education, helped to build a conception of childhood as a separate part of the life-cycle. Child labour was seen as a sad necessity but the view was gaining ground that paid work for children was wrong, as well as being superseded by technology. Humanitarians felt early labour stunted children's health and right to happiness. Others feared that the independence of wages made them resistant to authority.

The shock at the poor physical condition of working-class recruits in the Boer and First World War, when 40 per cent of conscripts were medically graded unfit for service, added to the view that children were a national asset. Most of all, the gradual introduction of universal, later compulsory education gave state agencies access to working-class children. Through demands for school attendance, medical inspection, classroom behaviour, permission to apply for jobs, they imposed standards of normal childhood experience, sometimes much at odds with parents or the children's own needs and expectations.

State and charitable agencies aimed both to protect and to control children's lives. In the late nineteenth century, a strong partisan like Dr Barnardo fell foul of the law in his efforts to remove children from what he considered incompetent parents. Yet strenuous efforts were made to uphold the ideal of the intact family. In the same period, sensational revelations over 'baby-farming' – the placing of infants with child-minders for a lump sum – were accompanied by proposals that all children not with their *biological* parents should be licensed and open to inspection.[37] Such views misunderstood the strategies of working-class survival which often spread childcare among relations and neighbours. Ironically, it also overlooked the fact that the vast majority of the infants being 'baby-farmed' belonged to domestic servants living in middle-class homes, the group most vulnerable to

[37]   *SC on Protection of Infant Life*, PP 1871, VII, pp. iii–vii.

seduction, to broken courtships, to bearing illegitimate children and entry into prostitution.

The twentieth-century experience of war and depression had brought greater awareness of the importance of nutrition in children's development while medical expertise gradually began to replace a more moral interpretation of parenthood. This strengthened the view that wives and mothers were responsible for their families' welfare and was confirmed by respectable working-class opinion within organised labour circles. Socialist ideas had helped shift the burden from working-class men's individual failure, particularly through drink, and to stress environmental factors and the poverty of low wages. Thus by the 1920s, the issue of wife abuse had faded as working-class men gained dignity through the labour movement.[38]

In a variety of contexts more state and voluntary agencies were impinging on working-class life over issues such as sexuality, health and child-rearing. The ambiguity of attitudes towards the working-class family runs like a thread through the history of this period. It may be strikingly illustrated by policy changes within the army where the officer class had complete control. In the mid-nineteenth century, a tiny fraction of soldiers were allowed to marry with official permission, called marrying 'on the strength'. The majority of men, quartered in inns and barracks, were served by local women with whom they often formed alliances. Such *ad hoc* arrangements had been exposed by feminists and working-class men in the campaign to repeal the Contagious Diseases Act. Under the acts, punitive measures against local women, including medical examination, had created a core of recognised prostitutes, 'Queen's Women'.

At the same time, the army was becoming more professional, shedding the amateur services of local launderesses, landladies and cooks although the domestic work which still had to be done was seen as unbecoming to soldiers. Furthermore, the new type of soldier was to be less brutalised, needing the civilising effects of home attachments. Therefore the logical solution was to allow marriage. Yet the soldier's duty and masculine persona was as a fighting man, not a responsible husband and father.

This paradox was solved by the imposition of a familial ideal *within* the army. The officers acted as heads of the regimental 'family', dispensing fatherly rewards and punishments. Officers' wives acted in

---

[38] J. Lambertz, 'Politics and Economics of Family Violence in Liverpool from the Late 19th Century to 1948' (unpublished MPhil thesis, Manchester University, 1983).

a maternal, philanthropic capacity. Many more men were allowed to marry 'on the strength' but their wives and children were incorporated under military discipline. Soldiers' wives were given the opportunity – compulsory – to earn money by doing laundry, cleaning and cooking, their quarters were provided and standards of housekeeping inspected. Their children were given schooling and medical services, but had to maintain certain standards of behaviour. All were expected to attend church and any breaches of discipline were punished by withdrawal of these privileges. Those soldiers who persisted in marrying without permission ('off the strength') had to maintain wives and children out of an income designed for a fighting man's individual support. Thus the concept of the *service family* was successfully imposed on that least familial organisation, the British army, until mass conscription in two world wars made the granting of a separation allowance paid directly to the civilian wife a necessity.[39]

In reality, the stability of working-class life increasingly depended on the level and regularity of the breadwinners' work opportunities and level of wages. The expanded scale of production increased the continuity of much employment but also undermined the monopoly of skilled craftsmen, reducing the division between the life style of the skilled and unskilled. Cyclical and technological unemployment was replacing chronic underemployment as the threat to twentieth-century individuals and families.

For those in work, shorter working days, Saturday afternoons off and Bank Holidays demarcated paid labour from a newly acquired leisure time. The development of working-class suburbs and rapid cheap transport further separated work from home. With the exception of a few volatile periods in the late nineteenth and early twentieth centuries, food prices fell and the standard of living rose.

In the more settled urban communities a working-class culture was emerging, more compatible with the mature phase of industrial capitalism. This took for granted the separation of home and work and organised working-class struggles took place over conditions of production, crucially the wage. The 'labour aristocrats', whether older style craftsmen or factory-based engineers, endorsed men's position as household heads. They had taken power in organisations like working men's clubs, first created by middle-class philanthropists. Here

---

[39]   M. Trustram, *Women of the Regiment: Marriage and the Victorian Family* (Cambridge, 1984).

respectable workingmen could gather, dressed in non-working clothes with watch, chain and bowler hat, removed from both work and the now female domain of home.

The labour movement solidified this view and, for example, took no part in late nineteenth-century marriage reform debates, a struggle left to organisations such as the Fabian Women's Group and the sole working-class women's voice, the Women's Co-operative Guild. The postwar family allowance proposals were actively resisted by trade unions, who feared an attack on the bargaining power of men's 'family wage' claims as well as on masculine authority in the home.

It is difficult to retrieve working-class women's own views of the family. There are flashes of insight during periods of controversy such as in the 1870s when the concept of 'the prostitute' was hardening into a fixed category rather than a life-cycle stage of variously short- and long-term liaisons, a development often resisted by local women.[40] The Women's Co-operative Guild was founded in 1884 to protect the interests of women in their central task of budgeting and shopping. Its membership, however, represented the top echelons of working-class families since Co-operative Societies refused to grant extended credit. These women sought better material conditions to fulfil their duties as wives and mothers. They campaigned for protection for their health by access to medical help and knowledge about reproduction. They stood out for equal grounds for divorce, confronting the male-controlled parent Co-operative Society on this issue. But these aspirations were firmly in the context of women's role within the family. It is significant, perhaps, that some working-class women did not enthusiastically embrace provision of services such as school meals, regarding them as a possible stigma on their children and derogation of their own role.

Interviews with working-class women looking back on their experiences from the early twentieth century reveal that many had no wish to continue the drudgery of the 'double shift', working for low wages in dead-end jobs as well as carrying home responsibilities. They were well aware that their ability and willingness to contribute to the family income might make men less enthusiastic about turning over the bulk of their wages to the household pool.

Nevertheless, women wished to be able to make the choice of how

---

[40]   J. Walkowitz, *Prostitution and Victorian Society: Women, Class and the State* (Cambridge, 1980).

much paid work to undertake, and some resented protective legislation and unequal pay which drove them into full-time marriage and maternity with such poor resources and weak bargaining power. For example, working-class women were quick to grasp that maintenance orders against their husbands' wages, which became available through the courts in the 1880s as part of a mechanism to allow separation without divorce (only, of course, for those women who were not deemed guilty of sexual irregularity), could be used to try and oblige a husband to maintain his wife and children *within* an ongoing marriage.

By the late nineteenth century, stable marriage was becoming part of respectable working-class culture with more emphasis on a formal marriage ceremony, although the older forms did not completely die out. When both parties had been married before, it was assumed that they had already achieved married status as long as each fulfilled their duties. A London woman explained that since the man she had married would no longer support her and her children, he was 'no husband to her and the one that worked for her she respected'.[41] Some women continued to avoid legal marriage, fearing a shift in the balance of power. One cohabiting woman refused marriage because she 'didn't choose to be knocked about, nor to see her children treated bad neither'.[42] All-female households, by pooling resources, could become a viable, if fragile further alternative 'family' while single or widowed men were more likely to go into lodgings.[43]

Nevertheless, the married state contributed to a respectable image as the concept of prostitution was transformed from what had often been a stage in the life-cycle to a specialised, full-time occupation catering to groups of mobile men such as sailors. In 1900, 88 per cent of people had been married at sometime in their lives, falling to 83 per cent in the 1920s, mainly because of the First World War, and rising again in the 1940s. In the twentieth century, despite the decline of regular church-going, more couples who could afford to do so were having church weddings, in a ritual expressing a traditional relationship, the bride, in virginal white and demurely veiled, being

---

[41]   Quoted in J. Lewis, *Women in England, 1870–1950* (Brighton, 1984), p. 11.

[42]   Quoted in I. Minor, 'Working Class Women and Matrimonial Law Reform, 1890–1914', in D. Martin and D. Rubinstein, *Ideology and the Labour Movement* (1979), p. 14.

[43]   D. Gittins, 'Marital Status, Work and Kinship, 1850–1930', in J. Lewis, ed., *Labour and Love: Women's Experience of Home and Family 1850–1940* (Oxford, 1986). L. Davidoff, 'The Separation of Home and Work? Landladies and Lodgers in Nineteenth and Twentieth Century England', in S. Burman, ed., *Fit Work for Women* (1979).

given away by her father.[44] For large sections of the working class, it can be said that in this period, particularly for women, marriage was moving from a shorter term contract to an all-embracing status.

During the second half of the nineteenth century, the age at marriage rose steadily reaching a high of 27 for men and 25 for women around 1900 and falling gradually during the next half century. In these later decades, marriages were less frequently broken by death, formal divorce was rare, migration much diminished and, despite the unknown quantity of separations, it is probable that family continuity was higher than before or since.

The essence of such marriages had become male financial support in return for wives' household management, cooking and sexual services. A married man expected to be able to turn all housekeeping and childcare over to his wife when he turned over ('tipped up') his weekly wage. Custom varied between industries and areas as to what proportion the husband kept for himself but the basic principles were similar. The traditional nineteenth-century pattern was for the husband to tip up everything to his wife – sometimes on the door step with neighbours as witness – when she would give him back pocket money ('spence' in the north) usually spent on fares, tobacco, beer or a sport, club subscription or hobby.[45]

Some household economies were separated to the point where a father might send a child out to buy a bit of food as relish for his meal alone. This practice often pegged family income to a set sum which was not increased as subsequent children arrived or with price rises, partly because it was all a man could do to keep up this level but also because the rigid division of labour kept him from appreciating the anxieties of managing at the margin. Illness or unemployment could have immediately disastrous effects where the basics of rent and food consumed almost the whole income. The development of national insurance schemes for unemployment and illness of the breadwinner helped ward off the worst consequences but it was only in the mid-twentieth-century economy of full employment and bonuses that men began to pay regularly for bigger items such as consumer durables.

[44]   D. Leonard, 'A Proper Wedding', in M. Corbin, ed., *The Couple* (Harmondsworth, 1978).
[45]   A. Gray, 'The Working Class Family as an Economic Unit' (unpublished PhD thesis, Edinburgh University, 1973).

A good husband was one who contributed regular and, where possible, sufficient, support and was not violent, particularly towards the children, although many men took part in family life far beyond this minimum. Despite long hours of work, many still came home for the main midday meal. They enjoyed playing with younger children, taking them for walks or telling stories. They might contribute produce or income from working allotments, keeping pigs or chickens, mending boots and household equipment. Men 'spoke for' relatives needing jobs at their place of work and in skilled trades might guide their sons into similar work. But all these were matters of choice and other legitimate masculine pursuits could take precedence: time spent with male peers in sport, politics, club or union activity, or, more damaging to domestic life, the public house. Expectations of masculine prerogatives and behaviour were strongly felt and, even where men were not contributing income, might be upheld. Many men did help with housework and childcare but they risked being dubbed 'mop rag' or 'diddy man'.

Women prided themselves on their ability to manage the budget and allocation of work so that even domesticated husbands had little understanding of what was actually involved. When the mother was incapacitated she would hand over management to a teenage daughter if no female relative or neighbour could be found to 'do' for the household. At any time, it is estimated that at least one third of working-class families could not have survived on the male wage alone. The hardest times in the family cycle were when the children were too young to earn and, after a period of relative prosperity as they reached working age, again in old age when grown children had left home.

A wife had to manage on what the breadwinner brought in plus resources she could mobilise. These included children's earnings, credit with local shopkeepers and small sums she could earn perhaps doing outwork or casual harvesting. Many such activities were extensions of household services, such as providing lodgings, taking in washing, child-minding, nursing the sick, attending childbirth and laying out the dead.

Many of these services were provided without money payment but as part of a reciprocal network among relatives and neighbours. In some cases these included the mother organising the services of her children such as running errands for neighbours. Below a certain social and income level, the pawn shop was an important source of day-to-day financial coping, and, for all households, the housewife's skill at shopping could add to familial assets. In larger towns, charities were a source of goods and services but it took expertise to know where to apply and how to turn gifts in kind to best account.[46]

In some areas like textile or pottery towns, there was more opportunity for married women's work but from mid-century the proportion fell, and until the Second World War only about 10 per cent were officially recorded as in paid employment. Household economy was most casual among the very poor and the incidence of female headed households varied inversely with income. Over the period, higher real wages for men made the most desperate measures less necessary. But women also lost control over such resources as children's time and labour which were increasingly diverted to school. Opportunity to act as handywomen slowly gave way as midwives were registered. The close relationship with the landlady which could carry over the rent was replaced by the impersonal council house tenancy.

Many women's greatest resource was their network of human relationships. Within the household they allocated tasks and regulated distribution of food, clothing and space. They had to balance rewards to fit needs of dependency and contributions of wage earners. Children often felt they were working for their mothers in services or cash. There is evidence that where theft took place among family members it was between husbands and wives, siblings or children and fathers; almost never would children steal from their mothers. Children's recognition of the mother's contribution to family survival may be partly responsible for the romantic vision of 'our Mam', particularly by working-class men.

Within the community, working-class women reciprocated goods and services with kin and neighbours and dealt with shopkeepers, rent collectors and, increasingly, schoolteachers and state officials. As towns became more settled, mothers and daughters were able to build up reciprocal services, handing on a tenancy, caring for grandchildren, being cared for in old age, although often living near by rather than in the same household. Women's strong material and emotional attachments within this female world may have been resented by some men. Neighbours were careful to leave the house before the master's return and closeness between female kin may account for the ready stock of mother-in-law jokes.

---

[46]   E. Ross, *Love and Labour in Outcast London: Motherhood 1870–1918* (Oxford, New York, 1993).

Women's informal power, born of extremity, was augmented the lower and more irregular the breadwinners' wage. Even then, it was set in a context of masculine pride and economic advantage. Out of meagre resources, it was thought rational to see the breadwinner receiving the lion's share of food. But there was also symbolic significance in the father's special chair, relish for his tea, money for individual spending, freedom from childcare and other privileges. Adult sons bringing in a wage might also gain this status in modified form and there seems to have been some conflict between growing sons and their fathers. Most mothers tried to give what there was left to their younger children. When times were hard many women survived on tea, bread and marge or 'kettle benders' (crusts steeped in water with salt and pepper). Since they seldom went out, they could do with the least clothing.

Wives at all levels prided themselves on their ability to keep the household at the highest standards according to neighbourhood norms. When families were large and the burden of care so great, there was little time and energy left for demonstrations of affection to children. Devotion had to be expressed in the fierce attention to cleanliness and behaviour which made many mothers seem harsh and joyless. In the long run, women could not do a great deal without their husbands' co-operation in handing over the highest possible sum. Wives felt justified in upbraiding men who did not make the best of themselves, spent resources on hobbies or paid too many rounds at the pub. Groups of wives would stand outside the local to claim the 'housekeeping' at the weekend when wages had been paid. Husbands expected their comforts to be considered, to have their meals ready as much to their taste as possible. A wife who was not able or did not bother to keep up these standards was demonstrably not living up to her part of the marriage contract.

A level of interpersonal violence seemed endemic among some sections of the working class, undoubtedly inflamed by close quarters and heavy drinking. Fighting between husbands and wives was accepted, with the women usually, but by no means always, the victims. The sparking points were rows over money and the wife's personal services, especially where a husband felt his 'manhood' had been infringed. During the depression an unemployed miner, usually the most considerate of men, whose wife had taunted him with the poverty and indignity of their home, 'sometimes vowed religiously that the day he got a safe job he'd give her the biggest hiding any woman ever had, just to show her who was really who'.[47] Some habitually tyrannical husbands and fathers seem to have had higher expectations for their lives and turned their frustrations on wives in terms of sexual jealousy. The mother's central position in the lives of her children built up an intense devotion and coloured men's expectations of their own wives. This may have fuelled the complicated dynamics which could turn the quondam devoted son into a demanding, even abusive husband. It is possible that sexuality was another contested area.

What evidence there is, suggests that few mid-nineteenth-century working-class families deliberately practised contraception, with the possible exception of textile areas where work for married women was built into the local economy. A fatalistic acceptance of children, a belief by both men and women in the husband's sexual rights, the importance of children as subsidiary earners and the belief that any discussion of sex was dirty and shameful, combined to produce ignorance and lack of motivation to limit family size. Fear of pregnancy and exhaustion made many women endure rather than enjoy sex. Undoubtedly many did try to bring on miscarriages, using herbal and patent remedies through information garnered from female relatives and friends.[48] They seem to have been unaware of the laws passed in the 1860s making self-induced abortion a criminal offence, although infanticide cases were given wide publicity.

For the late nineteenth-century generations, the introduction of compulsory schooling diverted children's help and earning capacity and the burden of large families was becoming more obvious. Babies who survived the first year of life now had a much greater chance of growing up, and lower infant mortality, which was finally achieved in the early twentieth century, made fewer pregnancies necessary to reach a reasonable completed family size. More secure work for men gave a rationale to planning family strategies. For example the fertility rate of railway workers fell rapidly following the expansion of promotion ladders. Since abstinence and withdrawal (coitus interruptus) continued as the most common form of contraception, some co-operation between husbands and wives was necessary.

Many women manifestly would have liked to have borne fewer children but did not know how. Their daughters and granddaughters vowed they would not be dragged down by spending an average

[47]   W. Brierly, *Means-Test Man*, 2nd edn (Nottingham, 1983), p. 205 (1st edn, 1935).
[48]   D. Gittins, *Fair Sex: Family Size and Structure in Britain, 1900–39* (1982).

of fifteen years pregnant, nursing and caring for babies and began to put pressure on husbands. By the mid-twentieth century the average of six living children (but the result of many more pregnancies and births) had fallen to just over two, filling only about four years of a woman's life with child-bearing. Whatever the constellation of remote and proximate causes, family size of skilled workers had already declined by a third before the First World War. More isolated areas where women's work was less available and the age of marriage lower, as in mining and agricultural regions, retained higher birth rates, but by the 1930s even unskilled workers' families were approaching the two to three child norm. Those with more than four or five children began to feel shamed, as if they were irresponsible or giving evidence of being 'too highly sexed'.

Ignorance, promoted by a code which proscribed all discussion of sexual matters, made many women terrified of childbirth. Even in the 1930s, maternal mortality rates had not fallen significantly and ill-health due to overwork, poor nutrition and multiple pregnancies was widespread. Midwives had begun to attend women in childbirth and no longer helped with household tasks, which had given the newly delivered mother the rest she craved. In any case, the fees were high, the expense of a doctor prohibitive to all but the best off. By the interwar period, more women began seeking expert help, expecting relief from pain and disablement, and by the 1940s about a quarter of working-class women's confinements were in hospital.

Babies were made much of, played with by fathers and older siblings, often sleeping in the parents' bed. Breast feeding for several years was common, both as a convenience and an attempt at contraception. But the toddler was abruptly ousted from these privileges at the arrival of the new baby and after about age 7 would be expected to contribute to the household according to strength and ability. In the interwar period the fall in family size meant that each child could receive more parental attention, for example birthdays began to be marked with gifts and special food. On the other hand, the circle of sibling companionship, help and competition dwindled. It should be kept in mind, however, that these advantages and disadvantages were still not the experience of the 40 per cent of children who remained in the 10 per cent of larger families.

Children's labour was used to run errands, mind little ones, and in household tasks such as black leading and polishing, washing up, turning the mangle and hanging out laundry. They helped with outwork done at home, fetching materials and delivering the finished article. Outside the home they did street selling and casual jobs of all kinds. 'Half-timers' continued to work in mills and factories up to the First World War and their money contribution could be vital to the household economy. Girls tended to do more unpaid housework and boys money-making activities, but all would contribute where necessary. But for some at least, the rising standard of living in the later nineteenth century lifted the pressure for children to earn and, combined with schooling, encouraged a form of separate childhood experience to develop.

Girls, held closer to household responsibilities and care of younger children, tended to play in mixed age groups. Their singing games, in urban streets or villages, presaged courtship and marriage. Boys moved further afield in age-banded groups. By the 1890s in the skilled working class they were freer from domestic tasks, the concept of a 'cissy' seems to date from this period. These children knew that they owed their existence and support to their parents, most of whom held strict notions of duty and obedience although harsh punishments seem to have been much less than has been popularly believed.

Children's culture, mainly in the streets and fields, contained elements of rebellion against adults in general, played out in pranks like knocking on neighbours' doors and running away, rather than confronting their own parents. Children were valued for their potential earning power but also for themselves, even if harsh material conditions might leave little energy for lavishing affection. Undoubtedly some adults, both parents and older siblings, abused their position of power. The late nineteenth-century founding of the NSPCC, although partly motivated by concern to organise working-class morals, was also a recognition of childhood vulnerability, and incest was made a criminal offence in 1908.

The education system also marked distinctions between the sexes. Girls' absence was condoned as necessary to domestic work while it was assumed that boys were playing truant and more severely treated. Domestic subjects for girls had been introduced from the 1870s although most of the content was unrealistic, advocating expensive and alien materials or couched in abstract terms. However, by the interwar period, domestic subjects in the curriculum were identified with the majority who were not going on to secondary school, tying aspiration to future homemaking, as with the 14-year-old girl who was eager to gain her housewifery certificate to 'show Mr Right'.[49]

Many parents, particularly mothers, had resisted the imposition of primary education in the first generations in 1870s and 1880s. They resented the loss of children's contributions to the household. As the school leaving age rose in the early twentieth century, the conflicts centred on the 11 to 14 year olds and children were torn between loyalty to home and expectations of the school. For example, children were punished for being tardy in the morning when they had to do housework or errands before school. When the scholarship ladder was introduced in the 1920s, many eligible scholars passed up their hard-won places to the mystification of middle-class teachers who could not understand the pressures even on better-off families.

Discipline was a particular flashpoint between school, parents and children. While there was some verbal and physical violence in many working-class homes, the systematic shaming, sarcasm and some-times brutal use of the cane in schools dismayed many parents, some of whom resisted by keeping children at home or changing schools. Children themselves were often caught between differing forms of punishment and reward which were difficult to reconcile much less resist although many truanted and a few, particularly older boys, joined in short-lived school strikes.[50]

Children growing up in tightly knit communities, the urban street or court as well as rural village, were often taken in by relatives and neighbours who might take responsibility for their welfare if their parents were for some reason unable to do so. A child noticed getting into mischief or in danger would be reported to parents or dealt with on the spot. They would often be given food and made to feel useful by doing small services for this wider circle, although the use of chil-dren's labour was always an incentive to have control over them. Children from a whole street might join in expeditions such as the annual hop-picking from London's East End into Kent and recent urban migrants sent children back to rural relatives for holidays. Despite the poverty and instability of many families, a child had a chance of being taken in and looked after somewhere, shared out for longer or shorter periods among grannies, aunties or, less often, neighbours. Informal adoption was not unusual and illegitimate

[49]   D. Scannell, *Mother Knew Best: An East End Childhood* (1974).
[50]   P. Thompson, 'The War with Adults', *Oral History*, 13 (1975), pp. 29–38.

children could also be absorbed, some raised by grandmothers and believing that their own mothers were elder sisters.

These arrangements were not always easy, stretching resources of the host family, sometimes resented by their own children and resulting in scapegoating of the intruder, but care of some sort was usually forthcoming and formal legal adoption was only introduced in 1926. Only in the very poorest families did children have to 'fetch ourselves up' by scavenging, stealing and relying on charity, or being taken in by poor law institutions, the fate of the late nineteenth-century 'street arabs' who slept rough and lived under their own rules.[51]

Parents, particularly mothers, were often instrumental in deciding when and where children took their first full-time jobs. The relatively late age at marriage meant that from twelve to fifteen years might elapse from the end of school to the time a young person married and moved to a home of his or her own. If young men had to move away they would go into lodgings. A large proportion of girls continued to go into residential domestic service leaving home at age 10 or 11. Although physically still children, in social terms they were little adults, hair pinned up under a cap and wearing a uniform, they were responsible for earning their own living. In striking contrast, they lived under the same roof with the daughters of the house who might be four or five years older, their better nourished physiques quite matured, but who were still considered schoolgirls in short frocks with hair down their backs.

By the twentieth century, domestic service was an aging occupation and more girls were going into manufacturing industry with a sprinkling in shop and clerical work. Like their brothers, they now lived at home, taking part in a growing youth culture in the street and music halls. Same-sex friendships flourished, a welcome change from the loneliness of residential service. After 1900, dancing became a special youthful pastime and dance halls were favourite meeting places for courtship. Groups of young men and women sauntered in certain parts of town on Saturday evenings taking part in courting rituals known by names such as 'the monkey parade' or 'clicking'. As late as the 1870s, rural courtship games such as 'Kiss-in-the-Ring' were being played on the outskirts of London, but two generations later young people were more likely to meet at the local Palais de Dance and pursue their lovemaking in the cinema.

[51]   T. Thompson, 'Thomas Morgan', in *Edwardian Childhoods* (1982), p. 21.

In the late nineteenth century, young people were beginning to have a little more spending money and a rudimentary form of teenage culture began to emerge, mainly based on distinctive clothing. In rough working-class areas, young men would form gangs to protect their territory and girl friends. Among girls, the circulation of women's magazines, but above all American films, encouraged romantic love. How far this replaced practical considerations in choice of a spouse is difficult to judge but may have influenced the generally less fatalistic outlook and higher aspirations for family relationships of post-First World War generations.

The long period when young people were living at home but physically and sexually mature and earning their own keep brought conflicts over accepting parental authority. Boys 'tipped up' until they began to earn men's wages at about age 18 and/or started serious courting, when they were usually allowed to pay board and keep back the remainder, a quasi-lodger status. More control was exercised over girls who were expected to continue to pay over their wages and help in the house. They were only allowed out on certain evenings to designated places and under a strict curfew. Their respectability in behaviour, language and sexual propriety reflected on the status of the family and could mark them as flighty, not worthy of marriage. This was a serious charge in a period when the sex ratio was unbalanced in men's favour, particularly in towns.

After the teens, when couples started to pair off, 'courting' and 'walking out' together could last for several years while saving for furnishings. Their behaviour was overlooked by others in the local community and taking the intended home to meet the parents marked recognition of the relationship. By the interwar period, the rise in the school leaving age and fall in age of marriage compressed this period by at least half. Fewer people lived in lodgings as better transport allowed them to travel further from home to work. Finding rooms was the greatest obstacle to marriage and the young couple, still sometimes but not as often expecting a baby, would start by living in the already overcrowded parental premises.

Rent was the biggest item in most working-class budgets, absorbing a disproportionately larger share the poorer the household. Model dwellings and later private and council houses on the new estates charged prohibitive rents and the health of families suffered in pinching to reach these levels. Amenities such as running water, bathrooms and lavatories only began to reach many working-class areas in the

1930s and reliable hot water supplies were almost unknown. Houses equipped with separate 'coppers' built over a brick hearth for heating large amounts of water were a feature of the better type. Since working-class housing kept to decent standards had never been a profitable investment, much housing stock was delapidated, making cleanliness almost impossible, graphically illustrated by the 35 per cent of children with head lice evacuated from inner cities during the Second World War. Housing available through building societies and local councils after 1920 further distinguished those who could attempt a better standard of personal hygiene; below a certain level, working-class people's bodies, clothes and surroundings were not only shabby but smelled of grease, dust and grime.

Gradually, new housing began to introduce separate sculleries with gas cookers instead of the closed grates or even open hearth cooking. Gas lighting replaced oil in town houses followed by electricity in the 1930s, but at a price. Living conditions were made more difficult by having to share water taps, lavatories or earth closets and middens between several families. Overcrowding within a one or two roomed home with large numbers of children, elderly relatives and lodgers made keeping order as well as cleanliness a Herculean task.

Rising living standards increased the amount and complexity of housework and childcare. More space, more furniture, china ornaments and utensils had to be washed, dusted and polished. Children's hair and bodies had to be washed more frequently, their clothes laundered, starched, ironed and mended, Sunday-best cared for. Tremendous energy was expended on making surroundings look bright and neat. Grates were black leaded, brasses, furniture and woodwork polished or scrubbed, window ledges, doorsteps and flags whitened and hearth stoned. This could only be maintained by holding to strict routine and division of labour. It emphasised appearances rather than antiseptic cleanliness; in popular wisdom: 'Keep the front doorstep clean. There's more passes by than comes inside.'[52]

Given these burdens, it is understandable why working people, particularly women, wanted indoor bathrooms, cooking facilities in a separate scullery and, most prized, a separate parlour only in use on Sundays and ritual occasions of Christmas, weddings and funerals. Here was a cool, orderly space where good furniture and precious ornaments could be displayed and cherished. The necessity to share

[52] E. Roberts, *A Woman's Place: An Oral History of Working Class Women, 1890–1940* (Oxford, 1984), p. 135.

housing and facilities, the anxiety every time water had to be carried through the downstairs' family's living room dropping on their newly cleaned oilcloth, meant that the rational proposals of interwar reformers for communal cooking and washing facilities were lost on women craving space of their own. More families were able to enjoy some of these amenities by the 1930s when pressure from the labour movement and women's groups had raised standards in council housing. Fewer children meant more space, and furnishings could be bought on hire purchase.

All working-class people below a certain income level suffered from ill-health due to overwork, undernourishment and unhealthy surroundings. But the tradition of reserving the best for the male breadwinner meant that non-earning children did with less and there is evidence that differential feeding was connected to the higher death rate of girls in childhood and early teens.[53] Married women's poor health, in particular, was omnipresent throughout the period, largely undetected as they were not eligible for medical attention unless as insured in their own right (only about 10 per cent). The early twentieth-century experiment of the Fabian Women's Group in supplying mothers of young babies with extra milk and the improvement of mothers' and children's health on the small but regular separation allowances when men were conscripted during the First World War were revealing. Food rationing and the special attention paid to children, child-bearing and nursing mothers during the Second World War produced even more dramatic results. The greatest improvements in family conditions were, together with full employment, due to the introduction of the National Health Service and social security system in the 1940s giving women and children direct access to medical facilities and supplementary foods rather than through the often unevenly divided as well as insufficient 'family wage'.

Those who survived into old age usually wished to remain self-sufficient as long as possible. Some were able to aid adult children by child-minding or providing house room. Many took lodgers whose rent sustained the household. These arrangements were eased by the early twentieth-century introduction of the old age pension for insured workers. But state recognition of a chronological age for retirement began to set a standardised category of 'old age'. Generations

[53] R. Wall, 'Inferring Differential Neglect of Females from Mortality Data', *Démographie historique et condition feminine*, Annales de Démographique Historique (Paris, 1981), pp. 119–40.

born before universal literacy were less capable of coping with such regulations and socially more dependent on their children.

By the twentieth century, more children were living to grow up and the pattern had shifted from about two-thirds of the (statistically rare) person over 70 living on their own to only one third, the remainder being with their spouse, kin, lodgers or themselves living as boarders. The needs of the dependent elderly could be shared between the still numerous adult children. Even so, the condition of the elderly person was not always enviable. Some felt they were taking resources from hard-pressed younger people and cases of neglect, even cruelty, have been noted. Those who were without relatives or neighbours still faced the indignity and rigours of the workhouse.

The working-class culture of the late nineteenth and early twentieth centuries centred on the local area, often the immediate street. Status and respectability differed according to local traditions and income levels. Maintaining that status was an important goal and gave a precious form of dignity to lives which had few other rewards. The attempts to provide elaborate funerals and mourning rituals through burial insurance, so inexplicable to middle-class observers, epitomises the craving for an honorific place. The vitality of kin ties in giving a sense of identity is shown in the pride given to family photographs and 'memory' or funeral cards.

Next to providing food and shelter, the most important function of the family was marking status through life style in the eyes of kin and community. Much of this was in the hands of women through gossip, in poorer communities, the street matriarchs or 'Queen Bees' standing in doorways, gathering in the corner shop or, at a more respectable level, peering from behind lace curtains. Standing well in the local status system brought solid returns in terms of credit, contacts and access to houses or jobs. It reflected the level of commitment of husband and father and the skill and personality of the wife and mother.

By the end of the nineteenth century, the status system among the skilled was somewhat more privatised. Shorter hours meant that men could have breakfast at home and spend more time with their families in the evenings. Their wives were full-time homemakers, paying ready money or saving with the co-op. They insisted on well-turned-out, well-behaved children with special attention to table manners and speech. Often the family's standards had been influenced by the mother's experience of domestic service. These families could afford Sunday rituals of special food and might attend church or chapel. They put on more elaborate meals for Christmas, weddings and funerals and were the consumers of new speciality foods like tinned salmon and peaches. They were beginning to enjoy seaside excursions or even longer holidays staying in lodgings.

People were still good neighbours but intense public sociability declined as living standards improved. Women living next door to each other for a life time on the best of terms might seldom cross each others' threshold and never called each other by first names. These were the patterns carried into the new housing estates of inter-war Britain. There, first, the mutual struggle with primitive shopping and other amenities might draw people together, but loneliness and isolation of non-working wives as well as high rents forced many to leave and pre-figured the post-Second World War conditions surrounding depressed young mothers.

Demographic changes in the interwar period and a decline in both lodging and residential domestic service had fostered the smaller household centred on the nuclear family, the average household size falling to 3.2 by 1951. Since the early nineteenth century, the category of *kin* as measured by prohibition on marriage, and with whom sexual relationships would therefore be incestuous, had been drastically pared down.[54] The means test for unemployment benefit introduced during the depression gave no recognition of wider kin ties and one of the most resented rulings forced parents to evict their adult children for fear of losing benefit. Yet even in this period, as Eleanor Rathbone demonstrated in her campaign for family allowances, the majority were not living in the ideal family-wage household of working father, full-time housewife and three dependent children. A quarter of households were married couples with older children, a quarter people on their own, while others had to cope with large numbers of children. There were families headed by the widowed and composite families of step- and half-siblings, although increasingly these were the result of separation and divorce rather than death of a parent.

An important minority pattern among large families was for the youngest children to benefit from more food, clothing, house room and opportunities for training provided by their elder siblings' earnings. Boys in this position were often able to move into better occupations. Girls were more likely to be kept more at home and remain

[54]   S. Wolfram, *In-Laws and Outlaws: Kinship and Marriage in England* (1987).

unmarried, tacitly accepting the care of elderly parents. In the earlier part of the period, if she inherited a good tenancy or the house, such a woman might have some independence in later life in a context where remaining single was not necessarily stigmatised. Her lot could be favourably compared to the eldest children, particularly girls, who carried a heavy burden of domestic responsibility and/or early wage earning. But the single woman without any income and responsible for elderly parents could also be heavily exploited. The estimated 300,000 in the 1930s carrying this burden were ignored by the state and without legal rights to inheritance.

As in the earlier period, family patterns varied widely. Some followed the peculiarities of occupation or area. In deep-sea fishing communities where men lived at home for a month or so between trips to sea, they took an active part in many domestic affairs. Then they would be gone for long periods and the women were virtually in charge.[55] In textile and pottery towns, many women worked for part of their married life, taking part in all-female shop floor entertainments and outings as well as their more traditional domestic role. In isolated mining communities, the exhausting and dangerous labour of the men built up a male-centred life at the pit. Women's separate existence had to cope with providing hot meals and baths for shift workers, washing coal-saturated clothing, struggling against the ubiquitous coal dust in poor housing whose rent was deducted at source by the company, leaving little flexibility for budgeting. Cheap coal and relatively high wages were some compensation and communities were tightly knit with wider family as an important adjunct in survival.

Within these patterns, particular circumstances determined individual destinies. For all income levels, migration which severed people from kin, unemployment, illness or death of the father or incapacity and death of the mother caused most hardship. In the 1920s, the son of a printer was set fair to follow that highly paid, most prestigious craft. His father's death left his mother with a pension too small to support herself and the three children. She had, however, inherited a cafe in London's dockland and here the household moved: the war-blinded father's brother with his pension, the old soldier who cleaned in return for board and lodging, likewise the simple-minded country boy who did the heavy work and a young orphaned maid. All but the two male servants ate with the family who shared the cafe food.

[55] P. Thompson, 'Women in the Fishing: The Roots of Power between the Sexes', *Comparative Studies in Society and History*, 27 (1985), pp. 3–22.

Later, the boy's father's employer, with backing from his union, gave him an opening as a journalist, a solid trade, the most precious form of working-class inheritance.[56] The sons, much less, the daughters, of the unskilled were seldom as fortunate.

The Second World War again focussed attention on the family as a national resource. The bombing of civilians and evacuation of mothers and children from cities, many billeted with middle-class families in the countryside, drew attention to the deprivations in the life of the poor. The family ideal was central to the war effort and women with children under 14 were exempted from conscription. Yet the need for women's labour resulted in a mass programme of communal feeding in schools, workplace canteens and the government's British Restaurants as well as intervention in food provision through rationing and food subsidies.

After the war, despite a spurt in marriage and much media attention to the importance of motherhood, many women continued to work in the buoyant postwar economy in an effort to realise prewar aspirations for better material conditions and retain the interest and companionship of wartime experience. They were the first generation to reap the benefits of health and energy from the lower birth rate. But for the most part, traditional forms were preserved. The birth rate rose dramatically as returning servicemen and women flocked to remake a home-centred life. Part-time employment for women became the popular solution to practical problems of combining work and home duties, maintaining masculine precedence and the division between the family and wider society.

Among the mid-eighteenth-century literate elite the perception of the family was paternalistic, formal and public. It included strict rules about which kin would be allowed to marry and have legitimate sexual relations. The legal dissolution of marriage, whether by church or state, was virtually proscribed. The powerful position of the master, husband and father was a model for most other institutions of society and state, a model summed up in the maxim: 'The World is but one great family.'

A century later, that conception had shifted, as separate or even antithetical spheres had become established, symbolised and encouraged by the removal of family life from the site of production as well

---

[56]   L. Heren, *Growing up Poor in London* (1973).

as political decision-making. There were now the vastly expanded public organisations of the state, voluntary societies, trade and professional associations, and market institutions; the masculine stage of the Great World.

By contrast, the family, from which men went out and to which they returned, was now seen as the bastion of the private and the moral, the location of dependent, often powerless, women and children. In the words of a mid-nineteenth-century attorney's wife and mother of nine children: 'Our family is a little world.'[57]

By the middle of the twentieth century that little world, no matter how diminished, continued as a potent source of personal emotion and identity, casting the light and shade of childhood, and containing the most immediate experience of love and hate, power and dependence, interpersonal altruism and interpersonal violence that most people would experience in their life time.

As in the past two centuries under review, people lived out their lives in a rich patchwork of situations, now upholding, now resisting prescriptions of an idealised family form. As in contemporary Britain, men, women and children sought affection, support and a sense of personal worth wherever they could be found, usually within, but sometimes outside, that protean entity, the family.

Acknowledgements
I would like to thank Judy Lown for her help in preparation of this chapter, Ludmilla Jordanova and Jane Lewis for their thoughtful comments and Paul Thompson for his advice and encouragement throughout.

[57] Rebecca Solly Shaen, 'Unpublished Diary 1800–1855', John Johnson Collection, Bodleian Library MS 18 and 19, fol. 318.

CHAPTER 3

Work

PATRICK JOYCE

I

This chapter cannot hope to provide an exhaustive history of work over the period. Rather, it takes what is probably the major insight of recent scholarship on industrial capitalism, and attempts to work out some of the consequences of this insight. The realisation that the factory and the machine should form a part and not the whole of our picture of industrialisation is a relatively recent one. Coming to terms with the diversity and irregularity of capitalist development involves therefore a critical account of older notions of social and political change predicated on now questionable premises. It also necessitates the attempt in turn to relate such change to a more adequate notion of the economy and work experience, a relation that is itself revealed as problematic. The attempt to balance old and new accounts – for it may be a question of balance rather than simple substitution – must therefore be historiographical and theoretical, as well as empirical. In, broadly, the first half of the chapter an empirical approach predominates, as the principal features of work are delineated. Towards the close of section two, problems associated with newer perspectives are raised in a speculative manner, which steadily becomes more historiographical in approach. However, we shall begin at the beginning, namely what people worked at in the past.

The vagaries of collection and classification that characterise census occupational statistics make them a notoriously uncertain guide to changes in occupational structure and the experience of work.[1] The category of 'field labourer', for example, obscures both the multiform nature of the labourer's means of livelihood and, even more, the

---

[1] For amplification of the statistics presented here see P. Deane and W. A. Cole, *British Economic Growth 1688–1959* (Cambridge, 1962), chaps. 2, 4, 6; B. R. Mitchell and P. Deane, *Abstract of British Historical Statistics* (Cambridge, 1972), chap. 2.

densely textured culture in which these means of livelihood were embedded.[2] However, the best guide to structural change is perhaps Deane and Cole's derivation of an industry structure from the occupational returns (Table 3.1).

This account can be deepened by Mitchell and Deane's classification of the labour force. In Tables 3.2–3.4 the principal occupations and occupational clusters have been chosen to illustrate developments. Of course, statistics classified by occupation, product and raw material tell us little about industrial groupings, and nothing at all about the forms of organisation within particular sectors or industries, be these domestic, workshop, factory, or intermediate forms.

From Table 3.1 it will be apparent that a decisive shift to manufacture took place in the first three decades of the nineteenth century. This development was an important characteristic of the half-century preceding 1831. Indeed, as early as 1701 it has been estimated that between a quarter and a third of the total adult male population of England and Wales were engaged in manufacture and mining, and that the value of output in these sectors was equal to that in agriculture.[3] Many of these would, however, have been primarily involved in agriculture. The distinction between these sectors in what is misleadingly called 'pre-industrial' Britain, is in fact an unhelpful one, and continues so to be for much of the nineteenth century as well. Nevertheless, the general shift in occupational structure will be apparent, even though it should be recognised that nineteenth-century industry was built upon the foundations of a highly sophisticated commerce and manufacture.

Though intermittently arrested, the decline of agriculture was inexorable, shrinking from 35.9 per cent of the total occupied population in 1801 to 8.7 per cent in 1901. With textiles in the van of early industrialisation, the second or capital goods phase both widened the base of manufacturing industry, as in shipbuilding and engineering, and multiplied the range of non-manufacturing industries and services, such as transport, mining and building. Table 3.2 indicates the acceleration of growth in these areas between 1861 and 1891. Among transport workers those engaged in road transport predominated: in 1891, 212,000 were employed in rail transport, 407,000 in road and 235,000

[2] R. Samuel, 'Village Labour', in R. Samuel, ed., *Village Life and Labour* (London, 1975). The author's plea for a complication and redefinition of the notion of the occupation in the countryside applies to urban workers as well.

[3] J. Rule, *The Experience of Labour in Eighteenth-Century Industry* (1981), chap. 1 for a useful discussion.

Table 3.1 *Estimated industrial distribution of the British labour force, 1801–1951 (millions of persons)*

	Agriculture, forestry, fishing	Mining and quarrying	Manufactures	Building	Trade	Transport	Public service and professional	Domestic and personal	Total occupied population
1801	1.7		1.4			0.5	0.3	0.6	4.8
1811	1.8		1.7			0.6	0.4	0.7	5.5
1821	1.8		2.4			0.8	0.3	0.8	6.2
1831	1.8		3.0			0.9	0.3	0.9	7.2
1841	1.9	0.2	2.7	0.4	0.9	0.3	0.3	1.2	8.4
1851	2.1	0.4	3.2	0.5	1.0	0.5	0.5	1.3	9.7
1861	2.0	0.5	3.6	0.6	1.2	0.6	0.6	1.5	10.8
1871	1.8	0.6	3.9	0.8	1.6	0.7	0.7	1.8	12.0
1881	1.7	0.6	4.2	0.9	1.9	0.9	0.8	2.0	13.1
1891	1.6	0.8	4.8	0.9	2.3	1.1	1.0	2.3	14.7
1901	1.5	0.9	5.5	1.3	2.3	1.3	1.3	2.3	16.7
1911	1.6	1.2	6.2	1.2	2.5	1.5	1.5	2.6	18.6
1921	1.4	1.5	6.9	0.8	2.6	1.4	2.1	1.3	19.3
1931	1.3	1.2	7.2	1.1	3.3	1.4	2.3	1.6	21.1
1951	1.1	0.9	8.8	1.4	3.2	1.7	3.3	0.5	22.6

Source: Deane and Cole, *British Economic Growth*, Table 31.

Table 3.2 Occupational structure of Great Britain, males, 1841–1921 (in thousands)

	1841	1851	1861	1871	1881	1891	1901	1911	1921
I									
Public administration	40	64	72	106	109	146	191	271	383
Professional occupations/									
subordinate services	113	162	179	204	254	287	348	413	415
Commercial occupations	94	91	130	212	352	449	597	739	904
II									
Transport and									
communications	196	433	579	654	870	1,409	1,409	1,571	1,530
Agriculture, horticulture and									
forestry	1,434	1,788	1,779	1,634	1,517	1,422	1,339	1,436	1,344
Mining, quarrying and									
workers in products of same	218	383	457	517	604	751	931	1,202	1,204
III									
Metal manufacture,									
machines, implements,									
vehicles, etc.	396	536	747	869	977	1,151	1,485	1,795	2,125
Building and construction	376	496	593	712	875	899	1,216	1,140	894
Textiles and clothing	883	1,079	1,025	983	933	1,002	980	1,071	724
Food, drink and tobacco	268	348	386	448	494	597	701	806	228
Total in these occupations	4,018	5,380	5,947	6,339	6,985	7,808	9,197	10,444	9,751
Total occupied	5,093	6,554	7,271	8,182	8,844	10,010	11,548	12,930	13,670
Total unoccupied	1,604	1,041	1,054	1,169	1,778	2,028	2,242	2,515	2,002

Notes: For 1841–91, the figures for the occupied population include children under 10 years; the total unoccupied figure does not. For 1921, the figures relate to those 12 years and over; for 1931, 14 years and over; and for 1951, 15 years and over. For these and many other reasons inter-decennial comparisons present great difficulties.

Sources: Mitchell and Deane, Abstract, p. 60; see also B. R. Mitchell, British Historical Statistics (Cambridge, 1988), p. 104.

Table 3.3 *Occupational structure of Great Britain, females, 1841–1921 (in thousands)*

	1841	1851	1861	1871	1881	1891	1901	1911	1921
Professional occupations/ subordinate services	49	103	126	152	203	264	326	383	441
Domestic offices and personal services	989	1,135	1,407	1,678	1,756	2,036	2,003	2,127	1,845
Agriculture, horticulture and forestry	81	229	163	135	116	80	67	60	90
Textiles	358	635	676	726	745	795	795	870	701
Clothing	200	491	596	594	667	759	792	825	602
Food, drink and tobacco	42	53	71	78	98	163	216	308	123
Total in these occupations	1,719	2,646	3,039	3,363	3,585	4,097	4,199	4,573	3,802
Total occupied	1,815	2,819	3,252	3,570	3,887	4,489	4,732	5,356	5,684
Total unoccupied	5,369	5,192	5,762	6,535	7,567	8,572	10,247	11,432	11,983

Notes: See notes to Table 3.2.
Sources: See sources for Table 3.2.

Table 3.4 *Occupational structure of Great Britain, males and females, 1921–51 (based on 1951 census categories)*

	1921		1931		1951	
	M	F	M	F	M	F
Public administration	261	78	141	3	214	21
Administration/managers in extractive/ manufacturing industries	287	25	350	26	347	30
Professional/technical	378	408	490	443	788	588
Personal service	372	1,845	516	2,129	512	1,610
Commerce, finance, insurance (excluding clerical)	1,180	579	1,621	701	1,357	856
Clerks and typists	581	492	778	648	932	1,409
Transport and communications	1,591	75	1,748	82	1,569	149
Agriculture, horticulture and forestry	1,341	107	1,282	71	1,105	114
Mining/quarrying	1,204	7	1,083	4	675	2
Metal manufacturing, engineering and allied trades	1,888	123	1,765	147	2,517	208
Building and construction	738	10	970	17	1,268	14
Textiles	314	634	324	663	220	413
Textile goods, clothing	155	544	164	544	135	474
Food, drink and tobacco	147	77	161	73	175	97
Total in these occupations	10,437	5,004	11,393	5,551	11,814	5,985
Total occupied	13,656	5,701	14,790	6,265	15,649	6,961
Total unoccupied	2,016	11,966	1,552	12,055	2,213	13,084

Notes: See notes to Table 3.2.
Source: Mitchell and Deane, *Abstract*, p. 61.

in waterborne transport. The late nineteenth century was still the age of the horse. The expansion of the food, drink and tobacco industries indicates the development of a mass-consumer market, increasingly served by large wholesalers and multiple-outlet retailers.

In the twentieth century, and especially after the First World War, the familiar story of the decline of the great staple industries becomes apparent. The relative decline of textiles became an absolute one after 1911. The great expansion of mining after 1881 became a contraction, especially in the 1930s, and domestic service, as staple a staple industry as any in the nineteenth century, suffered a similar fate. In 1911 these sectors accounted for a massive 20 per cent or so of the British labour force, but in 1951 only 6 per cent. Manufacturing industry, growing in step with the working population between 1831 and 1911, expanded its share from about a third of the total in 1911 to 39 per cent in 1951. The metal, machinery and vehicles group of industries expanded from 24.3 per cent of the total in manufacturing industry in 1891 to 45.5 per cent in 1951. Motor manufacture, consumer durables and light industry – especially along the London–Birmingham axis – announced the eclipse of the north by the south, so reversing the rise of the north between 1750 and 1850. The eclipse continues to near-totality, South Wales as previously being part of the metaphoric north.

New, science-based industries (the electrical industries, chemicals), together with the multiplication of service industries and the public sector, have given rise to the manager, the local government clerk, the shop assistant, the teacher and social worker, who have displaced their nineteenth-century forbears, the pitman, weaver and shipbuilder (see Table 3.4). The extraordinary growth of the professional and white-collar sectors is apparent from the 1880s and 1890s.

Changes in the structure of women's employment have been as marked as those among men. Domestic service, at 40.4 per cent of occupied women in 1881, has suffered the depradations of two world wars, the rise of consumer durables and the attenuation of middle-class living standards (or at least of the gap between middle-class and working-class standards). Not only the standards of the middle class *echt* of course: the battalions of Pooters in the later Victorian city have relinquished the services of the divisions of country girls, themselves turned away from the households of the early Victorian farmer. Textiles, and just as much dressmaking, approached the size of the domestic service sector. Dressmaking indicates the changeable and intermittent nature of the Victorian occupation, especially marked among women: Little Dorrit turns her hand to the trade, circumstances demanding and patronage permitting. The shape of things to come was apparent by 1881, when education took up a greater share than agriculture. In 1911 professional occupations and subordinate services (very much the latter), together with commerce and public administration, comprised just over 10 per cent of women's employment. Especially as clerks and typists women moved forward in the same 'white-collar' tide after 1911. Nonetheless, as late as 1951 the number in domestic service suggests a Victorian aspect to women's employment.

Though the ratio of occupied to unoccupied in the Victorian economy is much the same as today, this similarity masks fundamental differences. The proportion of males over 15 years who do not work is now three times greater than in the second half of the last century, a proportion made up of the retired old and the educated young. Work was begun early in the nineteenth century: the 1851 census indicates that 28 per cent of children aged between 10 and 15 years worked. This was in fact probably less than in the eighteenth century, when Defoe in 1723 remarked of the West Riding, 'scarce anything above four years old but its hands were sufficient for its own support'.[4] Probably, but we do not know: the 1851 indication is undoubtedly an underestimate, bearing in mind the importance of outwork and domestic production, of agriculture, and the unknown quantity of casual but often intensive child labour in the towns. Government legislation made little impression on this vast, hidden sector of the economy. It has been estimated that by 1911 the proportion of children aged between 10 and 15 at work had declined to half the 1851 level,[5] the decline of traditional sectors of the economy and legislation on workplace conditions continuing a process greatly accelerated by the enactment of compulsory education in 1880. In Flora Thompson's *Lark Rise*, children were no longer ruled by the gang-masters but by the Revised Code of Her Majesty's Inspectors. If childhood was often short in the nineteenth century, old age – for those who attained it – might be harsh and bitter. Age and debility brought either a change to lighter work and less earnings, or no work at all. The unskilled, or at least those without access to benefit societies, were hardest hit.

[4] Quoted in E. H. Hunt, *British Labour History 1815–1914* (1981), p. 9.
[5] Hunt, *British Labour History*, chap. 1, also for a discussion of the age and sex distribution of the labour force.

The other major difference in the structure of employment since the last century lies in the number of married women working. In 1971, 40 per cent of married women were at work; in 1911, 90 per cent had no paid employment. In 1851 more married women were at work, and the 1800 figure may have approached or exceeded recent levels. But, as for children's employment, the world of employment hidden behind the census enumerators' figures in the nineteenth century would undoubtedly reveal a much higher incidence of married women's labour. Nonetheless, the change in the course of the nineteenth century was striking if less marked and more uneven than sometimes supposed: later marriage and large families, combined with the effect of the erosion of domestic and outwork production, produced the segmentation of work and home, and the redefinition of the home as the site of unpaid, female labour, the workplace as that of paid labour. The Victorian cult of domesticity was in part a consequence and in part a cause of these changes. The labour of young, unmarried women and of girls was, however, a major feature of the nineteenth-century economy, showing only a modest fall between 1851 and 1911.

More than three-quarters of the population of Manchester, Bradford and Glasgow aged 20 years and over in 1851 were born outside these cities, and if these populations were swollen by the recent and massive Irish influx, then the other great cities were not wholly dissimilar. Over 50 per cent of the population of Birmingham were newcomers, the ratio of British to Irish immigrants being nine to one. Mobility was probably at its height between 1840 and 1890, though in the northern textile districts it was very marked before this period. The basic stimulus was industrial relocation, a process in turn stimulated by the growth of the railway system. After the 1880s the rate of mobility declined, and was replaced by another sort of mobility, that of the commuter, including the working-class commuter, by train and bicycle. Long-range mobility was important for certain groups: the agricultural young of both sexes, some of the urban skilled (though 'tramping' was in decline), and the Irish, Welsh and Scottish Highlanders. Boom industries and towns were a special magnet – Middlesbrough, St Helens, Bradford – and of course London was as always the greatest magnet of all. Cornish and Scots miners, as well as Lancashire cotton operatives, colonised the industry of the United States and further afield. Historians still have much to learn about this interplay of old worlds and new.

Short-range mobility was, however, of the greater significance, and a product of many factors other than the search for work and higher wages. Nonetheless, the experience of work over the period was for very many workers the experience of new, and especially urban, living environments. This chapter will lay special emphasis on the gradual and uneven nature of change at the economic level, but it needs to be remembered that if the accent on continuities is a necessary counter to received notions of change, then the experience of urban life did represent a considerable discontinuity in popular culture. Not that notions of a transition from stable, rural, 'traditional' communities to unknown and alienating urban life is any longer tenable. Recent work has done much to dismember the platitudes of earlier, chiefly functionalist, forms of sociology here. The emphasis is being shifted from the mobile worker as object to subject, handling transitions creatively in terms of the flexible resources of the obtaining popular culture.[6]

Not only was movement to the larger urban centres often short range, it was also progressive. The experience of the classic mill town, or any of the small or medium industrial towns, also needs to be differentiated from life in the great cities. Prior experience of particular towns, as of industrial life itself (whether in the form of pre-factory manufacture or semi-urban factory work), meant that change was not always the shock of the new it has been taken to be. High rates of mobility within towns often mask the minute distances of this movement, and the early consolidation of the 'charmed circle' of neighbourhood streets. In the town, so in the region and county: it is not generally realised that if in the 'shock centre' of factory industry, Lancashire, in-migration was considerable, then the county still retained more of its native-born population in the mid-nineteenth century than any other English county.[7] Most important of all, perhaps, the working-class family was itself the creative and adaptable medium of change, arranging accommodation and support, but

---

[6] The work of Anderson and Hareven shows how untenable the thesis of social breakdown is: M. Anderson, *Family Structure in Nineteenth-Century Lancashire* (Cambridge, 1971); T. Hareven, *Family Time and Industrial Time* (Cambridge, 1982). For an earlier, functionalist view of social breakdown see N. Smelser, *Social Change in the Industrial Revolution* (1959).

[7] J. T. Danson and T. A. Welton, 'On the Population of Lancashire and Cheshire 1801–1851', *Transactions of the Historic Society of Lancashire and Cheshire*, 11 (1858–9), p. 41.

especially finding work and easing the transition to it. The family but also the place of origin were the bases of the residential clustering of the newly arrived.

If the keynotes of the transition to urban, industrial life ought to be persistence and adaptation rather than the disintegration and abandonment of older cultures,[8] then certain things should be borne in mind. One needs to consider the pressures *acting upon* popular creativity and limiting available options. Spectacular rates of population growth in many towns, the unplanned development of these towns, poor social conditions, low and irregular wages and the pervasive insecurity of material life have to be remembered. It was mainly after the mid-nineteenth century that these conditions were changed, and even then change was irregular and gradual. As Anderson observes for mid-nineteenth-century Preston, the reciprocities of kin tended to be short term, calculative and instrumental. The contrast between Preston at this time and the 'traditional' working-class communities of the 1930s may be a telling one. The 'traditional' may be of relatively recent origin: 'it remains for future research to establish just when these solidary, collectivistic communities with their frequent exchange of services . . . through a strongly affective and close-knit kinship system really began to flourish to the full'.[9] The pre-1914 limitations placed by poverty on kinship and neighbourhood activities were considerable, the change developing slowly with relative affluence, a decrease in the death rate, increased population stability and community coherence, and the beginning of government welfare policies.

As yet these questions have not been extended to the forms of workers' communal self-organisation, let alone to the bearing of these forms on class consciousness. If and when they are extended then our periodisation and categorisation of working-class culture may need radical revision, a revision that may of course involve the undermining of Anderson's picture too, in the form of the extension far back into the nineteenth century of the forms discerned in the 1930s, namely the development of functional rather than instrumental kin ties, and the spread of community solidarity more actively beyond the basis of kin. But then, how adequate are our notions of working-class community forms in the 1930s? These notions, part of the 'rediscovery' of the working class taking place in the 1950s, owe much

[8] For the accent on popular creativity in another sphere, see P. Bailey, *Leisure and Class in Victorian England* (1978).
[9] Anderson, *Family Structure*, p. 178.

to works like Hoggart's *Uses of Literacy*, works that combine insight and romanticisation in about equal measure.

One also needs to guard against simplified notions of a transition from a customary, traditional popular culture to new forms of urban, industrial, working-class solidarity. The situation is probably more complex: the development of civic self-government and culture, the role of factories and employers in the ecology of the factory town and in the formation of neighbourhood identities, as well as the agency of employers in utilising and corroborating working-class ideologies of the family, all worked to complicate the picture, cutting across and contradicting simplified notions of the development of solidary and conflictual class identities.[10] We need accounts that will balance these pressures with counter-pressures making for continuity, especially the economic ones indicated later, namely the persistence of craft tradition and the often merely formal nature of changes in work organisation.

The question of class is also complicated by the question of the Irish, the oldest and most numerous of all the immigrant groups in Britain (and relative to their vast importance the least studied).[11] This importance is clear from mere numbers alone; around 3.5 per cent of the British population in the post-famine years. If by 1911 the number of Irish-born had fallen to 1.3 per cent this grossly underestimates the presence of the 'effective Irish', from the 1840s to the 1914–18 war, probably between 4 and 6 per cent of the labour force. The famine marked the growth of permanent settlement, and with it perhaps the clearest example of a migrant population adapting, and retaining, its own culture in the process of transition to urban life. Their confinement – by and large – to low-paid, unskilled occupations was a product of the twin disablements placed upon them by their proud, sorry history on the other side of the water, and British attitudes on this. But it also argues a preference for a rhythm and morality of work owing much to a peasant background and putting them at one remove from an ethic of material advancement and individual self-help. Just as in the sphere of work they colonised certain occupations (classically building) by their extraordinarily quick responses to the labour market

---

[10] For these developments, and a preliminary discussion of other questions raised in the section on mobility, see P. Joyce, *Work, Society and Politics: The Culture of the Factory in Later Victorian England* (Brighton, 1980), esp. chap. 3.

[11] This imbalance is at last being remedied, see, e.g., L. H. Lees, *Exiles of Erin: Irish Migrants in Victorian London* (Manchester, 1979), and the excellent survey in Hunt, *Labour History*.

(also by their willingness to accept lower wages and, occasionally, break strikes), so in the cultural sphere did the attributes of their background preserve a strong sense of difference from the host community. The 'effective' Irish invariably involved more than the first-born British generation. If ethnic antagonism perhaps lessened in England from the 1870s – the process was slower in Scotland – Catholicism and nationalist politics combined to accentuate differences of cultural background and resist assimilation. The integrity and longevity of Irish neighbourhood communities is very striking.

The question of labour mobility introduces a range of questions which have received little systematic discussion in the historical literature. The links between geographical mobility and social mobility, and the question of social mobility itself, have been neglected in the writing of British labour history.[12] Rather than social mobility itself, it is the related categories of the diversity and irregularity of the occupation that will be pursued here. By occupational diversity is meant the range of occupations stretching over an individual's work career, or characteristic of it at any one point. One may consider the question of irregularity in at least two senses: endemic fluctuations of the cyclical, macro-economic type, or of the localised kind, whether seasonal- or demand-specific fluctuations. Regularity may also be considered in the sense of work time, as pertaining to the working day, week or year. These related aspects of the occupation throw up a host of problems, only a few of which can be broached here. Before outlining historical developments, some general observations arising from the great and largely unacknowledged importance of diversity and irregularity are in order. The construction of models of social structure from the building blocks of occupations needs to be carefully scrutinised: the classification of occupations into social categories should be subject to the provisos that we still know little about the character of individual occupations, and even less about their meaning to individual work lives. In particular, labour and social historians' tendency to ascribe often quite elaborate cultural identities to general categories ('skilled' and 'unskilled', 'artisan' and 'proletarian', 'petty bourgeoisie') and specific occupations (miners, tailors, shoemakers) needs to be heavily qualified or totally undermined.

If a general progression to uniformity in the work life, more regularly

---

12   See the remarks of J. Kocka, 'The Study of Social Mobility and the Formation of the Working Class in the Nineteenth Century', *Le Mouvement Social*, 3 (1980).

provided work, and to regularity in the sense of work time is discernible over the period then it has been very uneven and incomplete. The endemic nature of diversity and irregularity in the 'pre-industrial' economy has been noted, taking this largely meaningless term to mean the first half of the period before the general but slow consolidation of factory production and the direct wage form, not that the factory was ever the dominant form or representative norm. The interdependence of agriculture, mining and manufacture was close, and the town–industry, village–agriculture, distinction fairly spurious. In the eighteenth century diversity was reflected in irregularity: in mid-eighteenth-century London a list of journeymen's wages reads, 'tailors – overstocked, out of business three or four months a year; housepainters – overstocked, out of business four or five months a year', and so on for a variety of occupations.[13] A century later in London Mayhew guessed that about a third of the workers in the generality of trades were fully and constantly employed, a third worked only part of the time, and a third were only occasionally employed.[14] The strategies workers employed to circumvent this irregularity are still largely unknown to us, whether they be alternative occupations (outside or within the wages system) or non-work alternatives.[15]

The causes of this irregularity were many, and they overlapped considerably. They ranged from the endemic casuality of many trades (dockworkers, porters), the increasingly widespread effect of the trade cycle in an increasingly interdependent capitalist economy, to the pervasive influence of seasonality. Seasonality was itself compounded of social habit, fashion and the weather. There was a marked tendency for those in related or adjacent sectors to be affected, too, in all manner of callings and ways: beggars, clerks and barristers might fall on hard times with their manual brethren.[16] Building is perhaps the classic example of climatic seasonality, textiles and clothing of fashion, but the effect was complex and very widespread. Right into the present century, for instance, the importance of the courts, Parliament, and the quality to the London trades was considerable. Withdrawal in the summer threw tailors out of work into 'cucumber time' (when

[13] R. Campbell, *The London Tradesman* (1747).
[14] As quoted in E. P. Thompson, *The Making of the English Working Class*, 2nd edn (1968), pp. 275–6. See chaps. 7–9 on work experience.
[15] 'Dovetailing', or the planned integration by workers of different occupations, was one work alternative, also trade-union regulation of casual labour.
[16] S. Webb and A. Freeman, *The Seasonal Trades* (1912).

cucumbers were all they could afford to live on); return for the Season threw housepainters and decorators onto their own devices.

Long-term developments in the organisation of production and the nature of demand, attended by changes in the design of work and workplaces, and in technology and in raw materials, did much to iron out these differences but it was perhaps not until as late as the turn of the present century that the economy as a whole lost its old heterogeneity.

The situation in the mid-nineteenth-century London trades Mayhew described is indicative; as is the continuing importance of outwork, indeed the *proliferation* of home-working in the sweated trades of London and elsewhere. Multi-occupation in the countryside continued to be important, if anything the spread of country and village industry in the mid- and late-nineteenth century complicating the picture further.[17] The picture was complicated enough already, and we return to the ambiguities of the designation 'field labourer' with which we opened: in 1892 it has been estimated that three-quarters of the field workers in Monmouthshire had work in woodcutting, quarrying and mining.[18] The means of livelihood in the countryside contained important aspects of a subsistence economy until very late (totting, foraging, gleaning, landholding, and use of common rights), and one suspects such aspects were not completely unknown in towns and industrial villages, whether in the form of pig and chicken keeping or the growth of food in allotments and gardens.

Even in the large and increasingly mechanised sectors it could be argued that workers exchanged one kind of instability for another. Aside from the trade cycle, the relative abundance of suitable labour throughout most of the nineteenth century, together with demand fluctuations in these trades (for example, shipbuilding and textiles), meant that irregularity of work might be marked, and with it to some degree diversity of occupation. As will be seen, the 'archaic' organisation of production in the ostensibly modern, large-scale industries meant that workers often functioned as both employees and employers, hence filling a variety of work roles.

As at one end of the scale so at the other the complexity and ambiguity of work lives and identities was marked. The history of what

---

[17]   See the essays in sect. III, vol. 1, of G. Mingay, ed., *The Victorian Countryside*, 2 vols. (1981).

[18]   Samuel, 'Village Labour'.

has been termed 'penny capitalism' is of importance here.[19] It was especially significant in itinerant distribution and the provision of household services. The hawker and knife-grinder were among many who provided a familiar, convenient and cheap service to a rapidly expanding population in the late nineteenth century. As with working-class retailing (stalls, shops, beerhouses), such activity was also an important recourse for aspirant or incapacitated workers. The longevity and vitality of the small-scale sectors of production will later be seen: in the Birmingham metal trades, for instance, a man might in succession be a journeyman, a small master, and self-employed. The building trades were riddled with tiny enterprises and worker-capitalists, as were the 'artisan' trades of the late nineteenth century producing for the cheap end of mass-consumer demand. Such were the workers of Bethnal Green, especially those in the furniture trades.[20]

The workers of Bethnal Green were both makers and vendors, exploiters and exploited, owners of the means and premises of production, custodians of the language of skill and of 'pre-industrial' work rhythms, and yet subject to unrestrained market forces which were part of both a local and an international economy. They were an integral part of the capitalist economy, yet outside the wages system, inhabiting a world in which the line between master and worker, capitalist and proletarian, was so indistinct as to be almost meaningless. Again, how is one to categorise another of the 'proletarians' thrown up by Samuel's indefatigable and inspirational research into the experience of work; the mid-nineteenth-century Yorkshireman who rented a few fields and covered them with 'day-hole' pits, and who was simultaneously mining entrepreneur, owner-carter, blanket weaver, joiner, farmer and beerseller.[21]

Brickfields, mines and quarries in fact reveal the profoundly fragmented character of so much work in the nineteenth century.[22] Extraordinarily numerous, very small-scale and exploited by micro-capitalists on an individual or co-operative basis, these ventures gave employment to considerable numbers, an employment unrecorded in the census and meshing with a vast range of primary, secondary

[19] J. Benson, *The Penny Capitalists: A Study of Nineteenth-Century Working-Class Entrepreneurs* (Dublin, 1983).
[20] R. Samuel, 'Artisans and Workers in South-West Bethnal Green' (unpublished paper). It is not without interest that Bethnal Green was a nursery of British fascism.
[21] R. Samuel, ed., *Miners, Quarrymen and Saltworkers* (1977), p. 19.
[22] *Ibid., passim.*

or alternative employments. The development of mining indicates that the growth of an unambiguous form of wage labour and of occupationally exclusive labour forces concentrated in specific geographical localities is a later one than is commonly realised. Even then, further work on the twentieth century may well reveal a good deal more ambiguity in the position of waged labour than we imagine. While north-east England led developments early on, and enclaves of 'independent colliers' were important in many localities (such workers being culturally but by no means occupationally homogeneous), it was not until the late nineteenth century that the micro-sector was fully eclipsed and the pattern, say, of South Wales became the dominant one. Until then, many of the British fields outside the north-east of England were primitive in organisation, inextricably mixed up with other industries and neighbouring town life (as in Lancashire), or subject to a high degree of labour mobility (as in central Scotland). As with the paradigm of South Wales in mining, so with that of textiles in the economy as a whole: only slowly and incompletely in the second half of the nineteenth century did other industries begin to approximate to its organisational and cultural forms.

Occupational exclusiveness and concentration are integral to our understanding of the formation of 'traditional' working-class culture and consciousness. When it is understood how uneven and late developments in fact were, it becomes apparent that this entire process of formation stands in need of some revision, and it is with such questions that this chapter will in part be concerned. Certainly, to the extent that the single and exclusive occupation, and the unambiguously waged and 'manual' occupation, came to dominate, the process of class formation at a socio-economic level was very late. Similarly, the process whereby industry and locality are held to have become fused as an aspect of class-conscious worker solidarity needs further questioning, for the nineteenth century in particular, and if for the nineteenth century then almost certainly for the twentieth too.

In terms of the regularity of work time a general process of convergence and uniformity is apparent, as in the matter of occupational diversity. One may similarly point to the decline of the 'artisanal' sector and customary work practices, but also to pressures in favour of 'rational recreation' and the reform of older time observances. Especially after the spread of factory and workshop legislation in the second half of the nineteenth century the regular five-and-a-half-day week became common, until in the 1890s the six-day week was in a minority. The regular, and increasingly shorter, day and week eventuated in the regular working year: it was the last quarter of the century that witnessed the rapid spread of (mostly unpaid) working-class holidays away from home.

Nonetheless, against these developments should be set the pronounced tendency to irregularity still conditional upon the prevalence of occupational diversity. Paradigms of development posited upon the factory system, especially textiles, such as E. P. Thompson's 'Time, Work-Discipline, and Industrial Capitalism' have been both influential and misleading.[23] If 'Saint Monday' was in decline after 1850 its obituaries have perhaps been too quickly written.[24] The increasing intensity of labour discipline and regularity of work rhythms seen in textiles do not seem to have been witnessed in the small-scale, mid-nineteenth-century industry of Birmingham and the Black Country. Even for the few large ironworks and mines, evidence for the speed-up of work and the imposition of labour discipline is not at all conclusive. Labour in the great cities and ports, especially in the trades less subject to sweating, also shared in these characteristics, and even in the sweated trades time irregularity would have been marked, even if intensity and discipline were pronounced where work was to be had and could be controlled by employers. The material and ideological segmentation of work and non-work time was therefore an extremely complex process: above all for women, perhaps, not only was the irregularity of the non-domestic occupation marked, but it was integrated in home life in very diverse ways. The home, and the disposal of time in the domestic sphere, were inextricably linked to the waged occupation, whether it be needlework, washing, straw-plait working, or any other of the host of occupations largely hidden from the historical record.

II

The opening section of this chapter will already have conveyed something of the diverse and irregular development of industrial capitalism over the period. Before considering the relationship between the development of the economy, the experience of work and the historio-

---

[23] *Past & Present*, 38 (1967).
[24] E. Hopkins, 'Working Hours and Conditions during the Industrial Revolution: A Re-Appraisal', *Economic History Review*, 2nd ser., 35 (1982).

graphy of labour in the final section it is first necessary to broaden and deepen this perspective on the economy, a perspective the consequences of which social historians have yet fully to work through. The contemporary re-evaluation of the nineteenth-century economy in particular, stressing irregularity and the incorporation rather than the supersession of different forms of industrial organisation, returns in many ways to the classic view of Sir John Clapham.[25] From Marxist and non-Marxist historians alike,[26] the tendency has been to reject unilinear, and indeed teleological, notions of a convergence upon large-scale, mechanised production as the defining mark of the economy. Working from the premises of Britain's early industrial start and long-sustained growth, its position of dominance in world markets, and from the absence of state intervention, the relative archaism of industrial organisation has been discerned. The cautionary prefix 'relative' is in order here, lest the spectre of Other Countries as the norm from which Britain represents a departure too easily deflects us from the recognition that the progress towards centralisation and mechanisation in Germany and France, for example, was also gradual, uneven and complicated by the persistence of the craft sector, and 'pre-industrial' forms of organisation, management and worker perceptions in the 'leading' sectors. Nonetheless, the term 'archaism' is useful and suggestive in countering anachronistic interpretations. It should not be understood as conveying a *telos* of modernity.

In pointing to the persistence and sometimes the regeneration of older forms of industrial organisation (small workshop, outwork), non-Marxist historians have rightly been chided for relegating these sectors to the category of the residual.[27] Diverse forms of industrial organisation have co-existed within the same period, industry and indeed firm (the Nottingham hosiery industry, for example, combining male factory work and female domestic work in the late nineteenth century). The significance of small-scale enterprises, of hand technology and muscle power, the prominence of manual skill, the multiplication of the domestic and sweated sectors, together with the attenuation of tendencies to centralisation in the new sectors, all com-

[25] J. H. Clapham, *An Economic History of Modern Britain*, 3 vols. (Cambridge, 1926–38), esp. vol. 2.

[26] See, for example, R. Samuel, 'The Workshop of the World: Steam Power and Hand Technology in Mid-Victorian Britain', *History Workshop Journal*, 3 (1977); B. Elbaum, W. Lazonick, F. Wilkinson and J. Zeitlin, 'The Labour Process, Market Structure and Marxist Theory', *Cambridge Journal of Economics*, 3 (1979), pp. 227–303: L. Hannah, *The Rise of the Corporate Economy* (1976).

[27] Editorial in *History Workshop Journal*, 3 (1977).

bine to force a reinterpretation of received notions. Reinterpretation is especially telling in the case of large-scale, mechanised industry. Here managerial hierarchies were weakly elaborated, capitalists' dependence on workers' skill and workplace authority was marked, and technology was of limited effect. Given the highly fragmented and decentralised pattern of ownership, inter-capitalist competition, and often intense fluctuations of output, employers were reluctant to bear the heavy overhead costs of mechanisation, a reluctance compounded by the generally obtaining situation of labour abundance. This tendency to rely on tried and proven methods, perfectly rational in the circumstances, meant that when questions of labour productivity were confronted it tended to be by means of the existing structures of production rather than by mechanisation and the wholesale reordering of work authority.[28] In effect these characteristics of production gave rise to a situation in which the skill and authority of workers was powerfully embedded in industry, but also one in which a considerable degree of interdependence might nonetheless also obtain between capital and labour, it being in the interests of both to cooperate given the mutual dependence of the two sides. As a consequence of these archaic forms of organisation it will be apparent that the 'pre-industrial' characteristics of labour were marked long into the nineteenth century and indeed beyond.

If the economic historians have been rebuked for extending only formal recognition to the limited extent of mechanisation, then this recognition of irregularity and continuity poses questions equally pertinent to classical Marxism's strikingly similar emphasis on the machine and the factory as the hallmarks of 'Modern Industry'. As one recent neo-Marxist critic of classical Marxism observes,

In volume 1 of *Capital*, Marx portrays a capitalist labour process in which capitalists essentially get their way. In introducing new divisions of labour and machinery and in intensifying work they meet with the resistance of workers . . . but the power of capital triumphs by virtue of the very technology at its disposal . . . The individual and collective actions of workers are apparently of no avail, as technological development reproduces the domination of capital over labour on an ever more oppressive scale.[29]

In criticising Marx and his most influential contemporary champion,

---

28   For a cogent expression of this reading of the economy, see A. Reid, 'The Division of Labour and Politics in Britain, 1880–1920', in W. J. Mommsen and H.-G. Husung, eds., *The Development of Trade Unionism in Great Britain and Germany, 1880–1914* (1985).

29   W. Lazonick, 'Industrial Relations and Technical Change: The Case of the Self-Acting Mule', *Cambridge Journal of Economics*, 3 (1979), p. 231.

Braverman,[30] the complex forces at work in shaping the division of labour are seen to involve a consideration of economic and social relations *within* the ranks of capital and labour as well as the relationship between capital and labour. Far from the labour process producing the de-skilling and homogenisation of labour, skill and control were redefined and renegotiated in the process of industrial change, a situation especially marked in British industry. The omniscience of capital has been similarly disputed in the critique of neo-classical emphases on the inherent rationality of market forces.

This recognition of irregular development similarly challenges all unilinear notions of change, perhaps the most influential of which recently has been the model of 'proto-industrialisation'.[31] While the redirection of attention to the agrarian origins of industry, the role of merchant capital and to the family as the locus of the construction of new social relations of production is to be welcomed, the usefulness of the model for the very diverse British case is to be questioned. Even within its own terms of reference, namely the putting-out system as a *distinct phase* instrumental in the progression to centralised, more advanced forms, the model's inherent assumptions and its applicability have recently been closely questioned.[32] There was a wide variety of ways of achieving what was anyway an extremely various end, and decentralised forms of production were every bit as important as centralised.

Turning now to change in the principal sectors of work, by the mid-eighteenth century the basic system of British agriculture was already well established. By 1790 landlords owned 75 per cent of cultivated land, occupying freeholders 15–20 per cent. The division between large landlord, tenant farmer and hired labourer represented a capitalist utilisation of resources that was reflected in the progressive deepening of capitalist social relationships in the nineteenth-century countryside. Nonetheless, these processes were complicated. The

---

[30] H. Braverman, *Labour and Monopoly Capital: The Degradation of Work in the Twentieth Century* (New York, 1977).
[31] H. Medick, P. Kriedte *et al.*, *Industrialisation Before Industrialisation: Rural Industry in the Genesis of Capitalism* (Cambridge, 1981).
[32] P. Hudson, 'Proto-Industrialisation: The Case of the West Riding', *History Workshop Journal*, 12 (1981); J. Zeitlin and C. Sabel, 'Historical Alternatives to Mass Production', *Past & Present*, 108 (1985).

basic agrarian social structure was accompanied by a dense under-growth of marginal cottage labourers and small plebeian independents and semi-independents. The account of occupational diversity and irregularity already given indicates further complexities in economic and social relationships. The basic distinction between the economi-cally advanced south and east and the less developed north and west was of great importance. Capitalist methods and social relations were advanced in the former: it was there that weekly wages, the decline of living-in and the spread of task work developed earliest; there too that the farmer household first ceased to be the focus of a shared culture, giving way to the differentiation of farmer and labourer styles and activities.

If these developments were well under way in the south and east in the early nineteenth century, in the north and west the situation was different. There living-in continued longer, as did annual hiring and yearly wage payment. For some categories of worker annual pay-ment was important throughout the century, though the phenomenon is best regarded as a transitional form between living-in and weekly wages. In Scotland and Wales, also in the south-west of England, primitive methods and variations on the theme of independent small-holding were common characteristics. Throughout the nation as a whole the importance of really small farming should not be underesti-mated: in 1831 the proportion of farms without hired labour to landless farm labourer families was only about one to five.[33] For all farm labourers the relationship to the farmer was always more than the cash nexus: the farmer, or landlord, might have to find a home, an allotment, a school and 'heaven knows what' for the labourer; and the wage was compounded of non-cash elements such as meals, fuel and fodder. Farmers might employ old or ill workers and periodic doles as well as bad-weather payments were quite common. There was still a 'semi-patriarchal' air to farmer–labourer relationships in Joseph Arch's time, and indeed Arch was seen by farmers as stirring up rancour by attempting to cut off 'unofficial' payments in favour of cash wages.[34] 'Semi-patriarchy' is not unhelpful either in describ-ing the landlord–farmer relationship for much of the nineteenth cen-

---

[33]   Clapham, *Economic History*, vol. 1, p. 113. Of 961,000 families engaged in agriculture 275,000 were occupiers (owners or farmers).

[34]   E. L. Jones, *Agriculture and the Industrial Revolution* (Oxford, 1974), chap. 10, esp. pp. 220–2.

tury, though there is very little paternalist about the other side of the agrarian triangle, the links (or lack of them) between the landlords and the labourers.[35]

This very brief survey cannot of course do justice to developments, but it does indicate that if customary rights and plebeian independence were everywhere in retreat the reduction of the worker to undifferentiated wage labour, even by the end of the century, was far from the mark. Similarly, the antagonisms between labourers and landholders would have been mediated by the many non-economic aspects of work experience, heightened there and softened here but nowhere adequately explicable in terms of a simple capitalist–proletarian opposition. After 1850 or so agriculture ceased to be the framework of the whole economy, and began to take on its twentieth-century form as an 'industry' among other industries. The high-farming of the mid-Victorian period accelerated mechanisation, though it was far into the twentieth century before the agricultural worker ceased to live by the sweat of his brow. The shift to owner-occupation, especially with the great land sales of 1914–27 when over a quarter of England passed from tenanted hands, the gradual but crucial involvement of the state, especially in war, together with the contemporary consolidation of holdings have all led to a quintessentially capitalist form of agriculture, characterised by high mechanisation, output and efficiency.

The organisation of production in the manufacturing sector over the period may be broadly characterised as the transition from mercantile to manufacturing or industrial capitalism, with the very great proviso that until the close of the nineteenth century the characteristics of the period of 'manufacture' were a powerful living presence within industrial capitalism. As late as 1840 the *predominant* form of the organisation of production was capitalist outwork,[36] steam and the factory as often acting as the multipliers of this sector as its competitor. Tendencies to increased scale and capitalisation, and to direct management, were under way between 1780 and 1830,[37] but it was only in textiles that anything resembling Marx's 'machinofacture' was evident before the third quarter of the century. Even then, the phenome-

---

[35] On landlords and farmers and landlords and labourers, see, respectively, the essays by T. W. Beastall and F. M. L. Thompson in vol. 2 of Mingay, ed., *The Victorian Countryside*. On the labourer and work see A. Howkins in the same volume.
[36] See Thompson's definition, *Making of the English Working Class*, p. 284.
[37] S. Pollard, *The Genesis of Modern Management* (1965), chap. 2.

Table 3.5 *Steam power in 1870*

	No. of works	Steam HP
Textile trades	6,426	414,748
of which *cotton factories*	2,371	280,602
all other factories	4,055	134,146
Clothing trades	15,543	189
of which *tailoring*	5,918	79
Ironmaking	2,022	221,543
of which *blast furnaces*	511	164,551
foundries	1,310	20,022
Metal working trades	5,074	51,405
of which *machinery manufacture*	1,762	36,473
Leather trades	10,646	2,566
of which *boots and shoes*	8,865	420
Mineral working trades (not mining)	2,887	19,144
Building trades	9,621	7,779
Woodworking trades	2,700	1,215
Food manufacture	5,274	7,546

Notes: The table is adapted from Samuel, 'The Workshop of the World', Table 1, p. 18. Samuel's interpretation of the returns tends to slightly overplay the limitations on concentration and use of steam power. See A. E. Musson, *The Growth of British Industry* (1978), p. 167.

non of uniform machines subject to the compulsions of a central power source was not seen to any extent in other industries until much later. Within textiles there were important differences as to scale and the rate of mechanisation. Within the manufacturing towns *par excellence*, the Lancashire and West Riding mill towns, the number of adult males employed in non-factory occupations was very considerable. Outside textiles and engineering, and excluding non-manual workers, in Blackburn in 1871, 33 per cent of men were so employed as against about 50 per cent in factory work. The figures for Huddersfield were 41 per cent and 40 per cent respectively.[38] Perhaps the best way of indicating the late and limited development of tendencies to concentration and the use of steam power is the factory returns of 1870 (Table 3.5).

Even in the 'leading' sector the limitations to size and technology are apparent (textiles, iron and metal working). Within cotton itself there were many small enterprises, and the crucial significance of the small workshop is strikingly apparent in tailoring, shoemaking

---

[38] Joyce, *Work, Society and Politics*, pp. 106–7.

and building. However, if the salience of the small is pronounced this did not mean that dramatic changes had not taken place in this sector before 1870. Capitalism in the early nineteenth century made progress less by machines and factories than by the increasing control of the small workshop by capitalist middlemen, through their power over credit, supply and distribution. The tempo and quality of workshop life was altered. The trades of London present the classic case of the destruction of livelihood and status brought about by intense competition and an overstocked labour market. Degradation to permanent journeymen status and to 'dishonour' became increasingly marked. Because mechanisation and factory concentration were absent this did not mean that the larger capitalist concerns did not increase the competitive tempo at all levels: as Behagg has shown for Birmingham large employers pressured small, and the effect upon the small master and journeyman was increasing antipathy to the large, especially when the small master was driven to the wall.[39] In building, Price has shown an analogous effect in terms of the early nineteenth-century development of 'general contracting'.[40]

However, if the absence of the factory did not mean the absence of change, it would nonetheless be wrong to overestimate the extent of this change. In building the extraordinary diversity of the industry, and the great numerical importance of small concerns, meant the continuation of established social relationships in industry. And in Birmingham the limited nature of the changes Behagg points to is revealed by Zeitlin and Sabel's account of the regeneration of the small-scale sector until well into the last quarter of the nineteenth century.[41] There the continuing vitality of decentralised, flexible specialisation brought with it the development of master–man co-operative methods. London is perhaps too readily seen as the paradigm for the country as a whole: the upturn in the mid-Victorian economy took the pressure off many in the trades, even in London, where the process of decline was anyway slow and irregular.[42] As we have indicated,

---

[39] C. Behagg, 'Custom, Class and Change: The Trade Societies of Birmingham', *Social History*, 4 (1979).

[40] R. Price, *Masters, Unions and Men: Work Control in Building and the Rise of Labour, 1830–1914* (Cambridge, 1980).

[41] Zeitlin and Sabel, 'Historical Alternatives'.

[42] For evidence of the decline of traditional trades as late as the 1890s, see G. Stedman Jones, 'Working-Class Culture and Working-Class Politics in London, 1870–1900: Notes on the Remaking of a Working Class', *Journal of Social History*, 7 (1974), p. 485.

the structures that replaced the traditional crafts mixed casualisation and sweating with the more complex forms apparent in Bethnal Green. In the country as a whole, in the 'artisan' centres of Birmingham and Sheffield (though less in the latter than the former), in the ports and the provincial cities and towns (including the 'classic' mill towns), as well as in the country districts, the continuity and vitality of small workshop production was marked,[43] and with it much of the vitality of older versions of the master–man relationship.

Completing this survey by returning to the large-scale sector, generalisation about the shape of change in the later nineteenth and twentieth centuries is difficult. One must avoid the exaggerated claims that the economy as a whole was converging upon a dominant form characterised by the factory and the machine, and that within the manufacturing sector itself tendencies to increased scale, technology and direct management were uniform in effect. At the same time, the thesis of 'combined and uneven' development should not be allowed to obscure movements in the above direction, though these cannot in any sense be regarded as an end goal of change. Change was gradual and cumulative, but also diverse in organisational form and non-linear in effect.

Tendencies evident between 1780 and 1830 were continued very slowly in the nineteenth century, though after 1850 with increasing emphasis as the engineering, vehicle building and metal working trades expanded, iron shipbuilding developed and mechanisation began to take effect in the home, consumer trades, such as shoemaking. Nonetheless, pressures towards direct managerial control and de-skilling were limited: recent research has revealed that the 1880–1920 period, often regarded as strategic in this respect, witnessed changes that were geographically and industrially very uneven. If inroads were made on the position of some workers with the creation of strata of semi-skilled and general factory labouring workers, all in all there was no draconian destruction of skill and reorganisation of the division of labour. Where employers were disposed to reorganisation, concentration and consolidation (and by no means all employers were), the effect of change was sometimes nullified by

---

[43]   I. Prothero, *Artisans and Politics in Early Nineteenth-Century London* (Folkestone, 1979), p. 338; Hopkins, 'Working Hours and Conditions'. For the relative strengthening of the artisan's position from the mid-nineteenth century, see R. Gray, *The Aristocracy of Labour in Nineteenth-Century Britain, c. 1850–1900* (1981), chap. 3.

union resistance.[44] It was only after the First World War that the emphasis on monopoly, scale and sophisticated labour management became marked.[45] Even so, heterogeneity still mattered: indeed, because the post-1918 forms of the division of labour have been relatively less studied than those of earlier periods, the tendency to recognise diversity earlier yet still retain implicit notions of modernity for the twentieth century is a dangerous one. There were important countervailing tendencies, such as the decline of the great staple industries and the rise of light industrial undertakings. Within supposedly 'mass-production' industries, above all the motor car industry, 'craft' methods continued to be important in the interwar years.[46] One returns, finally, to the necessity of balance: the accent on continuity and adaptation should not be permitted to mask contrary developments. The industrial worlds of 1820 and 1920 were very different: in the latter, workplaces were bigger, machinery more prevalent and sophisticated, the direct wage form had spread widely, and these imperatives involved in turn a more direct managerial involvement in the execution and organisation of work. Cumulatively, in the end a qualitative difference in the experience of work was involved. Perhaps the best way to reveal in concrete form the way change happened is to consider briefly the organisation of authority within the industrial enterprise.

The factory system that superseded the putting-out system was originally based not on direct control but on delegated authority, especially on sub-contracting. Outside the factory, too, in building, civil engineering and mining sub-contracting was of great importance. The sub-contractor hired the labour, supervised production and received the rate for the finished goods from the entrepreneur. Though in decline by the mid-nineteenth century this decline was protracted, for example in engineering and the iron and steel trades; and the development of direct management was further postponed by a

---

[44] Hannah, *Rise of the Corporate Economy*; for the employer's attempt at the imposition of control, see R. Price, 'The Structure of Subordination in Nineteenth-Century Relations in Production', in G. Crossick, R. Floud and P. Thane, *The Power of the Past: Essays in Honour of E. J. Hobsbawm* (Cambridge, 1984); for its patchy effect, see M. Holbrook-Jones, *Supremacy and Subordination of Labour: The Hierarchy of Work in the Early Labour Movement* (1982), chaps. 3, 5, see also chap. 2 on 'archaism'. The work of Reid, Zeitlin and J. Melling indicates clearly how limited was the reorganisation of work by capitalist employers in the 1880–1920 period (see bibliography).

[45] E. J. Hobsbawm, *Industry and Empire*, 2nd edn (1971), chaps. 9, 11.

[46] J. Zeitlin, 'The Emergence of Shop Steward Organisation and Job Control in the British Car Industry: A Review Essay', *History Workshop Journal*, 10 (1980).

transitional form, that of the 'helper system', whereby the worker hired, paid and supervised the underworker, though his (or her) work was usually done under foreman supervision. Such systems were prevalent in iron and steel, textiles, pottery, and were also seen in mining and building. However, sub-contract and the helper system did not compose a distinct phase, simply superseded in the late nineteenth century. They existed alongside direct management in various mixed forms and persisted into the twentieth century.[47]

Similarly, direct foreman supervision did not simply supersede delegated authority. Foremen might, for example, act as sub-contractors as well. The integration of the waged foreman into direct management was a long and difficult process. His control of production and personnel functions made him a kind of master in the workplace, and his equivocal position between capital and labour makes him a strategically vital, if largely unstudied figure in the history of labour.[48] Equivocation was probably as often tilted in favour of his own gang or team as in the direction of management. The foreman was the object as well as the subject of industrial conflict, as workers fought to limit, or expand, his role.

Under the pressure of management, but also trade unions, foreman power was diminishing prior to 1914. But its persistence is testimony to the power of delegated authority as opposed to direct control. It was only in the interwar years that the internal hierarchies of production managers, engineers, accountants and foremen began to become pronounced. The growth of personnel management, consciously elaborated welfare schemes, and 'scientific' management in general, was slower before about 1920 than is often supposed. Tendencies to consolidated control at the upper level of the hierarchy have been limited, too, moves to amalgamation and combination retaining strong federal characteristics. Before the Second World War centralised managerial and ownership structures were limited, though in the private and public fields this tendency has been marked since then.

This account of persistence and adaptation raises the general question of the degree to which we can term many nineteenth-century workers proletarians. What is meant by this term? Here the work of Kocka

---

47   H. Gospel, 'Managerial Structure and Strategy: An Introduction', in H. Gospel and C. R. Littler, eds., *Managerial Strategies and Industrial Relations: An Historical and Comparative Study* (1983).

48   See the pioneering work of J. Melling, '"Non-Commissioned Officers": British Employers and their Supervisory Workers, 1880–1920', *Social History*, 5 (1980).

on the German example is helpful.[49] The condition may be described as not only work for wages, but wage working for life for an increasing proportion of those who work manually, and for some who do not. Life-chances are determined by the market. Workers do not possess materials, tools, products, nor the premises of production, and their work is determined by those who do in the form of capital. Relations between wage workers and employers are based on contract and not on extra-economic compulsion or tradition. As Kocka argues, such a categorisation indicates a socio-economic class position: 'Working class on this level is not more than a potentiality, a category, and not a group.' Kocka's neo-Weberian analysis provides us with a framework for understanding class formation, and one, it should be added, in which the various stages are not considered as having a necessary or unilinear causal effect from economy to culture and politics, as tends to be the pattern in classical Marxism and its many derivatives. The stages of class formation are to be conceived of as class position: 'social class' in the sense of those sharing a common socio-economic position becoming aware of what they share and developing on this basis a common social identity; and class at the level of 'party', in terms of labour and political organisation.

One does not here wish to choose between different approaches to class, but this scheme does have the virtue of providing a relatively firm conceptual and empirical framework for understanding the structural co-ordinates of class formation. The Marxian emphasis on the development of class in Britain – at least as developed under the powerful influence of E. P. Thompson – does excessively stress struggle and agency as the primary and indeed prior category of formation. However, it should be emphasised that some of the most cogent criticisms of this position come from within contemporary Marxist circles.[50] This emphasis on struggle leads to problems. Certainly, class needs to be seen in cultural and political terms, ones of the playing out of cultural traditions and values in changing circumstances. It is a mental and cultural construct. But its construction will not be understood unless the socio-economic position is explored. If class position is not considered by attention to the question of proletarianisation, then one is led to ask in what sense is the phenomenon to

---

[49] J. Kocka, 'Problems of Working Class Formation in Germany: The Early Years, 1800–1875', in I. Katznelson and A. R. Zolberg, eds., Working Class Formation: Nineteenth-Century Patterns in Western Europe and the United States (1980).

[50] For example, P. Anderson, Arguments within English Marxism (1980), chap. 2.

hand a 'class' one, and more particularly a 'working-class' one (presumably one based on the perception of workers' shared experience as manual proletarians), rather than political tradition *per se*, or extra-proletarian identifications such as 'the people', or the primary producers.

Why should proletarianisation be a question? In one sense it is not. Some form of waged labour was a condition of probably a majority of workers before the beginnings of this period. And very few workers in the period as a whole were outside some form of dependency on the capitalist labour and commodity markets. But having said this, one has only scratched the surface of the problem. Above all, proletarianisation was not an annunciation but a process, as complex and uneven as the economy itself. If in general it was a process moving towards a more uniform socio-economic position for workers then the movement was constantly interrupted and sometimes contradicted. In terms of the experience of workers the effects were often profoundly ambiguous and contradictory. Wage and non-wage characteristics of labour were deeply embedded in each other, and capitalist wage work rarely took a pure form.

This discussion brings into focus much of what has already been said about the experience of work. The discussion of labour mobility has raised questions about the late development and ambiguous forms of supposedly 'traditional', solidary and conflictual forms of working-class community, forms usually taken as the benchmarks of a 'mature' working class. More directly in terms of class 'position', the discussion of occupational irregularity and diversity indicates that workers would have been taken out of wage dependency (outside production or within as small masters or self-employed) or subjected to strikingly different, often very indirect, forms of that dependency. Irregularity of work no doubt enforced economies of need of which the wage was only one aspect (along with kin support, credit, letting, charity, and so on). This in turn raises questions of the centrality of work, more particularly manual work, in the self-definitions making up class identity. The late and incomplete growth of uniformity here, as in the matter of coherent occupational communities, complicates the question further. Regularity of work in the sense of work time also suggests great variations in the conditions and experience of workers, especially in the ways in which they would have evaluated the meaning of work for their lives. The situation in agriculture, in penny capitalism and small-scale working-class enterprise in general, and in the 'artisan' trades, alike suggests the complexity and ambiguity of class position. In the case of Birmingham described by Behagg, one of especially marked conflict, we find that the journeymen he speaks of are very strange proles indeed: almost every skilled journeyman was in fact a kind of small master, employing underhands and independent, even in a factory setting, to the extent that the goods produced were often sold to the employer. The small master–journeyman association remained close.

And this indeed indicates much of the general situation. Given the persistence of outwork and small-scale production, also the archaism of industrial capitalism, the worker would often have employed assistants – perhaps kin and neighbours, sometimes paid, sometimes unpaid and unofficial. He or she may have possessed parts of the means of production, whether tools, premises or goods. Dependence should in fact be considered as a kind of spectrum: there are numerous examples of a fair degree of independence, and movement along the scale would often have been considerable, even for workers in seemingly dependent positions who in the course of time might move in and out of different situations, such as those of journeyman or operative, small master, and self-employed worker. The line between employer and employee would thus often have been indistinct, even in the most 'modern' of all industries, textiles. West Riding woollens was riddled with small units, as was the weaving side in cotton. In these works kin and neighbours might be employed, and the move back to overlooker or operative status might be abrupt. The renting of 'room and power' contributed to the possibility of setting up.

Finding a way through the thicket of questions thrown up by this appreciation of ambiguity is not easy. One way would certainly be a social history of the wage.[51] Wage work is very old, but before becoming the dominant form it emerged slowly out of a diverse system of non-wage work relations which continued to co-exist alongside it, serving as a basis for interests sometimes accentuating, sometimes counteracting, common interests based on the wage alone. As Hobsbawm has shown, only around the mid-nineteenth century, and then only in the more advanced industries, did workers begin to move beyond customary evaluations of the wage to apply systematically

---

[51] For a very interesting beginning in this area, see M. Sonenscher, 'Work and Wages in Eighteenth-Century Paris', in M. Berg, P. Hudson and M. Sonenscher, eds., *Manufacture in Town and Country before the Factory* (Cambridge, 1983).

the rules of the capitalist market game.[52] As with evaluations and industrial bargaining, so with material components was the emergence of the capitalist wage long delayed. The history of the monetarisation of the wage is unwritten, though it is clear that credit and customary non-cash components were of great importance long into the nineteenth century. Diversity of outgoings needs to be explored alongside diversity of income, as do the periodicity of the wage (weekly, monthly), and the almost totally neglected history of the mode and ritual of the moment of payment. It is clear that a systematic history of the wage would greatly alter our view of many things: of the nature of industrial disputes, of the perception of time and of workers' evaluations and representations of work.

It is perhaps in the more advanced nineteenth-century industries that especially interesting questions are raised, particularly in relation to the workings of authority in industry. The 'archaism' of the large-scale sector has already been described: given the skeletal nature of managerial hierarchies and the resulting dependence of employers on worker skill, initiative and work authority, it is clear that the position of the 'proletarian' worker was an odd one. Authority was delegated not only to a wide range of intermediary workers but to production workers themselves. Delegation therefore involved an extremely intricate network of relationships between employer, worker and helper (or underhand). Many aspects of these relationships are relatively unexplored: the 'sharing' of authority between worker and employer, the reshaping of authority as mediated in the worker–helper relationship (the latter often being kin or neighbours) and especially the corollary of delegation, the displacement of authority, and hence often blame, upon a wide range of intermediary, non-employer, figures within and without industry. In their actual work situation, and certainly in their own eyes, many workers were far from being powerless and dependent wage hands. But both situation and attitude led them therefore into relationships with employers that cannot be reduced to a simple capitalist–proletarian opposition. The irregularity of the economy has been shown, and the consequences for proletarianisation developed. But the logic of ambiguous class position bears directly on the worker–employer relationship as well: if historians have begun to extend that logic to other aspects

---

[52]   E. J. Hobsbawm, 'Custom, Wages and Work Load', in *Labouring Men* (1964).

of the work situation the central question of that relationship still remains to be revalued.

When the consequences of the thesis of combined and uneven economic development have been explored, ambiguity has in general, however, hardly been the keynote. Rather, the recognition that workers' skill, initiative and control have been deeply embedded in nineteenth-century industry has commonly brought with it an emphasis upon the 'pre-industrial' characteristics of labour – in the form of the culture of the independent and respectable 'artisan' – as the source of a resistant and oppositional culture.[53] This is only one side of the coin. Besides independence, and in fact inseparably connected with it, needs to be set the matter of worker–employer reciprocity.

The recent attention given to the 'archaism' of the large-scale sectors in the nineteenth century also points to the necessity of looking again at relationships between employers and workers. The fragmented and competitive nature of capital has already been indicated, as has the capitalists' reliance upon the worker for a variety of workplace functions. The generally conservative attitude of employers to labour, and to innovation generally, is also apparent. From this it is clear that not only were employers often not concerned to de-skill and subordinate the worker, but that workers' and employers' interests often met on what has recently been termed 'the terrain of compromise'.[54] This terrain is a ground very little worked upon by social historians.[55] Contrary to the tendency to exalt either unilateral worker action or unfettered capitalism, it is the area of interdependence between capital and labour that needs consideration. Indeed, whether one is dealing with this or any other period or country, the extent to which capital and labour have a basic interest in co-operation has been generally overlooked, overshadowed as it has been by the attention given the conflict inherent in the capital–labour relation.

It is not of course that the ground of compromise is either static or unconditional, and in all cases the limits of compromise must be borne in mind. As previously pointed out, the pressures acting upon the division of labour are broader than those *between* labour and capital alone (see above p. 151). The effect, for example, of internal divisions

[53] Price, *Masters, Unions and Men*, is a clear case of this.
[54] Elbaum *et al.*, 'Labour Process, Market Structure and Marxist Theory', p. 229.
[55] For a fuller account, see P. Joyce, 'Labour, Capital and Compromise: A Response to Richard Price', *Social History*, 9 (1984); *idem*, 'Languages of Reciprocity and Conflict: A Further Response to Richard Price', *Social History*, 9 (1984).

within labour and capital on the division of labour is equivocal and dependent on a wide range of factors, especially non-economic ones: such divisions can lead to aggression as well as compromise, for example, inter-capitalist competition leading employers to smash unions. Nonetheless, as a general perspective and as a guide to particular outcomes of the division of labour the perspective of interdependence and compromise is a valuable one. It certainly has much to tell us about the nature of Victorian industry, so marked by co-exploitation, and of the mid- and late Victorian years especially, given the relative stability of the economy, the lack of technological innovation and the application of labour-intensive methods.

The account so far given of the ambiguous nature of class position alerts us to the recognition that for many nineteenth-century workers the perception of the capitalist employer as a class enemy, and especially *the* class enemy, may have been ambivalent, indistinct or even non-existent. So much is apparent from the continuing ownership by workers of components of the means of production, the changing locations of workers along the employer–employee spectrum, the effects of the delegation of authority, variations in wage dependency and so on. In turn, the assumed centrality of the capitalist employer–proletarian worker opposition in classical Marxism's account of class formation is opened to interrogation. One can begin this questioning with reference to the fairly representative example of building. Given a heterogeneous category of owners, and an often indistinct line between masters and men, situations of conflict and alliance could be very diverse. The endemic warfare of large and small units is apparent, especially in local markets. Alliances of unions and employers against the unfair practices of petty contractors and scamping jobbers were as frequent as alliances of workers and small employers against the driving foremen of the large builders.

Conflicts and alliances are in turn linked to the question of the delegation and displacement of authority. In both the small- and large-scale sector conflict and hence blame could be displaced from employers to a wide range of intermediaries, whether managers, foremen, agents or indeed production workers themselves. In turn the possibility of alliances between co-exploiting workers and employers was marked. The question of middlemen is in fact vitally important. In the most advanced industry of all, cotton textiles, the example of speculating middlemen (merchants, factors, agents) – playing bulls and bears on the raw cotton market for instance – was held up for the common obloquy of masters and workers. The Cotton Famine in Lancashire was not known as such, but as the Cotton Panic. Speculation was one of many pretexts for joint action in defence of the interests of the trade.[56] In export industries in general blame for the industry's ills, and ameliorative agitation, were often directed by workers and employers alike to political and economic conditions overseas. If this was the case in textiles, where a capitalist employer class was most clearly delineated, then when the structure of so much nineteenth-century industry is considered the ambiguous and indistinct nature of the capitalist employer is even more apparent. For, as we have seen, capitalism in the nineteenth century made headway as much if not more by the tightening hold of the middleman rather than the large manufacturer. In the trades and in outwork, the worker as often confronted not the capitalist employer but the much more immediate figures of the merchant, the putter-out, the clerk, inspector and agent. These were the bearers of unfettered competition and degraded status. Thus for many workers the picture of the capitalist employer was fractured, indistinct and ambivalent.

But for many workers, also, the conception of the employer would have had a more immediate aspect, and one that if often ambivalent had a positive as well as a negative side. For the skilled trades especially, the notion of the integrity of the individual workmen was inseparable from the integrity of the trade. And the integrity of the trade involved notions of the community of interest of masters and workers in that trade. If, as seems likely, the early nineteenth century did not mark a great divide in the history of the non-factory sectors, then it follows from this that, if severely tested, notions of reciprocal rights and obligations between masters and workers were not completely ruptured either. Versions of the trade as a community therefore need to be traced throughout the course of the nineteenth century and later still. And, given the archaism of industrial organisation in the new industries, one can argue for continuities of perception as well, of notions of independence but also of worker–employer reciprocity. The latter question of cultural transmission raises complex questions which will be developed in the conclusion of this chapter.

As a way of broaching these matters, however, it is necessary to consider either neglected or misunderstood aspects of early nineteenth-century work culture and class perceptions, taking first the

---

[56] Joyce, *Work, Society and Politics*, p. 99.

language and rhetoric of the trade. Central to artisan notions of work were proprietorial valuations of skill as human capital. Such capital was invested in the trade as a common enterprise, the master investing organisational ability as well as working capital. What one discerns are probably very old notions of reciprocity between master and man in their separate but linked spheres,[57] the man seeing himself as on a par with the organiser of the trade. Reciprocity was a vital presence in the Birmingham Behagg describes. There the exaltation of 'industry' was pronounced; upon it depended the cultivation of morals, religion and 'civility'. But if the master who robbed his men 'rebelled against God', then so too did the men who robbed the honourable master. If the industrial and political action described for the Birmingham tradesmen was offensive (so rightfully reversing the trite association of small scale and peaceful), it was still essentially offensive reciprocity.

Notions of masters and men reciprocally linked in their own proper spheres are discernible in industries as different as mining and factory-based engineering (the latter in the early twentieth century).[58] They were clearly of great durability. Recent work on the Scottish colliers, the independent or 'honourable' miner,[59] begins to uncover a still largely hidden world. These workers regarded themselves as true independents, not wage hands, and because of this they were involved in all sorts of informal understandings with employers based upon a relationship of reciprocal equality. They had no basic quarrel with the small masters (upon which class identifications could have taken place) so long as the masters kept to their side of the bargain. Even when the bargain was disrupted from outside, with the development of big fields, large owners and immigrant workers, the gulf between the independent man and the mere wage hand was enormous. It showed itself in trade-union practice and cultural values as well as in attitudes to employers.

The second area to be considered is the conception of class relations discernible in earlier nineteenth-century radicalism. Notions of proprietorial skill and the employer as the manager and organiser of production carried with them the impetus to co-operative production

---

[57] R. A. Leeson, *Travelling Brothers* (1979), p. 273. Leeson underestimates the vitality of the small workshop production upon which collaborative notions were based.

[58] Holbrook-Jones, *Supremacy and Subordination of Labour*, pp. 56–7, 60.

[59] R. Harrison, ed., *The Independent Collier* (Hassocks, 1978), esp. A. Campbell and F. Reid, 'The Independent Collier in Scotland', and A. Campbell, 'Honourable Men and Degraded Slaves'.

among workers, and were closely linked to forms of artisan radicalism. The employer could in certain circumstances be regarded as dispensable, particularly under the severe conditions of unfettered capitalist competition in the early nineteenth century when many employers were abrogating the proper reciprocities of master and men. But it is necessary not to confuse these economic and political activities with class identifications having at their centre the opposition of capitalist employer and proletarian worker. Stedman Jones's recent work makes clear the danger of such anachronistic readings.[60]

Economic distress and exploitation were given a political and not an economic explanation, in terms of the artificial monopoly of the political system by the aristocrats and the capitalists. Capitalists in these terms were essentially middlemen, an understanding that in fact meshed closely with the objective situation of many workers. The fundamental opposition was between the working class or classes and the capitalists, who were composed of fundholders, merchants and factors as much as employers. The enemy was thus not employers as a class but oppressive and unjust employers. It was not masters who were opposed but capitalists.[61] The employer in fact had a decidedly *useful* role (in management and supervision), and what early nineteenth-century radicals like Thomas Hodgskin pointed to was not a picture of two opposed classes thrown up by a new system of production but rather a harmonious world of production inhabited by master and man. Indeed, the aristocracy was the chief enemy; and of particular importance may well have been the opposition of the 'industrious' classes and the idle and parasitic ones. The probable ambiguity of the terms 'working class' or 'working classes' stands in need of close consideration here, terms which may have partaken of the meaning of 'industrious' classes, a term which in its extension to the useful role of employers would have emphasised the common assault of the worker and employer on the non-industrious class *sans pareil*, the idle and parasitic aristocracy. Also, because employers were not identified as a class, it followed that they were differentiated individu-

---

[60] G. Stedman Jones, 'The Language of Chartism', in D. Thompson and J. Epstein, eds., *The Experience of Chartism* (1982). Stedman Jones shows the importance of continuity rather than discontinuity in the transition from populist and constitutionalist notions to supposedly class-based theories of exploitation within production, theories that turned upon the labour theory of value. Even if the 'new' reading was new, which is probably not the case, its hold was only over a minority of workers. The old, populist notions were very widely diffused in popular society.

[61] W. Sewell, *Work and Revolution in France: The Language of Labour from the Old Regime to 1848* (Cambridge, 1980), for a very similar situation in mid-nineteenth-century France.

ally, by their actual behaviour, and that the industrious, useful, honest and efficient employer would have been singled out for praise as much as his opposite for blame. Thus it is the utility of employers, their differentiation by individual merit and the continuing forcefulness of ideas of harmonious worlds of work that have to be kept in mind when considering the question of worker–employer reciprocities, and social relations in general, in the whole course of the period.

What, it may be asked, does all this talk of reciprocity mean when every schoolboy is aware that big nineteenth-century employers were to a man advocates of the cash nexus, paragons of bourgeois liberal individualism in its familiar garb of Benthamite utilitarianism and classical political economy? Well, there is something in this: but as a generalisation it is at best a simplification, at worst a travesty. To call the strategies and styles of large nineteenth-century employers 'paternalist' is to encounter difficulties: the development from extra-economic to economic forms of managerial control is certainly characteristic of the nineteenth century as a whole, and collective bargaining, trade-union recognition and economic incentives certainly contradicted the pure myth of individual paternalist responsibility. Paternalist strategies certainly worked in tandem with 'economistic' ones, and were always inseparable from authoritarian actions. But if we recognise the consequences of combined and uneven development for labour we should do so for capital as well: the limited nature of technical and organisational change was reflected in the personal style of the family firm, and this style – as in the case of so many of the characteristics of labour as well – argues fundamental continuities with eighteenth-century forms. Purely 'economic' styles and forms of coercion were in fact very slow to develop, as were the consciously developed (and self-conscious) welfare schemes that grew alongside these. It is also the case that what seem to us incompatible modes – paternalism and individualism – were in fact in the mental constructions of nineteenth-century employers perfectly compatible.[62]

This in turn argues that our Gradgrindian stereotype does not fit the bill. Just as bourgeois liberal culture was more diverse, lively, adaptable and contradictory than it is usually given credit for, so too was industrialisation not only not inimical to but actually productive of paternalist solutions. And these solutions were as much moral,

[62]   See the very interesting J. Seed, 'Unitarianism, Political Economy and the Antinomies of Liberal Culture in Manchester, 1830–1850', *Social History*, 7 (1982).

religious and political as economic. While it is idle to discount the vital importance of paternalism to problems of production it is also necessary not to reduce paternalism to solely economic terms. Indeed, much of the nature of nineteenth-century management was extra-economic in character: the control of time by work discipline, for instance, was inseparable from wider social and moral reform, and – given the nature of the family firm – relations between workers and employers spilled over far beyond the bounds of the 'economic'. With many reservations nonetheless – about the combined use of economic and non-economic forms of coercion, about the inseparability of paternalism and autocracy and about the sometimes intermittent and uneven use and incidence of paternalism – there seems little doubt that the use of the term is warranted. If nothing else it is a necessary prophylactic against the received wisdom concerning nineteenth-century capitalists. But more than this, it describes the actual practice of very many enterprises, and certainly describes the self-justification of employers, who, if they were led along the path of economic incentives, the end of extra-economic and punitive legal coercion, and formalised collective bargaining, were in general led unwillingly. For employers themselves, therefore, notions of reciprocal social and economic relations were quite central. The use of the term paternalism does not, of course, exhaust the meaning of worker–employer reciprocity. Far from it, as it only partly describes the situation in small workshops. But its applicability to the large concern – seemingly the least likely location – does argue the necessity of exploring anew the question of reciprocity and revaluing the historical weight of the worker–employer relation.

III

The history of labour has gone through remarkable changes in the past thirty years. Until the early 1950s or so the dominant mode of analysis was a sort of left Whig interpretation, owing much to the Webbs and G. D. H. Cole. Notions of evolutionary development dominated, as did the implicitly teleological mode of thought so often associated with such notions. Under the influence of the Webbs especially, the history of labour was construed as the development of a 'modern', organised and gradualist trade-union and party-political movement. The tendency to hagiography was marked, though struggle was usually ascribed to the early 'pioneer' days before the break-through into 'modernity' was achieved. Further to the left, with Cole and leftwards to the Communist party historians, varieties of belief in progress and scientific rationalism were also marked, though there the causal primacy of the economic 'base' invested the juncture of evolutionism and Marxian class struggle.[63]

The predominating emphasis in historial work tended to be on organisation and leadership, to the neglect of non-institutional forms of association and the culture and actions of the majority of workers. Political organisation, and to a lesser extent ideology, also tended to absorb interest. The history of history in recent years has seen an enormous and liberating expansion of range: particularly since the 1960s horizons have broadened, with the growth of oral history, women's history and much else. A massive amount of attention has been given to the nineteenth century, an attention which reflects the importance of the century for understanding industrial capitalism, but one which is surely disproportionate. This chapter, in its concentration on the nineteenth century, pleads the virtue of necessity but admits the vice of disproportion. The 'history of labour' is a term which at once conveys the strides that have been made. It is no longer credible to study the history of labour *in vacuo*. The study of institutions and leaders has been replaced by the study of the relationships *between* groups and classes, and by accounts of social interaction, whether at home or in the workplace.[64] Popular culture is now a serious object of study, as are the formal and informal agencies of 'social control'. There has recently been a welcome turn to the study of language and the constitution of ideology and consciousness, owing much to post-structuralist influences, especially that of Foucault. The interest in social domination has reversed the earlier epic and triumphal optimism of the Whigs.

This enormous growth of activity has recently bred a necessary reaction, particularly against the precipitate and unreflecting fusion of different aspects or levels of historical explanation and human experience. The disassociation of these aspects, thrown together in the unhappy term 'social history', and their subjection to analysis in their

---

[63]   The study of post-1945 historiography has recently begun; see R. Johnson, 'Culture and the Historians', in J. Clarke, C. Critcher and R. Johnson, eds., *Working-Class Culture: Studies in History and Theory* (1979); R. Samuel, 'British Marxist Historians I', *New Left Review*, 120 (1980); prefaces and contributions in R. Samuel, ed., *People's History and Socialist Theory* (1981).

[64]   For interesting comments, see B. Harrison, 'The Workplace Situation', *Times Literary Supplement*, 24 Oct. 1980.

own right is apparent in arguments for the 'relative autonomy' of the state and political processes from economic and social change.[65] More closely in the realm of work, the tendency to relate social and political change to economic processes is readily discernible in the central place given the division of labour in recent social history.[66] This is not the place to argue whether or not the historians involved share a common tendency to 'reduce' cultural phenomena to expressions of economic change. Given the breadth and diversity of approach among the wide range of historians involved this is unlikely. Nonetheless, the link between the division of labour and politics has been questioned in a radical fashion recently from the general perspective of the disassociation of the two spheres.[67] With this approach one can have considerable sympathy: the account of irregular and uneven economic development already given shows how problematic is the relationship between work experience and class consciousness as understood in the common 'economic' sense, a sense in which politics is closely involved as the outcome of economic 'position'. Similarly, the extreme diversity of the division of labour's progress and of the experience of work argues against the composition of 'basic' economic processes to which important structural changes in social attitudes and politics are supposedly related.

In the remainder of this section these two questions will be taken further – the consequences for 'social history' of irregular economic development, and the relationship of economic and political change. The first question has already been broached, though now it will be treated much more directly in terms of labour historiography. Necessarily in a somewhat arbitrary fashion, leading positions in the field will be picked out for consideration, including the argument for the 'autonomy' of politics, the position which perhaps has most in common with the thesis of uneven development. It is as well here to recall the advisability of a little scepticism in confronting this new

---

[65] G. Eley and K. Nield, 'Why Does Social History Ignore Politics?', *Social History*, 5 (1980). The title is representative of the genre, as is the journal of the general process of theoretical questioning.

[66] To the works of Joyce and Price already mentioned need be added those of R. Gray, *The Labour Aristocracy in Victorian Edinburgh* (Oxford, 1976); G. Crossick, *An Artisan Elite in Victorian Society: Kentish London, 1840–80* (1978); G. Stedman Jones, 'England's First Proletariat: "Class Struggle and the Industrial Revolution"', *New Left Review*, 90 (1975); J. Hinton, *The First Shop Stewards' Movement* (1973); K. Burgess, *The Challenge of Labour* (1980); and J. Foster, *Class Struggle and the Industrial Revolution* (1974).

[67] See, e.g., Reid, 'The Division of Labour and Politics'.

picture of the labour process: it is necessary to 'de-centre' the factory and the machine from our picture but not to displace them completely. And, if revisionism's characteristic defect of enthusiasm may be apparent here, there may be dangers too in the allied severance of work, society and politics. However, before turning to what we know, it is necessary to describe what we do not know. Only then will the open and provisional nature of the questions and answers indicated in this section be apparent.

In getting at these difficulties a good deal of the problem is that while we have an established labour history and an increasingly large corpus of theoretical work we still know surprisingly little about the history of work. It is possible to exaggerate the advances 'social history' has made over the narrower and more traditional concerns of labour history.[68] We still know little about the history of capital, a history without which the history of labour is literally inconceivable, and this is an ignorance one fears is reflected in the lack of attention given here to middle-class work life and evaluations of work. Indeed, for all workers, of whatever class, the central question of the linguistic, artistic and ritual ways in which work was represented is still largely unasked. Many omissions in the history of work have already been indicated, and others may be noted. We now know much more than we did about work processes, the forces acting on the division of labour, something too about workplace life and its relation to life beyond work, but what may be termed the interior life of the workplace is still largely opaque to us, the everyday arrangements of production and the customs and attitudes shaped in work. The little-known work of Messenger on the industrial folklore of mill life in the turn-of-the-century Ulster linen trade indicates the rich possibilities oral material and anthropological perspectives open up.[69] The book illustrates the difficulties of analysis too: for earlier periods such material is unavailable to us, but more than this the question of the links between work and the wider culture are not explored here. The interplay between these spheres in the generation of cultural representations of work, and of attitudes to its execution, is clearly of great concern for the history of work and the destination of social history. Reference to the mid-nineteenth-century Birmingham trades has

---

[68]   For the dominance of 'old' over 'new' in research work, at least to 1978, see V. F. Gilbert, *Labour and Social History Theses* (1982). Consulting the indexes of this volume is an instructive exercise.

[69]   B. Messenger, *Picking up the Linen Threads: A Study in Industrial Folklore* (Austin, Texas, 1975); see also H. Benyon, *Working for Ford* (1973).

already suggested the importance of religious and moral influences in the creation of work cultures.[70]

The interior, cultural life of production is, however, only one aspect. In the discussion of irregularity, proletarianisation and workers and employers numerous perspectives are opened up. Central to many of these is the necessity of a closer knowledge of what may be termed the material nature of work. What was the design of workplaces and the arrangement of machines? How was the working day broken up? What was the level of noise, dirt and disease, and how were workers affected outside work by, say, deafness or hereditary and perhaps caste-like occupational ailments and sensibilities? What was workers' influence over, and attitudes to, the products they made? What were the languages of the workplace? Extra-institutional perspectives are vital, but this does not mean that institutional ones should be neglected. Reid, for instance, has recently shown the interesting possibilities opened up for the study of trade unions by a detailed attention to the division of labour and union structure.[71]

The first of the four broadly different approaches to the relationship between the division of labour and cultural and political change to be reviewed is that between changes in the structure of work and the failure of an oppositional consciousness to emerge in the working class, chiefly the labour aristocracy idea.[72] Whether in the form of economic criteria (Hobsbawm), authority in work (Foster) or the more refined readings of ideological hegemony (Gray and Crossick), the labour aristocracy notion has been widely influential.[73] The idea, broadly, is of the separation out of a distinct stratum in the working class whose privileged material position or 'incorporated', subordinate ideology explains the relative quiescence of the working class as a whole. It is impossible to do justice to the variety of questions raised in the different approaches to the problem, which range from the bald and anachronistic question, 'why did the working class not

[70] For a very interesting discussion of the intersection of work and non-work life in the development of work practices and attitudes, and in the matter of workers' images of society, see J. Cousins and R. Brown, 'Patterns of Paradox: Shipbuilding Workers' Images of Society', in M. Bulmer, ed., *Working Class Images of Society* (1976).

[71] A. Reid, 'The Division of Labour in the British Shipbuilding Industry, 1880–1920, with Special Reference to Clydeside' (unpublished PhD thesis, Cambridge University, 1980).

[72] For full citations see Gray, *Aristocracy of Labour*.

[73] E. J. Hobsbawm, 'The Labour Aristocracy in Nineteenth-Century Britain', in *Labouring Men* (1964); Foster, *Class Struggle*; Gray, *Aristocracy of Labour*; Crossick, *An Artisan Elite*.

take the revolutionary path?', to the subtle exploration of culture and ideology in the attempt to explain the stability of capitalist society in terms not of coercion or privilege but of consent.

As the notion has been developed what seem to be its *necessary* material underpinnings have in fact largely been relegated in importance. Reid's work on the shipbuilding industry goes far to subvert these often shaky underpinnings: in place of a privileged stratum the very unclear line of demarcation between skilled and unskilled emerges, as do the sectional differences *between* skilled workers. Given this heterogeneity it is difficult to conceive of a cohesive, emergent stratum. The picture of irregularity in occupational life presented in the present discussion leads in a similar direction. Also, given the great range of variation between industries, simultaneity of emergence and internal coherence are again questions: it is difficult to give *any* specific identity to relations between the skilled and unskilled. More than this, the incomplete nature of proletarianisation, and the resulting ambiguity of master–worker relationships, raise quite fundamental difficulties.

The contrast between the relative quiescence of the mid-nineteenth century and earlier conflict tends to be posited on implicit notions of a 'mature' class formation from which mid-century developments are a departure. This is mistaken. When the ambiguity of class position is considered it is apparent that the 'respectability' and 'reformism' of the labour aristocracy are misconstrued in a wholly anachronistic manner. Rather than a departure from an (idealised) norm, they are in fact the 'rational' and historically appropriate expressions of the conditions of labour. So much is apparent from our consideration of the conception of class relations present in earlier nineteenth-century radicalism. The possibility of all manner of 'cross-class' alliances and reciprocities – in the field of work as well as cultural values – is only to be expected when class itself is so incompletely developed. This does not, of course, mean that social relations were not marked by often bitter conflict. However, it is ambiguity and continuity that are especially striking: rather than any major break around mid-century in the artisan trades it is continuity in the form of work-derived notions of independence and respectability that mattered,[74] continuity too in the organisation of production itself. Similarly, the political concerns of artisans seem to change little, and it is in fact probable

---

[74]   The perspective of Prothero is probably the correct one, *Artisans and Politics*, conclusion.

that changes in politics rather than in work mattered more here, namely the successful political adaptation of 'respectable' opinion, at governmental and extra-governmental levels. At best the labour aristocracy notion describes one among many sectional divisions in the working class (local, regional, sexual, etc.), most of which were not economic in character; and in all probability it is an elephantine anachronism.

The second position to be reviewed is the association between work and the presence of an oppositional consciousness in the working class, in particular the emphasis on workers' autonomy and control in industry and the extrapolation to oppositional work-based cultures, and eventually to politics. Elements, to some degree contradictory, of this position and the first one have been combined, for instance in the work of Gray and Hinton. For Hinton, the mid-Victorian 'aristocrat' retains the creative psychology of the producer, the practice of whose trade is a condition of personal and spiritual fulfilment. The ambiguities and tensions obtaining between the notions of resistant work cultures and exclusive privilege are perhaps not fully resolved in this work (just as the more general question of the labour aristocracy as simultaneously exclusive and yet the leaders of the working class as a whole is not resolved).[75]

In Price's recent work on the building industry the emphasis of work control at the informal, shop floor level dispenses with the 'labour aristocracy' notion altogether. For this we ought perhaps to be thankful, but what is put in its place is a rather unsatisfactory tendency to elevate work experience to a privileged position in the formation of class consciousness and politics. More especially, 'work control' is treated in a rather uncritical fashion as leading unproblematically to the consciousness of conflicting interests. This kind of approach is in fact widely diffused, most of all outside higher education in 'people's' history: some of the work of the History Workshop movement reproduces the characteristic emphases on class struggle and the agency of working people in their own history, emphases in turn owing much to the example of E. P. Thompson and the climate of the 1960s and early 1970s.

Now, this accent on autonomous regulation and independence is clearly very important: our examination of work makes this clear. But why 'work control' should be embedded in industry and what

[75] Gray, *Aristocracy of Labour*; Hinton, *The First Shop Stewards' Movement*.

the consequences of this are, are questions only partly answered by the emphasis on militant worker-cultures. The reasons for it are more complex: here one would invoke market structures, inter-capitalist competition and the terrain of compromise between workers and employers. As the account given here has already made plain, independence is inseparably related to questions of the compromise and co-operation obtaining between capital and labour. All this is to say nothing of the dubious extrapolation from work control to syndicalist politics in Price, nor the false dichotomy, widely prevalent, between the trade-union rank and file and the leadership, heroes of resistance on the one hand, villains of compromise on the other.[76] But the point to be pressed home here, indicating the contingent, contextualised nature of the link between work experience and social attitudes, is that the standing of the craftsmen and a strong attachment to unions is not at all incompatible with extremely positive attitudes to firms and employers, and indeed with non- or partly conflictual 'images of society'. Recent sociological work has shown this, amplifying what is readily apparent in the historical record.[77]

The third of the positions to be outlined is the association of change in the division of labour with transitions from one sort of work mentality to another, more especially a concern with the *loss* rather than the retention of control over the immediate work situation, a process held to have reached a significant stage in the 'leading sectors' of cotton and engineering by the mid-nineteenth century. This has been elaborated by Stedman Jones in his critique of Foster, and is further developed in the present writer's work.[78] Very briefly, what is at issue is the loss of the worker's technical indispensability and the development of a new tempo and organisation of production attendant on the machine, no longer on quasi-handicraft production. The cultural changes seen to arise from this break in craft control are in their work aspect understood as the transition from the struggle over control to that over the product, or wages. The outcome is a narrowing of horizons from the customary psychology of the craft that involves workers operating within and accepting the parameters of the capitalist organisation of authority in industry.

There is much wrong with this, as the account of industrial 'archaism' will already have indicated. More particularly, Lazonick's

[76]   Price, *Masters, Unions and Men.*
[77]   Cousins and Brown, 'Patterns of Paradox'; Joyce, *Work, Society and Politics, passim.*
[78]   Stedman Jones, 'England's First Proletariat'.

work on the cotton spinners shows how if technical indispensability was in part lost (and even then for the coarse not the fine spinners) then capitalist dependence on the spinners' supervisory capacity argues the retention of some real purchase on production and of elements of a 'craft' mentality.[79] The spinner–employer relationship ought in fact best be seen as a classic example of the interdependence of capital and labour spoken of here. Clearly, then, this approach tends to exaggerate both de-skilling and the degree of dependence experienced by workers. It also generalises too readily on the basis of supposed 'leading sectors'. The general theoretical background is also probably too imprecise and abstract for historical use, namely the Marxian notion of 'Modern Industry', and the supposed transition from 'formal' (wage-based) to 'real' (machine-based) capitalist control over the labour process.[80] Yet there are still considerable problems in ignoring the degree of real change that took place.

In the cotton industry, as well as in textiles in general, skills were lost and down-graded as well as retained and extended: beside the rather misleading figure of the cotton mule spinner should be set that of the handloom weaver. More than skill was, of course, lost or retained, namely communal identities deeply interwoven with the cultures of work: one thinks of situations of domestic production not only in textiles but in a wide range of industries. This complex movement of gain and loss may be too easily lost to view in the concentration on continuity and adaptation arising from the idea of uneven economic development. The sudden or gradual destruction of craft skill and standing was seen in a range of industries outside the vast textile sector. Whether as the product of technological change or managerial reorganisation of the division of labour, the factory, the workshop and outwork production saw changes that exposed the worker to a vulnerability and dependence in the labour market that has to be set beside the evidence for strength and independency. This degree of dependence has in turn been augmented by the often perilously insecure nature of jobs and wages. One has laid particular stress on the interdependence of capital and labour, but this should not obscure the fact this was so often not a relationship of equals: the effect of dependence and economic insecurity led to accommodations with capital based on coercion and necessity, the nature of which as yet remains obscure in the historical record. Under particular conditions

[79] Lazonick, 'Industrial Relations and Technical Change'.
[80] See Stedman Jones, 'England's First Proletariat', for this distinction.

these accommodations might go beyond mere 'pragmatic acceptance' to a more deeply ingrained deferential culture of poverty.

Thus, these aspects need to be on the agenda, though now severed from the idea of a linear and uniform process of de-skilling and loss of workplace control. The extension from concrete and immediate work situations to workers' evaluations of work also raises important matters that should not be minimised; though the extension seen in this third 'position' from relinquished craft control to the transition from craft, customary mentalities to skilled, market-orientated ones is, to say the least, problematic. If it did take place, such a change, even in the most 'advanced' sector of textiles, was partial and incomplete, involving the interpenetration and not the substitution of custom and the market. It must be said that the work that has taken up this sequence of developments (Foster, Stedman Jones, Joyce, etc.) has failed to work out the links in the chain. Also, the seminal essay of Hobsbawm on the decay of customary evaluations of work never in fact establishes the internalisation of new evaluations.[81] The reality of the link between work processes and evaluations is, of course, itself open to question, and the exploration of the destiny of customary attitudes will usefully be undertaken in terms of ideological pressures (from clergymen and employers, for example) that may not be related directly or at all to material changes. The whole area is, in fact, ripe for investigation despite the superficial appearance of overkill. It is necessary to bear in mind here the earlier reference to how little is known of the interior life of the workplace and of workers' and others' representations of work.

The matter of workers' evaluations or representations of work nonetheless introduces questions of transition that the emphasis on continuity and adaptation may miss. The stress on changes from customary to market-based criteria in industrial bargaining has been associated with the wider question of the transmission and acceptance of managerial authority in capitalist industry. The first of the positions outlined here, the labour aristocracy, can in fact be interpreted as a sub-species of the more general question of the consolidation of authority in capitalist industry in the course of the nineteenth century. One is at leave, however, to accept the problem but reject the labour aristocracy 'solution'. Similarly, it is feasible to reject much if not all of the traditional Marxist economic framework but still recognise

---

[81]   Hobsbawm, 'Custom, Wages and Work Load'.

that questions like the internalisation of capitalist industrial authority among workers are real questions.

Around the mid-nineteenth century the sequence of changes posited here in terms of bargaining and authority have been linked in historical scholarship to wider sequences, in particular the recognition by workers (and indeed capitalists) that industrial capitalism was no longer potentially transitory, but something increasingly seen as natural or at least irreversible, to be adapted to by workers rather than by-passed, evaded or forgotten[82] (though again, it must be said that the links between the widely separate areas of change involved in such transformations have been made in only the most empirically sketchy of ways). This sort of perspective on industrial capitalism as an economic and cultural *system* suggests parallels with developments such as the separation of work and non-work time, a process involving both ideological influences and the material decay of forms of production involving the family and home in which work and non-work time were not separated. Now, it will already be apparent that the thesis of combined and uneven development sets the cat among many of these pigeons. But, if our theoretical positions as much as our chronologies are in need of drastic revision, it is still the case that real changes were going on that can be too easily lost to view. Traditional Marxist positions if weak on solutions are strong on problems.

Before taking up at more length questions of transition and uniformity in the economic and cultural spheres (questions necessarily offset against the dominant emphasis on continuity and diversity here), positions that have a particular affinity with this dominant emphasis will be considered. The term 'position' is perhaps incorrect: the ramifications of the recognition of combined and uneven economic development are still being worked out. This chapter is indeed part of that working out. The older picture of the economy carried with it a corresponding picture of the working class, as increasingly homogeneous in condition and experience, whether as de-skilled proletarians or mass urban dwellers. Class consciousness issued fairly unproblematically out of this position. Classically Marxist in a technical sense, this reading has been dispersed widely in very often non-Marxist historical work, but especially in popular understandings of industrial society. The new reading of the economy and the division of labour leads in

---

[82] Hobsbawm, *Industry and Empire*, p. 123. For a theoretical position in Marx, unfinished but suggestive, that ties together some of these aspects, see C. Johnson, 'The Problem of Reformism and Marx's Theory of Fetishism', *New Left Review*, 119 (1980).

somewhat different directions. The lack of any markedly uniform or unilinear change indicates a multiform 'working class': tendencies to unity are always offset by tendencies to fragmentation; economic changes are always creating new sources of division among wage earners even as they undermine others.

The challenge posed to orthodox accounts is clear; namely, are the old categories still valid and merely need to be applied more carefully (in the sense that everything happened more slowly and unevenly than previously claimed), or, more radically, do we need a new set of explanatory categories altogether? The account given in this chapter would tend to suggest that the choice may not be quite so stark: the older readings have some validity when their teleological and deterministic aspects are discounted; new readings and categories need to incorporate rather than negate older ones. But of the necessity of new bearings in the history of labour there is no doubt.

The most fully worked out approach to alternative readings is to be found in the very suggestive recent work of Alastair Reid,[83] where the recognition of the importance of combined and uneven development is especially keenly present. This response does not represent a necessary implication of the recognition of uneven development, but as a coherently worked out if exploratory approach it does have the advantage of introducing the wide range of questions demanding attention. The basic idea here is that of intense competition between workers over the allocation of tasks and the definition of skills, a competition in turn arising from the relative abundance of labour and intense cyclical fluctuations in output and employment opportunities. Competition is seen to arise from insecurity in earnings and in the demarcation of tasks. Working very much in line with recent fashions in social history, economics and politics are held at arms length: the consciousness of class is seen as the outcome of specific historical processes in which ideologies and institutions play a crucial role, and not as a 'natural' response to underlying economic and social conditions. To quote from Reid, who elsewhere observes that the working class is spontaneously divided not spontaneously united,

The process of the containment of the working class does not then require 'special' explanations whether in the form of a labour aristocracy, social control or the cultural subordination of crucial strata, all of which tend to assume that, left to itself, the working class would be spontaneously united and revol-

---

[83]   A. Reid, 'Politics and Economics in the Formation of the British Working Class: A Response to H. F. Moorhouse', *Social History*, 3 (1978).

utionary due to its economic position. On the contrary, defeat is the normal not the abnormal condition of the working class under capitalism, for in the absence of consciously formulated politics and carefully constructed alliances, it is only able spontaneously to sustain temporary sectional revolts.[84]

This is certainly one response to the notion of uneven development, but it is not altogether a successful one. In order to develop further the questions raised earlier, and to evolve a hopefully more rounded response to the real nature of economic change, this position will be criticised, at first in terms of the particular case,[85] then the general problems it raises. Reid's approach is based upon shipbuilding, in which the division of labour was perhaps more sectionalised than in any other industry at the time. The sectional divisions envisaged are in fact rather narrowly derived from work-based studies of the division of labour and from the pattern of bargaining between workers and employers. What is missing is a sense of the *social* relationships between workers, outside work but also within the work situation. Within work one can conceive of the solidarities based on the individual shop, the enterprise itself, or the particular craft, and the general identification with craft workers as a whole. Rather ironically, the derivation of generalisations from studies of work-based sectionalism raises the charge of economic determinism: instead of the old orthodoxy of spontaneous unity a new one of spontaneous division on economic lines!

These points raise general questions, in particular the need to balance tendencies to fragmentation with those to unity. In this kind of approach the necessary tension between the two, seen to arise from a proper understanding of the great diversity of the economy, tends to be resolved arbitrarily in favour of the former. There is also the danger of wage labour being regarded as too abstract a category from which some form of collective consciousness could arise. Thus, such consciousness is always a product of ideology and politics. The position taken here is rather to identify wage labour as a category of great complexity and ambiguity, developing very irregularly, but not therefore to see it as too 'abstract' to be productive of social consciousness.

The picture of the working class presented in these accounts, in which the flux of cultural fission and fusion reflects the flux of the

[84] *Ibid.*, p. 361.
[85] H. F. Moorhouse, 'History, Sociology and the Quiescence of the British Working Class: A Reply to Reid', *Social History*, 4 (1979), pp. 488–90.

economy, tends to ignore or minimise the extent to which change and discontinuity set up new patterns in economic and cultural life that if not uniform and unilinear were, however, increasingly widespread and regular in their effect. In the discussion of the previous position under review these problems have been considered in some detail, especially as they relate to forces attenuating conflictual class consciousness. But exactly the same general point can be made about forces operating in the opposite direction. As well as extra-economic pressures making for unity there are crucial economic ones: strikes, for instance, frequently may have been sectional in character, but the first object of the exercise was more often the employer, not the worker. Strikes established continuities of memory and tradition which often cemented solidarities across a wider field than the occupation or 'section' alone. Similarly, the main fact about trade unions would not be that they were sectional-minded but that they existed at all. That they do exist is surely testimony not merely to 'conscious' politics and 'constructed' alliances but to shared work-derived experiences of a common socio-economic position – at an inter-trade and trade level – without which conscious stratagems would be illusory.

The point to stress is that tendencies to unity and a resulting class consciousness based on a common class 'position' can be geographically and industrially localised, emergent or declining at different times and under different conditions. To admit this, and to recognise the special importance of periods of political and economic crisis, is not to disallow the notion of class consciousness, unless we wish to apply hopelessly idealised criteria. Such a period of crisis was (roughly) the 1830s, and 1840s, such a place the cotton districts of south Lancashire. Recent research reveals how, across a wide range of trades, factory and non-factory, similarities of economic situation and political perception unified sectional experience.[86] The crisis was economic and political; and so was its resolution, in terms of the stabilisation of the mid-Victorian economy and the changed face that a once oppressive state now presented to workers. The point is that class *was* a product of economic as well as political change, and that it eventuated in behaviour and attitudes in which the 'economic' was inextricably bound up with the 'political'. Nor is it difficult to discern at this time a coalescence of diverse and sectional occupational exper-

---

[86]   See the copious R. A. Sykes, 'Popular Politics and Trade Unionism in South-East Lancashire, 1829–1842', 2 vols. (unpublished PhD thesis, Manchester University, 1982).

ience into a more common experience of capitalism as unbridled and amoral competition, a coalescence which found institutional expressions in politics and economics (Chartism and inter-trade-union co-operation for example) that unified workers not only across occupational but also geographical lines.[87] Historians, rightly, would now regard this consciousness of class as more fragile and less a matter of class 'made' (no longer in the making) than was once thought. But the question of continuity still asserts itself: if class feeling was a reality, where did it get to? It must be said that the accent on political autonomy, diversity and fragmentation does not handle the question of inherited organisational modes and cultural values very well.

It will also be apparent that the compartmentalisation of politics and economics creates problems. 'Class' is never the mere rising to consciousness of some underlying economic reality; it is always mediated by ideological and political means. But it is the terms of this mediation that are open to question, especially the accent on deliberate and conscious manoeuvre, choice and negotiation at a, broadly, 'political' level. Class consciousness and political choices themselves, are a product of a variety of contexts, ranging from work to family life, education and religion. These contexts repress or express class feeling and form attitudes in a thousand subtle ways, by gesture and language, ritual and symbol. It is upon this ground that conscious manoeuvre is exercised. If work is not the only ground upon which economics, class and politics are linked it is an important one. The example of artisan culture comes to mind. The care with which notions of a unitary 'artisan' culture have to be approached is indicated by the great irregularity and diversity of occupational life. Nonetheless, for many nineteenth-century craft workers, the trade does seem to have conferred important moral categories of honour, dignity and worth. The trade and the workplace also acted as collectivities focussing disparate areas of experience, connecting the sphere of work with home life, fellowship, education, politics and much else. And this conception of work was important for politics, just as all worker notions of justice, freedom and dignity are derived in large part from the experience of labour. In constituting many of the key categories of consciousness, rhetoric and language that, as it were, intervene between economic processes and political attitudes, such notions are surely integral to the constitution and meaning of political attitudes.

---

[87] To the works of E. P. Thompson, Prothero, Behagg, etc., already cited can be added that of D. Goodway, *London Chartism, 1838–1848* (Cambridge, 1982).

Such a key category in the nineteenth century was 'independence' which straddled work and politics. Derived in large measure from work, it was a central element in 'artisan' support for radicalism and Liberalism.[88] There is a danger that new currents in 'social' history will lead back to the old and narrowly conceived political history.

IV

In order to present a balanced account countervailing tendencies to irregularity and uniformity in the economy, and unity and fragmentation in social consciousness, have been traced, especially in the preceding section. Historical change produced divisions of labour in which old and new forms of production were combined, and in which the power of the past was profoundly influential. The industrial phase of capitalism co-existed with earlier forms of capitalist production and in turn generated new non-industrial forms. The rise of industry did not mean the ubiquity of machine-based factory production. But neither should it be inferred that this rise was illusory, nor that because of the unevenness of the economic structure industrial capital did not come to exercise political and economic dominance. The accent on continuity and archaism carries with it certain dangers, dangers to which revisionist historians of British business and the enigmatic 'industrial spirit' are prone.[89] Older modes of production and cultural structures may persist in a social formation, and if the salience of the new is less marked than we often suppose this does not mean that the dominance of the new may not be real, though it does mean that this dominance will have to be realised, and questioned, in more subtle ways than have yet been attempted. Whig interpretations on the one hand, both Marxist and non-Marxist, and fashionable, revisionist ones on the other, probably share a common avoidance of the necessary difficulties involved. In depicting the history of labour rather than capital, the history of the factory as presented here indicates somewhat analogous problems. While not until late and then incompletely did it come to dominate the experience of work, it affected the structure of production and the experience of productive life at all levels. Similarly, the imperatives of new forms of production were registered in politics and the political regulation of economic life.

[88] Prothero, *Artisans and Politics*, pp. 339–40; and J. Vincent, *The Formation of the Liberal Party, 1857–1868* (1966).

[89] M. J. Wiener, *English Culture and the Decline of the Industrial Spirit, 1850–1980* (Cambridge, 1981); A. Meyer, *The Persistence of the Old Regime* (1981).

Above all, perhaps, the factory exercised a sway over people's minds that has secured for it a central place in the cultural symbolism of the industrial countries to this day. In this sense the history of the factory is the history of myth, though nonetheless real for that. This, however, is a history that cannot be pursued now.

The purpose of the present exercise, while recognising the powerful, indirect effect of the factory, is to penetrate mythology and reconstitute contemporary situations and perceptions. Existing accounts are often inadequate, and it will be apparent that the picture of the economy presented here on the whole emphasises the shortcomings of notions based in economic terms on the paradigm of the factory, the machine and direct capitalist control of labour; and in social terms on notions of class formation predicated on an increasing homogeneity of economic and social condition and aspiration, and an increasing sense of economic class conflict. Instead, the extremely diverse socio-economic position of workers has been urged, a position explored in the consideration of irregularity and diversity in the occupation and in work time. Some of the consequences of this complex and open-ended process of proletarianisation have been indicated in terms of the diverse and ambiguous experience and perception of workers; perceptions such as that of the role of work and occupations in cultural self-definitions, the perception of industrial conflict, and the understanding of social relationships with other groups and classes. Instead of a putative unity of consciousness based on a common situation of wage dependency, what begins to emerge is a fragmented series of perceptions which are themselves disjointed and ambiguous in the sense that they cannot be comprehended by our current and crude dichotomies of dependence and independence, cultural fragmentation and unity, but in turn relate directly to the ambiguous nature of wage dependency. This general picture has in turn been supported by other aspects of this account of work: the late-developing and complex forms of supposedly 'traditional' working-class community life; the influence of the Irish; and in particular the question of the relationships of workers and employers.

Special attention has been given to this because the complexity of the socio-economic position of the working class is especially clearly revealed in the area of social relations with and perceptions of employers. It is in this area too that one is questioning a central tenet of classical Marxist positions, the crucial importance for class formation of the opposition of capitalist employer and proletarian workers. One is also doubting whether the relationships obtaining in any historical period between employers and workers can be sensibly read as involving an inherent and steadily intensifying tendency to conflict. Rather than one inbuilt and overmastering deterministic quality it is necessary to conceive of tendencies to conflict, compromise and co-operation as being fairly evenly balanced, outcomes being dependent on the historical context and particular balance of forces at play. In short, it is necessary to balance contradiction and conflict with an awareness of the reciprocity obtaining between employer and workers.

The importance of considering the shared perspectives of capital and labour has not generally been recognised. The emphasis on conflict alone obscures the degree to which the relationship of worker and employer was and is about mutual as well as opposed interests. Conceiving of this relationship as reciprocal in character helps to identify this central ambiguity by pointing up the fact that both sides were involved in recognising and accepting (or at least tolerating) the rights and prerogatives of the other if industry and employment were to continue. A bargain, sometimes conceived as a partnership, is involved, and if this bargain is conditional and unstable, it is nonetheless a persistent feature of industrial relations.[90] The reciprocal nature of the bargain extends far beyond economic matters alone, involving as it does notions of what is permissible and proper behaviour.

The anachronism of considering popular protest and trade custom as exclusively conflictual and economically class based has been suggested. Notions of the trade as a community of interests have been indicated, as have those of the utility and worth of employers, and it seems likely that these persisted into new forms of industry in the nineteenth and twentieth centuries, accentuated as they appear to have been by the archaic structure of the new. This continuity was reflected in the delegation and hence the complex ramification of authority in industry, also by such matters as pride in work, in tools and machines, and in the product itself (important in an age of the 'bespoke' product), matters that have too often been seen as solely conflictual in their implications. Customary notions of work were displaced by notions more closely related to the market, yet this was and has

---

[90]   For further consideration see Joyce, 'Capital, Labour and Compromise'; *idem*, 'Languages of Reciprocity and Conflict'.

since never been anything but a partial change. The change was managed in terms of the cultural capital workers had, and this involved both the independence and the reciprocities inherent in the ethic of the craft. How these transformations occurred is as yet unclear, but it can be suggested that we need to look closely at how new justifications of work built upon older ones and did not merely negate them. This process of handling and interpreting a deepening capitalist economy brought the potential for identifying interests as well as differentiating them. It was a double process that goes some way to explaining the mixture of militance and conservatism characteristic of the British labour movement. On the one hand, rights have been defended and elaborated. On the other, this has usually been within the terms of the prevailing economic and institutional order. In this respect, bearing in mind that the anti-capitalist challenge of the early nineteenth century seems to have been accompanied by little sustained attack upon the capitalist ownership and control of industry, the customary past may not be as different from subsequent developments as is often thought.

The stress on continuity has, however, to be related to the growth, after the 1840s especially, of justifications of work in which, for workers and employers, the conditions of marketplace bargaining began to co-exist with custom. These justifications were experienced in the older terms of independence and reciprocity, but they also led in new directions. These directions were ambiguous, because if they led to the assertion of new rights and to an increasing awareness that the social relations of labour and capital were economic in character and hence conflictual given the contradictions of the market, they were also counter balanced by the tendency to accept most of the prerogatives of capitalist ownership and authority, and to extend to the market itself a high degree of legitimacy in the regulation of economic life. Nevertheless, perceptions of the market and the economic as determining factors were always lived in terms of the cultural categories of inherited modes of perceiving the employment relation. For workers and employers that relation was rarely reducible to a simple cash nexus, but was rooted in the categories of independence and reciprocity. It is necessary to interpret the changes those categories have undergone in extra-economic as well as economic terms, and to see that they carry a potential for compromise and co-operation as well as for conflict. Conflict can be realised just as much in disrupted reciprocities as co-operation can be by the recognition of independence.

It is also in this area that older accounts of economic change and class formation are especially open to question. The thought given in this chapter to potential ways in which a new reading of the division of labour and of the experience of work might inform our accounts of social and political change has nonetheless indicated that there is a fairly close link between the experience of work and wider perceptions of social relations. This is not to say that work was or is the sole or main source of such cultural and political perceptions or of class identification: far from it, as will be clear from the preceding section. Nor is it maintained that there is a unilinear, deterministic relationship between socio-economic position, common consciousness and organisation: it is not the case that all things being equal, in the sense of an unambiguous and widespread form of wage labour obtaining, working-class consciousness and organisation will develop.

However, it needs to be emphasised that unless economic position and work experience are articulated with these other sources of class identity (education, home, etc.) then it is difficult to see how we can retain established notions of a 'working class'. If, for instance, we are dealing with political sources of class identification – such as the recognition of interests in common arising from antagonism with an adversary state – unless these sources are related in experience and ideology to the area of production then we are in fact dealing with political categories *per se*. One returns to the point about E. P. Thompson's influential ideas of class made earlier: we need to be clear in speaking of the 'working class' what it is to which we refer; a common consciousness arising from a shared and usually life-long condition of waged labour, involving a positive identification with the values of manual work, or political categories such as 'the people', the product of political traditions and alliances running across the imprecise boundaries between workers and others.

The latter is often compared with the former. Such political categories have been very important in British history, but it is difficult to see what they have to do with a working class strictly defined, or for that matter with class at all, a term connoting relations of exclusion, and super- and sub-ordination, as well as struggle and moral solidarity. The universalistic and inclusive moral tone of class vocabularies in much of the nineteenth century and later, for France as well as Britain,[91] if very marked was also often far removed from class in these senses. More generally, it may be that the categories of explanation needed would be 'social conflict' rather than 'class conflict', or 'plebeian' and 'popular' rather than 'working class'. Though socio-economic position does not necessarily lead to class consciousness and class organisation, it is difficult to conceive of the category of 'working class' having much historical relevance or empirical use if the socio-economic situation of workers, which surely has a considerable import on social consciousness, involves an almost endless series of fractured and disjointed economic positions and cultural perceptions.

It is suggested here that such is probably not the case, and that the roots of class consciousness that lie in work experience are very important, but to suggest this fragmentation and to pursue analysis in this direction is important too. The hold of the orthodox categories of both labour history and social history is breaking down, as the material of history is being released for recombination in ways no longer petrified within these categories. The same applies to issues in the history of work outside class formation and the relationship between capital and labour. Instead of an inherent logic of industrialisation in which economically rational market forces, or an omniscient capital and pliant labour, dictated an unswerving path from decentralised to centralised, more efficient, forms of mechanised mass production, historians are increasingly aware of the extra-industrial economic factors and the entirely non-economic factors that have shaped the division of labour and industrialisation. In the transition to factory production, for instance, the forces involved ranged from the distribution of agricultural holdings to the social and political environment of industry. This in turn suggests the role of popular taste, the agency of the family, custom and community, and the political and institutional context at a local and national level. Thus an economic history and a social history that refute the category of the economic when isolated from its human context have much in common. They alike seek to think anew the history of industrialisation and of work handed down to us by previous generations, which if answering to their times does not answer to ours.

---

[91]   Sewell, *Work and Revolution in France*, pp. 281–4.

POSTSCRIPT: THE MOST RECENT HISTORIOGRAPHY

A chapter in a multi-authored volume which happened to be the first to be submitted inevitably, by the time of publication, cannot take account of the most recent developments in what is an extremely active field of enquiry and debate. A brief discussion of the most recent literature may, therefore, be found useful.

This chapter seeks to explore some of the implications of a reading of the industrial revolution, the general character of which has recently, and most usefully, been set in the context of long-term changes in the interpretation of industrial development in Britain.[92] The arguments presented above are rather insistent in their emphasis upon the need to consider the employment relation as consensual as well as conflictual in character. Subsequently, this interpretation has been given weight and depth in the sociological literature,[93] and has begun to be developed further in historical writing.[94] Whether historical or sociological, investigations of the nature and history of work have continued to be powerfully informed by the literature on what has come to be called the labour process.[95] The attempt to build upon as well as go beyond the characteristic emphases of earlier labour process approaches to consider the institutional, social and political forces acting upon the division of labour has also been evident.[96]

There is still, however, much to be gained from a close consideration of work organisation and practices. In this chapter much attention has been given to the example of the spinner in cotton textiles. Since Marx's day this emblematic figure – part artisan, part proletarian –

[92] D. Cannadine, 'The Past and the Present in the English Industrial Revolution 1880–1980', *Past & Present*, 103 (1984).

[93] Above all in the work of M. Burawoy, *The Politics of Production: Factory Regimes under Capitalism and Socialism* (1985), and *Manufacturing Consent: Changes in the Labour Process under Monopoly Capitalism* (Chicago, 1979).

[94] For instance, R. Price, 'Conflict and Co-Operation: A Reply to Patrick Joyce', *Social History*, 9 (1984); C. Behagg, 'Myths of Cohesion: Capital and Compromise in the Historiography of Nineteenth-Century Birmingham', *Social History*, 11 (1986).

[95] For a useful guide to the labour process debates see P. Thompson, *The Nature of Work: An Introduction to the Debates on the Labour Process* (1983). For historical writing so informed, see R. Price, *Labour in British Society* (1986), also R. Harrison and J. Zeitlin, eds., *Divisions of Labour: Skilled Workers and Technological Change in Nineteenth Century England* (Brighton, 1985). The latter has much information on the picture of irregular and uneven capitalist industrial development presented in this chapter, as well as on the endemic sectionalism of skilled workers.

[96] For example, C. F. Sabel, *Work and Politics: The Division of Labour in Industry* (Cambridge, 1982); see also the review article by J. Zeitlin, 'Social Theory and the History of Work', *Social History*, 8 (1983), and G. Salaman and C. R. Littler, *Class at Work* (1984), chaps. 3–6. Burawoy's work also exemplifies this broadening of interests.

has been the subject of intense scrutiny. In presenting a picture of the reciprocal relations obtaining between workers and employers, I have drawn upon the example of the spinner, turning to recent research on the subject. Since then, cotton spinning has been subject to yet further scrutiny,[97] which deepens our understanding, yet further throws into relief the necessity for such detailed consideration of the labour process. It still remains the case that some rather large claims in the writing of social history are often based upon a very schematic understanding of work practice. It is necessary to move beyond the excessive concentration on the division of labour, and the labour process, however widely conceived, to consider work in its full cultural significance and context. Work is as much moral as economic. The need for such a fuller history of work has been a major concern of this chapter. In recent years there is every sign that such a history is forthcoming.[98] Attempts to devalue the history of work so conceived in favour of institutional approaches are already evident in the literature.[99] This redirection of labour history towards the history of industrial relations is surely both narrow and retrograde.

The chapter pursues the proletarian in order to explore what significance this elusive and ambiguous figure has for our understanding of class. In emphasising class 'position' or the socio-economic character of labour it to some extent underplays the significance of other forces acting upon the formation of social identities and the capacities for labour and political mobilisation and organisation. Other structural

---

[97] M. Freifeld, 'Technological Change and the "Self-Acting" Mule: A Study of Skill and the Sexual Division of Labour', *Social History*, 11 (1986). In the terms of the argument as conducted in this chapter this article would perhaps tend to switch the emphasis back to the independence of labour rather than the interdependence of capital and labour. However, of the deepening reality of capitalist control over the labour process in the later nineteenth century there should be no doubt. For this, and the resulting recognition of joint interests between labour and capital evident among skilled workers, see K. McClelland, 'Time to Work, Time to Live: Some Aspects of Work and the Re-Formation of Class in Britain, 1850–1880', in P. Joyce, ed., *The Historical Meanings of Work* (Cambridge, 1987).

[98] S. L. Kaplan and C. J. Koepp, eds., *Work in France: Representations, Meaning, Organization, and Practice* (Ithaca and London, 1986); B. Roberts, R. Finnegan and D. Gallie, eds., *New Approaches to Economic Life* (Manchester, 1985); Joyce, ed., *The Historical Meanings of Work*, especially the editor's introduction.

[99] J. Zeitlin, 'From Labour History to the History of Industrial Relations', *Economic History Review*, 2nd ser., 40 (1987). Zeitlin's case is not helped by the direction of his fire upon perhaps the weakest brigade in the anyway rather spectral army he confronts, namely what he terms 'rank and filism'. His account of 'history of work' or 'social historical' approaches is undiscriminating in the extreme.

factors are important, such as demographic change and socio-spatial patterns. Cultural and ideological elements such as gender, religion and ethnicity receive some but not enough attention here. In particular, the roles of the state and political systems need emphasis: for instance, the different paths taken by the English and German working classes clearly owe much to the more open state and party system in one, and the more closed or negative character of institutions in the other. In recent work on class formation in Western Europe and the United States this broad range of formative influences receives close consideration.[100] Nonetheless, the questions asked here about the process of proletarianisation remain of critical importance. What it is that the range of forces considered here is actually interacting with is too often assumed to be a uniform and homogeneous 'working class'. It is clearly anything but this, and once this is realised the social identities and capacities for action resulting from the range of formative influences considered, such as the character of the state, take on new and unexplored forms.

Whether these forms can be described by the concepts of class at all is now very much an open question. This root-and-branch rejection of class is evident in Reddy's recent work.[101] This has the merit of going beyond negative denials of class in attempting to put new interpretations in their place, rather than writing class off as a rather nasty and manipulative form of rhetoric,[102] a position characteristic of some liberal and many rightists perspectives. However, whether the answer Reddy comes up with in his extremely stimulating work is the right one is I think open to question.[103]

This chapter offers a measured and qualified defence of the notion of class. But this in turn only serves as a preface to a closer analysis of the concrete forms class took, and the ways in which it was, and is, always closely related to other forms of social identity and collective action; forms that were as important, and often more important, than

---

[100]   Katznelson and Zolberg, eds., *Working Class Formation*.

[101]   W. M. Reddy, *Money and Liberty in Modern Europe: A Critique of Historical Understanding* (Cambridge, 1987); see also *idem*, *The Rise of Market Culture: The Textile Trade and French Society, 1750–1900* (Cambridge, 1984).

[102]   P. N. Furbank, *Unholy Pleasure, or the Idea of Social Class* (Oxford, 1985).

[103]   P. Joyce, 'In Pursuit of Class: Recent Studies in the History of Work and of Class', *History Workshop Journal*, 25 (1988).

class itself.[104] This chapter draws on the work of Stedman Jones in emphasising political and populist sources of social identity and action. It seems to me that these were very important in British history, but that the existing terminology – for instance the term 'populism' – is altogether misleading for what it is that needs to be explored. Questions of terminology bear heavily upon questions of language and ideology. In the criticism of Stedman Jones's formalistic understanding of language and ideology that has been forthcoming there is a new and increasingly sensitive attention to the forms and deployment of language and ideology as these interact with social circumstances.[105] That class is again on the historical agenda for the British case may seem surprising: accounts of class formation in Europe and the United States still tend to look at the British case as one where the class question is sealed and settled. As the structure and outlook of class change with bewildering rapidity in the Britain of the 1980s this is far from being the case.

Finally, while concentrating upon particular aspects of the history of work, I have attempted to convey some impression, however inadequate, of the changing nature and experience of work over this lengthy period and across the span of many occupations. Recent work has done much to illuminate knowledge of aspects only briefly considered here,[106] and readers will find in the bibliography further reference to works in an area of study at once broad, diverse and challenging.

Acknowledgements

I wish to thank Dr Alastair Reid and Dr Jonathan Zeitlin for reading and commenting upon an earlier draft of this chapter. My special thanks are due

[104] Michelle Perrot is one of the few historians to have explored the concrete forms of a specifically 'working-class' outlook, where the sense of being a proletarian and a manual worker are quite central, 'On the Formation of the French Working Class', in Katznelson and Zolberg, eds., *Working Class Formation*. In a forthcoming book, *Visions of the People: Conceptions of the Social Order in England before 1914* (Cambridge, 1990), I attempt to consider this inter-relation of different sources of identity and action, as well as examine the different 'languages' of class: political, economic and imaginative.

[105] See especially R. Gray, 'The Deconstruction of the English Working Class', *Social History*, 11 (1986); also P. A. Pickering, 'Class Without Work: Symbolic Communication in the Chartist Movement', *Past & Present*, 112 (1986). For an account less sensitive to these matters and to the problematic character of class yet of much relevance to the relationship of work and class, see M. Savage, *The Dynamics of Working Class Politics* (Cambridge, 1987).

[106] On the experience of agricultural work, see K. Snell, *Annals of the Labouring Poor: Social Change and Agrarian England 1660–1900* (Cambridge, 1985); or on the experience of labour in the eighteenth century, see M. Berg, *The Age of Manufactures 1700–1820* (1985); J. Rule, ed., *English Trade Unionism, 1750–1850: The Formative Years* (1988).

to my colleagues at Manchester University, Dr John Breuilly and Dr Iorwerth Prothero. I also wish to thank Mr Keith McClelland, Dr John Seed, and Dr Richard Whipp for their comments. The advice of these scholars has contributed greatly to what value this chapter may have. None of them is responsible for its limitations.

CHAPTER 4

Housing

M. J. DAUNTON

'There are many ways of regarding the house', warned *The Builder* in 1881, 'and most of them, it must be confessed, are prosaic.'[1] This caution is salutary, but it may be that a concentration on two of the many possible approaches to the history of housing may avoid the perils of tedium. One is the relationship between design and society, between the physical form of housing and the social life it contains. The individual house could relate to the external environment in a variety of forms, with the threshold between private and public space drawn at different points and with more or less emphasis. The physical structure of the house might be articulated in a number of ways, with the internal space used in a more or less specialised or undifferentiated manner.[2] The second theme is the relationships which emerged from the ownership, management and occupation of housing. It is wrong to view houses merely as a collection of inert bricks and mortar, for they involved conflict over the distribution of income and resources between landlord and tenant, rates and rents, private enterprise and public initiatives. The outcome could affect not only the daily lives of residents, determining the amount they paid for accommodation and the terms on which it was held, but could also impinge on social structure and political debate. The emergence of a nation of owner-occupiers has very different social and political implications from a nation of tenants, and it is necessary both to explain how this change occurred, and to assess the consequences. These are two of many ways of viewing the house, but neither, it is hoped, is as prosaic as *The Builder* feared.

---

[1] *The Builder*, 40 (1881), p. 1.

[2] This is suggested by A. Rapoport, *House Form and Culture* (Englewood Cliffs, NJ, 1969), and W. Hillier and J. Hanson, *The Social Logic of Space* (Cambridge, 1984). These works are not sensitive to historical contexts; the best application to a precise time and place is R. J. Lawrence, *Le Seuil franchi: logement populaire et vie quotidienne en Suisse romande, 1860–1960* (Geneva, 1986).

STANDARDS AND DESIGN

Hermann Muthesius in 1904 remarked that 'in all its ideas and feelings, in its *mores*, its philosophies and in its whole outlook on life, England stands apart from the countries of the continent of Europe'. He went on to assert that

this difference is nowhere more striking than in the style of living. England is the only advanced country in which the majority of the population still live in houses, a custom that has survived all the political, social and economic changes that European civilisation has undergone in the past hundred and fifty years. Whereas on the continent these changes caused mass migration into the cities, where people became imprisoned in giant multi-storeyed barrack-like blocks, in England, where, indeed, industrial development had started so much earlier, they barely touched the inborn love of country life ... The Englishman sees the whole of life embodied in his house. Here, in the heart of his family, self-sufficient and feeling no great urge for sociability, pursuing his own interests in virtual isolation, he finds his happiness and his real spiritual comfort. Outside pleasures, the hubbub of the metropolitan streets, a visit to a Bierkeller or a cafe, are almost hateful to him.[3]

These comments are surely exaggerated, for not only were self-contained houses found in Belgium, but the public house was also a significant part of working-class social life in Britain. Muthesius had nevertheless raised some important points about British housing standards and design which intrigued both contemporary social commentators and modern historians.

Why, it must be asked, did England come to be so firmly associated with residence in self-contained houses? This was not the case, after all, in Scotland where the towns were characterised by 'giant multi-storeyed barrack-like blocks' as surely as in Germany. Britain thus presents a microcosm of the variation in housing styles within Europe, and these broad contrasts between two generic house styles in England and Scotland were further complicated by a number of other variations. The nature of a self-contained house in England or a tenement in Scotland would obviously vary between working-class and middle-class families, in size, standards, and the social use of the available space. The generic house type in England also varied regionally across the country, whilst it is also necessary to consider change over time. The distinction between the tenement and self-contained house provides the basic theme; class, place and time supply the variations.

[3]   H. Muthesius, *The English House* (Berlin, 1904–5; English edn, 1979), p. 7. The contrast noted by Muthesius forms a theme in D. J. Olsen, *The City as a Work of Art: London, Paris, Vienna* (1986).

I

Table 4.1 *Size distribution of dwellings, 1900–1*

		Percentage of all dwellings consisting of			
		1	2	3	4+
			rooms		
London	1901	14.7	19.8	17.8	47.8
Glasgow	1901	23.8	47.9	17.5	10.8
Berlin	1900	8.0	37.2	30.6	24.2
Paris	1901	26.7	30.1	21.8	21.4

Sources: Report of an Enquiry by the Board of Trade into Working-Class Rents, Housing and Retail Prices, PP 1908, CVII, p. 534; *Report . . . on the German Empire*, PP 1908, CVIII, p. 18; *Report . . . on France*, PP 1909, XCI, p. 16.

Housing in England and Scotland diverged in style, size and standard. Whereas English houses had a larger number of rooms assigned to specialised functions, Scottish tenements were closer to the European pattern of fewer undifferentiated rooms. In London about a third of dwellings in 1901 had one or two rooms, whilst in Glasgow the proportion was well over two-thirds, which was similar to the European capital cities of Paris and Berlin. The difference in both external appearance and internal layout was remarked upon in 1908:

There is little in common between working-class houses in Scotland and those in England. The typical residence of the working man, whether labourer or skilled mechanic, is, in England, a cottage of three, four or five rooms; in Scotland it is a flat of one, two or three rooms. The difference is reflected in the appearance of the towns. In an ordinary English industrial town, street after street of two-storey cottages built on an almost uniform plan are met with. In Scotland the cottage disappears and its place is taken by blocks of flats of two, three and four storeys; in Edinburgh, for example, the most usual type of tenement house is that of four storeys, each with four flats or sixteen in the block. As regards the flats themselves the rooms are generally much larger than those in an English cottage, and moreover, in nearly all tenements additional accommodation is afforded in one or two of the rooms, according to the number in the flat, by a 'bed recess', or space sufficient to contain a large bedstead.[4]

The housing styles and standards which emerged in England were associated with a favourable relationship between wages and rent. The ratio between the two variables may be expressed as 1.0 in England, with any lower number indicating a less, and any higher number a more, favourable relationship between supply and effective demand.

[4] *Report of an Enquiry by the Board of Trade into Working-Class Rents, Housing and Retail Prices*, PP 1908, CVII, p. xx.

Table 4.2 *Wages and rent levels in five countries, c. 1910*

	Index of weekly money wages	Index of net rent (ex. tax)	Ratio of wage to net rent
England and Wales	100	100	1.0
USA	230	207	1.1
Belgium	63	74	0.9
France	75	98	0.8
Germany	83	123	0.7

Source: M. J. Daunton, *House and Home in the Victorian City: Working-Class Housing, 1850–1914* (1983), p. 80.

The ratio was higher in the United States but consistently less favourable in Europe, most especially in Germany where rents were 23 per cent higher than in England although wages were 17 per cent lower. Belgian housing conditions and style were the nearest European equivalent to England, whereas Germany was particularly noted for the domination of 'giant multi-storeyed barrack-like blocks'. This relationship between wages and rent levels might similarly account for differences in housing standards and styles between England and Scotland.

In England, the least favourable ratio between wages and rents was in London and Plymouth, followed by Newcastle upon Tyne. London was, of course, a special case as the largest city in Europe, whilst Plymouth was unique amongst English towns for its pattern of residence in sub-divided large houses. The wage:rent ratio in most English towns ranged between 1.4 and 2.0, and any lower figure was an exception. In Scotland, however, the ratio did not rise above 1.2, and the large towns were trapped at the most unfavourable relationship between effective demand and supply which was found in England. Perhaps the most telling comparison is between Glasgow and Birmingham, the second and third largest towns in Britain. Birmingham had a wage:rent ratio of 1.7, whereas Glasgow had a wage:rent ratio of 1.2. The variation in the ratio had an immediate social and physical expression in the levels of overcrowding and the size of dwellings, for Scottish cities were consistently more overcrowded and dominated by smaller dwellings. How is this broad distinction between the two kingdoms to be explained?

Although Scotland had been a low-wage area in the early and mid-nineteenth century, this was no longer the case by the end of the century at least in the Lowlands. The unfavourable ratio between wages and rents found in 1905 would rather appear to be the result

Table 4.3 *Wages, rent, overcrowding and house size in British cities, 1905–11*

	Rent index 1905	Wage index (skilled builders) 1905	Ratio of wages to rent	Percentage of population in overcrowded conditions in 1911	Percentage of dwellings with three rooms or less in 1911
London	100	100	1.0	17.8	54.1
Plymouth	81	80	1.0	17.5	56.6
Newcastle	76	90	1.2	31.6	58.3
Sunderland	59	88	1.5	32.6	62.0
Bradford	59	83	1.4	9.3	43.2
Leeds	56	87	1.6	11.0	36.9
Burnley	53	85	1.6	9.5	16.3
Blackburn	50	87	1.7	4.4	5.3
Cardiff	59	92	1.6	4.8	22.2
Birmingham	59	98	1.7	10.1	33.7
Bristol	53	93	1.8	4.8	24.1
Leicester	48	94	2.0	1.1	6.1
Edinburgh	81	88	1.1	32.6	62.8
Aberdeen	68	79	1.2	37.8	74.5
Glasgow	76	91	1.2	55.7	85.2

Sources: Report of an Enquiry by the Board of Trade into Working-Class Rents, Housing and Retail Prices, PP 1908, CVII, pp. xxxviii–xxxix, l–li; 1911 Census of England and Wales, vol. VIII, Tables 3 and 4; 1911 Census of Scotland, vol. II, Tables XXXIX and XLV.

of the high level of rents, where the crucial variables were building costs and land prices. The cost of building was influenced in part by the regulations imposed by the Dean of Guild Courts which controlled building in Scottish cities, and in part by the structure of the Scottish building industry. A comparison between building regulations in Glasgow and London in 1904 indicated that in a building of two storeys, stone walls were 50 per cent, brick walls 25 per cent, and foundations 114 per cent thicker in Glasgow than in London. This difference in the cost of construction was exacerbated by the contrast in the size of building firms. Scottish builders tended to operate on a smaller scale than their English counterparts, and may in consequence have been less able to reduce unit costs of production.

It was also widely assumed that land prices were higher in Scottish than in English cities, reflecting a distinctive code of property law. Land in Scotland was normally held on a 'feu'. The original owner or 'superior' would grant the land to a 'vassal' in return for a fixed annual feu duty. The superior had parted with the freehold for an annual payment, and any future increase in value would be taken entirely by the vassal. The feu must therefore be distinguished from the short-lease system of England where there was a reversion of both land and building to the ground landlord at the end of the term. The lessor in England could balance short- and long-term considerations, for immediate development of the site at a lower ground rent would be compensated by the ultimate reversion of both site and building. In Scotland, no such compensation was possible and the superior, who was liquidating an irrecoverable asset, accordingly aimed to secure the highest possible feu duty once and for all. An English landlord who was selling the freehold would, in contrast, receive a lump sum which could be invested to produce both income and appreciation of capital. The legal system meant, it was argued, that Scottish land prices were higher than in both freehold and leasehold areas of England. The system of feuing and the construction of tenements were, asserted the Scottish Land Enquiry Committee, intimately connected:

> The exaction of high feu duties ... has ... a tendency to necessitate the erection of tenements in order to make it profitable to develop the land subject to these payments. The high price of land and the erection of tenement housing react upon one another, that is to say, the high price of land requires the erection of tenements to make the maximum use of it and to spread the burden of the feu duty over as many payers as possible, and conversely the power to erect tenements and to impose upon the land a very considerable property maintains the high value of the land.[5]

This analysis might, however, reflect the political desire of Liberals to explain housing problems by the land question rather than the realities of urban development.

Although a tenure similar to feuing – the chief rent – was found in Bristol, Sunderland and Manchester, tenements did not develop. Indeed, in continental cities tenements were constructed on freehold land. Feuing was a particular expression of a wider range of factors which influenced land prices. In England, a concentrated landownership pattern and tenant farms directed investible funds into capital accumulation, whereas in countries marked by fragmented ownership and peasant holdings funds were directed into purchases of land

---

[5] *Scottish Land: The Report of the Scottish Land Enquiry Committee*, p. 293.

whose price would consequently be inflated. Similarly, the price of building land in Berlin was high and rising in the late nineteenth century, in part because of the role of the municipality in purchasing land and holding it for development. The stricter planning controls in German cities could, as in Britain when 'green belts' were instituted, drive up the price of building sites.

Although the explanation is still problematical, the broad distinction between self-contained houses and tenements certainly led to adaptations of social life. Residence in tenements, much more than in self-contained houses, implied strict controls. The lack of privacy and need to share space could create problems, and 'where the number on the stairs is large the effect of a single undesirable family in lowering the general standard and making life difficult for the neighbours is correspondingly great'. This was of some importance for the owner as well as the residents, for tenements suffered from 'the grave disadvantage that the carelessness of one family may affect the whole tenement, and that it is more difficult to bring home responsibility to the defaulter than in the case of cottage property'.[6] The result was the creation of strict codes to regulate tenement life. The Burgh Police (Scotland) Act of 1892, for example, imposed various obligations governing the use of common space and facilities. Occupiers were responsible for cleaning stairs, landings and passages to the satisfaction of the sanitary inspector and a definite rota was established, but the most extreme form of control over property was the practice of 'ticketing' which started in Glasgow in 1866. A tin-plate ticket was fixed to the outer door of a property, stating the cubic contents and the number of occupants permitted. Houses were then visited by inspectors between midnight and 4 a.m. to ensure that the limit was not exceeded. Tenements required not only strict supervision; they also entailed close control by the owners. In a few cases this resulted in the use of resident caretakers on the lines of the *concierges* of Paris, but it was far more usual for house agents or factors to rely on assistants who visited the property. The problems of residence in tenements which 'necessitates a much greater degree of personal contact and communion than the English'[7] is certainly one explanation of the greater use of professional managers in Scottish cities.

[6] *RC on the Housing of the Industrial Population in Scotland*, PP 1917–18, XIV, p. 65.
[7] A. K. Chalmers, ed., *Public Health Administration in Glasgow: A Memorial Volume of the Writings of J. B. Russell* (Glasgow, 1905), p. 105.

There was a change over time both in the internal design of housing and in its relation to the external environment, and a crucial point in the analysis of urban form is the nature of the relationship which existed between the internal private domain of the house and the external public domain of the city. The important question becomes the nature, placement and permeability of the barrier or threshold between the two, for the transition may be sharp and abrupt or vague and ambiguous. It follows that the house should be considered not in isolation, but as part of a broader settlement system which underwent two changes during the period, one in the mid-nineteenth century and the other between the wars. But before explaining these changes, it is necessary to describe the settlement system which existed from 1750 until the readjustments of the mid-nineteenth century.

The price of urban land rose by perhaps 50 per cent between the 1780s and 1810s, which produced a more economical use of land, resulting in a dense packing of courtyards at the rear of houses on the main streets. A large part of the additional housing stock during the late eighteenth and early nineteenth centuries was the result of infilling of the existing built-up area or the sub-division of existing housing, with extensions to new land on the fringe of towns following the style which had emerged in the central districts. The result was a promiscuous sharing of facilities in the private domain of the house, a cellular quality of space in the public domain and a threshold between public and private which was ambiguous and permeable. The result could be the type of layout described by Engels in Manchester in 1844, where courts behind the main streets could be entered only by covered passages:

Of the irregular cramming together of dwellings in ways which defy all natural plan, of the tangle in which they are crowded literally one upon the other, it is impossible to convey the idea. And it is not the buildings surviving from the old times of Manchester which are to blame for this; the confusion has only recently reached its height when every scrap of space left by the old way of building has been filled up and patched over until not a foot of land is left to be further occupied.[8]

Wages and material prices in the building industry had started to rise in the 1790s, and this was exacerbated by the increase in land values. Although house prices increased from about 1800, they lagged

[8] F. Engels, *The Condition of the Working Class in England* (Panther edn, 1969), p. 81.

behind mounting costs during the Napoleonic Wars. It was not possible to raise rents in line with costs so 'the choice lay between squeezing profit margins or skimping on the use of materials, or both'.[9] Lower standards of construction, smaller houses and a denser use of land meant that in some ways living conditions in towns worsened between 1740 and 1820. But whilst there might have been some deterioration in the quality of housing, the quantity does appear to have kept pace with the mounting urban population. Of course, building was a cyclical phenomenon, with alternating periods of oversupply and shortage. It is difficult to separate the trend from the cycle in the census reports, but the average number of inhabitants per house in England and Wales remained fairly stable, at 5.67 in 1801, 5.68 in 1811 and 5.76 in 1821. There may have been severe temporary shortages in the troughs of the building cycle, and there may have been poorer standards of construction and increased density of land use, but 'on balance, it is likely that the secular pressure on living accommodation did not worsen in the industrial towns, and that in some it improved slightly'.[10] This ability of housing stock to keep pace with population growth is important given one of the characteristic demographic patterns of England: a newly married couple expected to establish a new household rather than, as in many cultures, to join an existing one. Unless sons delayed marriage until the death of their fathers, this pattern required a larger stock of housing than was necessary where residence in an extended family household was socially accepted. Since the age of marriage was in fact falling, there was a consequent increase in the demand for housing, and it would seem that supply was more or less able to keep pace so that housing shortages did not impose constraints on marriage and the formation of new households.

The houses built in the late eighteenth and early nineteenth centuries in industrial towns were fairly rudimentary. In Leeds, for example, cottages in the 1780s and 1790s were usually two-roomed, with a living room on the ground floor and a sleeping chamber above. In Liverpool and Nottingham, three-storeyed houses with one room per floor were more common. There was, in consequence, little differentiation in room use, and it was also usual for houses in a court to share facilities such as privies and water supply. In the course of the nineteenth

[9] C. W. Chalklin, *The Provincial Towns of Georgian England: A Study of the Building Process, 1740–1820* (1974), p. 225.
[10] *Ibid.*, p. 307.

century, the public and private domains were modified in a number of ways. The cellular layout of courts with their ambiguous areas of semi-private and semi-public space gave way to a more open texture. The dwelling became more enclosed and private, whilst the external domain became waste space or connective tissue which was made sterile or anonymous. The house itself changed in form so that the internal space was used in a more specialised way with a clear differentiation of function. The result was a realignment of the relationship between private and public so that space which was not encapsulated within the private sphere of the individual house became totally public and hence open to view and regulation. The threshold between the private and public spheres had been redrawn and made less ambiguous and permeable.

These changes cannot be precisely dated for there was a variation between parts of the country and even within a town. However, the trends had coalesced to produce the 'bye-law' housing which typified English towns between the Public Health Act of 1875 and the outbreak of the First World War. It was the product of a number of forces. One was a conscious desire to render public space socially neutral, and to bring areas of interaction under regulation. The space in the city between buildings, the interstices of the urban form, were rendered socially neutral waste space rather than social arenas in their own right. Birmingham Corporation in 1875, for example, banned the pleasure functions of the fairs from the streets of the town on grounds both of moral improvement and congestion. Recreational life was excluded from the public space of the town and transferred to specialised areas. The corporation therefore intervened in a positive as well as a negative sense in order to provide parks which formed so many moral enclaves in the town, with their regulations, railings and park wardens. This realignment of urban layout applied equally to housing. The change arose in part from a concern for public order and public health, for cellularity produced problems of control over cleanliness and criminality. The aim was to 'open up' the city in order to make it visible for inspection. In Liverpool, for example, a series of local acts from 1842 to 1889 exerted mounting pressure on the building of courts until eventually it was more economical to construct streets. The regulations also insisted that each house should have a private and exclusive open space at the rear. Instead of a court shared between a group of neighbours, each house came to lay 'between an anonymous and public space, which is the street, and an individual and private space which is the yard'.[11] The threshold between the public and private domains had been asserted.

The change was not merely the result of official regulations, but also of economic variables. The general level of prices reached a plateau in the mid-Victorian period, but fell steeply in the last quarter of the nineteenth century before recovering in the early twentieth century. The movement of building costs and house rents diverged from this general trend. The building industry was not marked by major technical and structural changes which produced gains in productivity, so that the variation in building costs was relatively slight. The index of house rents actually moved against the general trend in prices. Whilst prices fell by 25 per cent between 1870 and 1893, the rent index rose by 19 per cent. When prices started to rise in the early twentieth century, rents lagged behind the general level of inflation: prices rose by 24 per cent between 1898 and 1910, and rents by only 6 per cent. Real wages were buoyant up to the late 1890s, and it would seem that a large part of the gain was taken by higher rents, which reflected to a considerable extent the improved quality of housing. Robert Giffen suggested in 1884 that over the previous fifty years, working-class wages might have doubled, whereas rents had risen by 150 per cent. This still left a larger sum for other purposes, and he argued 'that the houses are better, and that the increased house rent is merely the higher price for a superior article which the workman can afford'.[12] This was confirmed by G. H. Wood in 1909, who assumed that half of the increase in rent since 1850 was accounted for by new features. The Scottish census provides a longer time series of house size than the English census, and this indicates the marked fall in the proportion of the population living in one-roomed houses from 26.2 per cent in 1861 to 11.0 per cent in 1901. It might be argued that in the second half of the nineteenth century, increased expenditure on housing, the rise of home-based consumption and the development of a culture of domesticity were significant responses to the rise in real wages.

There was not only a positive incentive for working-class families to accept new patterns of consumption, for there was also a defensive reaction. The fall in prices in the late nineteenth century produced pressure on the profit margins of industrialists, who responded by

[11] A. Errazurez, 'Some Types of Housing in Liverpool, 1785–1890', *Town Planning Review*, 19 (1943–7), p. 68.
[12] R. Giffen, *The Progress of the Working Classes in the Last Half Century* (1884), p. 13.

Table 4.4 *Rents, building costs, prices and real wages, 1851–1910*

				Real wage index	
	House rents	Building costs	Rousseaux price index	Wood	Bowley
			1870 = 100		
1851	73	90	83	85	–
1861	85	95	105	85	–
1870	100	100	100	100	–
1876	108	108	105	116	–
1882	114	102	92	114	122
1888	116	92	76	133	143
1893	119	93	75	142	157
1898	123	99	71	147	165
1903	129	99	78	–	165
1910	130	101	88	–	163

Sources: H. W. Singer, 'An Index of Urban Land Rents and House Rents in England and Wales, 1845–1913', *Econometrica*, 9 (1941), p. 230; B. R. Mitchell and P. Deane, *Abstract of British Historical Statistics* (Cambridge, 1962), pp. 240, 472–3, 343–5.

Table 4.5 *Distribution of population by house size in Scotland, 1861–1911*

	Percentage of population in houses with						
	1	2	3	4	5	6	remainder
				rooms			
1861	26.2	37.7	12.7	6.4	3.7	2.9	9.5
1871	23.7	38.3	13.9	6.7	3.8	3.0	10.4
1881	18.0	39.5	16.1	7.6	4.2	3.2	11.4
1891	14.3	39.4	17.9	8.3	4.6	3.4	12.1
1901	11.0	39.5	19.9	9.1	4.9	3.5	12.1
1911	8.4	39.5	21.1	9.6	5.4	3.7	12.3

Source: 1911 Census of Scotland, Vol. II, Table XLVIII.

intensifying the control over work in order to raise productivity. Higher real wages were bought at a social cost to the workforce, for the maintenance of money wages at a time of falling prices was only made possible by an intensification of the workload and a rejection of customary standards. The increased expenditure on accommodation and furnishings was in part a defensive retreat from the loss of autonomy at work, so that a culture based on the home and family came to replace a culture based on the workplace.

One indication of this readjustment in housing standards was the change in domestic technology. Gas for both lighting and cooking was introduced into working-class houses in the 1890s which was made possible by the development of the prepayment slot meter. In Birmingham, for example, the number of consumers rose from 63,339 in 1898 to 172,985 in 1914, the proportion with meters from 8.2 to 54.6 per cent, and the proportion with cookers increased to 63.5 per cent. The cost of cooking by gas was calculated in 1920 to be 120 per cent more expensive than an efficient coal range, but convenience and the ability to remove cooking from the kitchen to the scullery encouraged its adoption. Further, paraffin lamps could be replaced as the major source of light. The supply of piped water also became well-nigh universal. In Newcastle in the 1840s, less than one in twelve of the population had access to a piped water supply; in 1883/5, 33.1 per cent of households had an indoor and 32.7 per cent an outdoor piped supply; in 1914 every house had a supply. Baths were still rare, being provided in one eighth of the houses in Burnley in 1912. The major change permitted by piped water was the substitution of water carriage for conservance systems of waste disposal. By 1911, water closets provided the majority of conveniences in eighty out of ninety-five English towns with a population exceeding 50,000. The change was swift. In Manchester, for example, water closets rose from 26.4 to 97.7 per cent of sanitary conveniences between 1899 and 1913. But the change was not only in the mundane realities of gas cookers and water closets.

The front parlour in English bye-law houses became a shrine to respectability and domesticity, reflecting the emergence of 'privatised and family-centred values'.[13] It would contain the best furniture and perhaps a piano, and the occasions which could justify the use of the room and its fittings were precisely defined. The parlour was not to be used for relaxation. Rather, it should be interpreted as a more controlled and formal social environment. This applied both to family occasions and to relations with outsiders. Everyday meals and casual meetings with neighbours took place in the kitchen in an informal and unstructured manner. The parlour was used both to reinforce the family as a group and to regulate relationships with outsiders in a formal setting and according to established social conventions. The internal space of the house was used in an increasingly specialised and differentiated manner which replaced the earlier

[13] G. J. Crossick, *An Artisan Elite in Victorian Society: Kentish London, 1840–80* (1978), p. 146.

pattern of undifferentiated use of a single living room. In Scottish tenements, however, this was not possible and the fewer, larger rooms were used in a much more promiscuous manner, with a lack of distinction even between living room and bedrooms, let alone between formal and informal space.

In the twentieth century, a further realignment took place in both the private and public domains of English working-class houses. By the early twentieth century, concern for 'national efficiency' and the maintenance of an 'imperial race' made bye-law housing appear in an unfavourable light. The city had been opened out, the worst problems of order and disease solved. Wide streets on a grid-iron plan now did not appear as the solution to the disordered chaos of the cellular layout of the eighteenth and early nineteenth centuries, but were rather viewed as an expensive and dispiriting form of development. The emphasis was placed instead on a lower density layout on garden city lines. Suburban land would itself be cheaper; development costs could be reduced by constructing narrower roads; the plan could be irregular, taking full advantage of aspect and layout; and houses could be built in pairs or short blocks rather than in long, uniform terraces. These principles were adopted before the First World War for middle-class garden suburbs and London County Council's cottage estate at Tottenham but it was in the interwar period that the new design became paramount. The public sphere became less open and regained an element of cellularity.

In the private domain, there was a trend away from the specialised use of differentiated rooms. Most bye-law housing was narrow and deep, which led to restrictions on light and air. The aim of architects such as Barry Parker and Raymond Unwin was to abolish back projections and to move towards an internal layout which was less narrow and deep, allowing more light and air into the house, and paying greater attention to the aspect of the house made possible by the abandonment of a rigid grid-iron layout. These principles were incorporated in the Tudor Walters report establishing design criteria for council housing. The ambition might seem admirable, but the perceptions of the architects might well clash with the expectations of the residents. This was most obvious in the so-called A3 council houses without a parlour which offended the socially approved use of space. Raymond Unwin betrayed a deep insensitivity to the life style of the working class when he remarked that 'there can be no possible doubt that until any cottage has been provided with a living room large enough to be healthy, comfortable and convenient, it is worse than folly to take space from that living room, where it will be used every day and every hour, to form a parlour, where it will only be used once or twice a week'.[14] A large proportion of the council houses erected between the wars was indeed of the non-parlour type, which meant that local authorities were flouting 'the housing *mores* of the people'. The decision that two living rooms were an 'unjustifiable luxury' ignored the expectation of a distinction between everyday and special use. The Mass-Observation report on housing during the Second World War concluded that 'in this respect at any rate, the new houses built between the wars have proved themselves much less in accordance with the needs of the people who live in them than the old houses of the nineteenth century'.[15]

However, the future was to be dominated by the style proposed by Unwin, and bye-law houses have been increasingly modified since the Second World War in order to meet the new use of internal space. Anthony Bertram argued in 1935 that house design had developed from 'amalgamation' in the Middle Ages, when the Great Hall was used as a general purpose room, to disintegration into separate rooms for various functions and class of users, to reamalgamation in the twentieth century. The trend from differentiation to generalisation in room use characterised middle-class housing between the wars, so that working-class housing which had gained rooms in the nineteenth century converged with middle-class housing which lost rooms in the twentieth century. Although housing had by 1950 become relatively standardised by social class, this had by no means applied at earlier times.

III

The aggregate statistics given in the census confound the great country house of the aristocracy, the suburban villa of the prosperous middle class, and the cottage of the working class, which differed not only in size but also in the social articulation of physical form. At the top of the scale, the large town and country houses of the aristocracy and gentry were far more than places of residence, for they expressed in their design a particular conception of social relationships.

The 'social house', to use Mark Girouard's term, emerged in the

---

[14] R. Unwin, *Cottage Plans and Common Sense* (1902), p. 11.
[15] Mass-Observation, *An Enquiry into People's Homes* (1943), pp. 104, 107.

middle decades of the eighteenth century to replace the 'formal house' of the seventeenth century. In the formal house, the usual arrangement was to have a central public room or salon, from which radiated suites of rooms or apartments consisting of a drawing room or antechamber, bedchamber and closet. The rooms in the suite formed an 'axis of honour' which expressed etiquette and power. 'Since each room in the sequence of an apartment was more exclusive than the last, compliments to or from a visitor could be nicely gauged not only by how far he penetrated along the sequence, but also by how far the occupant of the apartment came along it – and even beyond it – to welcome him.'[16] The threshold between the private and public spheres within the house was defined not by rigid physical design, but according to the status of the parties. The communal public areas were of considerably less significance than the territories of the apartments, which formed the setting for social interaction rather than a strictly defined privacy. In the social house, the threshold was relocated. Suites of rooms were abandoned: bedrooms moved upstairs with a greater emphasis upon privacy; and communal public rooms became increasingly the setting for social relationships. The straight axis of honour gave way to a circuit of reception rooms.

The next stage in the evolution of the country house was the arrival of informality in the late eighteenth and early nineteenth centuries, so that 'houses were designed less for balls than for house parties'.[17] One trend was to bring the living rooms into closer connection with the outside of the house, by placing common rooms on the ground floor, with service areas in a separate wing rather than in the basement. The symmetry of the house was destroyed, but this was no longer functionally necessary with the collapse of the internal balance of the salon and apartment system, whilst romantic attachment to nature meant that 'to make a house lopsided became a positively meritorious gesture, an escape from artificiality'.[18] Nevertheless, the internal space was still used according to a strict code, for the Victorian country house was organised in four groups: family, guests, children and servants. Dr Franklin has remarked that 'the essence of Victorian planning was segregation and specialisation. Each group was allotted a separate territory, though with certain over-lapping between owner

---

[16]   M. Girouard, *Life in the English Country House: A Social and Architectural History* (1978), p. 145.
[17]   *Ibid.*, p. 218.   [18]   *Ibid.*, p. 219.

and guests; each territory except the nurseries was subdivided into a male and female side; each room was designed to fit a single precise function.'[19] The exact use of these rooms was associated with a strict ritual of organisation and hospitality but, unlike the 'formal house', did not define power and status. By the end of the nineteenth century a greater simplicity of plan and social convention was apparent, as the distinction between male and female domains weakened; the hold of ceremony relaxed; and the hall revived as the focal point of the house, marking a 'movement away from the minutely specialised and sealed-off spaces of high-Victorian houses'.[20]

The country houses of aristocrats and gentry mirrored the changing social relationships between the owner and his retainers and suitors, between family and guests, between servants and served. Although middle-class housing might not appear to have such explicit social purpose, certain of the changes in the country house were apparent. The trend in the nineteenth century was similarly towards the specialisation of rooms, the separation of the public from the private sides of life, and the creation of distinct spheres for women and children. A middle-class family pattern developed from about the 1820s which gave great significance to the home and domesticity, making it 'almost a sacred institution, the pivot not only of domestic comfort but of moral rectitude, the Christian commonwealth in miniature, in which the members of the family would be reared in those principles of honour, duty, industry, thrift and sobriety which would best conduce to their own well-being and to that of society at large'.[21] The home was in part a retreat from the stress of the world, a haven of order and security, and this was associated with two other trends: a retreat from the centre of towns to the suburbs; and a change in house style from the terrace to the villa.

The great majority of middle-class dwellings in Georgian England had been built in terraces of 'long narrow plots with their tall narrow houses'.[22] The houses in Bedford Square, erected between 1775 and 1780, provide an illustration of the grander type of middle-class terrace, which nevertheless followed the basic plan of even artisan housing: one room at the back and one at the front on each floor, with a passage or staircase at one side. The basement contained a service

[19] J. Franklin, *The Gentleman's Country House and its Plan, 1835–1914* (1981), p. 39.
[20] M. Girouard, *The Victorian Country House* (1979), p. 79.
[21] J. Burnett, *A Social History of Housing, 1815–1970* (Newton Abbot, 1978), p. 96.
[22] J. Summerson, *Georgian London* (1945), p. 49.

area for the kitchen, storage and servants; the ground floor accommodated the dining room and a sitting room; the first floor had a drawing
room at the front which possibly extended to the rear; whilst the
rest of the house was given over to bedrooms. In the larger houses,
a mews was provided at the rear for the carriage and horses. There
was little open space left on the plot, and gardens were usually provided communally in the square. 'The insistent verticality of the London house is idiomatic', which led a French visitor in 1817 to remark
that 'the agility, the ease, the quickness with which the individuals
of the family run up and down, and perch on the different storeys,
give the idea of a cage with its sticks and birds'.[23]

This style of development persisted in parts of London and provincial towns until the early years of Victoria, but a hint of the future
was already apparent in the plan for the Eyre estate at St John's Wood,
which was based upon pairs of semi-detached houses. Development
of the estate finally commenced in the boom of the 1820s when 'it
was the first part of London, and indeed of any other town, to abandon
the terrace house for the semi-detached villa – a revolution of striking
significance and far-reaching effect'.[24] Villadom characterised the
housing of the middle class in nineteenth-century cities, usually in
socially exclusive areas distinct from the lower classes. This permitted
a number of changes in design. The communal garden of the square
was replaced by a separate, private, garden. The common rooms of
the house which were used by all members of the family, and into
which guests might also be invited, were relocated on the ground
floor; the upper storeys were limited to the individual rooms of family
members. Leonore Davidoff has commented that

The growth of middle-class suburbs created larger areas of socially homogeneous population. This was, indeed, one of their primary appeals ... Control of the social, and thus also, spatial landscape was the very essence of
suburban design. The front and back entrance to the house denoted the difference between formal calling and visiting, as well as the watchful control of
tradesmen and servants ... The rules of etiquette were strictly observed in
controlling contacts and making acquaintances in the anonymous atmosphere
of new 'estate' building.[25]

Indeed, problems of social definition were felt acutely in the nineteenth century. Whereas in the eighteenth and early nineteenth centuries meeting places had been public with a 'singular comingling

---

[23] *Ibid.*, p. 51.
[24] *Ibid.*, pp. 158–9.
[25] L. Davidoff, *The Best Circles: Society, Etiquette and the Season* (1973), p. 74.

of the classes', this was less acceptable by the second quarter of the century, perhaps because barriers of rank and station were less obvious and needed to be asserted in a new manner. A society based on achievement required strict rules to legitimate social relationships. The result was a retreat 'towards greater exclusiveness, privacy and controlled social interaction'.[26] This was clearly associated with the change in the form of the city with the stricter definition of the threshold between public and private spheres, and it was also reflected in the emphasis upon the division between public and private life within the middle-class family. The house was interpreted as a refuge or sanctuary in which the husband recovered from the pressures of business, whilst the wife and children were sheltered from the world. Since it was no longer in itself a place of business, the house was 'feminised' and its social functioning left to the wife who was largely freed from the actual tasks of housework. Social life was virtually confined to private houses where it was controlled by a strict code of etiquette enforced by women. Indeed, the middle-class house and suburb were a collection of spatial and social arrangements to control accessibility.

Changes in architectural style were, until the late nineteenth century, cosmetic. By the end of the century a more radical change was occurring, and this was taken further between the wars. This was, as in the large country houses, a trend away from what J. J. Stevenson termed 'multifariousness' towards a more open and fluid organisation of space, and the replacement of display and ritual observances by 'rational' use. The distinction between family rooms and the public areas of the house was eroded; the separation of male and female territories was reduced; and the distinction between dining room, drawing room, morning room and study gave way to the more flexible use of fewer rooms. These changes were encouraged after the First World War by the greater difficulty of finding domestic servants, the impact of taxation, the weakening of the distinction between male and female roles and a fall in family size. The outcome was 'a growing convergence of standards between the established members and the new entrants to the class, reflected . . . by an increasingly standardised type of house appropriate for a small family with little domestic

---

[26]   *Ibid.*, p. 24. The nature of the middle-class house in London, and its contrast with Paris and Vienna, is described in Olsen, *The City as a Work of Art*, chaps. 7, 8 and 10.

help'.[27] The continuation of the trend away from diversity towards combination of rooms produced an increasing convergence between middle-class property and working-class housing constructed by local authorities, so that the main differences became location and detail rather than internal plan.

Houses for the lower middle class and working class were predominantly constructed in terraces until the First World War, until suburban semi-detached houses and council estates produced a change in style in the interwar period. Although the villas of the middle class before the First World War, and the local authority housing and suburban estates of the interwar period, all followed general national trends, the terraces of 'bye-law' houses built for working- and lower middle-class occupiers up to 1914 were by contrast marked by significant regional divergences. This forms a final variation on the theme of the self-contained English house.

IV

It has already been indicated that the rents of working-class houses in 1905 varied by a considerable margin and did not necessarily follow the level of wages paid in the town, so that the relationship between the wage and rent indices was highly unfavourable in Plymouth and Newcastle, and most favourable in Leicester. This regional divergence in the cost of supply and the level of effective demand produced marked discrepancies in overcrowding (more than two persons per room), which amounted to 31.6 per cent of the population in Newcastle in 1911, but only 1.1 per cent in Leicester. It also entailed particular regional adaptations of the working-class self-contained terrace house.

In the early nineteenth century, the back-to-back house had been a feature of many towns in the north and Midlands, but by the end of the century it had retreated to a limited area in the West Riding of Yorkshire. Construction of back-to-backs had been forbidden in the building bye-laws of many towns, but was defended vigorously by Leeds Corporation until it was outlawed by national legislation in 1909. In Leeds, the majority of back-to-backs had three or four rooms. The three-roomed houses had two storeys, with a living room and non-habitable scullery on the ground floor, and two bedrooms on the first floor. In four-roomed houses, an additional room was

---

[27] Burnett, *Social History*, pp. 191, 245.

provided either in the attic or by relegating the functions of the scullery to the basement to create two habitable rooms on the ground floor. Of course, back-to-backs could not have separate back-yards, but in the most sophisticated versions this shortcoming was avoided by the provision of a small forecourt which contained the entrance to a water closet located in the basement.

The back-to-back house divided the space under one roof vertically; by contrast, the Tyneside flat divided the space horizontally. These two-storey 'cottage flats' were largely confined to a narrow band on either bank of the Tyne, and the regional limitation of the style is shown by the census of 1911. In England and Wales in 1911, 2.9 per cent of the population lived in flats, whereas the level in Northumberland was 25.4 per cent and in County Durham 14.6 per cent. Flat-dwellers were highly localised even within the north-east, for in Gateshead 62.5 per cent and in Newcastle 44.5 per cent of the population lived in flats. The older cottage flats had only two rooms, but in the more modern form there were three rooms on the ground floor and four on the first floor, each with a scullery. The upper flat had a front entrance adjacent to the street door of the lower flat, and a back entrance to a separate yard containing a closet and coal shed. These flats were completely self-contained and, unlike Scottish tenements, did not possess areas which were used in common.

Although the level of overcrowding and the size distribution of housing in Sunderland was similar to Tyneside, this adjacent town had a distinctive house style. This was a single-storey cottage containing sitting room, kitchen, bedroom and scullery with, in some cases, a second bedroom in a back extension. The houses were self-contained, with separate back-yards and, in comparison with back-to-backs and Tyneside flats, had a low density of land use. In a typical pair of flats in Gateshead, 1,059 square feet of habitable rooms were constructed on 1,064 square feet of land, and in a typical back-to-back in Leeds, 700 square feet of accommodation on 768 square feet of land. In Sunderland, there was, in one standard cottage, 449 square feet of habitable rooms on a plot of 1,275 square feet, which was only 40 per cent of the density of development in Gateshead.

Elsewhere in England, working-class housing consisted of two-storey through terrace houses. The main distinction was between houses with and without a back extension. In the cotton towns of Lancashire, the 'two up, two down' was the dominant house type, whereas in the Midlands and south, the most common form of bye-law house had a back addition which contained either a scullery or a scullery and kitchen on the ground floor, and a bedroom on the first floor. These 'back addition' houses therefore had five or six rooms. The result was a marked contrast between a town such as Leicester, where only 6.1 per cent of the houses in 1911 had three rooms or less, and Sunderland where 62.0 per cent of houses fell into this category.

One response to a larger house size might be a high level of sub-letting, although this was by no means inevitable. Towns dominated by through houses ranged from Leicester, where there was virtually no sub-letting, to Bristol and Cardiff, where about a third of the population was sharing accommodation. Similarly, in towns with small houses, there was a contrast between Leeds, where only 0.8 per cent of the population lived in shared accommodation, and Sunderland, where the figure was 56.4 per cent. There was, in other words, a tension between the apparently self-contained architectural form and the need in some towns, and at points of strain in the family or local economy, to share space. The result might be tension, in both a social and financial sense. Mrs Pember Reeves remarked in 1913 that 'letting a whole house to tenants who are invariably unable to afford the rent of it is to contract out of half the landlord's risks, and to leave them on the shoulders of people far less able to bear them'.[28]

The variation in size and standards may largely be explained in terms of the relationship between wages and rent: the ratio of the indices of wage and rent in Newcastle in 1905 was 1.2, in Blackburn 1.7 and Leicester 2.0. This economic explanation may account for the existence of small houses, but not for the precise architectural form, for the vernacular house style might be the product of a number of almost fortuitous factors creating a local conventional architectural form. The Tyneside flat, for example, emerged in the 1860s as a formalisation of the earlier pragmatic solution to sub-dividing property in the central districts of Gateshead and Newcastle. Restrictions to the supply of land had created a dense packing of accommodation in the existing built-up areas, and when these barriers to expansion were removed in the 1860s, the outcome was the extension of the earlier style, suitably adapted to meet the requirements of the building regulations. In some towns, building regulations might force builders to

---

[28] M. Pember Reeves, *Round About a Pound a Week* (1913), pp. 37–8.

reject the local house style, such as in Liverpool where the balance was increasingly weighted against courts and in favour of streets. But in other cases, regulations might act to maintain the existing style. This was the case in Sunderland, where the bye-laws allowed single-storey houses to have thinner walls and narrower streets than two-storey cottages. The regional house style was produced by a complex mixture of market forces, public regulation, conventional expectations and builders' conservatism. The causes of the wide range in rent levels clearly demand further explanation, but there is no doubt of the consequence: the increase in the rent index between 1870 and 1910 was considerably less than the variation at one point in time; and the national aggregate census figures of house size and overcrowding similarly obscure the fact that at any one time the range between towns was as significant as the change over time.

THE SOCIAL RELATIONS OF HOUSING

Housing is a universal need, but the conditions under which it was supplied could have very different ideological and social consequences. Where accommodation was owned by employers, the housing and labour markets were combined, so that the supply of housing might be used as an element in the management of the workforce. Alternatively, housing could be supplied by a separate group so that the property and labour markets were distinct, which raises the question of how house capital related to other fractions of capital. Housing was a commodity in its own right, supplied under normal conditions of commercial profit, but it was also a necessity for the production of commodities in general. It was therefore an open question whether house capitalists would be protected as a separate interest group, or whether greater weight would be attached to raising standards and protecting tenants. The ownership of housing as a source of rent created a continuing relationship both with the state as a source of taxation, and with the tenants who had to pay. The balance between the house as a source of rent and rates could change, depending upon the political and social position of house capital in relation to other forms of property. The terms upon which housing was supplied to tenants could vary, depending upon the length of tenancies, the flexibility with which lets could be terminated, the legal powers of the landlord in evicting and securing payment, the management techniques which were developed. This relationship between landlord and tenant might be unproblematical but it could in certain circumstances become a significant focus for social conflict, and it was in any case an important element in the texture of everyday life. Another category of tenure united ownership and occupancy, a solution which might be deliberately designed to diffuse property ownership with ideological and social consequences. The provision of property to let might continue in a different guise of non-commercial state provision, which would change the criteria by which rents were determined, tenants selected and housing managed. It became a matter for a housing bureaucracy operating under rules determined by political decisions, rather than by a commercial response to the laws of the market. Tenure is clearly an important element in the social formation.

These tenures could co-exist at any one time, as well as change in their relative importance over time. At the beginning of the period, housing supplied by the employer was of greater significance, both in agriculture where the 'tied' cottage survives to the present and in the early factory colonies where many employers provided at least some accommodation for their workforce. In the nineteenth century, housing for all classes was normally supplied by a group of house capitalists, but this tenurial structure was transformed in a short period between the wars. There were three related changes: the private rented sector became largely a historical survival; local authorities emerged as the suppliers of new rented accommodation to the working class; and owner-occupation developed as the typical middle-class tenure. In England and Wales in the interwar period, 19.4 per cent of the additional housing stock was provided by private landlords, 31.5 per cent supplied by local authorities and 49.1 per cent owner-occupied. By contrast, local authorities had supplied only 0.5 per cent of the houses erected between 1891 and 1908 and 5.5 per cent between 1909 and 1915. Although in 1939 the private landlord was still the largest single source of accommodation, house capitalists had been pushed to the periphery of the market in new property between the wars. Although reconstruction after the Second World War gave a considerable role to the public sector, the trend towards owner-occupation revived in the 1950s and it is now the dominant tenure. These tenurial changes had important consequences, both at the level of the mundane realities of daily existence, and in the determination of the general social structure.

Table 4.6 *Tenure of housing, England and Wales, 1938 and 1961*

	Percentage of houses	
	1938	1961
Owner-occupied	34.9	42.3
Rented, public	11.2	23.7
Rented, private	53.9	27.8
Other	n.a.	6.2
	100.0	100.0

Sources: Report to the Minister of Health by the Departmental Committee on Valuation for Rates, 1939 (1944); A. H. Halsey, ed., *Trends in British Society since 1900* (1972), p. 307.

I

In 1750, housing was to a large extent an adjunct to the labour market, but in the course of industrialisation and urbanisation it came to be supplied independently of the employer as a separate fraction of capital. Employer-provided housing remained a common phenomenon in agriculture, but for industrial workers it was increasingly confined to isolated areas where no alternative was available. The provision of housing by employers where it was not dictated by necessity became rare in the course of the nineteenth century. Indeed, the only major area in which it did persist as an integral part of the wage bargain was in north-eastern England. A survey of 1913 found that 96.9 per cent of houses supplied rent-free by colliery companies were in County Durham and Northumberland. The wage bargain there started from the assumption that the colliery owner should provide a house, which was not the case in any other coalfield or industry where it was assumed either that housing should not be provided, or that it should be supplied in return for rent. It was a feature which the employers, though not the workmen, came increasingly to resent. Rent allowances had been introduced in place of rent-free houses when, during the boom of the early 1870s, the demand for houses outstripped the supply and workers were housed in non-company property for which a rent had to be paid. The allowance became a more or less fixed or historic figure whereas rents and house prices rose, and it was therefore increasingly in the owners' interests to switch from rent-free houses built at current costs to rent allowances paid at historic costs.

In County Durham in 1894, 78.1 per cent of married underground workers received a free house as against 17.2 per cent receiving a rent allowance; by 1912 the figures were 51.9 and 45.4 per cent respectively. The miners for their part realised that 'the advantages of having a rent-free house when no wages are being earned, which may sometimes be for very long periods such as in times of sickness and in times of strike, are too solid to be lightly given up'.[29] Miners preferred free houses for the very same reason that the owners were eager to switch to rent allowances: the real value of a free house was greater since a substantial differential had opened up between the rent allowed and actually paid. The north-eastern coalfield was an object lesson of the dangers to employers of allowing too intimate a connection between employment and housing: where the relationship of landlord and tenant, employer and employee, were compartmentalised it was possible to enter and leave the housing market without implicating the entire wage bargain.

The provision of housing by the employer might connect with the labour market in a different way: it might form part of a desire to construct a patriarchal community. This was not a primary motivation, as emerged clearly from the survey carried out in 1833 by the Factories Inquiry Commission which asked manufacturers 'Do the workpeople live in the houses of their employers; and if so, is any control or superintendence exercised for their moral and social improvement, or are any arrangements made to enforce domestic cleanliness?'[30] In the cotton industry of Lancashire, about half of the respondents provided no accommodation for their workmen; about another third provided housing for a minority of workers; which left about a sixth who housed a large number or a majority of the workforce. Amongst this small group with a major commitment to the housing market, only a handful utilised housing for 'moral and social improvement'. The view was rather that the tenants were 'generally of too high a class to be intruded upon', so that 'there is no control or superintendence over them when out of the mills: they are respectable and left to arrange their families and habits of life in the same manner as

[29] *Report of the Medical Inspector of the Local Government Board. Number 262. Dr L. W. Darra Mair's Report to the Local Government Board on the Sanitary Circumstances of the Whickham Urban District with Special Reference to the Housing Accommodation Generally and to Certain Back-to-Back Houses at Marley Hill in Particular* (1907), pp. 11–12.

[30] *Supplementary Report of the Central Board of His Majesty's Commissioners Appointed to Collect Information in the Manufacturing Districts as to the Employment of Children in Factories, and as to the Propriety and Means of Curtailing the Hours of their Labour,* Pt II, PP 1834, XX, p. 3.

all other classes who do not work in factories.'[31] In this context, the answer of the Ashworth family at Hyde stands out very clearly: 'The state and cleanliness of their rooms, their bedding and furniture are very minutely examined, and the condition of their children, their income and habits of life, are carefully enquired into, and remarks thereon are entered in books which are kept for the purpose.'[32] Such a policy was only possible in factory 'colonies' at an early stage of industrialisation, and such obvious and blatant methods of social discipline were to become redundant, if not counter-productive. Most employers were not interested, the policy was difficult of achievement in large towns, and more indirect influences proved highly effective. By the later nineteenth century, 'employer ownership of housing was limited in extent in the North, the factory itself rather than direct control of housing acted as the principal focus of workplace influence'.[33] Industrial discipline and control in Britain did not rely upon patriarchal or welfare capitalism which rather characterised the German, American and Japanese industrial economies. Employers in Britain in the course of the nineteenth century recognised unions and incorporated them into the system of industrial relations, relying upon a compact with separate organisations to which the workers had a commitment. The solution which developed in other countries might well involve the rejection of unions, and aim to incorporate the workers directly into the firm, which might well involve company provision of housing. This applied to welfare capitalism in America and corporate paternalism in Japan, but was not characteristic of the industrial system in Britain where most employers had a pragmatic response to the supply of housing and saw no virtue in denying the role of the speculative builder and the small property owner.

Subsequently, a few employers, such as the Rowntrees at Earswick, Cadburys at Bournville, and Levers at Port Sunlight, did again develop an interest in housing standards and provision. These initiatives must be distinguished both from the earlier generation of factory colonies in Britain, and from the experience in other countries. Edward Cadbury was insistent that Bournville should not be merely a company town, for the use of the employer's position as landlord as a means of control would be counter-productive. Rather, the emphasis was

---

[31] *Ibid.*, pp. 223, 263.   [32] *Ibid.*, p. 280.
[33] P. Joyce, *Work, Society and Politics; The Culture of the Factory in Later Victorian England* (Brighton, 1980), p. 121.

upon the need to supply housing of a higher standard than the market would provide in order to raise the efficiency of the workforce. Discipline would not be maintained and output increased by the American techniques of scientific management and the 'open shop', for 'any scheme which aims at lessening the worker's independence by drawing him from his Union is running counter to the very spirit of the times and will rouse the fiercest hostility'. Cadbury proposed instead that the 'test of any scheme of factory organisation is the extent to which it creates and fosters the atmosphere of co-operation, without in any way lessening the loyalty of the worker to his own class and its organisations'.[34] The proviso was vital. Patriarchal techniques were an assault upon the autonomy of the worker in the factory and the community. Instead of enforcing subordination, Cadbury's approach was to accept the existence of separate class organisations and to ensure that they were loyal rather than hostile to the firm. The strategy rested upon the general acceptance of unions within an institutionalised system of labour relations, and a general concern for 'national efficiency'. The housing standards which emerged from the intersection of demand and supply curves might not be adequate, and the emphasis in these housing schemes initiated by employers in the late nineteenth and early twentieth centuries was therefore placed upon raising the standards of the environment, usually by the encouragement of building associations and public utility societies rather than direct company construction.

The majority of employers in any case viewed housing as something with which they were only marginally concerned, with which they might become involved or not as circumstances dictated. The response was one of pragmatic necessity rather than firm commitment, but once the employer had felt compelled to build houses, they might be used to fulfil certain management objectives. This consideration applied to the shipyard of the west of Scotland. The new yards on Clydeside in the late nineteenth and early twentieth centuries were located away from existing settlements, which made it difficult to obtain a labour force and some shipbuilders entered the housing market as a pragmatic response. It was clear that 'housing was simply too costly and the workers too well organised to use accommodation

---

[34] E. Cadbury, *Experiments in Industrial Organisation* (1912), pp. xvii, 68–9, and 'Some Principles of Industrial Organisation: The Case for and against Scientific Management', *Sociological Review*, 7 (1914), p. 106.

as a manipulative or coercive instrument against a workforce',[35] and employers could indeed impose managerial prerogatives upon skilled men who were resisting mechanisation and systematic labour discipline without relying on the use of housing. But where housing had been supplied it was possible, for example, to provide subsidised dwellings for supervisory grades as part of a strategy to weaken the hold of unions over key occupations. Housing had been supplied for other reasons, but it could become part of the management strategy of the company.

The provision of housing by employers was relatively scarce for two reasons. On the one hand, there was a sufficiently well-developed building industry to supply the houses and a large group of small investors to purchase them. On the other hand, the social structure did not require stabilisation by patriarchal and *dirigiste* methods. A separate group of petty bourgeois property owners had emerged in Britain in the course of urbanisation and industrialisation, which raises vital questions in the social history of housing. How is house capital to be located as a separate fraction of capital in the social structure? What was the nature of the relationships between landlords and their tenants? Historians have paid more attention to production than to consumption, to getting than to spending, and this applies to housing perhaps even more than to other commodities. Although rent was the largest single expenditure of most families, more attention has been paid to the determinants of the building cycle than to the social relationships created by the ownership and management of house property.

II

The predominant house tenure for all classes which emerged in the nineteenth century was rental from private landlords, and the investment of relatively small sums in housing appealed to a particular social grouping. In the UK in 1913–14, house property and business premises comprised 14.1 per cent of all property passing at death, but amounted to 45.4 per cent in estates of £100 to £500, 33.8 per cent in estates of £500 to £1,000 and 26.8 per cent in estates of £1,000 to £5,000. The ownership of house property in British towns was characterised

[35] J. Melling, 'Employers, Industrial Housing and the Evolution of Company Welfare Policies in Britain's Heavy Industry: West Scotland, 1870–1920', *International Review of Social History*, 26 (1981), p. 293.

by highly fragmented smallholdings. In Blackburn in 1895, for example, there were 3,365 owners, of whom 1,070 or 31.8 per cent held property with a rateable value of £15 or less. The largest single owner possessed only 1.1 per cent of all rented property in the town, the largest five owners only 3 per cent. Housing was a characteristic investment of members of the petty bourgeoisie who left less than £5,000 at death, and there were very sound reasons why this should be the case. Investment in housing was 'more than a search for profits and rents', for it formed part of a 'careful plan of life-cycle related saving'.[36] A typical middle-class family passed through a property cycle. Early manhood was spent in paying off debts and creating a trading capital; this was a period of earned income and net payment of interest. Middle age was marked by the liquidation of debts and the accumulation of capital in both the business and in other investments; this was a period of earned income and net receipt of interest. In later middle age, unearned income from rents and interest dominated as active involvement in business was abandoned. The wealthier families might invest predominantly in stocks and shares, whereas the less wealthy would concentrate upon local, secure and tangible assets. Although the structure of the portfolio differed, the aim was the same: provision of income for old age, a widow or an unmarried daughter. The less wealthy members of the middle class were particularly attracted to investment in housing. Usually, their businesses had been small scale and precarious with an intense localism of concern, and this goes far to explain 'the characteristic investment of surpluses in highly secure and local outlets, especially urban property'.[37] The owners of house property, it was reported in 1834, were 'generally retired tradesmen, widows and persons of small property',[38] and this remained the case until 1914.

The petty bourgeoisie was vital to the provision of housing, but was at the same time politically isolated and expendable, as became increasingly apparent at the end of the nineteenth century and in the early twentieth century. The ideology of the petty bourgeoisie hampered the development of a national political presence designed

[36] R. J. Morris, 'The Middle Class and British Towns and Cities of the Industrial Revolution, 1780–1870', in D. Fraser and A. Sutcliffe, eds., *The Pursuit of Urban History* (1983), p. 295.

[37] G. J. Crossick, 'Urban Society and the Petty Bourgeoisie in Nineteenth-Century Britain', in Fraser and Sutcliffe, eds., *Pursuit of Urban History*, p. 320.

[38] *Report from His Majesty's Commissioners for Inquiring into the Administration and Practical Operation of the Poor Laws, Appendix B2, Answer to Town Queries*, vol. II, PP 1834, XXXVI, p. 75.

to protect its interests, and, in this respect, the lower middle class in Britain differed from its counterparts in Germany or France. Industrial capitalism had evolved more gradually in Britain, so that the polarisation of large and small capitals was less stark. Further, there was in Britain 'no traditional ideology of a pre-industrial petty bourgeois kind around which discontented groups could focus', so that 'there was no distinctive consciousness in relation to industrial or commercial capital'.[39] The shopkeeper radicalism of the early nineteenth century had little rationale by the later years of the century, and its denunciation of monopoly and privilege had become identified with the ideology of laissez-faire and free trade. Whereas in Germany the petty bourgeoisie urged state protection of the small man against large-scale business, in Britain there was a failure to develop a distinctive political voice which would move beyond a merely negative rejection of municipal socialism to a positive demand for state protection of private landlords. The political activity of the lower middle class remained, like its characteristic investment, localised. This was not serious when it had been possible for ratepayers to mobilise on a local political stage and institute a period of retrenchment, but by the end of the nineteenth century countervailing forces had emerged on the local political stage; there was a need to fulfil the requirements of central government; and the most significant issues had become matters of national politics at Westminster rather than local politics at the town hall. Private landlords were threatened in the late nineteenth and early twentieth centuries both by a deterioration in their fiscal position and by a curtailment of their legal powers over tenants. A rectification of these grievances would required national legislation, but the landlords lacked a distinctive political voice and their claims were ignored by political parties with other interests to serve. Ratepayers' associations and the United Property Owners' Association tended to concentrate on a negative opposition to municipal socialism and state interference, and they were increasingly linked with utility and railway companies who joined the landed interest in a general defence of property. The specific interests of house property were swamped, and pragmatism was overwhelmed by doctrinaire assertion.

Houses were not only a source of income for their owners, but also for the local authorities, and rents and rates were clearly in conflict

[39] G. J. Crossick, 'The Emergence of the Lower Middle Class in Britain: A Discussion', in G. J. Crossick, ed., *The Lower Middle Class in Britain, 1870–1914* (1977), p. 44.

as rateable value lagged behind expenditure from the late nineteenth century. Between 1893/4 and 1898/9, rateable value in England and Wales increased by 7.9 per cent and the income from rates by 23.9 per cent, creating pressure on the rate base which could be resolved only through a change in national fiscal policy, either by introducing local taxes on other sources of income, or by passing responsibility on to central taxation. The implications were serious for private land-lords: the increased burden of local taxation explains about a quarter of the 40 per cent decline in property values in Edwardian London; and it coincided with a number of other unfavourable trends. The housing boom of the late 1890s created a high level of vacant property which made it difficult to pass the incidence of taxation from the owners to tenants, particularly at a time of stable or falling real wages, whilst high interest rates imposed a further strain on profits. It is not surprising that property values in Glasgow fell by 36.2 per cent between 1901 and 1912. The normal cyclical downturn in the property market was overlain in the Edwardian period by a crisis in local taxa-tion which had serious consequences for house capitalists.

The debate on the fiscal crisis was cast in such a way that the needs of private landlords were ignored. The Liberals denied that real pro-perty as a whole was overtaxed in relation to other sources of income, but insisted that the burden *within* real property had shifted away from land and towards the owners and occupiers of houses. The solu-tion was to increase the taxation of land, in the belief that landowners were gaining an unearned increment from an increase in site values created by the activities of the community. This would both provide revenue, and remove the incentive to 'hoard' land for the maximum gain, so that the burden of rates would be reduced, land prices would fall and builders would be able to solve the housing problem. Whereas the Liberal approach viewed house owners and their tenants as opposed to ground owners, the Conservative interpretation differed: real property as a whole, both land and houses, were considered to be overtaxed in relation to other sources of income; the solution was to widen the tax base and increase the contribution of central government. The Liberal and Conservative theories of local taxation were based upon different views of the place of small house owners in the social formation. The Conservative approach assumed a unity of interest between rural land and urban ratepayers and house owners in opposition to industrial and mercantile capital, whilst the Liberal approach viewed house owners and their tenants, industrialists, mine owners and rural tenants as opposed to the landed interest. Central government grants-in-aid were denounced by Liberals as a device to permit land to escape from its equitable contribution to taxation. The problem which was to face house owners at the end of the nineteenth century was that the Conservatives failed to implement their approach to local taxation, whilst the Liberal land campaign foundered upon its own impracticalities.

Conservative practice in the 1890s belied its promise by providing aid for rural interests and neglecting the concerns of the towns. Instead, Conservative policy turned in another direction which was to lead to the ultimate sacrifice of the small house capitalist. This was the creation of a 'rampart' of small proprietors to protect large estates and capitals. House capitalists could not fulfil this role, for they were an unpopular group and protection of their interests might bring other property into disrepute. It was more sensible to deny their claims and instead to create a class of owner-occupiers with a stake in the existing order of society. Conservative policy was thus designed to encourage owner-occupation, rather than to rectify the grievances of private landlords.

Practical action to reduce the burden of local taxation on house owners was aborted in the years before the First World War by the Liberal land campaign. This had a number of serious flaws. The share of rent in national income was declining, and the unearned increment was not as significant as the land campaign assumed. The conflict between house owners and landowners was also exaggerated. In leasehold towns they were distinct, but inclined to see themselves as co-operating in the development process; in freehold areas the two interests were united in one person. The valuation of land was in any case a practical impossibility. The land campaign foundered, but the pursuit of this particular solution to the problem of local taxation had resulted in a long period of deterioration in the fiscal position of house property. Indeed, neither the Conservative nor the Liberal approaches had been designed with the needs of house capitalists in mind.

Conservative doctrine grew out of the grievances of agriculturalists and the Liberal programme stood for the interests of industrial, mercantile and finance capital. Between the landed interest on the one side and the millowners and merchants on the other lay another fraction of capital: urban house capital, made up of a mass of property owners who assumed most of the rate burden and lacked a definite political attachment. Their interest was commensurate with the Conservative complaint about finance-and-mercantile capital's immunity from the poor rates, and with the Liberal outrage at the landowners' evasion of the municipal burden.[40]

The political isolation of house capital was thus a product not only of petty bourgeois ideology, but also of the interests of the major political parties.

The position of the house capitalist did not only deteriorate fiscally, for there was also a shift in the legal balance of power in favour of the tenant. The landlord in England could use the common law of distress which allowed the seizure of goods to the value of the outstanding rent. In 1838 this was supplemented by the Small Tenements Recovery Act which provided a more expeditious means of removing defaulting tenants in houses with a gross rental under £20 a year, but landlords felt that the process was too time-consuming. A tenant might owe two or three weeks' rent; the landlord might give one week's notice to quit; this would be followed by notice that the landlord would apply for a warrant of ejectment; a magistrate could then order possession in twenty-one days. The landlord stood to lose two months' rent in addition to the cost of obtaining and implementing the warrant. The general feeling amongst property owners was that the law of distress should be abandoned and a speedier process of eviction substituted, for the ability to secure vacant possession and to relet was more highly valued than the right to seize the goods of a defaulter. However, the trend to the First World War was, on the contrary, a curtailment of the power to levy distress without any compensating easing of the process of eviction. The emphasis was placed upon security of tenure rather than speed of repossession, the Increase of Rent and Mortgage Interest (War Restrictions) Act of 1915 marking the definitive shift in the balance of power against landlords. Tenants were given security of tenure so that the tenancy could be terminated only for specified causes, and these restrictions were further extended in 1918 and 1923. The trend of legislation in England in the late nineteenth and early twentieth centuries was to curtail the power of the landlord over his property and to give increased protection to his tenants.

However, changes in the legal code do not provide a complete picture of relations between landlords and tenants, for there were a number of possible techniques of property management, so that ownership and control might be combined or divided, and tenancies

---

[40] A. Offer, *Property and Politics 1870–1914: Landownership, Law, Ideology and Urban Development in England* (Cambridge, 1981), p. 165.

might be short and flexible or long and rigid. The contrast between England and Scotland is once again instructive, for not only architectural styles but also techniques of property management were highly distinctive. One divergence was in the length of lets. In England, in the course of urbanisation, most working-class property came to be let on weekly tenancies with yearly and quarterly tenancies confined to middle-class properties. Labour mobility was not hampered by long tenancies, and landlords were able to collect rents at the same interval as the payment of wages. Weekly tenancies had spread from sub-divided property at the bottom of the market in the eighteenth century so that by the mid-nineteenth century most working-class property in England was held on short lets. In Scotland, however, the trend towards short lets was frustrated by an institutional and legal context which could be modified only by legislative intervention. Long lets remained the dominant form of tenancy in Scotland in the nineteenth century, and short lets were confined largely to the unskilled working class. In Glasgow in 1905/6, 83.5 per cent of houses with a rental of less than £20 a year were let on yearly tenancies. These tenancies expired at fixed removal dates, usually 28 May, and the decision to take a property was made four months or so before the tenancy commenced. The result, it was argued, was a discrepancy between the housing and labour markets which hindered labour mobility and imposed strain on working-class budgets because of the discrepancy between the intervals at which rent was paid and wages received. The explanation of this divergence between Scotland and England was sought in certain legal and institutional rigidities. One was the system of payment of rates.

In England, the occupier of a house was in theory liable for the payment of rates, which led to serious problems of collection in the early nineteenth century. It was unrealistic to expect working-class tenants to find the money to pay rates in a lump sum, and frequent changes of residence made it difficult to locate the occupiers who were liable for the rates on a house for a portion of the financial year. The payment of rates on small properties was in consequence more or less voluntary. The solution was to introduce 'compounding' of rates, by which the *owners* of small houses would pay the rates in return for an allowance; the tenants would reimburse the landlord by an addition to the weekly rent. However, compounding was not uniformly welcomed, for both political and fiscal reasons. Politically, it was argued that direct payment of the rates created a sense of responsibility, and the Reform Act of 1867 made this a precondition of enfranchisement. The experiment did not work, for direct collection was administratively complex and imposed serious strains upon working-class budgets, and in 1869 compounding was reintroduced. Fiscally, there was a desire by local authorities to reduce the commission of perhaps 20 per cent paid to landlords, as a response to the crisis in local government finance in the late nineteenth and early twentieth centuries. In Scotland, by contrast, rates were levied separately upon owner and occupier, and compounding had scarcely developed, so that both parties made direct annual payments in a lump sum. This placed a strain upon working-class budgets, and also, it was argued, checked the development of short lets, for it was necessary to maintain the identity between the financial year and the period of tenancy. Pressure for the introduction of compounding mounted at the end of the nineteenth century, for it offered a means of increasing the yield of the rates, easing the budgetary difficulties of tenants, and permitting the introduction of short lets. Whereas in England, owners of working-class property defended the practice of compounding against local authorities who saw the reduction of allowances as a contribution to the financial crisis, in Scotland, local authorities and working-class tenants wished to introduce compounding against the wishes of the owners. The difference arose both because allowances in Scotland would be set at a low level which would not compensate the owners for their increased responsibilities, and because landlords were hostile to the change in the pattern of tenancies which would be facilitated by compounding.

The second major reason why long lets survived in Scotland was the greater security given to landlords by the Scottish legal system. The law of hypothec meant that the tenant's furniture, furnishings and tools were liable to 'sequestration' or removal immediately after entering into possession, as security for rent not yet due. This gave the landlord security for the credit implied by long lets, which was not provided by the English law of distress, and it was argued that the abolition of hypothec would necessarily result in short lets. These legal and institutional divergences perhaps do not provide a complete explanation of the pattern of long lets in Scotland; after all, both France and Germany had longer tenancies than England. However, the desire in the early twentieth century to bring Scotland into line with England directed attention towards the system of collection of rates and the legal power of landlords. The House Letting and Rating (Scotland)

Act of 1911 provided greater flexibility in tenancies, introduced compounding and limited the process of sequestration. Landlords were
opposed to these changes: short lets, they argued, raised the cost
of management by increasing the turnover of tenants; the payment
to their agents for collection was more than the 2.5 per cent received
from the council; an increase in rates could be passed to the occupiers
only by raising rents, which would at best cause animosity and at
worst prove impossible. But the Act of 1911 was not an unmitigated
loss for Scottish landlords, for they had one gain which their counterparts in England had failed to achieve: a process of summary eviction.
The level of litigation in landlord–tenant relations in Scotland was
considerably higher than in England. In London between 1886 and
1890, one warrant of eviction was issued for every 1,818 inhabitants,
whereas in Glasgow in 1889 one warrant was issued for every 54
inhabitants. These warrants for eviction applied overwhelmingly to
the minority of monthly let property, and there was not a single tension in landlord–tenant relations in Scotland. The tenants of yearly
property wished to introduce a more flexible system of house letting,
whereas the owners of monthly let property wished to obtain a more
summary process of eviction. The Act of 1911 gave the tenants of
yearly property what they wanted, but at the expense of the legal
position of the unskilled working class in monthly property, for in
future they could be evicted in a more peremptory manner. Scottish
landlords had to face unwelcome change in their position in the better-
class property but had some compensation at the bottom of the market.
Certainly, this debate over the house-letting system had politicised
landlord–tenant relations in Scotland much more than in England,
and the Act of 1911 merely resulted in the continuation of tension
in another form.

The management of house property could follow a number of forms,
and this provides a further point of contrast between England and
Scotland. Landlords might deal with their tenants in person, or could
rely upon intermediaries. In English towns, one possibility was to
use rent collectors who visited houses on a part-time basis. Usually,
their responsibilities were limited and the main tasks of management
were still in the hands of the owner, but from the middle of the nineteenth century a specialist group of house agents emerged. They had
a wide involvement in the property market, in the sale of houses,
the letting of accommodation, the collection of rents, the levying of
distress on defaulters, the supervision of repairs, the payment of rates

and insurance. The use of house agents entailed the separation of ownership from control, and the owner could, if he wished, pass the entire management of his property to a house agent, who might even guarantee payment of the rent and remove the risk. The rule-of-thumb methods of small proprietors could be replaced by professional rigour and an increase in the scale of units of management. It is important, however, not to exaggerate the significance of the emergence of professional agents in England. Tenants did not necessarily suffer a deterioration in their position, for agents could adopt a more flexible attitude since they could spread risks and had more effective techniques of vetting applicants. Certainly, personal management remained the norm, for the ownership of house property and the desire for personal control formed an interlinked set of attitudes in England, given the intense localism of interest of the lower middle class and the strong personal attachment to property. The pattern in Scotland was different. The degree of separation between the ownership and management of working-class housing in Glasgow was considerable, with perhaps 80 per cent of properties in the hands of house factors who took responsibility for finding tenants, collecting rents, removing defaulters, undertaking repairs and paying rates, in return for a commission ranging from 4 or 5 per cent in monthly lets to 2.5 per cent in the better annual lets. The greater reliance upon professional agents reflected two features of the Scottish property market which overruled the desire for personal control. One was the greater tension which existed as a result of the legal and institutional framework; the other was the complexity of control of tenements with their shared space and facilities.

The deterioration in the fiscal and legal position of private landlords from the late nineteenth century meant that greater weight was attached to the improvement in urban conditions financed by the rates and to tenants' rights than was accorded to the protection of private landlords as a separate fraction of capital. This was apparent in the passing of the Act of 1915, which intensified the prewar trends to create a fundamental change in the housing market. The rents of all houses whose rateable value did not exceed £35 in London, £30 in Scotland and £26 elsewhere were not to be increased above the rent paid on 3 August 1914. Controls on rents also necessitated controls on mortgages, which were not to be called in or to charge higher interest rates. The Act was to apply for the duration of the war and six months afterwards. The result was a redistribution of income from landlords and mortgagees towards tenants. Although owners had fewer losses arising from unlet property and arrears, the increased cost of repairs and management further eroded profit margins beyond the already straitened prewar circumstances. Mortgagees in turn were unable to recall their money and obtain the higher rate of interest earned by other investors. Private landlords and mortgagees consequently suffered an erosion of their income and they were one of the few sectors of property sacrificed by the government during the war. The isolation of landlords was clear before the war with the erosion of the legal power over tenants, and the deterioration of their fiscal position; it was reinforced by the Act of 1915; and the development of policy between the wars did little to rectify their grievances. Indeed, in 1919 and 1920 rent restrictions were extended to higher value property, although an increase of respectively 10 and 40 per cent on prewar rents was allowed. Some relaxation was introduced in 1923, so that rents could be decontrolled whenever the landlord came into possession, but in 1931, 69.1 per cent of the housing stock in England and Wales still had controlled rents. Tenants of these houses were paying much less in real terms for their accommodation, but the redistribution of income was somewhat random and poorly focussed, and rent-controlled houses were used less efficiently than if rents had risen with prices and income. The incentive to 'ration' accommodation was reduced, so that small families might remain in large houses. The unsatisfied demand was squeezed out into alternatives such as furnished accommodation, whose price was thus increased. Identical houses might have controlled and uncontrolled rents but there was no guarantee that the poorest tenant rented the cheapest house, for it was simply a matter of sitting tenants gaining at the expense of newcomers to the property market. The government was caught in a dilemma. Rent controls had been required to prevent landlords charging scarcity rents at a time of housing shortage during and after the war; but the rent controls, by depressing earnings from house property, hindered the provision of new houses to end the shortage.

The building boom of the 1930s with its new basis of owner-occupation did clear the way for some liberalisation in 1933 before controls were again extended at the outbreak of the Second World War. Houses for middle-class occupiers could be decontrolled immediately, for it was assumed that private building for owner-occupation had removed the shortage. Houses for the lower middle class and artisans would continue to be decontrolled on vacant possession, but it was now accepted that the private landlord would not return to provide new working-class housing at the bottom end of the market. Control was maintained, and the private landlord in ordinary working-class housing was abandoned. In many countries, the private landlord has been incorporated within a regulated market, accepted as one of the range of instruments available to supply housing. This did not occur in Britain. The private landlord had been in an isolated and ambiguous position in the debate on local taxation between the Liberals and Conservatives before 1914; he was in a similar plight in the interwar period as the Conservatives came to rely upon the 'ramparts' strategy of owner-occupation, and Labour emphasised the role of local authorities as the normal source of new working-class housing. Private landlords were thus in an ambivalent and isolated position.

Private landlords ceased to dominate the market in new accommodation between the wars, although their preponderant role in the housing stock erected before 1914 made them the largest single category of owner right up to the Second World War. This period of retreat and decline awaits a historian who will assess the shifts and stratagems of a social group in decline. How, it might be wondered, did the structure and social composition of ownership change? Landlord–tenant relations in the new era of controls and security must have adapted and possibly the role of professional management increased. The demise of the market in private mortgages would impose financial strains, and presumably the squeeze of profit margins continued with the maintenance of rent controls and the mounting burden of rates. Landlords might respond by reducing expenditure on repairs, which led to a deterioration in the housing stock, or by resorting to spurious procedures for securing vacant possession or levying charges for 'key money'. These are all important matters, but historians have concentrated on the arrival of council houses and owner-occupation rather than the demise of the private landlord. The result is an imbalance in the analysis of the housing market of interwar Britain which urgently needs to be redressed.

III

Additions to the housing stock between the wars were divided more or less equally between rented and owner-occupied property. The decline in the share of rental from about 90 per cent to half of new construction was significant, but so was the remarkable increase within the rented sector of council housing. The Housing Act of 1919 marks the emergence of local authorities as the major suppliers of both new working-class and rented accommodation, and these connections between class and tenure, public enterprise and rental, were novel features of the interwar period, affecting both the immediate relationship between landlord and tenant, and the social structure in general. The interpretation of the change in the role of public provision of housing is a contentious issue, and the debate over causation has important implications for an understanding of the social consequences of council housing.

The assumption which is often made is that the mass council housing programme after the First World War may be understood in terms of the internal logic of policy. The definition of the housing problem in terms of slums distinct from the rest of the urban fabric, produced by the faults of lack of regulation in the past rather than the faults of the current urban economy, led to a policy of excising these 'plague spots', and then leaving the market, aided by philanthropy, to provide new housing under the guidance of regulations designed to prevent the recurrence of insanitary conditions. The argument might then continue by suggesting that when this policy was implemented, it clashed with reality: slums could not be so easily defined as separate 'plague spots' distinct from the rest of the urban fabric, while the high cost of cleared land in central areas prevented private enterprise or even five per cent philanthropy from providing replacement housing. The result was the acceptance of a larger role for the council in providing both replacement and new housing, on suburban rather than inner city sites. It would be wrong to deny that such a logic of change in housing policy did take place, at least in London. Caution is, however, needed. Although this might accurately describe the trend in policy in London, it does not fit the development of policy in Birmingham where a different set of policy prescriptions emerged by the First World War. There was a well-developed alternative to council housing which had many adherents before 1914.

A leading exponent of this alternative policy was J. S. Nettlefold, a member of the Birmingham City Council. He condemned municipal house-building on the grounds that it drove out private enterprise, and argued instead that the role of the municipality was to facilitate the work of builders by supplying cheap land. This might be brought about by national policy designed to force land onto the market which was a leading feature of the Liberal government's programme before the war. The council might acquire large tracts of undeveloped land at a cheap price, lay out streets on low-density garden city lines, and provide the necessary services. The municipality was to plan the development and to provide the infrastructure, but not to own the houses which would be supplied by private enterprise or by tenant co-partnerships which the residents were to run themselves. Nettlefold's opposition to council housing arose not only from his belief that the outcome would be to drive out private enterprise, but also on moral grounds. A common aim amongst Edwardian progressives was the need for the state to remove defects in the social system so that people could then take charge of their own lives; to go further would be to make men dependent rather than independent. The role of the state was not to house people, but to ensure that the normal person could house himself, for only on these terms was it possible 'to secure the conditions upon which mind and character may develop themselves'.[41] The provision of council houses could therefore be seen less as a solution to a social problem than as a means of creating a dependent and demoralised population. This was a view which was shared by some members of the Labour party, which by 1914 had not been fully converted to state welfare. The adoption of a large-scale programme of council housing after the First World War can, therefore, not be taken for granted.

The postwar housing programme has been viewed as 'an ad hoc response to an immediate political crisis',[42] providing an antidote to revolution at the end of the First World War. This required concern for quality as well as quantity, for the new houses had to be of a design superior to anything supplied in the past, in order to show that aspirations could be met under the existing order. The abandonment of the housing programme in July 1921 when only 170,000 houses had been built of the 500,000 proposed was, on this analysis, an expression of the erosion of the power of labour with the end of the postwar boom. This is to see council housing as a political creation, a concession consciously granted by the state to purchase social stability, with the working class viewed as passive recipients. An alternative approach would accord the working class an active role in destroying the private market which then necessitated state intervention. This account would place emphasis upon the rent strikes of 1915 which resulted in the

[41] L. T. Hobhouse, *Liberalism* (1911), pp. 158–9.
[42] M. Swenarton, *Homes Fit for Heroes: The Politics and Architecture of Early State Housing in Britain* (1981), p. 81.

imposition of rent controls, a decline in profits and a reluctance by private investors to enter the housing market. The Act of 1915 did not, it is argued, remove the source of grievances, for militancy developed amongst tenants as a result of problems of intimidation, shortages of accommodation and the cost of lodgings. Rent strikes occurred after the war, and it is argued that this made it inexpedient to remove controls, which resulted in the persistence of shortages and necessitated state intervention to supplement private enterprise. House capitalists before 1914 were, it is argued, in a politically marginal position and their survival depended on the inertia of the working class which ended in 1915. This is to give the working class a positive role in the creation of policy: the government was prevented from decontrolling the private market to restore housing to an economic footing; the working class achieved council housing as a positive victory, rather than received it as a coercive instrument. A third approach would view council housing as the resolution of a contradiction within capitalism. The minimum requirements of housing had been increased by legislation, which opened a gap between the rental needed by the owner to secure an adequate rate of return, and the occupier's ability to pay. The increase in standards meant that either the ratio of rent to wage would rise, or the rate of return would fall. This, it is suggested, was occurring before the First World War, but since housing was essential for the 'reproduction of labour power', it became necessary for the state to intervene directly to provide accommodation.

These three interpretations are perhaps not mutually exclusive. There is no doubt that the government did exploit the ideological potential of council housing, but as a secondary consequence rather than the primary stimulus, for the provision of housing to secure social stability would be an expensive, slow and cumbersome strategy. The interpretation neglects the strains which had emerged within the housing market, whether from the Edwardian erosion of profit margins, or the distortions of rent control after 1915. The second interpretation is surely correct to emphasise concern to protect tenants, and to stress the significance of rent control in depressing returns and prolonging shortages. But it is possible to exaggerate the importance of tenants' movements in the retention of rent controls. The government was aware of the dangers of allowing a sudden movement of rents to match the general level of prices after the war, based on an assessment of political expediency rather than the strength of tenants' organisations. Tenants simply outnumbered landlords, who in any case lacked a clear political voice, and this assessment of the situation after the war was a continuation of the prewar trends which had weakened the position of the private landlord. There was, after all, no reason why the burdens of control should not be compensated by tax benefits or subsidies incorporating the private landlord within a comprehensive housing policy. But rent control and housing policy were not integrated, and the policy was rather to react to the continuation of controls by developing alternative instruments. Of course, the distortions of wartime rent control were not entirely novel but rather continued a prewar erosion of profitability. There is indeed some justice in the view that a higher priority was given to the quality of housing than to the survival of house capitalists as a separate fraction of capital.

Whatever the reasons for intervention in 1919, the role accorded to council housing thereafter was radically different during Labour and Conservative administrations. The Conservatives had before the First World War favoured council housing as a solution to the housing problem as an alternative to the Liberal land campaign, but they were less sympathetic in the interwar period. Neville Chamberlain's Housing Act of 1923 viewed council housing as a temporary expedient until the housing shortage was removed, at which point both rent controls and local authority building could end. In the 1930s this policy did change. The Housing (Financial Provisions) Act of 1933 accepted that private building for owner-occupation had removed the shortage for middle-class and prosperous working-class families, so that controls could be abandoned and the supply of accommodation left to the free market. The nature of private building had changed from sale to landlords to sale to occupiers, which was welcomed and encouraged by Conservatives. However, this strategy could not work at the bottom of the market, where rent controls should be a permanent feature. Additions to the housing stock at the bottom of the market would be left to the filtering down of surplus housing, whilst local authority building should replace slums rather than provide 'general purpose' housing. The slum clearance schemes of the 1930s were new in scale, for the number of houses closed or demolished in England and Wales increased dramatically from 27,564 up to March 1934 to 245,272 between April 1934 and March 1939. The result was to define council housing as a low-status tenure. The approach of the Labour party was different. State initiative should be the normal rather than emergency method of supply; rent control should be permanent, with rent courts to establish fair rents. The Housing (Financial Provisions) Act of 1924 affirmed the commitment of the Labour government to subsidised local authority housing, and although it was to be abandoned by the National governments of the 1930s, this view of the housing market returned to the fore during the postwar Labour government.

The social purpose of council housing has been viewed in a number of ways both by politicians at the time and by historians since. This debate cannot be separated from what might appear to be a more mundane matter: how did councillors go about their new tasks of managing the houses which had been supplied? How should local authorities act as landlords? Local authorities could not, as private landlords, act upon purely commercial considerations, and this created a dilemma. Housing could be seen as an aspect of social policy, which might create the danger of a mounting financial deficit on the housing account. It might indeed be difficult to reconcile estate management, financial probity and social policy, particularly when the emphasis turned to slum clearance and tenants who were 'least eligible in the eyes of the private owner'.[43]

The establishment of rent levels raised complex issues of redistribution between areas and families. The scheme of 1919 limited the contribution of local taxation, and placed most of the cost upon central government. This meant that depressed areas with poor housing could be subsidised by prosperous areas with good housing, and finance was progressive with need. Subsequent legislation established fixed limits to the assistance from central government, the contribution of local taxation was increased and finance was now regressive with need. This created a serious problem for depressed regions such as the north-east of England, where low rateable values and poor housing conditions entailed a dilemma that construction would increase the rate in the pound with serious consequences for the tenants of working-class housing. Local authority housing was now subsidised from regressive local taxation rather than progressive national taxation. Councillors were willing in the early 1920s to adopt progressive principles at the expense of the national taxpayer, so that rents could be determined by the ability of the tenant to pay; they were less

---

[43] Ministry of Health, *Annual Report for 1929–30*, quoted in R. Ryder, 'Council House Building in Co. Durham, 1900–39: The Local Implementation of National Policy' (unpublished MPhil thesis, University of Durham, 1979), p. 246.

enthusiastic when it was at the expense of the local ratepayer. The reduction of rents for some tenants, particularly those rehoused from slums in the 1930s, would imply one of two things. An increased contribution from ratepayers was one possibility, which had political dangers and fiscal limits. Alternatively, the rents of other council tenants could be increased according to their ability to pay, which would involve unpopular means testing and resentment of the subsidisation of slum-dwellers. In Birmingham in 1939 the result was a rent strike by aggrieved council tenants which forced the council to abandon the policy. Rent policy therefore involved complex political issues of redistribution of income between council tenants, and between council tenants and other ratepayers.

The determination of rents was associated with the selection of tenants and their allocation to estates. Tenants of houses built under the Act of 1919 were largely drawn from the better-paid working class and some white-collar workers. Although the subsidy was progressive with need between areas, there was a tendency for the benefit to accrue to the more affluent families who could afford to pay the balance of rent unprovided by the subsidy. Councils developed criteria of 'housing need', but there was still a concern for ability to pay the rent and whether a tenant was 'desirable'. Enquiry Officers or Health Visitors might be employed to inspect the applicant's rent book and present house, to establish whether any rates were outstanding, and to determine the level of income. Selection became more difficult with the need to rehouse slum clearance tenants, and the emphasis was rather placed upon allocation. Families would be categorised as respectables or roughs, as desirable or undesirable tenants, and the sifting of the free market was institutionalised so that certain families could be allocated to 'problem' estates. Once the tenants were installed, the councils had to develop policies to protect the property, and to socialise the tenants into life on the new cottage estates. Partly, this was a negative process of excluding public houses and issuing rules which banned certain activities, but there was also a more positive encouragement of desired behaviour such as gardening. The supervision of the estates could be undertaken in a number of ways. It was rare in the interwar period for councils to adopt the 'intensive' system of management which combined the collection of rents and responsibility for repairs with welfare questions. On the whole, councils seem to have relied upon despatching rent collectors to the estates, who had a narrowly defined responsibility. This neglect of welfare considerations was also reflected in the design of the council estates in the interwar period.

The creation of suburban cottage estates had a number of consequences for families moving from well-established inner city districts. The ties of kinship which were so important for child-minding and assistance in times of difficulty were disrupted by the movement of nuclear families to the fringes of the town. Families from one area were dispersed to a number of estates rather than concentrated in a single location. It was also difficult for ties of kinship to develop once the population had moved to an estate, for the system of housing allocation would not permit a newly married couple to reside on an estate until they met the criteria of housing need, when they would not necessarily be allocated to the same estate as relatives or friends. There was also a change in the relationship between work and home, which intensified these social consequences. Journeys to work became longer, and women might be removed from sources of supplementary income which existed in the inner city. The estates were also notoriously lacking in amenities such as clubs, cinemas and churches. The number of shops was limited, and they were more expensive and less varied than the stores and markets of the central areas. One solution to these various problems was to build blocks of flats in the central areas, such as the Quarry Hill scheme in Leeds, but this was at the expense of rejecting the tenants' preference for self-contained houses. It was only at the end of the 1930s that council estates were planned in a social as well as technical sense, prompted by a growing concern for anti-social behaviour and vandalism. The substance as well as the shadow of garden city planning was sought with the realisation that the larger estates should be planned as self-contained communities. The failure to implement such a policy in the 1920s and 1930s entailed the purchase of better housing conditions at a considerable social cost.

Council estates provided suburbanisation for the working class to complement the suburbanisation of the middle class, but reflected a divergence as much as a congruence of experiences. The tenure on council estates was seen as inferior to owner-occupation by the middle class, and the two tenures were kept physically distinct. Suburban life imposed additional costs of transport to work and recreation, which the middle-class families could afford much more readily than the working-class ones. Indeed, it was discovered in Stockton that the standard of health on the new council estates was actually lower than in the slums because of the strain imposed upon working-class budgets. Middle-class households were more often self-reliant, dependent upon one wage earner, whereas working-class households were more closely involved in ties of kinship, and reliant upon supplementary incomes. Suburban residence might therefore disrupt the working-class family economy to a far greater extent. The suburbanisation of the interwar period had come about for different reasons, with divergent tenures and social consequences.

IV

Owner-occupation was, until the 1920s and 1930s, more often talked of than achieved. The desire to own one's home was a component of the ideology of the labour aristocracy, a symbol of status, independence and respectability, but there were also serious drawbacks, not only for the working class but also the middle class. The repayment of capital and interest generally exceeded the rent of a similar house; ownership did not necessarily provide the attraction of long-term capital gain which has been an important benefit in the inflationary period since 1945; nor was the reduction in tax liability a significant consideration at a time of low levels of direct taxation. Owner-occupation could be viewed as a source of inflexibility rather than a tax-effective investment, for it was easier to move to a rented house which fitted the family's current financial position and stage of life. Owner-occupation has become a firmly entrenched element in British mentality, but it is certainly not to be taken for granted as a self-evident means of providing accommodation. Before the First World War, owner-occupation was a response to particular features of local housing markets rather than a general phenomenon, and the ideological consequences could be very different from those perceived by recent Conservative politicians. This may be illustrated by the example of South Wales. In the commercial centre of the region, at Cardiff, only 7.2 per cent of houses were owner-occupied in 1914. The radical change came after the First World War, and by 1934, 35.4 per cent of all houses in Cardiff were owner-occupied, predominantly in middle-class areas. However, the incidence of owner-occupation had already attained such a level before 1914, in the very different circumstances of working-class ownership of houses, financed by co-operation in building clubs, in the mining valleys in the hinterland of Cardiff. The ideology differed from that normally associated with owner-occupation, for it was based upon mutuality rather than individualism, in a climate of political militancy rather than conservatism, amongst the working class rather than the middle class. Not only the scale but also the nature of owner-occupation changed in the interwar period, when the connection between class and tenure became more apparent.

The increase in owner-occupation had two dimensions: the decision of private landlords to sell existing property; and the sale by speculative builders direct to owner-occupiers. In England and Wales in 1938, 1.4 m out of 5.3 m prewar houses, and a further 1.4 m houses built between the wars, were owner-occupied. The first category is easily explained, for private landlords faced with an erosion of their profit margin were likely to benefit by selling to sitting tenants or to property companies who would secure vacant possession for resale. Owner-occupation was the largest tenure in new houses, accounting for 49.1 per cent of construction between 1919 and 1938. This was made possible by changes in economic variables; the extent to which it was encouraged by government policy in order to modify social and political attitudes is less clear.

Building costs fell between 1925 and 1933 from an index of 111.1 to 90.0, and interest rates fell from 6 to 4.5 per cent. This entailed a fall in the weekly cost of purchasing a three-bedroomed non-parlour house from 12s. 1d. to 7s. 8d. at a time when real wages for those in work improved significantly. The building societies were highly liquid, and the terms of borrowing were eased, so that in the 1930s the societies were willing to lend 90 or 95 per cent of the value of the property, for twenty-five to thirty years. Owner-occupation was taken further down the income scale, and there was a danger that both the market for loans and for houses were becoming saturated. The outcome was to bring building societies and builders together in the so-called 'builders' pools' by which builders created a fund to guarantee the societies against defaulting borrowers. The result was that the societies were less concerned than they otherwise would have been about either the value of a house in relation to a loan, or the ability of the purchaser to keep up payments. The interests of the purchasers tended to be neglected, and this led in the late 1930s to a legal challenge against the 'builders' pools' and a spate of 'mortgage strikes' in the London area. The attempt to meet the demand for new housing in the interwar period by extending owner-occupation to successively lower income levels had run into serious problems by 1938. 'The mistake made by building societies', argued one leading official looking back in 1942, 'had been that they had a greater regard for the builder-vendor than the buyer-borrower.'[44]

Building societies were central to the growth of owner-occupation between the wars. In the same way that local authorities controlled the allocation of resources in the public sector, so did building societies in the private sector. The access to housing was fundamentally different from the private rental market before 1914. The building societies favoured recent property of conventional form in areas of stable social structure which were sought by the average, stable family in secure employment. This had various social consequences. The housing market was differentiated between those to whom the building societies would lend, and those whom local authorities would house. Both created their own procedures for the allocation of resources which differed from renting a house from a private landlord in the free market. Those who met neither criteria were forced into a private rented market which was in decline, and which favoured sitting tenants rather than new entrants. The social consequence of the spread of owner-occupation, it has been argued, was the emergence of a class of debt-encumbered households which opposed economic and social change endangering the value of property. Many Conservatives did indeed expect owner-occupation to create social stability, and it was welcomed on the right and regretted on the left that 'home ownership eroded socialist zeal and led to wider electoral support for the Conservative cause'.[45]

This connection between owner-occupation and social stability can be over-drawn, for there were signs by the late 1930s that the spread of home ownership was creating tensions. Instead of producing a 'rampart' of small owners, the practices of builders and building societies seemed to be calling property into disrepute. The expected social consequence was, therefore, not to be taken for granted. But many commentators at the time and historians since *have* taken it for granted, and have often gone a step further to assume that the spread of the tenure was consciously encouraged to produce a socially content and Conservative electorate. The assumed social connotations of owner-occupation were, on this account, not the incidental outcome of a process occurring for other reasons, but the consequence of

[44]   Quoted in E. J. Cleary, *The Building Society Movement* (1965), p. 223.
[45]   M. Pinto-Duschinsky in V. Bogdanor and R. Skidelsky, *The Age of Affluence* (1970), p. 61.

government policies designed to modify social and political attitudes. Does this argument have any validity?

The encouragement to owner-occupation is usually seen as the result of the operation of the tax system which favoured investment in building societies and owner-occupation and checked investment in the rented sector. There were two issues. Should borrowers receive tax relief on their interest payments? Should investors in building societies pay tax on their incomes? The first aspect is the one which is usually stressed, for mortgage tax relief has become of increasing importance to most owner-occupiers in the recent past. In the 1920s and 1930s it was more complicated. Since owner-occupiers enjoyed a 'real' income from their houses, they were expected to pay tax on this hypothetical revenue from which could be deducted an allowance for repairs and interest charges. Private landlords were taxed on the actual rent received, and could similarly make deductions. Both could therefore reduce their tax liability by the payment of interest, but the private landlord had no incentive to make a loss on his source of income simply to avoid tax. The owner-occupier did have an incentive. The hypothetical revenue was calculated by reference to the rental of controlled prewar houses, which deflated the 'real' income received. When actual payments were deducted, many owner-occupiers were making an apparent loss, which reduced the tax liability on their salary. Tenants who paid income tax could not reduce their liability which might therefore provide some encouragement to become an owner-occupier. They might, however, be paying a controlled rent below the market level which would remove the incentive; this 'subsidy' was being paid by the landlord rather than the state. The system of tax benefits and rent controls was therefore biased against the owners of private rented property who received fewer tax advantages than owner-occupiers, and who also were paying a form of subsidy to many tenants.

The tax system also placed investors in building societies in a privileged position. The collection of taxes on small investments in building societies was difficult, and in 1894 it was decided that societies should pay the tax direct on half of the interest in order to remove the obligation of the Inland Revenue to collect from each investor. Individuals taxed at the full rate benefited, whilst investors whose income was below the threshold could claim a refund. In 1916, this agreement was amended so that tax was deducted at the rate of 3s. in the pound on all interest instead of the standard rate of 5s. in the pound, with no right to reclaim tax. Investors who were liable to tax had a strong incentive to place funds in building societies, and so contributed to the very liquid position of building societies in the 1920s and 1930s. This tax policy attracted a larger proportion of savings into housing, but it was not necessarily a deliberate policy to benefit owner-occupiers. A number of other factors need to be considered in order to understand why the societies changed their market. The building societies had been willing to lend to the owners of rented property before the First World War, supplementing the private mortgages supplied by solicitors which formed a major part of the money entering investment in housing. The controls introduced in 1915 distorted the market in mortgages, for interest rates in the rent-controlled houses were fixed and mortgages could not be recalled. This biased the market against lending to the private rental sector after the war: the private mortgage market largely disappeared as solicitors turned to other outlets for the funds in their care; and building societies developed as institutions catering for owner-occupiers. The landlords were in any case less likely to be seeking further loans, not only because the tax system was biased against them but also because of other ways in which governments failed to protect their interests. The burden of the rates fell on investment in housing more than other sectors, squeezing profit margins which were further eroded by rent controls. Private rental was also reduced by the impact of slum clearance, for between 1932 and 1939 over 300,000 houses were demolished with compensation to the owners which had been much reduced in comparison with the terms which had applied before 1914. This amounts to saying that the mild fiscal advantages to owner-occupation were less significant than the burdens placed on the private rental sector and the failure of the government to take action to redress the balance. In the circumstances, the building societies whose liquidity had been encouraged by the tax benefits to investors turned towards owner-occupiers as their natural market.

The 'property owning democracy' which started to emerge in the interwar period was neither a traditional nor a natural feature of the British social structure; it was a recent phenomenon which involved, as surely as council housing, the intervention of the state. It was not something to be taken for granted, and one of the interesting features of housing policy after the First World War was the willingness of governments of all political complexions to permit the erosion of the private landlord. The tenurial structure which emerged was, in international terms, a curious one. In other countries, there was a willingness to come to the aid of the private rental sector, and the British emphasis upon the role of the local authorities might be complemented by encouragement to housing associations. The social consequences of the tenurial system which emerged were confusing and complex. It would certainly be wrong to suggest that the result was the creation of three interest groups or housing classes – owner-occupiers, council tenants and private tenants. Although each sector did have its own particular methods of allocation and control which affected social life, there were also important social differences within each sector. The prosperous council tenants might resent paying higher rents in order to assist refugees from slum clearance schemes. The beneficiaries of rent control might pay a low rent for a house identical to one for which a new tenant entering the housing market for the first time was paying a market rent. The owner-occupier who had strained his resources and bought an overvalued house in the late 1930s might not be as staunch a supporter of the ethic of property ownership as those who were benefiting from the tax system to a greater extent. Although the crude notion that each tenure formed a housing class with common interests does not hold, there is no doubt that the changes in the market for accommodation between the wars led to complex and often anomalous shifts in housing access and cost which form a major theme in the social history of Britain.

CONCLUSION

The most important single date in the history of the social relations of housing in Britain, F. M. L. Thompson has suggested, was 1915, and the imposition of rent control was 'arguably the most decisive single stroke of policy in the present century'.[46] The implications, he insists, were profound and far-reaching, involving an interference with private property rights and the operation of the free market; sucking the state into controlled tenancies, rent tribunals and council housing; precipitating a retreat of private landlords from the provision of rented property; and inducing state subsidy of owner-occupation with its consequences for residential immobility and the sterilisation of savings in bricks and mortar. He concludes that if one wanted

[46] F. M. L. Thompson, 'Trying to Raise the Rent', *Times Literary Supplement*, 22 July 1983, p. 785.

to pick out one single origin of the fundamentally stable, unprotesting, unenterprising and conservative society of late twentieth-century Britain one could do worse than start with 1915. There is, of course, a danger that a single turning point has been emphasised and continuities neglected. The willingness of the state to sacrifice house capital in 1915 had clear origins before the First World War in the erosion of the profitability of rented property, the stricter control over distress and the failure to rectify the inequitable incidence of local taxation. The Act of 1915 was nevertheless important in converting prewar tensions into postwar crisis, and a new tenurial pattern emerged whose implications are vital for an understanding of twentieth-century Britain. Economically, the result has been to increase the proportion of capital invested in housing; socially, it has created an adherence to the existing system of property relations and consolidated a Conservative tenurial constituency; politically, it has involved the state in complex technical issues of taxation, rents, mortgages, building society finance and local authority housing. The creation of this new tenurial structure has been one of the major factors in the social history of twentieth-century Britain, both at the level of everyday life and of the social structure in general.

The significance of housing for an understanding of the social history of Britain was in many ways greater in 1950 than in 1750. By the end of the period, life was more home-centred. John Ruskin commented that 'Our God is a Household God as well as a heavenly one',[47] and the allegiance to the first deity only strengthened after he wrote. This was associated with the rise of owner-occupation, which dominated middle-class, and increasingly working-class, ambitions and investments. It was also linked with a change in leisure patterns towards the home and the family and away from communal pastimes. The culture of domesticity had strengthened its hold over British society since the mid-nineteenth century.

The share of resources devoted to housing increased, with a particularly large rise in the interwar period. In the 1870s and 1900s, investment in dwellings was respectively 19.8 and 18.7 per cent of UK gross domestic fixed capital formation, and 1.6 per cent of the gross national product in both decades. In the 1920s, investment in dwellings had risen to 25.8 per cent of gross domestic fixed capital formation and 2.4 per cent of gross national product, with a further increase in the

---

[47] Quoted by Burnett, *Social History*, p. 109.

1930s to 32.9 and 3.4 per cent. The changes in tenure in the interwar period implied a reduction in the rate of interest paid on the capital invested in housing, for owner-occupiers invested their own funds without a monetary return, whilst local authorities did not seek a commercial profit. Although housing was responsible for a larger share of domestic investment, it also formed a lower share of total consumers' expenditure. These changes entailed a considerable improvement in housing standards, but there were some implications which were less beneficial. Labour mobility was reduced, by the disinclination to leave a rent-controlled property; the need to secure 'points' on the waiting list of a particular local authority; and the high cost of buying and selling houses. Large local authority estates produced strains on the working-class family economy, and in the view of some eroded independence. The development of a property-owning democracy encouraged the sterilisation of savings in houses, with harmful effects on industrial investment. There has been considerable debate amongst economic historians on the impact of overseas investment before the First World War on the performance of the British economy. In the interwar period, capital exports collapsed, but it was investment in housing which increased rather than investment in industry. It is time that economic historians considered the balance sheet of investment in housing since the First World War as assiduously as they have analysed overseas investment before the First World War.

The outbreak of the Second World War led to the reimposition of rent controls, which were continued by the postwar Labour government. In the period of recovery after the war, the emphasis was upon building as many houses in the public sector as possible, and it was only in the 1950s that the trend towards owner-occupation reappeared, with a consensus in both the Conservative and Labour parties that the housing market should be a dual one, based upon owner-occupation and council housing. This consensus was to continue, with a variety of emphases, until the Housing Act of 1980 which gave the tenants of council houses the right to buy in order to join the ranks of owner-occupiers. The number of council tenants started to fall for the first time since the end of the First World War, and a new tenurial revolution commenced. One side-effect of this change in housing policy since 1980 has been to cast a new light upon the social history of housing. The development of policy can no longer be seen as an inexorable trend towards the triumph of the council house as a solution to the housing problem. This now appears much less self-evident, and the range of alternatives debated before the First World War is back on the political agenda. The doubts of the 'new' Liberals about the provision of state housing as a threat to the self-respect and independence of the working class appear less absurd in the 1980s than they did twenty or thirty years ago when much of the history of housing was being written. The desirability of tenants running their own estates, and the virtues of housing associations, are now being stressed. And the necessity for the demise of the private landlord is being questioned to a greater extent than at any time since the First World War. Perhaps it is correct to argue that 1915 does mark the most significant break in the history of housing in Britain; what is also true is that the outcome has been increasingly questioned since 1980 as assumptions about the social relations of housing are revised.

CHAPTER 5

Food, drink and nutrition

D. J. ODDY

As long as the state of domestic agriculture was the principal determinant of food consumption, the population of Britain depended on a limited range of food materials which were available on a markedly seasonal basis. While traditional forms of food preservation persisted, this meant that dietary patterns were circumscribed by the availability and durability of foodstuffs. Thus the predominant food material in all parts of Britain on the eve of the industrial revolution was some kind of bread-grain, either wheat, barley or oats, surpluses of which were processed to produce beer and spirits. Animal food was preserved by the liberal use of salt. Bacon or pickled meat, salt fish, butter and, to a lesser extent, cheese fell into this category. Green vegetables were seasonal in supply, as were pulses, roots or bulbs such as onions, though the latter were capable of storage for some time. Nevertheless, every year brought the 'hungry gap' of the late winter and early spring when supplies of vegetables were exhausted, a pattern which was not entirely eradicated in country districts on the eve of the Great War in 1914.

Even before the industrial revolution, there were growing differences in what people ate or drank which reflected changes in their style of life. In predominantly agricultural areas, where the majority of the population lived, it was still usual to process food in the home and the self-reliance of families which kept animals and brewed and baked for themselves made it appear that little change was in sight. Yet the consolidation of landholdings and changes in agricultural techniques of the eighteenth and early nineteenth centuries were turning many countrydwellers into a rural proletariat dependent on wage labour as the principal source of income and with little, if any, access to land of their own on which to produce food. As a self-sustaining ecosystem, rural society was nearing its end. For most of the nineteenth century only the vestiges of a peasant economy remained, largely confined to the more remote upland or marshland regions. Change was at its most extreme where industrial development in textiles, metal production and engineering during the later eighteenth century was beginning to create an urban society dependent almost entirely upon the marketplace for food supplies. As the nineteenth century progressed, reliance on the marketplace grew not only as the towns expanded but also to meet the needs of the semi-rural but commercialised communities of miners, fishermen and shipbuilders, and the various crafts and trades of market towns. In the absence of economic groups largely self-sufficient in food, and with an increasing number of areas where local food production could no longer meet demand, it became necessary for the bulk of the population in Britain to obtain their food supplies through a commercial marketing system at a very early date. Large-scale specialised food marketing for the growing industrial and urban areas came into existence before the end of the eighteenth century, with the traditional network of corn markets being supplemented from the 1790s onwards by a rapidly growing and often long-distance trade in potatoes and livestock and with a more localised but expanding trade in dairy products and vegetables.

Despite these developments, the supply of food did not increase smoothly. The mid-eighteenth century was thought of by contemporaries as a period of plenty. Not only was bread cheap, it was cheap enough to encourage the brewing and distillation of grain in large amounts. For some people, in London at least, the torrent of gin resulted in ill-health and death rather than the well being which commentators assumed came with the extreme cheapness of food materials. Though the legislation of 1751 reduced the consumption of spirits somewhat, the era of cheap food which had begun in the 1730s was almost at an end as population increased and industrial demand grew. Prices began to rise from the late 1760s and the period until the end of the Napoleonic Wars was one of dear food. Fluctuations in price were very marked and reached such heights in 1795–6 and 1800–1 that T. S. Ashton thought them of 'famine' proportions.[1] During the first half of the nineteenth century, prices of foodstuffs continued to reflect the stresses which a rapid growth of population placed on the market. In the pre-railway era there were limitations on the long-distance movement of foodstuffs and the food retailing system was

---

[1] T. S. Ashton, *Economic Fluctuations in England, 1700–1800* (Oxford, 1959), pp. 25–6.

only embryonic. The high prices of food and numerous food riots during the period of the Napoleonic Wars, and the widespread adulteration of commodities such as bread, tea and beer, which continued into the second half of the nineteenth century, indicated that the food supply was barely adequate to meet growing demand. The expensiveness of food and the narrow range of food materials limited the diet for the majority of the population both in quantity and variety and also made it vulnerable to interruptions in supply. Nevertheless, there were no great dearths during the industrial revolution, even though high prices around 1840 led to the decade later acquiring the epithet 'Hungry Forties'. The one major crisis resulted from the potato blight but was confined, principally, to Ireland. In Britain, the failure of the potato crop was limited to the western Highlands (1846–7) where the potato had achieved an importance almost as great as it had in the Irish diet. The resulting food shortage was prevented from becoming a famine by the hasty improvisations of the Highland Relief Board. One later food crisis occurred in the early 1860s, during the Cotton Famine in Lancashire. This resulted from a lack of purchasing power rather than a failure in food supply, and was also contained by the extensive use of charitable relief.

Food prices began to fall from the end of the second decade of the nineteenth century due, initially, to the improved productivity of British agriculture. Later, as free trade policies were adopted and transport facilities improved, produce from the New World and other newly cultivated regions began to reach Britain. The widening of markets, coupled with the beginnings of modern food technology and improvements in retailing, led to a greater variety of foodstuffs becoming available in the diet. This process began in the late nineteenth century and by the interwar years rising expectations placed increasing emphasis on the availability of tinned foods and imports from the tropics and southern hemisphere which had been transported in refrigerated ships. The culmination of this trend was the almost complete eradication of seasonal constraint upon food choice, but that lay beyond 1950 and depended upon the new low-temperature technology of the postwar food industry and the growing domestic ownership of refrigerators and freezers in the 1960s and 1970s.

Changes in economic organisation over such a long time span as two centuries were a major influence upon food consumption. The growth of industrial and commercial employment and the creation of an urban domestic environment reduced ties with the land and increased dependence upon commercial sources of food supply. This made gifts of food between countrydwellers and, more especially, presents to relatives, friends and patrons in towns an important part of social intercourse. Surviving correspondence of the late eighteenth and early nineteenth centuries mentions gifts of hams, chickens, pigeons and various game birds though fruit, notably apples, was common in the autumn.[2] Domestic sources of food production declined rapidly as a consequence of the adoption of an urban life style, and eighteenth-century gardens became a prime source of building land on to which towns expanded. Changes in agricultural organisation in the late eighteenth and early nineteenth centuries had a similar but less obvious effect in reducing the availability of non-marketed food. The supply of milk, potatoes, vegetables, pigs and chickens to agricultural labourers' homes were all affected by changes in the organisation of land and their loss or the reduction of their contribution to the diet remained a major rural grievance until the end of the nineteenth century. Domestic baking and brewing underwent a marked decline in the first half of the nineteenth century as house space, fuel and time available proved inadequate to maintain such traditional activities. During the second half of the nineteenth century, the introduction of multiple outlet firms in food retailing to which the sale of commodities such as tea, margarine, cheese, butter and bacon were central indicated the extent to which non-market sources of food production had declined.

I DIETARY AND CULINARY TRADITIONS IN BRITAIN

For the majority of the population, housing, income, and hours of work were major constraints upon the cooking and serving of food, so that to be concerned with meals reflected leisure, wealth and the availability of domestic labour. During the period of industrialisation, arrangements such as the timing of meals and the style of menus changed as significantly as did many other aspects of people's lives. Longer hours and increased regularity of work, the separation of workplace from home and, later in the nineteenth century, the widespread attendance of children at school, all influenced patterns of eating and drinking just as much as the conditions of housing, the provision

[2] For examples, see James Woodforde, *The Diary of a Country Parson 1758–1802*, ed. John Beresford (Oxford, 1978), or A. Bell, *Sydney Smith: A Biography* (Oxford, 1982). Both also illustrate the reverse flow of food from the great houses, such as Castle Howard. This might include exotic fruits like pineapples and melons.

of domestic kitchen equipment and the availability of fuel did. Whilst at higher income levels the preparation and serving of food reflected decisions and choices consciously taken, more generally it was a response to what circumstances permitted.

Before industrial and urban life styles became widespread, dietary habits varied markedly by region and social class. In southern England, the concern with 'wheaten bread, strong beer, and butcher's meat' limited the variety of meals and the influence of cooking. Meat, for those who could afford it, was almost an obsession. Perhaps the Rev. George Woodward's elder brother Tom was exceptional in eating little if anything other than meat. The Rev. George Woodward thought Tom 'an uncouth relation' and 'asked him once, how he managed about suppers, as he never eat cheese or apple pie; he said if he did not happen to be where there was meat, he often eat no supper at all, but smoked his pipe instead of it'. The views of foreigners confirmed the Englishman's preference for meat. Earlier, in the 1690s, Henri Misson had commented: 'I have known people in England that never eat any bread, and universally they eat very little; they nibble a few crumbs, while they chew meat by whole mouthfuls.' On such a table the puddings, both savoury and sweet, made up for the lack of bread and provided the cereal content of the meal.[3]

For the poor it was generally accepted that 'bread makes the principal part of the food of all poor families and almost the whole of the food of ... large families'.[4] Its quality varied markedly. Calculations based on weights of ingredients suggest that the loaf contained only 28 to 30 per cent water, so that it was generally of a drier texture than today. This doubtless helped its keeping qualities though, to modern palates, much of the bread eaten in the eighteenth and early nineteenth centuries would be thought stale because baking was much less frequent. Bread also depended on the availability of suitable yeast. In the countryside, its scarcity might mean that loaves were unleavened or more akin to soda-bread. In poor seasons blame was put on the flour. The Rev. Sydney Smith wrote of the harvest at Foston in 1816: 'Corn is rather bad than dear but makes good unleavened bread; and the poor, I find, seldom make any other than unleavened

---

[3] Sir Frederic M. Eden, *The State of the Poor*, 3 vols. (1797), vol. 1, p. 587; D. Gibson, ed., *A Parson in the Vale of White Horse* (Gloucester, 1982), p. 73; H. Misson, cited in J. Stead, *Food and Cookery in 18th Century Britain: History and Recipes* (1985), p. 26.

[4] Rev. David Davies, *The Case of Labourers in Husbandry Stated and Considered* (1795), p. 21.

bread, even in the best seasons.'[5] Many meals were made up of bread and tea alone, while the general demand for white, wheaten bread meant that barley and oatmeal used as porridge or 'hasty pudding' were in decline in the late eighteenth century. Moreover, the price of fuel in southern England was already forcing poor people to buy bread from the baker rather than bake it themselves. The use of the potato in the south was limited until the nineteenth century because, as the Rev. David Davies explained:

Wheaten bread maybe eaten alone with pleasure; but potatoes require either meat or milk to make them go down: you cannot make many hearty meals of them with salt and water only. Poor people indeed give them to their children in the greasy water in which they have boiled their greens and their morsel of bacon.[6]

Davies was not against potatoes as he realised that they would help poor people to feed a pig but felt rather that such dietary change was unlikely to be accepted in the south. Potatoes were more commonly eaten in the north and west of Britain. Sir Frederic Eden contrasted the southern diet of tea, twice a day, best wheaten bread and a little bacon with that of the north: 'In point of expence, their general diet as much exceeds, as, in point of nutrition, it falls short of, the north country fare of milk, potatoes, barley bread and hasty-pudding.'[7]

Until the end of the eighteenth century such a diet extended south into the Midlands and into Wales and the West Country, though there were already signs of change. At Burton-on-Trent, Eden observed that 'oatmeal forms a great part of the food of the labouring classes: it is boiled with milk into a sort of hasty-pudding', though wheaten bread 'is now beginning to be introduced on particular occasions, by those who can afford it'.[8] The universal respect for white bread extended into Scotland, though there most baked goods were of barley meal rather than wheat and Eden's north country fare was translated into oatmeal porridge, potatoes, and milk or cheese, with kale the ever-present vegetable. In Scotland as in the north of England, the practice of farm servants living in was still widespread in the nineteenth century, which meant that many ate at the farmer's table, though 'boarding out' became more common at times when food was dear.

---

[5] Bell, *Sydney Smith*, p. 106.   [6] Davies, *Case of Labourers*, p. 36.
[7] Eden, *State of the Poor*, vol. 1, p. 14.   [8] *Ibid.*, p. 812.

The adequate organisation of the domestic economy of the agricultural labourer's family in southern England depended, in Davies's view, upon having sufficient funds to obtain a pig below market price from a farmer, obtaining credit to buy flour by the sack and having 'sufficient garden ground for planting a good patch of potatoes'.[9] Domestic brewing, similarly, required families to use at least a bushel of malt every month to obtain 28 gallons of small beer, and the cost of materials and fuel (plus the cost of the equipment for young men setting up their own families) meant that from the late eighteenth century brewing as well as baking began to decline in many rural areas. 'How wasteful, and indeed how shameful for a labourer's wife to go to the baker's shop' thundered William Cobbett,[10] but the decline in traditional self-sufficiency continued and from the mid-nineteenth century only pockets of resistance to shop products remained. Cooking and meal preparation took on a more limited form in rural districts in the nineteenth century and was mirrored in the newly urbanised areas by the disappearance of home-made soups, broths and pottages where these had formerly been traditional. Once this pattern of change is understood, it explains Maud Davies's comments in her 1906 survey of Corsley that wives cooked only once or twice a week during the winter, but perhaps more often when potatoes were plentiful, though 'it was exceptional to find a woman who ... cooks every day'.[11] Indeed, the fact that people were satisfied to eat bread with cold meat or cheese and beer as regular everyday fare in much of England may well have limited the growth of culinary arts in Britain as much as any other factor.

Eating three meals a day was the accepted pattern everywhere in Britain by the eighteenth century. Exceptions were the isolated instances of those Oxford colleges which retained the medieval habit of dining at 11 and supping at 6, although Parson Woodforde noted in his diary that New College had begun to dine 'at three o'clock every day, Sundays excepted, which is half after three then' during the summer of 1768.[12] Even menus at workhouses, hospitals and schools confirmed the general arrangement of three meals a day. For many, the hours of these meals were determined by work, the main meal of the day being a midday dinner eaten at home, though there

[9] Davies, *Case of Labourers*, p. 23.
[10] William Cobbett, *Cottage Economy* (1821), p. 82.
[11] Maud F. Davies, *Life in an English Country Village: An Economic and Historical Survey of the Parish of Corsley in Wiltshire* (1909), pp. 214, 216.
[12] Woodforde, *Diary of a Country Parson*, p. 51.

were groups of workers such as farm labourers, shepherds, carters, miners and fishermen whose tasks took them away from the family at that time. The midday dinner was remarkably flexible in terms of its timing and arrangement. Urban artisans ate at midday, as travellers who ate at inns frequently did, but among the better-off classes, in town and country alike, dinner was usually later at 2 or 3 o'clock. The Drummonds[13] thought that the dinner hour gradually became later during the eighteenth century, which meant that suppers of cold meats were unlikely to have been eaten before 9 or 10 p.m., especially if the new practice of tea drinking around 5 or 6 o'clock was adopted. Among the classes who could afford it, eating in quantity was, without doubt, one of the pleasures of the eighteenth century so that dinner could be a lengthy and complex occasion. Only in exceptional circumstances, however, would they be as lengthy as Parson Woodforde's entertainment of his farmers on tithe audit day. In 1799, they stayed with him until 11 p.m. 'and went away highly pleased' having consumed 'two legs of mutton boiled & Capers, Salt-Fish, A Sur-Loin of Beef roasted, with plenty of plumb & plain Puddings &c', and substantial amounts of punch, wine, rum and beer to wash it down.[14]

Although some of the more fashion-conscious people paid attention to the French pattern of serving meals in successive courses, 'English service' was still general until after the Napoleonic Wars, so that for a family dinner 'Boiled Rabbits Smothered with Onions, French Beans stewed, Apple Pudding, Pease, Leg of Grass Lamb roasted' might all appear on the table together. Occasionally, a 'remove' dish would be brought to the table to replace another, in which case it would frequently be an opportunity for a soup or fish dish to be replaced by poultry or game, but generally people chose what dishes they wanted, while the rest of the food stood cooling. Sometimes salads and a dessert were available from a sideboard, though by the 1780s cookery books were already introducing the idea of separate courses. *The Ladies' Assistant* included in its Bills of Fare 'Family Dinners of Two Courses' which ranged from 'Four and Five' to as many as 'Eleven and Fifteen' dishes on the table.[15] Within twenty years or so of the battle of Waterloo, however, the French achieved a sweeping victory over fashionable eating habits. Though popular works such

[13] J. C. Drummond and Anne Wilbraham, *The Englishman's Food*, revised edn, ed. Dorothy F. Hollingsworth (1957), pp. 211–12.
[14] Woodforde, *Diary of a Country Parson*, pp. 589–90.
[15] Charlotte Mason, *The Ladies' Assistant*, 6th edn (1787).

as *The Family Oracle of Health* (1824) still recommended the simpler, traditional eating practices, French dishes, French service by courses at dinner and, above all, French chefs had become the dominant influence among the leading families and London clubs. Alexis Soyer, who became chef to the Reform Club between 1839 and 1851, epitomised this transformation. Not only did soup and fish now act as a first course and precede the second course of meat dishes, but the coupling of entrées with the older English practice of 'removes' gave a progression to meals which culminated in the menus suggested by Mrs Beeton from 1861 onwards.[16] At the same time, nineteenth-century mealtimes began to change. Professor John Burnett has drawn attention to Queen Victoria's preference for eating late in the evening: amongst the fashionable, social emulation rapidly converted dinner to an evening meal from the 1840s onwards, counterbalanced by the development of the 'English breakfast' eaten at 8 or 9 in the morning. A substantial morning meal was already well established north of the border: as early as the 1770s, Dr Johnson commented favourably on the tea and coffee, honey, conserves and marmalades which accompanied the scones and bannocks. Such patterns were well fitted to the activities of landed estates and country house parties, but they also suited the mercantile, professional and industrial middle classes whose business activities were becoming separated from their places of residence. In consequence, supper, as it was known in the eighteenth century and earlier times, disappeared except in the form of a late snack or drink, while the long gap between the two principal meals of the day came to be filled by a light lunch at 1 or 2 p.m. and, in fashionable houses after the 1840s, by afternoon tea.

From the 1870s or 1880s a further refinement in eating habits was the introduction of service *à la russe*, in which courses instead of containing a number of dishes were reduced to one or two only, and the recognised order of the meal familiar today – soup, fish, entrée, roast, dessert – became standardised in its varying degrees of complexity. Once established, this combination of evening dinner and service *à la russe* created a distinction in eating habits which persisted into the late twentieth century, between the middle class who adopted these patterns and the working class who continued to regard dinner as a midday meal to be eaten at home if at all possible. If the male

[16] For the best account of these changes, see John Burnett, *Plenty and Want: A Social History of Diet from 1815 to the Present Day* (1966; revised edn, 1989), chaps. 4 and 9.

head of a working-class family could not eat at home during a working day, it was quite likely that his wife and children would only eat a meatless meal. Sunday dinner was regarded as the highlight of the week, symbolised by the cooking of the main purchase of butcher's meat. Only in the event of severe privation was the attempt to maintain the status of the Sunday dinner abandoned.

One variation of these patterns which bestrode the social class barriers was the 'high tea', originating on Sunday evenings and normally eaten by the middle classes without the attendance of servants. It retained many of the characteristics of the suppers formerly eaten in the English style. The reaction against this formless meal by the faster members of society from the 1880s onwards excited the charge of 'hedonism' from R. C. K. Ensor,[17] but among the working classes its popularity widened in northern England and Scotland as the 'meat tea' which encompassed the diverse needs of children returning after school and the male wage earner coming home from work. Among the poorer classes it could be limited to the cooking of a bloater or herring, but on excursions or on holidays it might become the occasion for the combination of fish and chips, a dish which, it has been claimed, originated in Oldham in the 1860s. Whatever variation the form of the high tea took, the essential feature was the extension of a meal based predominantly on bread, butter and tea by the inclusion of some kind of fish or meat usually cooked in a frying pan.

These patterns of eating remained largely unchanged until the outbreak of the Second World War apart from the austerity occasioned by the 1914–18 war. If anything, they became more uniform during the interwar years as the cost of living fell and a wider section of the working classes began to imitate middle-class behaviour. When Sir William Crawford published *The People's Food*, his surveys in 1936–7 suggested that the typical Briton was a dweller in a largish town eating three cooked meals a day.[18] Breakfast, eaten between 7.30 and 9 a.m., typically consisted of porridge or breakfast cereals followed by eggs and bacon and bread or toast and butter. It was accompanied by tea since coffee was a breakfast drink for only a small minority. The midday meal was still commonly regarded as dinner, despite the changes in fashion in the nineteenth century, and more than half the families Crawford surveyed still took it at home. The overwhelming majority

[17]   R. C. K. Ensor, *England 1870–1914* (Oxford, 1936), p. 143.
[18]   Sir William Crawford, *The People's Food* (1938).

of them ate it as a cooked meal of meat, potatoes and vegetables rather than a salad or a snack, and the main course was followed by a pudding, again normally a cooked dish. Social differentiation was more pronounced at the evening meal which, whether referred to as dinner or supper or tea, separated the middle classes, who repeated the midday pattern of fish or meat with potatoes and vegetables, from the working classes who did not uniformly do so. For them, the distinction between high tea and supper eaten later at around 9 p.m. meant that some ate cooked food at about 6 p.m. and others later, but the variety of foods consumed – fish, meat-based dishes, cheese or cheese dishes, all usually with potatoes – defies generalisation. One other distinctive feature of the evening meal was the replacement of the cooked puddings eaten at midday. Among middle-class families fruit or cheese was sometimes eaten but it was commoner to complete the meal with bread and butter, or buns, biscuits, cakes and pastries.

Any suggestion of a trend in the interwar years towards a more standardised arrangement of meals and menus does conceal a number of variations. For instance, much regional variety in foods and cooking methods remained. Perhaps the greatest contrast was that between Scotland and England. The large-scale Carnegie Survey in 1937 showed that Scottish families still ate considerably more root vegetables, potatoes and baked goods (rolls, buns and scones) than English families but far less green vegetables and fresh fruits. This was a long-standing difference between Scottish and English diets and a pattern which continued into the postwar era.[19] There was also still a marked variation by income level and social class. First, among the fashionable society of the upper middle classes who still employed domestic servants, there was the retention of evening dinner *à la russe* in some semblance of its Victorian and Edwardian formality. Second, the interwar years were a period of high unemployment so that, at the other end of the social scale, lack of income was an inhibitor of social change. Among what Crawford termed 'Social Class D' with incomes of less than £2 8s. (£2.40) per week, therefore including many semi-skilled and unskilled labourers' families as well as various classes of pensioners and the unemployed, patterns of food consumption were not far removed from the restricted diet based on bread and

---

[19]   M. Steven, *The Good Scots Diet* (Aberdeen, 1985), p. 136.

potatoes common in the nineteenth century.[20] In this group, breakfast was much more likely to be bread with butter or margarine or dripping than bacon and eggs, though Crawford's survey suggested that almost one third of them did eat such a breakfast. Two thirds of his Class D families also ate a cooked meal of meat and potatoes at midday, but for tea and/or supper, bread, buns, cakes, biscuits and pastries with butter, margarine or preserves were the principal foods. Even so, a contrast with nineteenth-century dietary patterns was becoming apparent. With food processing and retailing much more highly developed during the interwar period, all classes in society were beginning to experience a greater variety of food materials through the use of industrially created foods such as margarine, breakfast cereals, preserves, meat or fish pastes, confectionery, cornflour products and canned fruits and vegetables.

If the overall trend in the twentieth century was towards a common experience in eating patterns, the principal agency in narrowing the gap between rich and poor was the social effect of war. For most of the 1914–18 war, the rationing of food for the civilian population was avoided until, from 1916 onwards, the problem of maintaining supplies during the U-boat campaign against merchant shipping made the government recognise that calls for voluntary restraint in the consumption of bread, meat and sugar were insufficient. By 1918, when 'war bread', consisting of high extraction flour mixed at times with other grains and even soya or potato flour, had become general, and shortages of sugar had been commonly experienced, the government introduced rationing of meats and fats which, by the summer of 1918, had been extended to most foodstuffs. The rationing system continued to the end of 1919 but had been completely abolished by 1921, when its principal legacy was the reduction in ostentatious eating which had characterised some sections of fashionable society before the war. While some scientists have tended to see the development of a food policy in the First World War as a triumph for the application of scientific principles, it seems more likely that the real achievement of the war was that full employment gave increased, regular incomes to many families, particularly through the employment of married women, while the hesitant extension of state control over food did little more than modify the sharing-out of food on the basis of price.

[20] For a discussion of the term 'restricted diet', see D. J. Oddy, 'Urban Famine in Nineteenth-Century Britain: The Effects of the Lancashire Cotton Famine on Working-Class Diet and Health', Economic History Review, 2nd ser., 36 (1983), pp. 68–86.

Wartime gains by working-class families, which interwar unemployment never managed to eradicate, gave confidence to the food-rationing plans laid down between 1936 and 1939 by the Board of Trade. Their success was ensured by the dominant influence in the Ministry of Food of Professor J. C. Drummond as Scientific Adviser from 1940 to 1946.[21] Bread and potatoes remained unrationed throughout the 1939–45 war, though bread prices were controlled and the flour extraction rate raised to 85 per cent to produce the 'National Loaf'. The rationing scheme concentrated on imported foods and, apart from sugar, mainly those which were of animal origin such as meat, cheese and butter. Some imported processed foods were separately rationed by a 'points' system which retained a certain amount of free choice for consumers, but the purchase of most foods required customer registration with local shopkeepers. The control of food supply went still further towards limiting the scale of eating formerly enjoyed by the rich and tried valiantly to induce the acceptance of unusual (and frequently unwelcome) foodstuffs, as when the Food Advice Division of the Ministry of Food urged the adoption of cookery using dried and dehydrated forms of such foods as eggs and milk.

With the end of the Second World War in Europe and the Far East in 1945, there was no early relief from the restraints imposed on the supply of food, and food rationing was not finally removed until 1954. In the immediate postwar years, Britain faced problems of sterling convertibility and the sudden cessation of Lend-Lease Aid. American dried egg disappeared from British shops and the cost of North American wheat led to bread being rationed between 1946 and 1948, while the wartime rations of meat and fat were further reduced. The Ministry of Food's substitutes, snoek and whalemeat, were flatly rejected by the population and the tightening of constraints upon food supply brought an outcry from the Housewives' League on behalf of women facing the intractable problems of near-fatless cookery. By 1950, the crisis had passed and the beginnings of relaxation were apparent: in January, milk rationing ended, in May, the points-rationing scheme was abolished and by the autumn eggs and flour were two more of the growing number of foods to be decontrolled. Above all, the ending of the five-shilling (25 pence) price limit on meals in hotels and the lifting of the restriction on the number of courses in restaurant

---

[21] For an appreciation of Drummond's influence, see Drummond and Wilbraham, *The Englishman's Food*, pp. 448–55, though the system of rationing is explained much more clearly in Burnett, *Plenty and Want*, chap. 13.

meals presaged a return of eating as an enjoyable social activity after ten years of stringency.

II DRINK

It is such a commonplace that water is a necessity of life that historians often overlook the deficiencies in its supply in the past. Yet water shortages were real problems for many people in the eighteenth and early nineteenth centuries. In the 1780s, *The Ladies' Assistant* commented that pump-water in London contained impurities from 'cellars, burying-grounds, common sewers, and many other offensive places', while water from the Thames or the New River could be 'very often muddy, or taste strongly of weeds and leaves' when it was obtained from water-sellers. Even in the countryside, the preservation of rainwater or the use of water from ponds and ditches presented distasteful problems of 'smell, taste and colour'. Against the needs of a growing population, water shortages, particularly in the rapidly developing urban areas, remained a problem throughout the nineteenth century. Outbreaks of cholera and other waterborne diseases drew attention to these shortcomings and stimulated some reforms but piped water on constant supply became widespread only from the 1880s onwards. In London, less than half the houses received water on a constant-supply basis in 1886–7 and it was not until 1906 that the system developed by the Metropolitan Water Board was virtually complete. In the provinces, industrial demand for water frequently took precedence over the needs of the individual, with the result that deficient sanitation persisted in urban areas of the north-west, north-east and Midlands up to the early twentieth century. The majority of urban areas in Britain had piped water supplies by 1914, though only 38 per cent of the parishes in rural England had even partially piped systems by that time.

It is not surprising that in these conditions 'drink' meant alcoholic beverages. As Dr Brian Harrison has shown, it was common belief that water required purification with spirits and that, generally, intoxicants were important aids to physical stamina, virility and health.[22] During the industrial revolution, when water supply in towns was intermittent, there were few alternatives to alcoholic drink. Milk was

[22]   See B. Harrison, *Drink and the Victorians* (1971), chaps. 2, 14–15 for this section; also E. S. Turner, *Taking the Cure* (1967), and A. E. Dingle, 'Drink and Working-Class Living Standards', *Economic History Review*, 2nd ser., 25 (1972), pp. 608–22.

not as readily available in the towns as is sometimes supposed. Its price in London doubled between 1790–4 and 1813–20, but came down with the proliferation of 'town dairies' or cowsheds during the 1820s and 1830s. The milk trade also remained notorious throughout the nineteenth century for the practice of adulteration and giving short measure – sure signs of the inadequacy of supply. Other non-intoxicating drinks such as tea and coffee were dear until the 1830s, while the availability of such alternatives as soda water (which first appeared in the 1790s) or commercially produced ginger beer (from the 1820s) was limited. In the circumstances, the annual consumption of beer and spirits rose without check to a peak in 1875–6 of just under 1.5 gallons of spirits and over 34 gallons of beer per head of the population. In both cases there was a sharp fall in the late 1870s, after which spirit consumption remained at an annual level of about 1 gallon per head and beer at about 28–30 gallons per head until the end of the century. In Dr A. E. Dingle's view, the peak in drink consumption in the 1870s resulted from the fact that purchasing power had outstripped the supply of consumer goods; but as food prices fell in the 1880s and 1890s, drink became relatively more expensive. Consumption of alcohol declined as new purchasing patterns emerged and the further reduction in drink consumption after 1900 reflected the desire to maintain new standards in spite of falling real wages. Some recovery in spirits drinking occurred in the early years of the Great War but, overall, the decline in alcohol consumption continued. By 1931, consumption of spirits was down to 0.2 gallon per head, only 20 per cent of the level in 1831, and beer consumption was 13.3 gallons per head, just under 62 per cent of the level a century before.

The consumption of alcohol provided a chance to forget pain or hardship and may thus have seemed a necessary accompaniment to life for many people during the industrial revolution. Moreover, the use of alcohol on occasions such as craft-drinkings, at funerals, baptisms and marriages or when courting, frequently symbolised the establishment or termination of some formal economic, legal or social relationship. Venues for drinking met many needs among the various social classes. Inns catered mainly for travellers but the ginshop or beerhouse provided workingmen with space, warmth, light and an opportunity for a considerable range of social activities. Drinking to excess was widespread. Dr Harrison suggests that in the 1830s one third of London's factory employees observed 'Saint Monday' by their absence from work after weekend drinking; the practice continued to be observed well beyond the middle of the century among higher-paid craftsmen in the provinces but fell into decline between 1880 and 1913 as holidays became regularised.

Within the second quarter of the nineteenth century there arose a desire to curb excessive alcohol consumption. In view of the consumption trends, it is difficult to believe that the temperance movement had a direct effect of any magnitude, especially as there were a number of other influences contemporary with the temperance campaign which may have affected drink consumption. The mid-nineteenth century saw some marked improvements in water supply, more milk became available as the large dairy companies began to develop long-distance milk traffic on the railways, and there was a growing popularity of 'cordials', ginger beer and non-intoxicating bottled drinks. Above all, the better supply of water facilitated the growth of tea consumption. Coffee held its popularity until the mid-century and the use of cocoa grew (the modern kind having first appeared in 1828), but tea, popularised by the temperance reformers from the 1830s and the adoption of afternoon tea drinking by the upper classes in the 1840s, became the principal drink of the British. Its cost fell as taxes were removed. From the 1860s green Chinese tea gave way in favour of the black Indian tea to which milk began to be added. It became the beverage for temperance eating houses and temperance hotels, for workmen's refreshment rooms, for railway travellers and, before the end of the nineteenth century, for city clerks and suburban housewives alike in the new tea-shops run by the Aerated Bread Company and J. Lyons and Company. From the 1870s onwards, the success of the temperance movement lay in the regulation of licensed premises, the reduction of hours when alcohol was for sale, the removal of music licences and the exclusion of children from licensed premises. The temperance question remained a political issue until the Great War but its relevance declined rapidly in the interwar years.

One further aspect of drinking remains to be explored. Drinking and eating to excess was undoubtedly regarded as normal behaviour by those who could afford it in the eighteenth and the first half of the nineteenth centuries. Some idea of the effect of overindulgence on British physique can be gained from the work of cartoonists like Rowlandson or Gillray: similarly, 'John Bull' was always portrayed as a substantial figure who would be regarded today as being considerably overweight. Some of the disadvantages of distended girth were apparent to John Bull's contemporaries in the eighteenth and nineteenth centuries: the popular remedy was spa-water. Although some bathed in it (from which the sea-bathing mania of the late eighteenth century developed), the popularity of drinking spa-water was considerable. A surprising number of resort towns were created by this fashion – Bath, Harrogate, Knaresborough, Buxton, Tunbridge Wells and Epsom among those popular in the eighteenth century, with Woodhall, Droitwich, Strathpeffer, Matlock, and, above all, Malvern gaining favour in the nineteenth century. Bottled water from favoured resorts reached London: Glastonbury water was eagerly sought after in the 1750s, while a century later Schweppes' Malvern water or Lea and Perrin's 'Malvern Seltzer Water' were available in the metropolis.

As a response to overindulgence in alcoholic drink, the temperance movement was therefore only part of a wider reaction to excessive consumption which began to develop in the second quarter of the nineteenth century. Abstemiousness took on a number of forms: in the 1830s and 1840s there was some interest in vegetarianism; G. R. Porter thought the upper classes had become more moderate in their use of alcohol by 1851; moreover, the image of well being began to change. John Bull's paunch had lost favour by the 1860s and dieting or 'banting' as it was known after the publication of William Banting's *Letter on Corpulence* in 1863, became popular. To be fat was old-fashioned. As sports using animals gave way to more athletic activities during the last quarter of the nineteenth century, further dieting fashions, such as the 'grape cure', caught the public's imagination. There was an upsurge of interest in fruit-eating diets at the turn of the century whereas fruit had formerly been avoided by many and generally proscribed as 'bad' for children. By then, water-drinking had lost much of its earlier support, though 'taking the cure' at continental spas remained fashionable during the Edwardian years while it retained royal patronage. With the disappearance of the excesses of the Edwardian table during the Great War, 'nature philosophy' renewed the appeal of abstemiousness and the first nature-cure establishment began to cater for wealthy clients in 1925.

III FOOD CONSUMPTION

There is very little quantitative evidence before the middle of the nineteenth century on which estimates of food consumption in Britain can be based. Agricultural statistics began to be collected in the 1860s

Table 5.1 *Weekly food consumption per head of the population based on food supply estimates, 1889–1938*

Dates	Bread (lb)	Potatoes (lb)	Sugar (lb)	Fats (lb)	Meat (lb)	Milk (pt)
1889–93	6.7	3.4	1.4	1.2	2.1	2.5
1894–8	6.8	3.1	1.5	1.4	2.2	2.6
1899–1903	6.8	3.2	1.5	1.5	2.3	2.9
1904–8	7.0	3.6	1.5	1.5	2.2	3.3
1909–13	6.9	3.6	1.5	1.3	2.1	3.3
1920–3	5.8	4.0	1.4	0.8	2.0	3.3
1924–8	5.6	3.3	1.8	0.9	2.1	3.4
1929–33	5.8	3.3	1.7	0.9	2.2	3.3
1934–8	5.4	3.0	1.7	1.0	2.2	3.4

Sources: These quinquennial mean figures are calculated from the annual series *Agricultural Statistics* and the *Statistical Abstract of the United Kingdom.*

but it was another twenty years before they became comprehensive. From the late 1880s to the outbreak of the Second World War, therefore, it is possible to utilise these figures together with food imports as the basis of the nation's food supply, and to suggest average food consumption per head of the population. Table 5.1 gives these estimates in summary form. From 1940, however, an annual monitoring of food consumption was begun by the Wartime Food Survey which, on an annual sample of 7,000–8,000 families, produced the first comprehensive statistics for Britain. Before 1940 similar assessments can only be made by relying on family budget material. While these sources can give a more sensitive indication of food consumption at the family level than the very general averages resulting from supply estimates, it must be recognised that family budget surveys were very limited in scope and only rarely allow regional variation to be shown. Furthermore, since there was no overall plan in their collection, the user of this material faces long and irregular intervals in its availability which makes any interpolation uncertain. It must also be accepted that the ascertainment of food consumption levels was seldom, if ever, the prime reason for the enquiry being made. Nevertheless, before the 1880s, family budgets provide the only quantifiable evidence of ordinary people's consumption as distinct from institutionalised diets from sources such as hospitals, workhouses, prisons, schools or the armed forces. Evidence derived from a number of budget surveys

Table 5.2 *Weekly food consumption per head based on family budget evidence, 1787–1937*

Date	Number of families	Bread (lb)	Potatoes (lb)	Sugar (oz)	Fats (oz)	Meat (lb)	Milk (pt)
1787–93	119	9.0	0.5	2	1.5	0.3	0.5
1796	32	5.6	5.1	3	3.5	0.6	2.8
1841	23	7.0	4.4	9	4.8	0.8	1.6
1863	493	10.9	3.9	7	5.1	0.9	1.4
1890s	153	6.5	2.0	15	5.2	1.8	1.5
1900s	2,332	6.6	3.0	16	7.7	1.2	1.8
1937	1,046	3.8	3.2	17	11.6	1.4	2.8

Sources:

1787–93	Davies, *Case of Labourers.*
1796	Eden, *State of the Poor.*
1841	*Journal of the Statistical Society*, 4 (1841–2), for William Neild's budgets. Several other contemporary budgets have been combined with Neild's Manchester and Dukinfield families.
1863	Dr Edward Smith's surveys in the fifth and sixth *Reports of the Medical Officer to the Committee of Council on Health*, PP 1863, XXV, and 1864, XXVIII.
1890s	This group contains diets from several surveys (including those by Charles Booth and B. S. Rowntree) collected between 1886 and 1901.
1900s	These surveys between 1902 and 1913 include the Board of Trade's 1904 inquiry (Cd. 2376) on which the cost-of-living index was later based.
1937	Figures for England only based on a recalculation of the original returns. See Rowlett Research Institute, *Family Diet and Health in Pre-War Britain* (Dunfermline, 1955).

which allow food consumption to be calculated has been assembled in Table 5.2.

Both the Rev. David Davies and Sir Frederic Eden, who were the originators of the eighteenth-century surveys, took considerable pains over the accuracy of their enquiries. Together, they provide a cross-section of rural life in England, since the majority of Davies's families were from southern England and the largest group in Eden's were from the northern counties. These figures quantify the regional difference in diet discussed on pages 255–6 and show the lower bread consumption in the northern counties being offset by the increased use of potatoes, milk and oatmeal (which has been left out of Table 5.2 for brevity). The budgets for the 1840s and 1860s reveal quite similar patterns of consumption. By that time, potatoes had become established in the diet on a nationwide basis, and the principal change from the late eighteenth century was the growing use of sugar, though meat consumption was also beginning to creep upwards. By the mid-nineteenth century sugar consumption had reached half a pound (0.2 kg) per head per week. At the conclusion of the first phase of industrialisation, then, the British diets consisted principally of starchy foodstuffs such as bread and potatoes but with some luxury foods such as sugar becoming regularly used.

For the later nineteenth century, the Drummonds postulated a model of dietary change in Britain. In their seminal work, *The Englishman's Food*, they wrote that it seemed

to be related to a rising standard of living for the falling curve representing bread and flour is complementary to the rising curve for sugar and sweetmeats. It is also related to a rise in the consumption of meat. These relationships reflect the fact that bread is the staple food of poverty and that people eat much less of it when they can afford to buy meat and to indulge in the type of dish with which sugar is eaten.[23]

The consumption figures shown in Table 5.2 agree substantially with this theory. Bread consumption fell as a greater variety of other foods began to enter the diet. So did potato consumption, which stabilised at around 3 lb (1.4 kg) per head per week as potatoes came to be eaten more as an accompaniment to meat. Between the 1860s and the 1890s, meat consumption probably doubled and began to exceed 1 lb (0.45 kg) per head per week before the 1914 war, while sugar, which also reached 1 lb (0.45 kg) per head per week, showed the most rapid rise in consumption of any foodstuff. During the twentieth century bread consumption continued to fall but the growth in sugar was slowing down. The major increases in consumption were in animal foods – fats, milk and, to a lesser extent, meat. A summary table of this nature, however, cannot reveal the increasing variety of foodstuffs, particularly branded goods, which many households had begun to buy.

Aggregate consumption figures suggested by Table 5.2, while reflecting the diet of ordinary people better than the estimates given in Table 5.1, leave a number of questions unanswered. They do not, for instance, make any distinction between urban and rural life styles, nor between social classes, nor between members of the family.

What little evidence there is for the eighteenth century shows no significant dissimilarity between town and country diets. By the mid-nineteenth century, when urban life styles had become quite distinct from rural, the difference in consumption patterns had become more obvious and remained so until the early twentieth century. Table 5.3

[23]   Drummond and Wilbraham, *The Englishman's Food*, p. 299.

Table 5.3 *A comparison of weekly food consumption in urban and rural working-class family budgets, 1863–1913*

	Date	Number of families	Bread (lb)	Potatoes (lb)	Sugar (oz)	Fats (oz)	Meat (lb)	Milk (pt)
Urban	1863	125	9.1	2.4	8	4.7	0.8	0.8
	1902–13	2,031	6.7	2.9	16	8.0	1.3	1.7
Rural	1863	377	11.6	4.4	7	5.2	0.9	1.6
	1902–13	301	5.7	4.4	13	5.1	0.9	2.0

Sources: As Table 5.2.

makes a limited comparison between urban and rural diets from the 1860s to the First World War. By 1914, urban families ate less bread and potatoes but more sugar, fats and meat than rural families, which suggests that dietary change was occurring earlier in the town than the country. Up to 1914, rural workers continued to live on a diet high in starchy foods; though they ate more potatoes and drank more milk than townspeople, their consumption of foods of higher social status (mainly animal products) was lower, and they were slower to benefit from the new international trade in food materials or the new branded goods produced by the food industry.

One shortcoming of all such evidence, whether from family budgets or supply estimates, is that the distribution of food within the family is seldom revealed. Yet circumstantial evidence points to a marked imbalance in food consumption within the family which must be understood for Tables 5.2 and 5.3 to be interpreted correctly. For example, in his report on the 1863 survey, Dr Edward Smith wrote: 'The remark was constantly made to me, ''that the husband wins the bread and must have the best food''.'[24] Because contemporaries accepted priorities of this kind as part of the normal patterns of behaviour in families where manual labour formed the basis of employment, such variations in food consumption were never measured and seldom commented on, though Smith concluded: 'The important practical fact is however well established, that the labourer eats meat and bacon almost daily, whilst his wife and children may eat it but once a week, and that both himself and his household believe that course to be necessary, to enable him to perform his labour.' James Hawker's reminiscences confirm this point. Writing of his childhood in

[24] *6th Report of the Medical Officer of the Privy Council, PP 1864,* XXVIII, p. 249.

Table 5.4 *Weekly food consumption differentiated by sex, c. 1894*

	Number of diets	Bread (lb)	Potatoes (lb)	Sugar (oz)	Fats (oz)	Meat (lb)	Milk (pt)
Men	21	3.4	4.6	15	5	4.1	2.0
Women	6	3.3	1.4	21	6	1.0	0

Source: 'The Diet of Toil', *Lancet*, 1 (1895), pp. 1629–35.

Northamptonshire, he remembered the hardships of the 1830s and 1840s: 'With respect to a bit of meat i never se any the First ten years of my Life, only on Sunday.'[25]

Dr Thomas Oliver's study of food consumption in the 1890s[26] is therefore interesting not only because it surveyed men like shepherds and navvies who frequently took their meals outside the family but also because it included those women who were the principal bread-winners in their families. Unfortunately, his sample was very small but as shown in Table 5.4, there was a marked difference in food consumption by sex. The men ate far more meat, milk and potatoes than women who in turn ate more sugar and fats than men. In effect, the men were eating cooked meals of meat and potatoes (and also porridge, which is why their milk consumption was so high) which provided adequately for their needs, while the women, in spite of working in lead factories and cotton mills, largely confined themselves to eating bread with jam or treacle and drinking tea. This self-limitation of women's diet was apparent at times of economic crisis, as during the Lancashire Cotton Famine of the early 1860s,[27] but was almost certainly a permanent feature of life in lower-income families. It was noted in the early 1900s by Mrs Pember Reeves in south London and by Maud Davies in her study of Corsley in Wiltshire. In York, Rowntree's summary of it was:

We *see* that many a labourer, who has a wife and three or four children, is healthy and a good worker, although he earns only a pound a week. What we *do not* see is that in order to give him enough food, mother and children

[25] G. Christian, ed., *James Hawker's Journal: A Victorian Poacher* (Oxford, 1978), p. 71.
[26] 'The Diet of Toil', *Lancet*, 1 (1895), pp. 1629–35.
[27] For examples of diets, see Oddy, 'Urban Famine'; Dr G. Buchanan's 'Report on the Health of the Distressed Operatives' noted one case of a death from scurvy, see *5th Report of the Medical Officer of the Privy Council*, PP 1863, XXV, App. V, 1, p. 309.

habitually go short, for the mother knows that all depends upon the wages of her husband.[28]

There is little sign that this pattern was modified to any degree in poorer working-class families before the outbreak of the Second World War and, indeed, the 'Hungry England' debate began in 1932 with the death of a married woman who had been denying herself food. After the war, nutritionists began to express the view that rationing had achieved a fairer distribution of food by raising an awareness of individual needs. Even if this was so, quantities of animal food in the rations were so small that many married women continued to resort to an unbalanced distribution of food within the family as a way of eking out provisions. It was not until the early 1950s, when rationing was at an end and the number of married women working outside the home began to rise, that these long-standing patterns of self-denial began to break down.

IV NUTRITIONAL STATUS

While the enquiry into the conditions of the poorer classes which began in the late eighteenth century was always concerned that the diet should be adequate for the performance of a day's work, the arguments were inconclusive since there was no standard available at the time against which contemporary diets could be assessed. By the mid-nineteenth century, however, when Dr Edward Smith's surveys were undertaken, the knowledge of physiology had advanced sufficiently for him to carry out analyses on foods to assess their carbon and nitrogen content and to recommend dietary intakes in terms of their adequacy. Smith thought 4,100–4,300 grains of carbon and 190–200 grains of nitrogen was a daily minimum requirement, against which he was immediately able to identify groups of people in various urban handicraft trades whose diet seemed inadequate. Recalculated into more recognisable terms as an energy intake of 2,800 kilocalories (11.7 megajoules) and 80 grams of protein, Smith's recommendations can be compared with twentieth-century recommended allowances. In 1932, the Ministry of Health published *The Criticism and Improvement of Diet* which accepted that an adult man in sedentary work needed an energy intake of 3,000 kcals (12.6 MJ) per day and 37 grams of 'animal protein'. These figures were hotly disputed during the early 1930s

[28]   See Magdalen S. Pember Reeves, *Round about a Pound a Week* (1913); B. S. Rowntree, *Poverty: A Study of Town Life* (1901), p. 135 n. 1; Davies, *Life in an English Village*.

Table 5.5 *Daily nutrient intake analysis of family budget evidence, 1787–1937*

Date	Number of families	Energy value (kcal)	(MJ)	Protein (g)	Fat (g)	Carbo-hydrate (g)	Iron (mg)	Calcium (g)
1787–93	119	1,990	(8.3)	49	31	380	8.4	0.25
1796	32	2,170	(9.1)	62	43	382	11.7	0.47
1841	23	2,300	(9.6)	62	51	399	13.1	0.39
1863	493	2,600	(10.9)	66	60	450	14.9	0.44
1890s	153	2,240	(9.4)	65	70	342	11.1	0.35
1900s	2,332	2,400	(10.0)	65	71	375	12.1	0.46
1937	1,046	2,540	(10.6)	76	96	343	13.7	0.65

Sources: As Table 5.2.

by the British Medical Association's Nutrition Committee which thought them to be too low and proposed instead that an 'average' man required 3,400 kcals (14.2 MJ) per day and 50 grams of 'first-class protein' (i.e. from animal foods). Later the Committee on Nutrition of the BMA (1950) and the Department of Health and Social Security (1969) reduced the recommendations used in the 1930s to levels not dissimilar from Smith's original calculations in 1863. Such variations can be explained partly by the improvement in scientific knowledge, partly by the political conflict over minimum living standards in the 1930s, and partly by social changes through which a more sedentary life style has developed since the 1930s.

Table 5.5 shows a nutritional analysis of the family budget evidence arranged in Table 5.2 on page 269. This analysis suggests that during the industrial revolution diets with energy intakes of around 2,100 kcals (8.8 MJ) per day were not unusual, that they drew mainly on carbohydrate sources for energy with low intakes of protein and fat and that they were deficient in calcium and, for some groups of the population, in iron. For many people, diets limited by income and availability of food materials meant low nutritional status, poor health and restricted physical growth. It is difficult to disentangle the relationships between nutritional status, physical environment and the incidence of infectious diseases, but tuberculosis and gastro-intestinal fevers were endemic for most of the nineteenth century and nutritional deficiency diseases such as rickets and scurvy were also present. At times of crisis when money was short or harvests failed and food prices rose, such diseases could reach epidemic proportions with typhus, the famine fever, among them.

During the later nineteenth century, diets began to improve with energy intakes rising to a range of 2,240 to 2,600 kcals (9.4 to 10.9 MJ) per day. Some increase in consumption of protein and fats occurred, though calcium deficiency persisted until well into the twentieth century. From the point of view of the medical historian, Professor Thomas McKeown[29] has suggested that the marked decline in a number of infectious diseases which occurred during the second half of the nineteenth century was attributable principally to the improvements in diet though, since he never quantified this improvement, his argument rests on residual reasoning. The improvement in Table 5.5 seems too small to justify such a claim and fits better with the Drummonds's belief 'that the opening of the twentieth century saw malnutrition more rife in England than it had been since the great dearths of medieval and Tudor times'.[30] The very high infant mortality rate up to 1911 confirmed that there were large sections of the population whose diet, however imprecisely its influences could be separated from a deleterious physical environment, was inadequate to maintain health. At the turn of the century, family incomes needed to reach 30s. (£1.50) or more per week before energy intakes began to exceed 2,500 kcals (10.5 MJ) per day and, though these diets could be achieved by families in the middle and lower middle classes and the better-paid among the working classes, they still showed the deficiencies of calcium that characterised most nineteenth-century diets with low intakes of milk and other dairy products.[31] The debate about physical deterioration in the early years of the twentieth century, though unreal in its principal premise, expressed fears about physical growth and development which proved to be well founded in the light of a series of reports which began to emerge with the introduction of medical inspections in schools. The common feature among them was the recognition that many children in the poorer areas of towns attended school ill-fed and exhibited recognisable signs of defective nutrition.[32] The effect of this in adult life was finally confirmed when, following the Military Service Acts of 1916, conscription provided the

[29] Thomas McKeown, *The Modern Rise of Population* (1976), chap. 7.
[30] Drummond and Wilbraham, *The Englishman's Food*, p. 403.
[31] D. J. Oddy, 'Working-Class Diets in Late Nineteenth-Century Britain', *Economic History Review*, 2nd ser., 23 (1970), pp. 318–20.
[32] See *Annual Report of the Chief Medical Officer, Board of Education*, PP 1911, XVII, para. 314.

opportunity to assess physical status. Two million men born in the late nineteenth century up to 1900 were medically examined: as a cohort they had been infants in British families coeval with Booth's and Rowntree's investigations and their physical status in 1917–18 depended largely upon their nutritional status in infancy and childhood. Only 36 per cent were placed in Grade I as having 'attained the full normal standard of health and strength' which their average measurements suggested was 5 ft 6 in (1.67 m) in height, 130 lb (59 kg) in weight and with a chest girth of 34 in (86.4 cm). The most obvious restriction on physical development was seen in the recruitment of 'bantam' battalions consisting of men whose failure in physical development left them below 5 ft (1.52 m) in height.[33]

Shortages of food during the 1914–18 war were only temporary and had no discernible effect on nutritional status. Paradoxically, in a period of rising money incomes and full employment, there was no obvious check to the 'continuous decline in the percentage of children returned as poorly nourished', even though 2–3 per cent of children still showed a 'serious degree of rickets' when they entered the school population.[34] Despite the problems of unemployment in the interwar years, there was a distinct upward movement in nutritional status, with surveys carried out in the 1930s suggesting that most families obtained an energy intake of over 2,500 kcals (10.5 MJ) per day, a level at which most deficiencies in minerals and vitamins had disappeared, so that the publication of Dr John Boyd Orr's assessment of the nation's diet in 1936 caused much alarm in the Ministry of Health. Orr's view that half the population had a less than adequate diet for optimum health and physical growth was incomprehensible to government departments still immured in the minimum concept of the nineteenth-century poor law.[35] Orr's contention seemed to be borne out by surveys in depressed areas where unemployment was high, such as South Wales, which showed lower energy intakes of about 2,200–2,300 kcals (9.2–9.6 MJ) per day. These were similar to nineteenth-century levels of energy intakes, though even in such cases the greater variety of foods beginning to enter the diet was having its effects. More sugar (over a pound per head per week in

[33] *Report upon the Physical Examination of Men of Military Age by National Service Medical Boards*, PP 1919, XXVI, pp. 22–3.

[34] *Annual Report of the Chief Medical Officer, Board of Education, for 1918*, PP 1919, XXI, p. 13.

[35] J. B. Orr, *Food, Health and Income*, 2nd edn (1937), pp. 7–12, 55–6.

the 1930s), more fats, and double the amount of milk common in the nineteenth century reduced grosser deficiencies, though anaemia and rickets remained problems in poorer areas throughout the inter-war years. Despite these improvements, medical inspections of nearly 1.7 million children carried out annually in the 1930s showed around 11 to 12 per cent were undernourished. This aggregate figure concealed considerable variations between areas least affected by the depression and industrial areas where unemployment was heavy. For example, in London the proportion undernourished was less than 6 per cent but reached 18.3 per cent in the West Riding and 22.5 per cent in the county of Durham. The blackspots, as might be expected, were Jarrow with 29.6 per cent and Pontypridd with 24.2 per cent undernourished. The overall trend of improvement, however, was unmistakable: between 1920 and 1940, children in the elementary school population showed a secular gain ranging between 2 to 3.5 in (5–9 cm) in height and 5 to 13.5 lb (2.3–6.1 kg) in weight.[36]

The attempt to maintain prewar standards of nutrition during the Second World War was largely successful. Energy intakes for urban working-class families fell back to just under 2,300 kcals (9.6 MJ) per day in 1942, recovered to almost 2,400 kcals (10.0 MJ) in 1944 and, once the postwar crisis in food supplies had passed, to almost 2,500 kcals (10.5 MJ) a day by 1952.[37] Although the rationing scheme hit animal foods hardest, particularly by restricting fat consumption, it was seldom that recommended daily intakes were not achieved, and the nutritional status of the population improved on balance as nutritional policies were implemented to expand welfare milk schemes, the school meals service, communal feeding provisions through works canteens and British Restaurants and to fortify foods such as bread and margarine.

Nevertheless, the restrictions placed on diet by wartime rationing emphasised an inherent contradiction between needs and wants. By the end of the 1940s, the population eagerly awaited a return to freedom of choice which would make the diet more varied and more palatable. The pent-up demand for sweet foods was so great that when chocolate confectionery and sweets were de-rationed in April 1949 the Ministry of Food was forced to restore rationing until February

---

[36] See D. J. Oddy, 'The Health of the People', in T. C. Barker and M. Drake, eds., *Population and Society in Britain 1850–1980* (1982), pp. 130–3.

[37] Drummond and Wilbraham, *The Englishman's Food*, Appendix C, p. 469.

1953, and to keep sugar on ration until the September of that year.[38] Britain was not finally free from food rationing until 1954 and the changes in consumption which followed lie outside the scope of this chapter. The removal of restrictions on food consumption, the increasingly sedentary nature of life, large-scale advertising of foods and advances in food technology all pointed towards a period of self-indulgence in Britain. Coupled with such changes in the 1950s came the first warnings of their effects – obesity and tooth decay in children and coronary heart disease amongst adults.[39]

---

[38] See D. F. Hollingsworth, 'Rationing and Economic Constraints of Food Consumption since the Second World War', in D. J. Oddy and D. S. Miller, eds., *Diet and Health in Modern Britain* (1985), pp. 255–73.

[39] Ministry of Education, *The Health of the School Child 1954–55* (1956), and J. N. Morris, 'Coronary Thrombosis: A Modern Epidemic', *Health Education Journal*, 14 (1956), p. 36, cited in Drummond and Wilbraham, *The Englishman's Food*, p. 462.

CHAPTER 6

Leisure and culture

H. CUNNINGHAM

I TIME FOR LEISURE

The most obvious way of providing some parameters for the history of leisure is to regard leisure as time; it is the time which is left over after work and other obligations have been completed. Any hope, however, that such an approach will provide clear and unambiguous statistics of the changes in the amount of leisure time available to the population must, for a number of reasons, be discounted. First, there were always jobs in which working hours contained within them periods of leisure of an episodic or more or less regular character; examples include the workshop trades of the nineteenth century, such as printing, in which there was time for drinking and other workshop pranks, and in the twentieth century shipbuilding where the scale of the enterprise made it impossible for supervisory staff to prevent card-playing at work. Secondly, there were jobs in which the working hours were never rigorously defined by the clock, and for which it is difficult to establish accurate figures for hours of work; such jobs, whose hours varied according to the day of the week and the season of the year, included agriculture, and all small workshop and domestic work. Significantly women were a large part of the workforce in many of these jobs. Thirdly, figures for hours of work exclude overtime, and until the 1920s there are no statistics to facilitate an accurate assessment of its extent; what is certain, however, is that overtime working has increased in the twentieth century and to that extent eaten into the apparent growth in leisure time. Finally, there are numerous conceptual difficulties enshrined in the phrase 'other obligations'. What do these include? If we think of leisure as a period of time, it is as 'free time', time in which people were able to choose what they did; but obviously people did not experience all non-work time as free. On the contrary, much of it was taken up with domestic chores, or for some people in the nineteenth century, say, with a sense of obligation to attend church or chapel. What these obligations were may have changed over time, but their existence makes any division of time into work time and leisure time manifestly oversimplified. Time-budget studies, which examine how people spend their time, are available on any scale within our two centuries only in the 1930s with the work of Mass Observation, and it is not easy to know how much time to subtract from leisure time for 'other obligations'.[1]

Despite these qualifications it is important and necessary to establish as firmly as is possible the changing patterns in working hours. These hours must be studied on a daily, weekly and annual basis.

So far as daily hours are concerned, the notion of a normal working day from 6 a.m. to 6 p.m. with two hours for meals seems to have become established in most industries in the middle years of the eighteenth century; this was a reduction from the hours which had been usual in the seventeenth century, and there is some evidence of the norm being accepted, not only where there was an employer with whom to negotiate, but also in the domestic trades, such as handloom weaving, where the hours of work were notoriously irregular. The establishment of this norm was to be of crucial importance over the next century for it provided a benchmark which workers could use to resist the considerable pressures to increase the hours of work. With some exceptions, organised trades were able to keep to, or within sight of, the norm. As J. C. Hobhouse claimed in 1825, ten and a half hours, and in some cases eight and a half hours in winter, was an ordinary day's work for 'machine-makers, the moulders of the machinery, house-carpenters, cabinet-makers, stone-masons, brick-layers, blacksmiths, millwrights' and many other craftsmen.[2]

It was against this norm that factory textile workers measured their lot. By the early nineteenth century the working day in these factories lasted from 6 a.m. to 7 p.m. or 8 p.m. with only one hour for meals; that is to say twelve or thirteen hours of actual work as opposed to the ten-hour norm. The factory movement may be seen as sanctioned and motivated by a desire to return to the norm, an achievement

---

[1] J. Gershuny, 'Technical Change and "Social Limits"', in A. Ellis and K. Kumar, eds., *Dilemmas of Liberal Democracies: Studies in Fred Hirsch's 'Social Limits to Growth'* (1983), pp. 23–44.

[2] *Hansard*, 13 (1825), p. 1008; M. A. Bienefeld, *Working Hours in British Industry* (1972), pp. 1–81.

ultimately reached in the Ten Hours Act of 1847, with the 1833 Factory Act providing a half-way stage with a sixty-nine-hour week.

The textile factories were not alone in suffering an extension of hours in the early nineteenth century. Coalminers, whose hours in the eighteenth century were relatively short, six to eight hours a day, were by 1842 nearly all working a twelve-hour day, with only very short breaks for refreshment; the extension of hours seems to have occurred in the 1830s, a decade when many workers were under considerable pressure to work longer hours. Agricultural workers, too, suffered a sharp decline from relatively short hours in the eighteenth century to the point where, in 1840, they were 'as much tied to regular hours as the factory labourer'.[3]

If we take stock at mid-century, many workers in organised trades had successfully clung to the norm established in the eighteenth century, and in 1850 worked a sixty-hour week.[4] Equally, the various pressures brought upon government by the factory movement had resulted in a return to the norm for textile factory workers by mid-century. In mining, agriculture, domestic service, in the 'dishonourable' sections of the artisan trades, and in all domestic work, the eighteenth-century norm had been breached, and hours were longer – and are peculiarly difficult to tabulate; but from day to day, it may be said with some confidence, they provided little opportunity for leisure.

In the century between 1850 and 1950 a clear pattern becomes discernible in changes in the hours of work: reductions in hours were concentrated in three periods, the early 1870s, 1919–20 and 1946–9. Broadly speaking, the nine-hour day was achieved in the first period, and the eight-hour day in the second; in the third period 'normal' weekly hours fell from 47.1 in 1945 to 44.6 in 1950, but overtime eroded half of this gain.[5] The campaign for the nine-hour day started in the building trade in the 1850s, but success was limited until the economic boom of the early 1870s when most organised trades made the break-through to a fifty-four-hour week and by and large were able to maintain that position in the subsequent depression. The campaign for the eight-hour day was even longer in gestation than that for the nine-hour day. Despite all the pressure mounted in the 1890s

---

[3] Bienefeld, *Working Hours*, pp. 26–7, 30, 58; H. Cunningham, *Leisure in the Industrial Revolution c. 1780–c. 1880* (1980), pp. 62–3.

[4] Bienefeld, *Hours of Work*, p. 77.

[5] Department of Employment and Productivity, *British Labour Statistics: Historical Abstract 1886–1968* (1971), p. 160.

and beyond, reductions in hours were insignificant on a national scale until the sudden achievement of success in 1919–20 when some 7 million workers obtained reductions averaging six and a half hours a week; the normal working week was reduced from fifty-four hours to forty-eight. These norms concealed numerous variations between and within trades and between regions. In 1924, for example, average hours worked ranged from 49.9 in cement to 40.3 in tobacco.[6]

Hours of work, therefore, tended to increase, marginally for some but significantly for others, in the period up to and including the 1830s. Thereafter the trend was downwards, but it was highly discontinuous; that is to say, the break-throughs to shorter hours were concentrated in a small number of years and were irreversible. The most widely accepted explanation for this pattern is that the demand for leisure was weaker amongst most workers than the demand for higher wages, and that normally a favourable bargaining position would be used to increase wages; hours reduction, it is argued, reflected not so much a positive demand for more leisure as an attempt in conditions of boom to insure against future unemployment.[7] Certainly workers have been more inclined to take the fruits of collective bargaining in the form of increased wages than as leisure time. Nevertheless, the demand for more leisure, for its own sake rather than as an insurance against unemployment, can be consistently heard throughout the nineteenth and twentieth centuries. It was manifest in Leonard Horner's questionnaire on the effects of the 1847 Ten Hours Act when the vast majority welcomed the shorter hours even if they implied lower wages. South Wales miners, of whom it was said in 1873 that 'they want short hours and more leisure', appear indeed to have taken out some of their higher wages in increased leisure in the succeeding half-century. And in the interwar period trade unions certainly never considered increased leisure if it meant a fall in wages, but some did campaign for more leisure in preference to higher wages.[8]

Collective bargaining was unquestionably the chief means by which hours of work were reduced. Parliamentary legislation was of marginal

---

[6] *Ibid.*, p. 97.
[7] Bienefeld, *Working Hours*; M. Hodgson, 'The Working Day and the Working Week in Victorian Britain 1840–1900' (unpublished MPhil. thesis, London University, 1974); see also J. Myerscough, 'The Recent History of the Use of Leisure Time', in I. Appleton, ed., *Leisure Research and Policy* (Edinburgh, 1974), pp. 3–16.
[8] Cunningham, *Leisure*, p. 149; W. J. Hausmann and B. T. Hirsch, 'Wages, Leisure and Productivity in South Wales Coal Mining 1874–1914: An Economic Approach', *Llafur*, 3 (1982), pp. 58–66; S. G. Jones, *Workers at Play: A Social and Economic History of Leisure 1918–1939* (1986), pp. 15–33.

importance by comparison. In the nineteenth century it was never used overtly to control the hours of adult males. It was important, as we have seen, in bringing hours in factory textile work back to the ten-hour norm by the mid-nineteenth century, but the extension of factory acts thereafter was often as much to regularise as to reduce hours. The key break-throughs were achieved without parliamentary aid, and Acts such as those in 1874 (reducing the hours of factory textile workers to fifty-six and a half), 1902 (a further reduction of one hour a week for textile workers), 1909 (restricting underground work in the coalmines to eight hours), the 1934 Shop Act and the 1937 Factories Act (limiting legal hours for certain categories of workers) had only a marginal effect on the overall national statistics.

Parliamentary legislation had a similar marginal role in the implementation of changes in the working week. The fundamental trend here was towards regularity of hours, but it was achieved only haltingly and with persistent anomalies. In the workshop trades of the eighteenth and nineteenth centuries it seems to have been a norm to concentrate work in the latter part of the week with Saturday as a handing-in day. This meant that Monday and sometimes Tuesday were holidays or generally light days. The celebration of Saint Monday has of course been fully documented, and to the extent that it was observed 'universally wherever small-scale, domestic, and outwork industries existed; ... generally ... in the pits; and sometimes ... in manufacturing and heavy industry' it must modify the account of daily hours of work which we have given.[9] Certainly Monday disappeared as a holiday only slowly, and there is much evidence that even in the late nineteenth century productivity was noticeably lower on Mondays than on other days of the week. How far the Saturday half-holiday was an alternative to the celebration of Saint Monday is difficult to determine. In Birmingham that seems to have been the intention.[10] Elsewhere – and this is a point on which more research is needed – Saturday may always have been some form of half-holiday, and may have survived the pressure to lengthen hours of work which we rightly associate with the early industrial revolution. Even in cotton factories, for example, in 1816 it was normal to stop at 4 p.m. on

[9]   E. P. Thompson, 'Time, Work-Discipline, and Industrial Capitalism', *Past & Present*, 38 (1967), p. 74.
[10]   D. Reid, 'The Decline of Saint Monday, 1766–1876', *Past & Present*, 71 (1976), pp. 76–101.

Saturdays, and in 1833 in Yorkshire woollen mills work stopped two hours earlier on Saturdays than on other days. The Factory Act of 1850, in laying down a 2 p.m. end to work on Saturdays, may have been recognising and endorsing a holiday that was rooted in custom. It is significant that the organisation most prominently associated with the campaign for the Saturday half-holiday, the sabbatarian Early Closing Association, was concerned with the hours of shop-workers; were they perhaps out of line with a general observance of the sense that work ought to end early on Saturdays? What is certain is that trade unions began to put early (or earlier?) closing on Saturdays at the forefront of their demands from mid-century so that by the early 1870s it had to a large extent been achieved by building workers, and by the early 1890s was a norm of all workers. It had been achieved more by collective bargaining than by parliamentary legislation.

If some regularity had been introduced to the working week by the later nineteenth century, can the same also be said of the working year? In the sixteenth and seventeenth centuries there had been a sharp decline in the number of holidays which were recognised and observed, but they had not been entirely eliminated. They continued to be observed, with some regional variation, around Christmas or New Year, at Easter and Whitsuntide, at the local fair, feast or wake, and to some extent on such national days as the 5th of November and Shrove Tuesday. It is of course difficult to distinguish, amongst colliers for example, between holidays and unemployment, and such holidays as were observed may have had to be paid for by extra work in the preceding days or weeks; this, however, seems to have been a price people were prepared to pay, and what is most worthy of note is the extent to which holidays were preserved right through the early phase of the industrial revolution. The most significant and best-documented example is industrial Lancashire where holidays centred on the annual wakes were maintained in the classic period of the industrial revolution.[11] It is true that many activities associated with particular local holidays, bull-running at Stamford, for example, or football in Derby or harvest festival dinners, were under consider-able pressure, and that some were abolished; but they were often replaced not with work but with some form of activity better geared

[11]   R. Poole, 'Oldham Wakes', in J. K. Walton and J. Walvin, eds., *Leisure in Britain, 1780–1939* (Manchester, 1983), pp. 71–98.

towards winning the support of respectable people. The holiday itself was retained.

Regional variations were of crucial importance in the evolution of holiday habits. In most parts of the country holidays had always been considered as particular days rather than as a stretch of days. Such holidays were the most vulnerable; they could be picked off one by one, especially in areas where labour organisation was weak, as in the agricultural south. The cotton districts of Lancashire, by contrast, were able to build on their success in maintaining the wakes and took the lead in pressing for the formal recognition of such holidays in the late nineteenth century. They were not as yet holidays with pay, but their existence established a precedent which others later could follow. It was in the areas where holidays were measured by the day that the Bank Holidays Acts of 1871 and 1875 were of most significance.[12] They were not the first legislative recognition of holidays – that had happened in the 1833 Factory Act – but they were the first in which the state's involvement was widely recognised and applauded; and hence, too, they had significance as a precedent.

In the late nineteenth and early twentieth centuries employers increasingly conceded holidays to their workforces. Brunner Mond, Lever Bros., the Gas Light and Coke Company, the London and North-Western Railway Company and the Royal Dockyards had all done so by the 1890s. In 1897 the Amalgamated Society of Railway Servants negotiated one week's paid holiday after five years of service. Other unionised workers, in coal and iron, for example, were putting forward similar claims before the First World War. It was undoubtedly, however, the war itself which made the issue a national one. The Ministry of Reconstruction discussed the question, somewhat indecisively, in 1917, and nearly all industries put forward claims for holidays with pay. By the beginning of the 1920s general and district agreements covered an estimated 1 million manual workers. The next major advance came in the late 1930s when union pressure by April 1938 had raised the number of manual workers with holiday pay agreements to 3 million (out of a total occupied population of 18.5 million of whom a further 4.75 million non-manual workers had secured agreements). By September 1938 the number of manual workers with holiday pay agreements was up to 4 million, and by 1945 it had reached 10 million, most of whom had a two-week holiday. The Departmental

[12] J. K. Walton, 'The Demand for Working-Class Seaside Holidays in Victorian England', *Economic History Review*, 2nd ser., 34 (1981), pp. 249–65.

Committee on Holidays with Pay of 1937 and the Act which followed in 1938 were more a reflection of union pressure than a major factor in securing the advance.[13]

The achievement of holidays with pay followed the same pattern that we have discerned in hours of work: the major reductions came discontinuously, and in this case in two clearly identifiable sets of years, the period immediately following the First World War, and that immediately before and during the Second World War. Broadly speaking these may be seen as coinciding with booms in the trade cycle, but it nevertheless required very positive pressure from the unions for any success to be achieved. The extent of that success must not be exaggerated. The workers who were most likely to have won holidays with pay were those in strong unions and those either employed by or under the legislative protection of government – the 1938 Act covered industries where there were wage-regulating bodies established by government. Casual or part-time workers, many of whom were women, were without benefit of holidays with or without pay, and the habit of taking holidays was dependent on the movements of the trade cycle; not all of those who were entitled to holidays with pay spent time away from home.

The hours of work of the working classes are relatively easy to establish in comparison to those of the middle classes. There are no national statistics and only the most scattered and perhaps unrepresentative information. Three trends may perhaps be distinguished. First, within the professions and the civil service hours were relatively short and imprecise until late in the nineteenth century. As late as 1875 daily hours in the civil service were 'generally from 10 to 4 or from 11 to 5'. In the private sector clerks worked rather longer hours, in the London and North-Western Railway Company, for example, from 9 to 5, and we can perhaps assume a gradual normalisation of a 9 to 5 day.[14] Secondly, amongst businessmen, the days of heroically long hours lay in the later eighteenth and first half of the nineteenth centuries. As the second and third generations came to the fore they relaxed their hours until they too began to internalise the 9 to 5 norm. In the early twentieth century the elite of Manchester's middle class,

---

[13] S. G. Jones, 'Trade-Union Policy between the Wars: The Case of Holidays with Pay in Britain', *International Review of Social History*, 31 (1986), pp. 40–67; Department of Employment and Productivity, *British Labour Statistics*, Table 34.

[14] *Civil Service Inquiry Commission*, PP 1875, XXIII, pp. 21, 458–61.

both businessmen and the professions, travelled in from Alderley Edge by the 8.25, 8.50 or 9.10 train, and returned home by the 5.7 or 5.45.[15] Thirdly, at the lower end of the middle classes, amongst shopworkers, hours were notoriously long and remained so. After over half a century of effort to curtail hours, a House of Lords Select Committee in 1901 could only confirm that many shops were working eighty to ninety hours a week. In 1881 the Shop-Assistants Twelve Hours' Labour League had been formed, the name itself indicative of the situation: in the cotton factories they had been campaigning for ten hours, and sometimes eight hours, in the 1830s. It is in fact by no means obvious that for shopworkers the trend in hours from the mid-nineteenth century was progressively downwards. The high hopes entertained in the 1840s and 1850s that shops could be persuaded to reduce their hours overall and in particular to close early on Saturdays had dimmed by the mid-1880s when the Early Closing Association admitted that only a minority of shops in London accepted the half-holiday. The shift thereafter towards a legislative solution was only very partially effective, and amounted to no more than a succession of select committees, bills and permissive acts. The 1911 Act did, however, enact a half-holiday – though with some exceptions.[16]

Persuasion seems to have been more effective for warehousemen and clerks. The Stock Exchange started early closing on Saturdays in 1843. By the end of 1848 closure at 4 p.m. on Saturdays had been achieved in City of London and West End banks, and in Manchester, banks, solicitors' offices, local government offices and warehouses also closed at that hour. By 1857 there was 2 p.m. closure for workers in solicitors' and other law offices. The Bank of England's Saturday closing hours were reduced from 3 p.m. in 1860 to 2 p.m. in 1886 to 1 p.m. in 1902. This seems to indicate that such workers' hours paralleled those of the better organised manual workers.

So far as annual holidays were concerned, however, blackcoated workers undoubtedly had the advantage. There may have been a reduction in holiday time in the early nineteenth century, though the evidence on which this is based is confined to the Bank of England which closed on forty-four days in 1808 and on only four in 1834. By 1845, however, the trend had been reversed and Bank workers were getting six to eighteen days' annual leave, depending on their

---

[15]   K. Chorley, *Manchester Made Them* (1950), pp. 114, 136.
[16]   W. B. Whitaker, *Victorian and Edwardian Shopworkers* (Newton Abbot, 1973).

length of service.[17] Evidence given to the Civil Service Inquiry Commission of 1875 indicated that clerks working for insurance companies, solicitors, banks, railway companies and the civil service were all getting at least two weeks' holiday a year. They had achieved this some three-quarters of a century before the bulk of manual workers.

Work time undoubtedly became more regularised and standardised over the period 1750–1950. Work became more clearly separated from leisure, and there was a diminution though not an elimination of leisure on the job. The ideal, though not always the actuality, of two weeks' holiday in the summer had become widely accepted by 1950. Parliament recognised certain days as holidays, and in that way gave legitimacy to the demand for leisure. The notion of what constituted a fair day's work changed from 6 a.m. to 6 p.m. with two hours' break for meals to the point where people began to think in terms of hours per week – and then progressively reduced that from sixty to fifty-four to forty-five. Alongside these changes, however, there were significant continuities. In the eighteenth century the holidays associated with fairs and wakes, often lasting a week, occurred in the summer, as did the holidays of the twentieth century. The days which Parliament recognised as holidays were, with the exception of the August Bank Holiday, days which had always been observed as holidays. The ways in which people in the twentieth century spent Christmas Day or Guy Fawkes Day may have changed, but the time of the year was still the same. And although the extent of a fair day's work changed, the notion itself survived.

We must conclude, however, at the point at which we began. Statistics of hours worked have always been collected for a purpose other than the benefit of the historian. They exist for those periods and those trades in which there has been a campaign of some kind to prevent the increase of or to reduce the hours of work. These campaigns fall into two groups. On the one hand there were campaigns whose focus was Parliament, and in which the aim was to legislate on behalf of some underprivileged group, children in cotton factories, for example, or shopworkers. At the opposite end of the scale were those campaigns led by trade unions representing the most skilled and best-organised workers. The consequence of this, however, is that we know relatively little about many workers, manual and non-manual, who neither aroused the concern of parliamentary reformers

[17] J. Giuseppi, *The Bank of England: A History from its Foundation in 1694* (1966), pp. 35, 100–2.

nor belonged to a trade union. As we have seen it was the latter type of campaign which achieved most success in controlling the hours of work, but it left behind it many unorganised workers. Neither campaign, of course, did anything on behalf of those who were not formally employed. These included, most notably, women whose work was housework, for whom the separation of work and leisure was often meaningless, and whose hours of work defy calculation. The statistics are in their way beguiling, but we need to remember as much what they omit as what they include.

II LEISURE CULTURES

How did people spend their leisure time? Insofar as leisure time can be seen as free time, time in which the individual is relieved from the pressures of work and other obligations, the choice of how to spend leisure time can be seen as distinctly personal. Indeed, some would argue that to the extent that it is not a personal choice it is not in any positive sense leisure, but merely adherence to social custom or obligation. Choice, of course, is constrained by material circumstances and by the availability of facilities, but within those constraints, on this argument, there is nothing to stop the chimney sweep foxhunting or the peer attending a low music hall. It is the beauty of leisure that it enables individuals to escape from the pressures that otherwise circumscribe their lives.

This idealist approach to the study of leisure may recommend itself to philosophers, but to historians it has rarely seemed to accord with reality. In a more down to earth way, many have suggested that the key analytic tool for the study of leisure activities is a distinction between the rough and the respectable. The implication of this distinction is that the respectable of all classes had more in common with each other than they did with the rough members of their own class; and presumably vice versa. The problem with this kind of analysis is a simple one: whereas historians of this school seem to have no difficulty in distinguishing what was rough from what was respectable, people at any point in time agonised endlessly over the distinction. With some activities, of course, there is no difficulty; we can easily place membership of a teetotal society on the one hand or rat-catching on the other. But there were many other activities, going to the theatre, for example, which were not manifestly rough or respectable, or rather which may have been rough to some but not to others.

The rough/respectable division is in fact an extraordinarily crude tool for the description of social reality; the fact that contemporaries made the distinction is, of course, of interest, but in adopting it themselves historians have confused the history of moral fears with the history of lived experience.

The latter can best be approached through a culturalist analysis. In this view leisure activities did not float freely in a stratosphere above the world of work and daily life; on the contrary, they were intimately related to and derived from that world. Boundaries of class, of gender, of age and of geography were therefore likely to be reproduced in leisure; and leisure activities may themselves have reinforced or shifted those boundaries, and not merely passively reflected them. In this approach, which will be the one pursued here, the analysis of leisure activities involves the identification of different leisure cultures. These leisure cultures, it must be emphasised, were not hermetically sealed against each other; there were overlaps and influences from one to another. Nor were any of these cultures ever static; they were constantly changing, both in themselves and in relation to other cultures.

The word 'culture' is sufficiently problematic to demand some explanation of the senses in which it is used. Culture here means a way of life and the values and attitudes embodied in that way of life. A leisure culture can be said to exist when a significant part of the population, measured either in influence or numbers, can be seen to follow a particular way of life in its leisure time. The different leisure cultures which will be studied here will be the culture of the leisured classes, urban middle-class culture, reformist culture, artisan culture, rural popular culture and urban popular culture. Finally, we must consider whether any form of national leisure culture existed, either alongside the other leisure cultures or superseding the differences between them.

The phrase 'the leisured or leisure classes' has been traced back to the 1840s, and may well have existed earlier. In 1868 Anthony Trollope was confident that England possessed 'the largest and wealthiest leisure class that any country, ancient or modern, ever boasted'.[18] At the end of the century Thorstein Veblen subjected them to the most trenchant analysis they would ever receive in *The Theory of the*

---

[18]   A. Trollope, ed., *British Sports and Pastimes* (1868), p. 18.

Leisure Class. Veblen argued that the fundamental reason for the development of a leisure class was that only in conspicuous leisure and in conspicuous consumption could the wealthy achieve the status that they sought. The key word to latch onto here is 'conspicuous'. Leisure for the leisure class was not something carried on in privacy; its function, to establish status, demanded that it be seen, both by fellow-members of the class and by an envious or admiring excluded public.

Since no leisure class could exist without plentiful time and money with which to display its leisure, and since the function of that display was so fundamental to its social position, it is difficult to determine whether there was any separation of work and leisure within the class. It is sometimes said, in romantic vein, that pre-industrial workers made no distinction between work and leisure, and did not know when one started and the other stopped. It would be much nearer the mark to say this of the leisure class. Since by definition, though with some qualifications which we will come to, they did not work in any sense in which the rest of the population would understand work, it followed that their duties and obligations in life lay in a highly ritualised leisure whose demands they often bemoaned.

The leisure class existed at the level of the nation and of the provinces. At the national level it could most readily be observed in the London Season whose origins can be traced back to the sixteenth and early seventeenth centuries. Initially, and indeed until the 1880s, this was as much a political as a social occasion; as it was put in 1718, 'Publick Business, and Publick Diversions, have the same Season.'[19] The diversions included the patronage of forms of high culture, particularly opera, a patronage which was frequently cited as one of the justifications for the existence of the leisure class. In a circumscribed political world the numbers involved were relatively small – some 300–400 families in the eighteenth century, compared to the 4,000 families who participated in the more purely social London Season of the late nineteenth century. Until the later nineteenth century entry to London 'Society' was carefully guarded and its social functions were mostly private. Thereafter, it became easier to buy one's way into 'Society'.[20] This reflected a change in the nature of the leisure class. It becomes less easy to identify a class whose members manifestly did no work; by contrast, public attention began to focus on a plutocracy whose male members worked, but so success-

---

[19] *Free-thinker*, no. 68, in *Oxford English Dictionary*.
[20] L. Davidoff, *The Best Circles: Society, Etiquette and the Season* (1973).

fully that they could spend fortunes in their leisure. Veblen distinguished between conspicuous consumption and conspicuous leisure, and argued that the former was becoming of greater utility in the maintenance of status than the latter; it might be more accurate to say that in the twentieth century conspicuous consumption within leisure was the hallmark of the leisure class.

The London Season formed one clearly demarcated phase in the annual life of the leisure class; the remainder of the year was centred on the country houses in a mixture of activities some of which were thoroughly exclusive while others entailed a carefully calculated patronage of more popular occasions. Shooting was the most exclusive of sports, and in the mid-eighteenth century began to take on its modern characteristics: birds were shot on the wing, systematic game preservation started, as also did the careful recording of the number shot – Lord Malmesbury, for example, shot 6,737 partridges and 4,113 pheasants between 1810 and 1830. As game preservation reached new heights poaching gangs became an increasing feature of rural society.[21] If poachers might be said to have a love–hate relationship with game preserves, fox–hunters simply hated them. Like shooting, fox-hunting was a sport invented by the gentry in the eighteenth century, but unlike shooting it was, in ideology at least, open to 'peer and peasant', and its social function was to knit together rather than divide rural society. In the late nineteenth century, as in London Society, the plutocracy began to supplant the aristocracy as its leaders.[22] There were other sports which took the leisure class away from the immediate environment of their estates, horse racing, for example, and then in the nineteenth century, as transport improved, yachting which 'in Victorian and Edwardian times ... was conspicuously and without embarrassment associated with flamboyant displays of personal wealth'.[23]

From the middle of the eighteenth century the London Season had its provincial counterparts. Frequently, assize week would provide the occasion for a gathering of county notables and a round of social and cultural activities. There existed also in the larger provincial centres – and perhaps particularly those in southern Britain – the

---

[21] P. B. Munsche, *Gentlemen and Poachers: The English Game Laws 1671–1831* (Cambridge, 1981).

[22] R. Carr, *English Fox Hunting: A History* (1976); D. C. Itzkowitz, *Peculiar Privilege: A Social History of English Foxhunting 1753–1885* (Hassocks, 1977).

[23] A. W. B. Simpson, *Cannibalism and the Common Law* (Harmondsworth, 1986), p. 14.

'urban gentry' who in a modest way provided a lower echelon of the leisure class. In the nineteenth century such people living on income from capital tended to gravitate towards the spas and more select seaside resorts. They were disproportionately female and old.[24] In contrast to the national leisure class, there was no firm structure to their year, nor any flamboyance in their leisure. They maintained their status by careful observance of the formalities which helped to distinguish them from those who had to work for their living. In the later nineteenth and twentieth centuries a new category, the retired, began to fuse with this older, modest, provincial leisure class, together to form a substantial proportion of the population of the southern and coastal towns in which they congregated.

Such people had little in common with the national leisure class, and it may be doubted whether they should be included within the leisure class at all. It was luxury and its overt enjoyment, not modest affluence, which characterised the leisure class in its higher reaches. One mark of that luxury was the role accorded to women. Within the leisure class it was always legitimate for a man to have certain duties, such as running the estate, which were scarcely distinguishable from work; increasingly, we have suggested, it became possible for them to be more obviously part of the world of work, at least in certain sectors of the economy, and most obviously in the City of London. Women, however, although they might have certain duties as hostesses, had to be kept rigidly separate from any money-making task. In their leisure, and in their conspicuous expenditure on it, particularly in their dress, their function was to testify to the wealth of their menfolk.

Other social groups might emulate or aspire to the luxury of the leisure class. Even as far down the social scale as the upper working class, it was a mark of status that a woman should have no employment; clearly, however, such women did not fall within the leisure class. We must reserve that distinction for families all of whose members were able to participate in the life style of the class, whether on a national or a provincial basis. The class itself exercised much energy and ingenuity in trying to establish its own boundaries, whether by the protocols of London Society or by the rigid formalities of visiting cards. What it could not prevent was the copying of its manners and dress by those without the means to sustain the life

---

[24] J. K. Walton, *The English Seaside Resort: A Social History, 1750–1914* (Leicester, 1983), p. 99.

style; but members of the class quickly gained the sixth sense to enable them to distinguish the impostor.

In contrast to the culture of the leisure class, urban middle-class culture, in its origins, was distinctively provincial. In the first phase of its development, up to the end of the eighteenth century, it was a culture which was more obviously urban than middle class. It expressed many of the values of the urban gentry, who themselves, as we have seen, may be considered part of the leisure class and its aristocratic way of life. The remarkable expansion, however, in the second half of the century of cultural institutions which were expressly designed to serve the interests and needs of the provincial urban well-to-do is indicative of a new cultural formation. Its existence can be documented from figures for theatre-building; whereas there were ten purpose-built theatres erected in the larger provincial towns between 1736 and 1760, there were at least one hundred and probably more erected between the 1760s and the 1820s.[25] The music festivals in the provinces, which made their appearance from about 1760 in, for example, Salisbury, Derby, Leicester and Sheffield, are another indicator. In London it was not until the first half of the nineteenth century that the patronage and market for classical music passed from the aristocracy to the upper middle class; the provinces may be said to have led the way. The new culture is visible, too, in the classical style of its architecture and in the design of squares which were emphatically the territory of the wealthy. For this culture was unashamedly exclusive; entry to the Assembly Rooms and circulating libraries, to the botanical gardens and even the walks, was confined to the wealthy. When we think of this culture our minds are drawn inexorably to Bath which did indeed exhibit many of its features. But it would be quite wrong to think of the culture as finding a home only in the more select spas of southern England. Liverpool, for example, had an Assembly Room described in 1760 by the Master of Ceremonies at Bath as 'grand, spacious, and finely illuminated; here is a meeting once a fortnight to dance and to play cards; where you will find some women elegantly accomplished and perfectly dressed'.[26] There were subscription libraries in Liverpool from the

---

[25]   C. W. Chalklin, 'Capital Expenditure on Building for Cultural Purposes in Provincial England, 1730–1830', *Business History*, 22 (1980), pp. 51–70.

[26]   Quoted in C. P. Darcy, *The Encouragement of the Fine Arts in Lancashire 1760–1860* (Manchester, 1976), p. 8.

1750s, in Warrington in 1760, in Manchester in 1765, in Lancaster in 1768 and in Rochdale in 1770. Further north in Edinburgh this culture arguably reached its apogee, both in physical form and in intellectual distinction, doubtless in part because there it was effectively the culture of a capital city.

Towards the end of the eighteenth century the intellectual dimension of this urban culture became more pronounced. So also did its masculinity. Like-minded men turned typically to the club or society as a forum within which to pursue their interests – chess, for example, or music. The most distinctive institution, however, to emerge in these years was the more widely based discussion club, the literary and philosophical society. In Manchester, for example, one was founded in 1781, and in the early nineteenth century at least a dozen towns had sufficient impetus behind their societies to erect special buildings, often incorporating a museum. If we project this culture forward into the testing second quarter of the nineteenth century, its leaders can be seen turning away from a provincial pursuit of high culture towards a direct concern with the social and political problems of their own towns; they formed statistical societies and diffused useful knowledge. They became a culture anxious to influence the ways of life of the working class from their narrow but powerful middle-class bridgehead, and were more concerned with the supply of leisure to others than with the enjoyment of it themselves; as such, their efforts will be considered later.

The emergence of this male, intellectual, socially concerned and distinctly middle-class urban culture was one sign of the fracturing of the urban cultural formation of the eighteenth century. It was under further and wider challenge in the late eighteenth century for its lack of seriousness, for its essential frivolity. The interlocking impact of the evangelical revival, the French Revolution and British radicalism posed a threat to the essence of eighteenth-century urban culture: its urbanity, its stress on manners and behaviour as opposed to feeling. William Wilberforce in his *Practical View* (1797) was to contrast 'the prevailing religious system of professed Christians, in the higher and middle classes in this country, . . . with real Christianity'. The shock waves were to be felt far into the nineteenth century. So far as middle-class urban culture was concerned they took two forms. First, particular activities, theatre-going, for example, or novel reading, or cards, or even cricket, now had to be scrutinised to see if they served any purpose which God, rather than Society, would approve. Many such activities became taboo, or so carefully circumscribed as to be changed in their essence. Secondly, the sociability which had been so highly prized in the eighteenth century now ceased to be a virtue. The attractions of a life lived in public within a defined and exclusive society gave way to an emphasis on domesticity. It would be a gross oversimplification to ascribe the origins of the nineteenth-century middle-class worship of home, and of the associated division between the male public sphere and the female private sphere, exclusively to ideology; there were other pressing material reasons for its emergence in the increasingly class-divided and insalubrious industrial towns. The effect, undoubtedly, was to shift the emphasis of middle-class urban culture away from sociability towards domesticity, and away from frank enjoyment of leisure towards a more calculating performance of duty. There were, of course, happy and relaxed evangelical homes; middle-class society as a whole, however, now took its pleasures more seriously, and took fewer of them.[27]

In the easier mid-Victorian days there was some relaxation of the harsher views. In the 1860s and 1870s press and pulpit endlessly discussed the legitimacy of this or that activity and of leisure in general. What might be called the official view was, of course, that the purpose of leisure, or as it was called in preference recreation, was to re-create a person for the more serious business of life, work.[28] As such, it is worth noting, recreation was essentially only necessary for those who worked, that is to say men, or, as we shall see, for those who were about to become men, boys. Leisure was justified not for its own sake, but for its ulterior function in re-creating men for work. Under the umbrella of this official view, however, more and more activities became legitimate, and were doubtless enjoyed for their own sake. Novels could be read, provided they were suitable; cards could be played, provided there was no hint of gambling; even the theatre became legitimate as plays with middle-class characters and conventional morality became the norm, and theatres themselves, in the 1880s, became effectively middle-class enclaves. In *The Church and the Stage* (1886) W. H. Hudson had no doubt that 'the broad ground of the essential sinfulness of all pleasure is already abandoned'.[29]

It was in physical activity, however, that the change was greatest.

[27]   D. M. Rosman, *Evangelicals and Culture* (1984).
[28]   P. Bailey, '"A Mingled Mass of Perfectly Legitimate Pleasures": The Victorian Middle Class and the Problem of Leisure', *Victorian Studies*, 21 (1977), pp. 7–28.
[29]   Quoted in M. Baker, *The Rise of the Victorian Actor* (1978), p. 59.

The suspicion of pleasure in the late eighteenth and early nineteenth centuries was linked to an elevation of intellectual or 'rational' recreation and a denigration of physical enjoyment. Sport conjured up images of a flamboyant aristocratic life style and gambling, or of the corrupt seediness of pub-based prizefighting. Middle-class urban culture, primarily in the form of the public school, was able from mid-century to transform the nature and image of sport. As ever, the justification for this had to be some ulterior purpose. As the Prospectus of the Harrow Philathletic Club put it in 1853, 'The encouragement of innocent amusements and recreation must tend greatly to the maintenance of order and discipline throughout the School.'[30] Numerous other justifications were also available: sport encouraged team spirit, it fostered qualities of leadership, especially valuable in the administration of empire, it took boys' minds off sex and it was the best training for war. As rules were drawn up and enforced, moreover, sport became an analogy for middle-class male life: a competitive struggle within agreed parameters. The middle class not only imposed a new ideology on sport; they were also in the period up to 1914 the chief beneficiaries of the expansion of facilities. In the mid-Victorian period, anxiety to establish the respectable credentials of sport had led to the deliberate exclusion from participation of anyone who was not middle class; in 1866 the Amateur Athletic Club barred from membership anyone who 'is a mechanic, artisan or labourer'.[31] This kind of formal exclusion did not last long as the potential contribution of sport to class harmony became part of its ideological baggage, but other forms of exclusion were equally effective; facilities for sport cost money, and were for the most part beyond the reach of the working class. There was, of course, a gradation in the expense of sports; in some, like yachting, the working class could at best spectate from a distance; in others, like golf, they were admitted, if at all, in special artisan hours; in others, like football and cycling, they came to participate in the sports only some years after the middle class had been dominant. There can be no dissent from the view that up to 1914 'the "sporting revolution" belonged, in the main, to the middle classes in their leafy suburbs'.[32]

In the twentieth century middle-class leisure culture became more

---

[30] Quoted in J. A. Mangan, *Athleticism in the Victorian and Edwardian Public School* (Cambridge, 1981), p. 224.

[31] P. Bailey, *Leisure and Class in Victorian England* (1978), pp. 124–46.

[32] H. E. Meller, *Leisure and the Changing City, 1870–1914* (1976), p. 236.

suburban than urban. For women, that had always been the case, and in the seclusion of the suburbs they had been able to develop some degree of autonomy in their leisure pursuits, in tennis and golf, for example, when the men were at work; at weekends men took precedence. New opportunities were to open up in the interwar period, provided most notably by the suburban Odeons of the 1930s, which were carefully styled to appeal to middle-class women. And as families increasingly retreated to suburbs from city centres, men, too, looked to the home environment for their leisure; work was urban, leisure suburban. And the more that process continued, the more exclusive middle-class leisure became.

The improvements in communications which facilitated the growth of the suburbs also made it easier to escape from them, and the middle-class suburban culture colonised other areas. An early example, in the late nineteenth century, was the matinee at the urban theatre; middle-class women could make a sortie to the town by special trains, carefully cocooned against too much contact with the workaday world. More significantly, middle-class families escaped in the summer to rented seaside houses, recreating there the weekend life of the suburbs. Care had to be taken, of course, in choosing the resort or the area of the resort, but an appropriate degree of exclusivity could normally be achieved. An alternative was to escape further afield, to the Highlands of Scotland, or to Europe. Over a million Britons took their holidays in Europe in 1930, the more fashionable of them drawn to the Riviera.

Middle-class urban leisure culture, then, was a shifting entity. An eighteenth-century specifically urban pursuit of pleasure turned in the nineteenth century to an anxious scrutiny of the legitimacy of particular pursuits and to a corresponding emphasis on domesticity rather than sociability. Gradually there was a relaxation, but it occurred within the safe boundaries of school and suburb. Indeed the most obvious and continuing thrust of the culture was towards social exclusivity. Within the wide middle-class boundary, lines to demarcate status were carefully drawn, and the upper and lower middle classes would never meet in leisure. What they had in common was an attitude to leisure and a view of its social function: in leisure people could meet others of similar social status in environments, whether private or public, which were in accordance with the canons of respectability of the day. In its upper reaches it was hard to distinguish middle-class urban culture from the culture of the leisure class. Many of its members contributed to and fostered high culture. But in the nineteenth century in particular, in its seriousness of approach towards leisure, it can be seen specifically as a class culture, reinforcing the class's sense of distinctness. In the twentieth century it shared in the nationwide acceptance of leisure, but it did so within its own boundaries.

There was always a minority within the middle classes anxious to reform the leisure of the working classes or to provide them with cultural goods. The reformist leisure culture, however, was something different. It refers to those within the working class who tried within leisure hours to create an all-embracing culture which offered a genuine alternative to what we shall later describe as popular culture. It was reformist because it had a missionary urge to bring others within its ambit; but it would do so by the example of a lived culture, not by the paternalism of the middle classes. It took two distinct, but not unrelated, forms, one religious, the other secular, thus including all those described by Richard Hoggart as 'the purposive, the political, the pious, and the self-improving minorities in the working-classes'.[33]

Methodism was the seed from which the religious reformist culture grew. From its origins it engaged directly with popular culture, and the preaching of the Wesleys, of George Whitefield and of their followers diverged sharply from the paternalist sermon of advice. The crowds who listened were being urged to throw off their old cultural associations and to embrace a new way of life. The new religious life provided its own entertainment – its 'love feasts' – and eased the transition by yoking its hymns to traditional popular tunes. From the late eighteenth century Primitive Methodism ensured that there would be no wholesale shift from militant sect to inward-looking denomination, and in the industrial villages which provided its most fertile soil it established a way of life which thrived on a sense of embattlement with the world. The most spectacular conflicts were fought over the celebration of fairs and other key dates in the popular recreational year, but at the heart of the war itself lay alcohol and the pub. Temperance, especially from the 1830s in its more aggressive manifestation as teetotalism, became the flagship of the religious reformist culture. The teetotal meeting was itself a conversion experience, and in its dramatic ritual an entertainment which the popular culture could

[33] R. Hoggart, *The Uses of Literacy* (Harmondsworth, 1958), p. 11.

scarcely rival.[34] Like any other revivalist movement it had difficulty in maintaining momentum, but there was always the possibility of new initiatives; the most significant, in the late nineteenth century, was the Salvation Army which, in southern towns in particular, fought again the battles for a new leisure culture of the people based on the Christian faith.

The secular reformist culture prided itself on its rationality, and avoided therefore the emotional extremism of the religious culture. But it was no less opposed to the traditions of popular culture and in a succession of forms offered an alternative way of life. In the Owenism of the 1830s and 1840s participants – and it was part of the oppositional character of this culture that it included women and children – created a set of institutions and occasions which made them independent of church and state; they had their own rites of passage, and they celebrated the birth of Paine in preference to that of Christ. But this was exceptional. The weekly club or society, meeting for the purposes of self-improvement or for the promotion of some cause, was the more usual format for the culture. Even in its quietest forms it was engaged in politics, and at times, as in the struggle for control of the Mechanics' Institutes in the 1830s, the political content was quite overt. But its dominant characteristic was its belief in education through mutual association. It was evident in the mutual improvement societies, in the impetus for education within Chartism, in the secular societies of the second half of the nineteenth century, in some of the working men's clubs, in the Co-operative movement, in the Clarion movement, in the Workers' Education Association and in the Left Book Club. Although rooted in the pursuit of knowledge, it was also a pioneer in the development of rambling, cycling and holidays.[35] It attracted to its various manifestations an articulate minority of the working class and, to an extent which remains to be investigated, members of the lower middle class.

The two forms of the reformist leisure culture were often in opposition to each other. Where the one was emotional, the other was rational. The withdrawal from politics of one was matched by the other's deliberate engagement in radical politics. But they are more properly seen as variations on a theme rather than opponents of each other. For not only were there points of overlap between the two

[34] B. Harrison, *Drink and the Victorians* (1971), pp. 129–32.
[35] H. Walker, 'The Popularisation of the Outdoor Movement, 1900–1940', *British Journal of Sports History*, 2 (1985), pp. 140–53.

forms of this culture, most obviously in the shape of self-improving people within the labour movement who were also Methodists; in addition the two forms had a common enemy in the convivial, pleasure-seeking, pub-based culture from which personally they sought escape and which collectively they hoped to reform.

Artisan leisure culture was based, as the name suggests, on a particular type of work, and its rise and decline paralleled that of the artisans.[36] In the eighteenth century and in the first half of the nineteenth it flourished, but as the artisans themselves became more absorbed into the structure of capitalist industry they began to lose the characteristic feature of their culture: independence. Independence in the work situation – the sense that they were their own masters – was reflected in the leisure culture where it took the form of a rejection of any patronage from above; as the artisans made their own goods, so also they made their own culture. If the work situation was one factor leading to independence, masculinity and age were others; this was a leisure culture of adult males. Women were admitted to participation only rarely and on sufferance, and the young, the apprentices, who had once had a culture of their own, were now firmly subordinate.

At one level artisan leisure culture had much in common with the secular reformist culture. It shared with it a certain intellectuality and rationality. In the town in which it has been most closely studied, Birmingham, artisans formed debating societies and clubs and attended the theatre.[37] The friendly society and the trade union both had their strongest roots among the artisans, and they were instinctively radicals in their politics. But the culture was entirely lacking in missionary zeal; it existed for itself, and had no desire to spread its way of life more widely. Moreover it had none of the distaste for the pub which marked the secular reformist culture. Indeed, artisans were notorious for their drinking habits, both on and off the job. The celebration of Saint Monday was particularly associated with artisans – and with drinking. Independent colliers, for example, regularly took a holiday on the Monday after pay day, and spent it in drinking, often associated with sport and gambling of a kind no respectable person would contemplate.

[36]　See E. J. Hobsbawm, 'Artisan or Labour Aristocrat?', *Economic History Review*, 2nd ser., 37 (1984), pp. 355–72.

[37]　J. Money, *Experience and Identity: Birmingham and the West Midlands 1760–1800* (Manchester, 1977), pp. 80–120.

Towards the mid-nineteenth century the heavy-drinking artisan culture became isolated to certain trades and regions. A more respectable, even family-based, culture began to replace it; middle-class observers of the early London music halls delighted to see artisans and mechanics, smoking their clay pipes, sitting at the tables with their wives. In perception the artisan was now becoming the 'labour aristocrat', a respectable, hard-working member of society who took his pleasures seriously. The clubs which artisans joined in Edinburgh, for horticulture, golf and bowling, and their participation in the 'patriotic' Volunteer Force, suggested a new conformity to the norms of middle-class society. The clubs, however, retained their own independence, and the artisan Volunteers took an instrumental attitude to a Force laden with ideological baggage; they joined it for the recreation.[38] And insofar as artisan leisure became more respectable, it was a respectability generated from within the class and for the class, not one imposed from outside.

The artisan or labour aristocrat of the later nineteenth and early twentieth centuries had enough independence in the work situation to be able to maintain a culture marked by the same quality. But after the First World War it becomes increasingly difficult to identify an artisan sector, and the 'skilled worker' sector which replaced it was less independent and less clearly defined. In certain trades, in shipbuilding, for example, the male camaraderie of those who had served an apprenticeship continued in work and carried over into leisure, but, outside these pockets of survival, artisan culture ceased to exist as an independent entity; the leisure of skilled workers became indistinguishable from that of other participants in urban popular culture.

In the mid-eighteenth century there was a vigorous popular leisure culture in rural areas. The calendar provided a customary annual cycle of recreation, normally reaching a peak in a feast, wake or fair which drew everyone in a district together in celebration. These events attracted travelling showmen on their familiar circuits, and were to that extent part of a commercial culture, but they were also integrated

[38]   R. Q. Gray, 'Styles of Life, the "Labour Aristocracy" and Class Relations in Later Nineteenth Century Edinburgh', *International Review of Social History*, 18 (1973), pp. 428–52.

into rural social structure. The gentry sometimes actively patronised, sometimes smiled benevolently, sometimes let well alone, and only rarely opposed these customary recreational occasions. The initiative for them normally stemmed from below, and, like the skimmingtons and charivaris, they were tolerated because they tended to reinforce rather than challenge the existing social order.[39] The game laws might be ignored for a day, but that was a price worth paying for their observance at all other times.

Towards the end of the eighteenth century this rural popular culture came under pressure from a variety of interlocking directions. Enclosure put space at a premium, and often made the survival of a particular form of recreation dependent on the whim of the gentry. The latter, as they aspired towards the standards of the national leisure class, had less and less time for what they now perceived as the juvenile behaviour of their social inferiors; as patronage became more necessary, it was increasingly withdrawn. Harvest suppers, clipping suppers and 'hopper feasts' were suppressed. Hours of work, as we have seen, became longer, and farm labourers often worked six full days a week and enjoyed only two holidays in the year, Christmas Day and Good Friday. As the balance of society as a whole tipped towards the towns the customs of rural society appeared to be without value or relevance, and the socially accepted rural popular culture of the mid-eighteenth century was shattered beyond repair.

Some voices were, however, raised against the movement of the times. William Hone's *Every-Day Book* in the 1820s provided a platform for those who wished to see rural sports maintained under proper patronage. The 'primitive customs' of the Hungerford Revel, for example, backsword or singlestick, running races for girls, and climbing the greasy pole, were said 'to promote cheerful intercourse and friendly feeling among the residents in the different villages'.[40] Such support for 'the old customs' was to become much more vocal and active at mid-century, leading to a full-scale repatronisation of rural popular culture – and in the process its transformation into something new. There was a reassertion of control over friendly societies; honorary members took over the management, and at Whitsun the customary revels were transformed into a respectable public celebration

[39] M. Ingram, 'Ridings, Rough Music and Mocking Rhymes in Early Modern England', in B. Reay, ed., *Popular Culture in Seventeenth-Century England* (1985), pp. 166–97.
[40] W. Hone, *The Every-Day Book*, 2 vols. (1878), vol. 2, p. 700.

centring on the church.[41] Maypoles made a comeback, but now shorn of any sexual or subversive connotations; the local children danced round them while their social superiors looked on benevolently. This repatronisation of rural culture doubtless provided agricultural workers with a welcome break in their working lives, but it was a culture of which they were supposed to be the beneficiaries, rather than one in whose making they were themselves active.

There were ways, however, of expressing independence. Improvements in transport put the rural inhabitants of all but the most remote regions within reach of a town and of urban values. At least once a year most people could make an expedition to their nearest large town, as they did to Oxford for St Giles's Fair. And within the rural areas themselves there existed something of an underground or secret rural popular culture. Long after the state had banned animal sports they continued in rural areas. More acceptably, the world revealed by Thomas Hardy in Wessex or George Sturt in Surrey or Joseph Ashby in Warwickshire or more recently in oral history pointed to the ability of rural labourers to create a culture for themselves. Its most dramatic expression, 'discovered' by the folklorists, was in song.

To emphasise folksong, however, would be to romanticise rural popular culture. For many, way into the twentieth century, both the hours for leisure and the means to pay for it were restricted. In Corsley in Wiltshire in the early twentieth century the family and the pub were the two main foci for social life, the latter used mainly by young unmarried men. Football in winter and cricket in summer were the main recreations. In a modest way the village did offer some facilities for recreation, but, significantly, they bore little relation to the rural popular culture of the eighteenth century. Elsewhere, a survey on the eve of the First World War found less of a positive kind to report. From a small village in Leicestershire it was reported 'there is no reading-room, no young men's class, no mother's meeting, "no anything!" There is no one to get up a good football or cricket club. The young fellows who remain in the village have nothing to do in the winter evenings but to "go to the public and play cards".'[42] The sense of what there might be, of things which would be provided

---

[41] A. Howkins, 'The Taming of Whitsun: The Changing Face of a Nineteenth-Century Rural Holiday', in E. and S. Yeo, eds., *Popular Culture and Class Conflict, 1590–1914: Explorations in the History of Labour and Leisure* (Brighton, 1981), pp. 187–208.

[42] M. F. Davies, *Life in an English Country Village: An Economic and Historical Survey of the Parish of Corsley in Wiltshire* (1909), pp. 276–83; B. S. Rowntree and M. Kendall, *How the Labourer Lives: A Study of the Rural Labour Problem* (1913), p. 228.

rather than spontaneously generated, is indicative of the pervasive poverty of the rural leisure culture.

Urban popular culture in these two centuries of rapid urbanisation can best be understood if we distinguish three approaches to the analysis and composition of such a culture. The first approach emphasises activities for which participants had to pay, and in which their essential role was that of spectator, audience or reader. Included would be theatres, circuses and fairs in the eighteenth and early nineteenth centuries, and, later, music halls, professional football, horse racing, the popular press, seaside excursions and cinemas. In this approach the emphasis is on the scale of commercialisation, the size of crowds, the distancing of stars and professionals, and on the role of technology. From the point of view of supply, urban popular culture in this approach can be seen as mass culture; it is less obvious that it should be so seen from the point of view of the participants. In the second approach the people are seen as the prime agent in generating leisure activities. There might be some commercial or voluntary input towards the provision of facilities, but the activity itself was of and for the people. The most significant institution was the pub which was the location for much besides the consumption of alcohol. The activities included brass bands, mass choirs, many flower shows and the allotments which provided the basis for them, fishing, and pigeon-fancying. In this approach activities were generated within a community or neighbourhood, though they might take the participants outside in the competitiveness which was one of the hallmarks of this type of urban popular culture: pub competed against pub, club against club. Stars and professionals were absent, and there was little formal separation of performers and spectators. In this approach the participants were mainly adult males. In the third approach women move centre stage, and attention is drawn to the much hazier division between work and leisure for most women. The focus is not on activities, but on space, and in particular the space of the home and of the street. Women's leisure, listening to the radio, for example, was not an activity demarcated as leisure but something that was done to the accompaniment of work – housework. In its more social aspect, in the street, its most typical form was chatting, and here too work, discussing prices, for example, was in no way distinguished from other forms of talk. There were, of course, activities of a more manifestly pleasurable kind in which women participated, such as going to the cinema, but the characteristic of this component of urban popular culture was that it was heavily based on a sense of neighbourhood.

Each of these approaches emphasises a different aspect of what can legitimately be described as urban popular culture. It could be argued, of course, that there were three different cultures, but equally the overlap between the three will be evident. The pub, for example, was commercialised, and in some of its forms, particularly in the twentieth century, it might more appropriately be studied within the first approach. Brass bands, similarly, could be big business. Besides the overlaps, it is tempting to think of a chronological progression from the last two of these components of urban popular culture to the first. This progression has often been seen in moral terms: from a working-class self-generated leisure culture (good) to a commercialised 'mass' culture (bad). It will be argued here that it is more fruitful to see the three components coexisting over time.

It will be immediately apparent that the approach to urban popular culture which has received most attention is the first, and our initial task must be an attempt to establish the level and type of participation in it with a particular focus on age and gender. This, of course, is a task beset with difficulties; information is scattered and often unreliable. At the beginning of the period an urban popular culture which was manifestly both urban and popular was only just emerging. There were still traces of what Peter Burke has called 'traditional popular culture', that is, an urban culture centred round calendar festivals; but this was of decreasing vitality.[43] Secondly, there still remained, and long remained, elements of what we can only think of as rural culture within towns. When Joseph Strutt in 1801 in *The Sports and Pastimes of the People of England* included a section on 'Rural Exercises generally Practised', his examples were frequently taken from towns, and in particular London. Finally, a firm division between polite and popular culture was of new growth. In the seventeenth century, in Bristol, for example, there was still a strong sense of civic and communal identity involving all.[44] This can be seen breaking down in the eighteenth century and is most evident in civic authorities' withdrawal from the ceremonies which had traditionally marked the beginnings of fairs, and in their increasing contempt for the town waits.

[43] P. Burke, 'Popular Culture in Seventeenth-Century London', *London Journal*, 3 (1977), pp. 144–8.
[44] J. Barry, 'Popular Culture in Seventeenth-Century Bristol', in Reay, ed., *Popular Culture*, pp. 59–90.

It was indeed in the fairs and in the theatres and showmanship with which they were associated that we can first see an urban popular culture. In London the theatre of the fairs which had enjoyed considerable prestige in the first half of the eighteenth century began to lose its middle-class patrons, and by the 1780s 'was now purely devoted to the entertainment of the populace and the diversions of children'.[45] And towards the end of the century, both in the provinces and in London, there was a decline in the social status of theatre-goers, and if theatre sizes are anything to go by, a rise in their numbers. In London the south bank was the location for a number of massive theatres serving the neighbourhood, and the populace had also invaded the hallowed precincts of Drury Lane and Covent Garden – most famously in the Old Price Riots of 1809 at the latter. Both in the capital and elsewhere there was an enormous popular appetite for the melodrama which flourished from the early nineteenth century; it could be enjoyed not only in the legitimate theatres, but also in the theatre of the fairs and in temporary structures put up by travelling troupes. There was little formal distinction between drama and other forms of entertainment which might be seen in these buildings, in particular circus, a late eighteenth-century invention, pantomime and hippodrama.

Who attended this entertainment? The most famous account which we have is Mayhew's description of the costermonger audience in the threepenny gallery of the Vic. Most of them were lads aged between 12 and 23. 'Young girls, too, are very plentiful, only one-third of whom now take their babies, owing to the new regulation of charging half-price for infants.'[46] At the penny gaffs, attracting attention from the 1830s, the youth of the audiences was again the subject of much comment. Fairs, too, like the flourishing Greenwich Fair in the 1830s and 1840s, naturally appealed to the young of both sexes. The audiences for the more established theatres may have differed according to the time of the week or year. The proprietor of the Coburg Theatre claimed in 1832 that 'On Monday nights ... we have the working classes generally, and in the middle of the week we have the better classes.' The wide variety of entertainment on offer over the year in Bristol's Theatre Royal in the later eighteenth and in the first half of the nineteenth centuries was a reflection of different

[45] S. Rosenfeld, *The Theatre of the London Fairs in the 18th Century* (Cambridge, 1960), p. 65.

[46] H. Mayhew, *London Labour and the London Poor*, 4 vols. (1861–2), vol. 1, p. 20.

audience tastes. Theatres, too, could aim to distinguish different parts of their audience by theatre design and by seat pricing. John Hippisley, submitting a scheme for a new theatre in Bath in 1747, said of the existing theatre: 'nothing can be more disagreeable, than for Persons of the first Quality, and those of the lowest Rank, to be seated on the same Bench together'. The extent to which these schemes of differentiation within a theatre were successful in the period before the mid-nineteenth century is doubtful. When the Select Committee on Dramatic Literature in 1832 found that it was 'generally conceded' that there had been 'a considerable decline ... in ... the taste of the Public for Theatrical Performances', the 'Public' it was thinking of was the upper and middle classes; drama in this period came as near as it ever would to being popular.[47]

The Select Committee also lamented a decline in 'the Literature of the Stage'. And other forms of literature besides drama were becoming more popular and more pervasive. This, indeed, was the first literate rather than oral popular culture. Events were advertised by print, and news was conveyed by print. The expanding newspaper press of the eighteenth century reached a largely middle-class readership, but the chapbooks and broadsides, some of which sold over 1 million copies, were bought by the new literate popular culture. London alone in the early nineteenth century boasted seventy-five printers who sold broadsides and chapbooks, and there were other major centres of production and distribution, for example, Edinburgh and Newcastle. It is impossible to establish an accurate profile by age, gender and class of the readership of this expanding quantity of print. Men, until the late nineteenth century, had a higher rate of literacy than women, and they may have had easier access to literature. They were probably also the main readers of the popular Sunday newspapers, which by 1850 were read by one adult in twenty; for Sunday was much more a day of leisure for men than for women.

Sporting literature was a sub-genre of popular literature, and with its emphasis on 'manly' sports may be assumed to have reached a dominantly male readership. Similarly, participation in and spectating of commercialised sports was largely, though not entirely, male. Most sports, of course, had a rural origin and often a rural location, but a nearby town could vastly increase the number of spectators. In

[47] SC on Dramatic Literature, PP 1831–2, VII, p. 3, q. 1270; Hippisley quoted in S. Rosenfeld, *Strolling Players and Drama in the Provinces 1660–1765* (New York, 1970), p. 181.

a frontier town like Merthyr Tydfil, for example, the inhabitants could easily walk out to see the foot racing and pugilism for which the region was famous.[48] Prizefighting, with its dubious legal status, necessarily sought secluded locations, but the organising centre of the sport was urban. William Hazlitt went to Randall's in Chancery Lane when he wanted to find out about a fight, and his description of subsequent events is built round the journey to Reading, followed by a 9 mile walk to Hungerford. The crowd there was mainly 'rustic', 'for the *cockneys* had been distanced by the sixty-six miles',[49] but sporting events nearer at hand could count on a large urban crowd. Horse racing was enormously popular. Attempts in the eighteenth century to control its spread by force of law seemed to have borne little fruit, and towards the end of the century the upper classes simply sought seclusion in the stands which they had built. Derby Day, as the descriptions indicate and as Frith's painting confirms, attracted all classes and both sexes, but it may have had a special status as a holiday. We know that in the 1840s in Lancashire colliers attended four or five race meetings a year, but not whether their wives accompanied them. Nor do we know who attended the race meetings in Kentish Town, Bayswater and Sadler's Wells in early nineteenth-century London or later the ring of suburban courses which gained a reputation for corruption and ruffianism. Another popular spectator sport was pedestrianism. When Captain Barclay in 1801 wagered 5,000 guineas that he could walk 90 miles between York and Hull in twenty-one and a half hours, 'Thousands of spectators on foot and on horseback attended . . . and he was loudly huzzaed, and carried on the shoulders of the multitude',[50] many of whom had doubtless placed a bet themselves. Probably they were dominantly male. Was this also true of the 'crowds of people' watching rowing matches on the Thames, whose numbers astonished Joseph Strutt, or of the more than 100,000 who were said to watch rowing on Tyneside in the 1840s? Cricket in an urban setting, as William Howitt's account of a 20,000 crowd at Nottingham in 1835 indicates, could certainly attract families.[51]

Families, too, were the main clientele for the commercial urban plea-

---

[48] G. A. Williams, *The Merthyr Rising* (1978), pp. 28–9.
[49] W. Hazlitt, 'The Fight', in *Selected Essays*, ed. G. Keynes (1948), pp. 83–103.
[50] [W. Thom], *Pedestrianism* (Aberdeen, 1813), p. 108.
[51] J. Strutt, *The Sports and Pastimes of the People of England* (1830 edn), p. 89; A. Metcalfe, 'Organized Sports in the Mining Communities of South Northumberland, 1800–1889', *Victorian Studies*, 25 (1982), p. 479; W. Howitt, *The Rural Life of England*, 3rd edn (1844), pp. 527–30.

sure gardens which flourished in the first half of the nineteenth century. There were at least sixty-five of them in London alone, some of them very small, and attached to pubs. According to taste, resources and season, they offered music, fireworks, balloon ascents, zoos and bowling greens. Dickens described one such garden in the 1830s: 'What a dust and noise! Men and women – boys and girls – sweethearts and married people – babies in arms and children in chaises – pipes and shrimps – cigars and periwinkles – tea and tobacco.'[52] As in their excursions down river to Greenwich or Gravesend or up river to Richmond, a broad spectrum of working- and lower middle-class families enjoyed and paid for a day's outing.

The picture we are building up of sport and of entertainment – theatre, circus, pantomime, the fairs, popular literature and the pleasure gardens – makes it evident that there was a large popular audience for commercialised entertainment in the period 1750–1850. This was already a spectator society. So far as sport is concerned, however much allowance we make for exaggerated numbers, there can be no doubt that spectators were there in their thousands. The key difference between this period and a later one may be that spectatorship later became more regular, weekly in the season, rather than annually or spasmodically when there was an event worth watching. But in the theatre, attendance was already quite as regular as it was to be later in music hall or cinema; attendance once or twice a week was common in the larger towns. When we turn to the following century, 1850–1950, the figures for attendance become more reliable, and their general trend is upwards, but it is important not to forget the extent of spectatorship and commercialised entertainment in the eighteenth and early nineteenth centuries.

Music hall was the first new form of entertainment to make its mark in the century 1850–1950. Yet immediately one must qualify its novelty. Charles Morton's opening of the Canterbury Hall in Lambeth in 1851 was to gain him immediate and retrospective attention, but there were important precedents in the saloon theatres which had flourished since the 1830s and in the 'music halls' – so named – which already existed in the larger provincial towns. What indeed was striking about the 1850s and 1860s was the multiplicity of forms in which people could experience what was eventually to become standardised as 'music hall'. The analysis of the songs, which has obsessed com-

---

[52]   C. Dickens, *Sketches by Boz* (1836), scenes, chap. 9.

mentators, has distracted attention from the range of entertainment on offer in the halls; dance, acrobatics, mime drama and clowning, as well as the occasional associated facility, a museum, art gallery or zoo, were part of the 'variety' of the halls from the beginning. And of course there was alcohol. On a small scale, basically at the level of the pub with a back room, entertainment of this kind had long been on offer, and, more important, it long continued to be on offer. As both Booth in London and Rowntree in York noted, there continued to be many pubs with music and singing. The emergence of music halls which were architecturally indistinguishable from theatres came relatively late, during the second great wave of music hall building in the late 1880s and 1890s when chains of ownership were becoming common. It was in the 1890s, too, that there was an attempt, only very partially successful, to win middle-class audiences. Until then, with the exception of a handful of halls in central London, the audiences had been almost exclusively working and lower middle class. Outside London all halls were centrally sited, but they drew their audiences from a wide geographical span.[53] As audiences, their behaviour does not seem to have been particularly novel. There was certainly greater spatial distance between performer and audience as the halls became larger and more formalised in their seating arrangements, but the working class had been familiar with large auditoriums in the theatres of the first half of the century, and both there and in the music hall they insisted on their right to be heard.[54] The music hall audiences, that is, never became passive consumers.

Cinema can be seen as superseding music hall as the most popular form of entertainment, but there was a long period of overlap. Music hall was indeed 'the commercial cinema's first home'.[55] From 1906 onwards, however, cinema acquired its own homes, some 4,000 of them by 1914. Until 1934 we can only guess at the number of admissions; an average of 7 or 8 million a week seems plausible for the years immediately before 1914 – or about 400 million admissions a

[53] D. Hoher, 'The Composition of Music Hall Audiences, 1850–1900', in P. Bailey, ed., *Music Hall: The Business of Pleasure* (Milton Keynes, 1986), pp. 73–92.

[54] D. Reid, 'Popular Theatre in Victorian Birmingham', in D. Bradby, L. James and B. Sharratt, eds., *Performance and Politics in Popular Drama* (Cambridge, 1980), pp. 65–89; P. Bailey, 'Custom, Capital and Culture in the Victorian Music Hall', in R. D. Storch, ed., *Popular Culture and Custom in Nineteenth-Century England* (1982), pp. 180–208.

[55] R. Low and R. Manvell, *The History of the British Film*, 5 vols. (1948–79), vol. 1, p. 36.

year. By 1934 the corresponding figure was 903 million, and it continued to climb steadily, reaching a peak of 1,635 million in 1946; by
the end of our period the downhill trend had started. Who composed
these audiences? For the early years we are dependent on much anec-
dotal evidence, all of which suggests that the audiences were dominantly working class, of all ages and both genders. In Robert Roberts's
Salford, married women, 'who had lived in a kind of purdah since
marriage', were to be seen on their way to the cinema escorted by
their husbands, and in the auditorium itself children helped read out
captions which were beyond the reach of their illiterate elders. Cheap
shows cost as little as 1d. or 2d., and in Birmingham adolescent boys
usually went twice a week.[56] The character of the audience did not
change markedly. In 1934, 43 per cent of cinema admissions cost less
than 6d., and another 37 per cent less than 10d. Those who went
regularly, that is at least once a week, were young, working-class,
towndwellers and were more likely to be female than male. In 1950
the lower ones social class the more likely one was to visit the cinema.
It is true that in the 1930s there had emerged a distinct middle-class
suburban cinema audience, but it remained separate – and a minority.[57] It is difficult to exaggerate the dominance of cinema as a form
of entertainment. In 1950 out of 1,611 million admissions to forms
of taxable entertainment, 1,333 million were to the cinema; the remainder included theatre, music hall, football, cricket, horse racing and
dog racing.[58] Imported films dominated the screens. Even before the
First World War Britain's contribution to film releases within the
country was at best 15 per cent. By 1926 it was only 5 per cent. Protective legislation raised the figure to 20 per cent in 1933, but the overall
dominance and popularity of American films was undeniable.

Reading matter, by contrast, continued to be produced within Britain, and in ever-increasing quantities. By 1900 daily newspapers were
read by one adult in every five or six, and Sunday newspapers by
one adult in three. In 1920 one adult in two read a daily paper, and
every four adults read five Sunday papers. By 1947 every ten adults
were reading twelve daily and twenty-three Sunday papers. The
number of books published rose from 6,000 in 1901 to 18,000 in 1951,
and sales grew even more dramatically from 7.2 million to 26.8 million

---

[56]   R. Roberts, *The Classic Slum* (Manchester, 1971), pp. 140–1; A. Freeman, *Boy Life
and Labour* (1914), pp. 108–60.
[57]   J. Richards, *The Age of the Dream Palace* (1984), pp. 11–31.
[58]   H. E. Browning and A. A. Sorrell, 'Cinemas and Cinema-Going in Great Britain',
Journal of the Royal Statistical Society, ser. A, 117 (1954), p. 135.

within the period 1928–39. By the mid-1930s libraries had not only come within the reach of effectively the total population, but also the number of books issued per head of population in the library areas had risen from 0.92 in 1875/7 to 2.23 in 1913/14 to 3.69 in 1934/5.[59] Two points need to be made about this increasing consumption of print. On the one hand, we think of it as mass consumption, and our attention is directed towards the rise of national newspapers to the detriment of the provincial. On the other, however, there was a remarkable expansion of a specialist press. This catered not only for all kind of hobbies, but also for two key sectors of the popular market, the young and women. Boys were the first to benefit with the penny dreadfuls of the 1860s being challenged by *The Boys' Own Paper* from 1879, and subsequently by numerous imitators. Despite or because of their public school stories they were read by many within the working class. Girls soon had equivalents to the boys' papers. Women, surprisingly, were slower to benefit from cheap print. That there was a market was quickly evident. *Woman*, founded in 1937, and priced at 2d., was selling over 750,000 copies a week within a year.

The seaside holiday is, on one argument, a dubious contender for inclusion in urban popular culture, for it represents in some ways an escape from the city. But the manner of that escape suggests that in essence urban popular culture was being transposed to the seaside. There was a long tradition of so doing. We misunderstand the history of the seaside holiday if we think of it as something initiated by the middle class and in due course imitated by the working class. Liverpool during the War of American Independence reported a decline in the number of seabathers, who normally came in their thousands from the interior of Lancashire, because of fear of the press gang.[60] From London the escape by water to the Thanet resorts and in the early nineteenth century to Gravesend long preceded the coming of the railway. The major increase in demand, however, came only in the later nineteenth century, and it was only then that the seaside holiday became a recognisable part of urban popular culture. Even then there were distinct regional differences. The week at the seaside which many working-class Lancastrians had come to enjoy by the 1880s was unique; elsewhere a day trip was the norm. The expansion

---

[59] T. Kelly, *A History of Public Libraries in Great Britain 1845–1975* (1977), pp. 517–18.
[60] G. Williams, *History of the Liverpool Privateers and Letters of Marque with an Account of the Liverpool Slave Trade* (1966), p. 302.

of demand can be seen in the increasing number of visitors to Blackpool in season: it rose from 1 million in 1883 to 2 million in 1893 to 4 million in 1914 to 7 million in 1939. The visitors soon came from further afield than Lancashire, and if they stayed beyond a day, as was increasingly likely, they found homely surroundings in the lodging- and boarding-houses. On the beach and in the public areas of the resort, too, they would find music and entertainment transported from the urban fair or wake. The holiday camp, although it existed long before Billy Butlin's initiative at Skegness in 1936, enjoyed its greatest growth thereafter. By the late 1930s there were 200 such camps, providing for 30,000 people weekly. Ten years later, in 1949, their growth had been such that they could accommodate 70,000.[61] After the Second World War over half the working class was taking a holiday away from home, women as much as men, and the great bulk of these were at the seaside. Like the cinema, it had come to be both familiar and glamorous at the same time.

Spectating at professional sport offered the same qualities. It was, as we have seen, common before 1850, and to some extent what happened thereafter was a switch from one sport to another; rowing, for example, ceased to be a major spectator sport, and amateur athletics could never claim the crowds of the professional pedestrianism which it replaced. Football, on the other hand, a new sport, attracted numbers which rose with barely a hiccup from the late nineteenth century up to 1950. The average football cup tie attendance is reckoned to have risen from 6,000 in 1888–9 to 12,800 in 1895–6, to over 20,000 in the first round in 1903. In 1908/9 English First Division matches were watched by 6 million people, with an average crowd size of 16,000, compared to 14 million watching in 1937/8 with an average crowd size of 30,000. We can become bemused by the escalating figures to the point where we exaggerate the importance of football spectating. In Scotland spectators as a proportion of the total population were about double those in England, but still in the pre-1914 period only about 14 per cent of the male population of a particular locality.[62] It was, of course, dominantly, though not exclusively, a male pastime, and it was regionally concentrated in the Lowlands of Scotland, northern and Midland England and to a lesser extent London, whose clubs,

[61] C. Ward and D. Hardy, *Goodnight Campers! The History of the British Holiday Camp* (1986).
[62] R. Hay, 'Soccer and Social Control in Scotland 1873–1978', in R. Cashman and M. McKernan, eds., *Sport: Money, Morality and the Media* (Kensington, New South Wales, n.d. [1980?]), pp. 231–6.

especially Arsenal, came to the fore in the 1930s. Other sports could attract crowds of similar size. Between 1891 and 1910 the average crowd size at eighty-one county cricket matches was over 14,000, and numbers continued to rise in the interwar period. Horse racing crowds reached 70,000 or 80,000 on Bank Holidays, and attendance at greyhound racing in the London area alone rose from about 6.5 million in 1928 to about 9 million in 1932. Once again, however, the figures can deceive; a mid-twentieth-century survey showed that nationally 90.5 per cent of men and 96.9 per cent of women never attended greyhound racing.[63]

Figures of this kind provide the easiest access to the history of urban popular culture in the period between 1850 and 1950. They may, however, be more significant for the light they shed on leisure as an industry than as an indicator of how urban people spent their leisure time. In particular, they do not necessarily point to any great change towards a spectator society, for spectating was already a common activity before 1850. And when considered not as tens or hundreds of thousands, but as a proportion of the available population their significance in the social life of the people can be placed in perspective.

The pub had close ties with this commercialised aspect of urban popular culture which we have been considering. It was itself a commercial undertaking, increasingly under the control of the major brewers. It was the main location for what was by a long way the single biggest item of leisure expenditure, alcohol. And it carried out its services under the eye not only of the brewer but also of government. Despite this, the pub also managed to be the main organising centre for the self-generating culture. Of course, the publican was often the sponsor of activities which he viewed simply with an eye to profit, and some of these activities were on a large scale. In the late eighteenth and early nineteenth centuries there were numerous orders prohibiting pubs as the venues for travelling entertainers, cockfights, horse races, football matches and other traditional sports.[64] But in addition what the pub offered was a space for socialising; clubs of all kinds met in pubs. In song and in music workingmen could participate and if they were good earn a drink or something more. The community generated by the pub expressed itself in the annual outing which continued to the end of our period. As Rowntree con-

---

[63] B. S. Rowntree and G. R. Lavers, *English Life and Leisure: A Social Study* (1951), pp. 125–6.
[64] P. Clark, *The English Alehouse: A Social History 1200–1830* (London, 1983), p. 258.

cluded in his second survey of York, 'Public-houses provide facilities for people to meet for recreation and social intercourse under conditions chosen and created by themselves.'[65] Above all, within the pub men could participate in a variety of competitive activities. These included darts, draughts, bowls, card-playing and gambling of all kinds. The pub was the organising centre for many sports, and far from diminishing, its role was on the increase; in the mining communities of south Northumberland pubs provided facilities for only 3 per cent of reported competitions in 1876, but for 39 per cent in 1885.[66]

This participant competitiveness was indeed a key feature of urban popular culture, and its significance is grossly underplayed in those accounts which focus exclusively on music hall, cinema and spectating generally. In the mid-Victorian period the south Northumberland miners competed in bowling, quoits, pigeon flying, dog racing, handicap foot races and clog dancing. For none of these is there a satisfactory national history; indeed such a history would miss the point that these activities, many of which might be enjoyed in many parts of the country, had their meaning precisely in their localness. It is true that as communications improved many of these competitions became regional or national. Brass bands, for example, were competitive from their beginnings on a significant scale in the 1840s. At the first Belle Vue, Manchester, contest in 1853 there were eight bands from Lancashire and Yorkshire. The Bramley Band in 1859 competed at Hull, Darlington, York, Sheffield, Chesterfield and Birmingham. With the Crystal Palace contest of 1860 organisation had become national. But competition still continued on a small and local scale; in the 1870s in the smaller Lancashire contests the prize was often meat.[67] Competition was extended to activities which were not of their nature competitive, for example, flower and vegetable growing and fishing, but it expressed itself most naturally in competitive sport, and in the leagues and knock-out competitions which characterised it, especially in its popular urban forms. Alongside the hundreds of thousands of spectators of professional football we need to remember the estimated 10,000 players of the game in the early twentieth century. And for the mid-twentieth century we might note as typical the High Wycombe British Legion and Ex-Servicemen's Club which with 1,000 male and 200 female members was by far the largest club in the town:

[65] B. S. Rowntree, *Poverty and Progress: A Second Social Survey of York* (1941), p. 366.
[66] Metcalfe, 'Organized Sports', p. 482.
[67] J. F. Russell and J. H. Elliot, *The Brass Band Movement* (1936), pp. 78–133.

it organised 'cricket matches, billiards and snooker competitions, darts teams and fishing competitions. Many cups and prizes are played for by club members.'[68] For the individual and for the club this participant competitiveness provided something to strive for and to achieve, and contributed to personal and local self-esteem in ways which the world of work could not match.

The urban popular culture focussed on the home and the street offered different kinds of satisfaction to a different part of the population. The dominant masculinity of the world of participant competitiveness had its parallel in an equally dominantly female world. We must not, of course, exaggerate. Just as women were to be found in the pubs and clubs, so there was also a degree of family leisure in which all members participated. Indeed one of the chief characteristics of twentieth-century leisure was the extent to which it became organised round the home and the family. Technology played its part in this: radio and the motor car, and increasing comfort and space in the home, all contributed to more leisure time being enjoyed as a family or in the home. Radio, for example, which could be found in less than one quarter of all households in 1928, was present in over half in 1934, and was effectively universal by the late 1940s.[69] For women, however, neither home nor family could ever be unambiguously leisure, for they were also work. The Women's Health Enquiry Committee of the 1930s found that 65 per cent of their respondents had two hours' 'leisure' a day, 'but this is spent in shopping, taking the baby out, mending, sewing and doing household jobs of an irregular kind which cannot be fitted into "working hours"'.[70] Equally, women were less likely than men to be able to take their leisure away from the home and family. Teenage girls had always had some independence, though both in time and money to spend, less than teenage boys; in the twentieth century, for example, they were the main frequenters of dance halls, often dancing together. The cinema, too, attracted more women than men. But most working-class women were confined, for their leisure as for their work, to the home and the street, and there is increasing evidence from the later nineteenth and early twentieth centuries that they created their own separate female culture there. In a mid-twentieth-century Yorkshire mining town the facilities for leisure were more outside than

[68]   Rowntree and Lavers, *English Life and Leisure*, pp. 377–8.
[69]   M. Pegg, *Broadcasting and Society 1918–1939* (1983), pp. 7, 48.
[70]   M. Spring Rice, *Working-Class Wives: Their Health and Conditions* (1981), p. 108.

inside the home, 'and as the leisure facilities outside the home are for males rather than females, the husband and wife move for the most part in different spheres'.[71] It remains to be established when such a culture can first be identified and when it began to wither away, but there is enough to suggest that it existed as a key component of the 'traditional working-class culture' which many have associated with the period from 1870 to 1950. Whether it can be called a leisure culture is dubious; it was essentially a female network of support based on the separation of male and female worlds after marriage. It was more likely to exist where women did not have jobs outside the home, but even in Lancashire much evidence points towards its existence.

The distinction between the three approaches to urban popular leisure culture has value to the extent that it identifies different and mutually exclusive worlds of leisure. As we have just seen, popular urban leisure was to a considerable degree fractured along lines of gender. But from the point of view of lived experience, separating out the first approach has its disadvantages and can draw lines of division where none existed. This may be seen most clearly by looking at the history of gambling. From one perspective it can be studied within the first approach; it was big business, and its clientele by the 1930s had come to include the majority of the working class. On the other hand, the gambler was an active participant; mass betting, indeed, has been described as 'the most successful example of working-class self-help in the modern era'.[72] Nor was the gambler exclusively male. Women bet, too, and the filling in of football pools became something of a regular weekly family occasion. Gambling simply cannot be fitted into any one of the three approaches. It is examples such as these which make it possible to speak, with appropriate qualifications, of the existence of an urban popular leisure culture.

As we have seen, many aspects of urban popular culture are most appropriately analysed in terms of class. Such an analysis can be challenged on two grounds. First, it can be argued that in many leisure activities the classes mixed in a free and unconstrained way. Here we encounter again an analysis couched in terms of a division between the rough and the respectable. The rough of all classes, it is said,

---

[71] N. Dennis, F. Henriques and C. Slaughter, *Coal Is Our Life: An Analysis of a Yorkshire Mining Community* (1969), p. 170.

[72] R. McKibbin, 'Working-Class Gambling in Britain 1880–1939', *Past & Present*, 82 (1979), p. 172.

could meet at the horse races, just as the respectable of all classes could, as is well documented,[73] find themselves next to each other in the choral societies of the later nineteenth century. Such occasions, it may be counter-argued, were either infrequent, and on that ground acceptable (Derby Day was only once a year), or of relatively minor importance in the context of the full range of leisure activities in which people engaged; that is to say, they were minority activities, not unimportant on that account, but equally not so important as to provide a key to the analysis of leisure.

The second challenge is to assert that in the twentieth century urban popular culture formed the basis of a national leisure culture in which all classes participated. There could be no consciously national leisure culture without mass communications, and the latter, of course, were under the control of capitalists or government. A national leisure culture, then, did not in any 'natural' way evolve out of an initially working-class urban popular culture; nor, on the other hand, was it simply imposed from above. It was, rather, the shifting outcome of ongoing tensions and negotiations between urban popular culture and the media. We can most readily identify this national leisure culture in certain days, events and stars. The most notable day was Christmas which, with the partial exception of Scotland, began from the mid-nineteenth century to be celebrated universally and in a common way. Sporting events, too, the Grand National, for example, or Cup Final Day (different, of course, in the different nations), became nationally recognised. Stars, whether W. G. Grace or Gracie Fields, were national figures – not only nationally known, but also seen as representative of the nation. The media played a large part in creating this national culture. The Christmas Day royal broadcasts in the 1930s, for example, were heard by an estimated 91 per cent of listeners.[74] Royal occasions, indeed, were a key element of this culture, for they were deliberately national and they were holidays. To an extent this popular national culture may be seen as originating in the mid-nineteenth century, in the Crystal Palace, for example, but the ritual associated with it only became routine in the later nineteenth and early twentieth centuries. The routine, however, was annual or even more spasmodic, and for that reason its overall significance in the history

[73] D. Russell, *Popular Music in England, 1800–1914: A Social History* (Manchester, 1987), pp. 199–208.
[74] A. Briggs, *The History of Broadcasting in the United Kingdom*, 4 vols. (Oxford, 1961–79), vol. 2, p. 272.

of the way people spent their leisure was less than that of those other leisure cultures which we have described. The artisan and rural popular leisure cultures became absorbed within urban popular leisure, but the other leisure cultures, rooted as they were for the most part in class, survived, and provided the key day-to-day leisure experiences for their members.

III THE SUPPLY OF LEISURE

We have so far looked at leisure activities from the point of view of the consumer or participant. We now need to ask how those activities were made available. There were four main ways. First, the state both created a legal framework and acted as a direct supplier. Secondly, there was much self-made leisure, whether we think of this as communal or associational on the one hand or personal and family based on the other. Thirdly, voluntary bodies and philanthropists were key agents in the supply of leisure for others. And finally, there was leisure supplied on a commercial basis. Needless to say, these neat categories are susceptible to fragmentation. Sheet music, for example, supplied on a commercial basis, provided a necessary resource for much individual and communal self-made leisure. But the four categories provide the best means of analysis of the supply of leisure. They must be supplemented by a fifth section on employment in leisure.

The state had always been concerned with the supply of leisure, but it is tempting in a Whiggish way to see the nature of that concern changing. Whereas in the early part of our period its main concern was to control supply, chiefly by licensing, it can be argued that later its role was more positive and that it became a direct supplier of such facilities as parks, libraries and playing fields. There is an element of truth in this interpretation, but in seeking to understand the role of the state it is preferable to unravel the motives for its intervention in the supply of leisure, rather than to divide its activities into two separate spheres, negative control and positive supply.

One such motive was prestige. At the national level this entailed support for both the production of high culture in the present and the preservation of the high culture of the past. In the eighteenth century royalty played the most significant role in this respect. The foundation of the Royal Academy in 1768, for example, was a mark of royal favour for artists, and had nothing to do with opening up opportunities for the public to enjoy painting; at its first exhibition in 1769 the Academy charged an entrance fee as it did not know of 'any other Means than that of receiving Money for Admittance to prevent the Room from being fill'd by improper Persons'.[75] Royalty could also claim to be protecting drama, though with increasingly dubious justification as monopolies of all kinds came under criticism; in the eighteenth century the patents already granted to Covent Garden and Drury Lane in London were extended to certain theatres in the provinces. Direct parliamentary subsidy for high culture did not begin, ironically, until the dawn of the age of laissez-faire. Parliament granted £35,000 for the purchase of the Elgin Marbles in 1816, and £60,000 in 1824 for the founding of a National Gallery. Between 1821 and 1840 over £750,000 from public funds was spent on the upkeep, collections and expansion of the British Museum. By the 1830s it had come to be recognised that state aid was necessary to maintain or at least subsidise museums throughout the country. From the 1860s governments began to draw back from subsidising high culture, perhaps because of uncertainty about taste, and it was not until the Second World War and its aftermath, with the establishment of the Arts Council in 1945, that there was a substantial increase in state support for high culture, and that it came to include opera and drama. Until then the dominant attitude, even for the relatively favoured galleries and museums, was summed up by a Royal Commission in 1929–30: 'In general it is true to say that the State has not initiated . . . The attitude of the State to the National Museums and Galleries has for the most part been a passive and mainly receptive attitude.'[76]

Public funding required more justification than had royal patronage. The public now could not be denied right of access. In 1810 admission to the British Museum was made free and unlimited, with dramatic impact on the number of visitors:

1809	15,197
1824–5	127,643
1835	230,000
1846	825,901

[75] Quoted in S. C. Hutchison, *The History of the Royal Academy 1768–1986* (1986), pp. 37–8.

[76] *RC on National Museums and Galleries*, PP 1929–30, XVI, Pt. I, p. 10, quoted in J. Minihan, *The Nationalization of Culture: The Development of State Subsidies to the Arts in Great Britain* (New York, 1977), p. 182.

These figures lead us on to the second motive which governed state supply of leisure, a concern for public order and social harmony. In July 1832, only weeks after the 'May Days' crisis of the Reform Bill, Sir Robert Peel argued in favour of public funding of the National Gallery in these words:

> In the present times of political excitement, the exacerbation of angry and unsocial feelings might be much softened by the effects which the fine arts had ever produced upon the minds of men ... He therefore, trusted that the erection of the edifice would not only contribute to the cultivation of the arts, but also to the cementing of those bonds of union between the richer and the poorer orders of the State, which no man was more anxious to see joined in mutual intercourse and good understanding than he was.[77]

It was this type of thinking which lay behind both the positive supply side of the state's role and the negative control side. Government could never be unaware of leisure's possible contribution to social or even international stability. In 1919 a Home Office report on revolutionary activities highlighted sport as a stabilising factor, and later in the inter-war period the government was fully alert to the political implications of England versus Germany football matches; football players, not always willingly, became part of the machinery of appeasement.[78] The supply of facilities for leisure by the state was never a free gift; it came with the same ideological and social wrapping as the licensing laws.

It is, moreover, easy to exaggerate the amount of state supply. The typical pattern was not for the government of the day to take an initiative, but for a pressure group within Parliament to be appeased by the appointment of a select committee. The best that could be hoped for as an outcome was a permissive act which a local authority could implement if it wished. Central government, that is to say, provided a legal framework within which museums or libraries could be built and run out of the rates; but it was as much concerned to protect the ratepayer as to encourage the provision of a facility. Not surprisingly, the buildings were often slow to appear on the ground. Up to the First World War libraries stemmed much more from philanthropy than from rates, and even at that date were within reach of only 60 per cent of the population. The same was true of museums and parks. Local authorities, nevertheless, played an increasingly important role in the provision of leisure. They shared the same

---

[77] *Hansard*, 14 (23 July 1832), p. 645, quoted in Minihan, *Nationalization of Culture*, pp. 56–7.

[78] S. G. Jones, 'State Intervention in Sport and Leisure in Britain between the Wars', *Journal of Contemporary History*, 22 (1987), pp. 163–82.

Table 6.1 *United Kingdom local authority expenditure on recreational facilities as a percentage of total local authority expenditure, 1903–50*

Dates	Public libraries and museums	Parks, pleasure gardens and open spaces
1903–4	0.6	1.0
1905–9	0.7	0.9
1910–14	0.6	1.0
1915–19	0.5	0.8
1920–4	0.4	1.0
1925–9	0.4	1.8
1930–4	0.5	1.3
1935–9	0.6	1.3
1942–5	0.5	0.9
1946–50	0.7	1.3

Source: Calculated from *Statistical Abstracts of the United Kingdom.*

motives as central government, namely a concern for prestige (in their case in relation to other local authorities) and a worry about social order, but they added to them a more compelling motive, a desire for prosperity. The seaside resorts led the way in the last quarter of the nineteenth century, investing in sea defences, promenades, piers, golf courses and concert halls as they sought to improve their attractiveness to visitors. In the interwar period seaside municipalities were engaged in the development of 'Dreamland' in Margate, 'Pleasure Town' in Blackpool and the 'Amusement Park' in Eastbourne. Other towns were less ambitious, but their expenditure on baths, washhouses, parks, pleasure gardens, open spaces, public libraries and museums rose steadily. For England and Wales local authority expenditure on these items was £3,225,000 in 1914, £5,049,000 in 1920 and £13,364,000 in 1939.[79] Considered, however, as a proportion of all local authority expenditure there was no clear upward trend over the first half of the twentieth century, suggesting that there was little change in the level of priority accorded to the provision of recreational facilities (see Table 6.1). Significantly, perhaps, the item of expenditure which had shown most tendency to rise was that for open spaces, reflecting a national concern with physique as much as a desire to improve leisure facilities.

A continuing element in the state's supply of leisure was its concern to control and monitor the use of space. The home, as a private space, was beyond its physical reach, and was in any case, from the point

[79]   *Ibid.*, pp. 177–8.

of view of authority, a safe and recommended location for the spending of leisure. The pub was much less safe and hardly at all to be recommended. Licensing of retail outlets for the sale of alcohol was the state's major intervention in the leisure market, and was intended to preserve public order and provide some means of monitoring the leisure of the poorer sections of society. From the 1770s and 1780s, as social and political tension mounted, there was a major campaign in England to get rid of the smaller ale-houses; the ratio of licensed victuallers to population declined.[80] In addition, the pub's hours of opening could be controlled, and from the First World War onwards so also could the strength of the alcohol consumed within it, but it was widely suspected as a space where political and social dissension could be hatched and illegal pastimes enjoyed. The public parks, museums and libraries were supported precisely because they were public, open to scrutiny and controlled by bye-laws. They quite deliberately aimed to enforce a certain standard of behaviour. The space provided by theatre, music hall and cinema was potentially more dangerous, but the power or threat of licensing of both building and activity made them relatively acceptable. The censorship of both plays and films, even though the latter was not under direct government control, ensured that public entertainments adhered to acceptable moral and political values. Fire regulations, too, for example those imposed on music halls in 1878, not only reduced the dangers of fire, but had the added advantage of driving out of business many of the smaller and, it was assumed, less salubrious halls. From the point of view of public order any leisure activity which was carried on in a large licensed building was acceptable. It was leisure which took place outside these spaces which posed the threat; streets, rivers, canals and privately owned rural areas were spaces where there was almost constant feuding between the state and the people. The use of urban streets or squares as the site for fairs, for example, was disputed in almost every large town in the later nineteenth century. Sometimes the fair was abolished, only to reappear on private land, sometimes it was moved to a less sensitive area of a town. Young males were constantly being harassed for swimming in rivers and canals, or playing football or pitch and toss in the street, and would automatically station a look-out for protection against a police raid. The privatisation of land by enclosure had severely curtailed the amount of land avail-

---

[80] Clark, *English Alehouse*, pp. 45–58.

able for recreation or public use both in rural and in urban areas, and attempts to preserve or reclaim it led to some notable battles, most famously the mass trespasses of the 1930s.

It is possible to put a progressive interpretation on state supply of leisure, particularly in the twentieth century when it might be thought to be responding to democratic demands. But whereas licensing came naturally to governments and was extended, supply, with the financial costs it entailed, was inevitably low on any government's list of priorities. Governments therefore always looked to market forces or to philanthropy as the preferred supplier, and themselves undertook that role most readily when the prestige or safety of the state was at stake. What is surprising is how frequent those occasions were. Increasingly from 1750 the way in which people spent their leisure was licensed and framed by the state, a fact reflected in the immense riches of the sources for the history of leisure held by the state.[81]

Self-made leisure requires less attention here because it was so closely connected with the different leisure cultures that a separation between supply and demand becomes artificial. It nevertheless requires emphasis, for it is easy to forget about it altogether. The more self-made it was, the more local or domestic it was likely to be, and therefore the harder it is to find information about it. In its communal or associational form it was a major means of supply of leisure in the middle-class urban culture, typically in the form of subscription concerts and libraries and of clubs, for example, for chess. The club or society was an organisational form of enormous significance in the supply of leisure; it brought together a group of people, normally men, for the pursuit of a single activity or for leisure more generally. In Bradford in 1900, for example, there were thirty choral societies, twenty brass bands, an amateur orchestra, six concertina bands and a team of hand-bell ringers.[82] Some clubs were offshoots of other organisations, whether the pub or churches and chapels or political bodies. In Rochdale, for example, and doubtless elsewhere, the churches and chapels were crucial suppliers of leisure right up to the First World War with their young men's and ladies' classes, their debating societies and numerous other activities. The Clarion Cycling Club in the same town sur-

---

[81]   E. Higgs, 'Leisure and the State: The History of Popular Culture as Reflected in the Public Records', *History Workshop*, 15 (1983), pp. 141–50.
[82]   Russell, *Popular Music*, p. 2.

vived into the interwar period as another example of the associational supply of leisure, though in this case with a symbiotic relationship with commercial supply.[83] Rambling clubs, holiday clubs, sporting clubs of all kinds, hobbies clubs, and the workingmen's clubs all suggest the importance of this form of non-profit-making association in the supply of leisure. At the family and individual level reliable information is even harder to come by. Much leisure enjoyed within the family depended on commercial sources of supply, of games, pianos, books and a huge array of hobbies, but all these required some input and organisation to make them into 'leisure'; in themselves they were inert. There is good evidence that the market for such goods took off in the eighteenth century, doubtless mainly within the middle class, but in music and hobbies in particular there came to be a considerable degree of activity in working-class homes; by 1910 there was one piano for every ten or twenty people, far more than the middle class could absorb.

Voluntary bodies and philanthropists were less single-minded than the state, but as with the latter it is both tempting and misleading to divide their activities in the supply of leisure into two groups, a negative controlling one and a positive supply one. Into the first group would fall such organisations as the Vice Society (1802), the Royal Society for the Prevention of Cruelty to Animals (1824), the Lord's Day Observance Society (1831), numerous temperance and teetotal societies and the National Council of Public Morals (1911). The second group might include philanthropists and employers who funded parks, libraries, brass bands and football clubs, the Mechanics' Institutes and Lyceums, the Pleasant Sunday Afternoon Association, the Girls' Friendly Society (1874), the Boys' Brigade (1883) and their numerous imitators and descendants. Such a division obscures the factor uniting the two groups, a concern to direct and mould other people's leisure by control of some sort over its supply. This motivation was rooted in a sense that aspects of the leisure of the people were dangerous to the morals and livelihood of individuals and of society. Drink, obscene literature, immorality on stage or screen, improper Sunday observance and cruelty to animals occur again and again on the target list of reformers. Analysis of the various campaigns for reform has suggested that there may be cycles of anxiety with

---

[83]   P. Wild, 'Recreation in Rochdale, 1900–40', in J. Clarke, C. Critcher and R. Johnson, eds., *Working-Class Culture: Studies in History and Theory* (1979), pp. 140–60.

the same concerns emerging with only slight variations in each cycle; gambling, for example, in the twentieth century began to rival, and even replace, drink as a perceived cause of downfall. These cycles of anxiety have been identified most clearly in the eighteenth century (the successive societies for the reformation of manners), and in the late nineteenth and early twentieth centuries when much of the focus was on the leisure of young people.[84] Rather like the trade cycle, it is sometimes easier to identify or apparently identify the cycle rather than to account for it. An alternative explanation is that the groups active in the reform of popular leisure maintained a fairly constant level of activity, and that the cycles were periodic panics which temporarily involved a wider section of society.

The hope of weaning people away from bad habits by the provision of counter-attractions came to the fore in the 1830s, and has rarely waned since. Initially the bad habits were perceived to be of a sensual and physical nature, and the counter-attractions, or perhaps more accurately alternatives, deliberately cultivated rationality and the intellect. Quiet and elevating pursuits, modelled on the best contemporary middle-class practice, were recommended and offered. 'Rational recreation' offered a solution to some of the most intrinsic social problems of the mid-nineteenth century. Not only would the bad habits themselves disappear or at least diminish, but in the process people of good will from different classes would meet fraternally (they were mainly men) and come to understand each other's point of view. From the mid-nineteenth century onwards physical activity in its reformed public school guise could be added to the acceptable counter-attractions, and soon became the chief amongst them. What is remarkable is the persistence of the language and ideology of rational recreation right to the end of our period. The group at which it was aimed might change (youth has been the major recipient of it in the twentieth century), but the nature of the concern did not.

The amount of leisure provided under these auspices was enormous. Parks, libraries and similar institutions, as we have seen, were frequently the outcome of philanthropy. In Glasgow, for example, where the ratepayers on three occasions in the second half of the century refused to provide funds for a public library, Stephen Mitchell, a tobacco magnate, left £70,000 for a library which opened in 1877.

[84] J. R. Gillis, 'The Evolution of Juvenile Delinquency in England 1890–1914', *Past & Present*, 67 (1975), pp. 96–126; G. Pearson, *Hooligan: A History of Respectable Fears* (1983).

Edinburgh had to wait until Carnegie offered £50,000 in 1886. In Manchester T. C. Horsfall raised the funds for an Art Museum, opened in 1884, hoping that if the different classes could take their leisure and recreation in common it would 'diminish the dangerous gulf which lies at present between class and class, especially in Manchester, and give them a common interest and mutual appreciation'.[85] Bristol acquired a municipally owned museum, library and art gallery between 1895 and 1905, all through private benefactions. Some of these civic institutions were less than totally successful in their counter-attractiveness; parks, for example, tended to be planned on too grandiose a scale, too far from the most densely populated areas of towns. They were monuments to the benefactors as much as facilities for the people. But other activities provided by voluntary organisations were unquestionably popular. Much church and chapel activity should probably come under this head, rather than in the self-made category, for it was organised from above for people deemed to be in need. Of these, the most important were the young. Sunday schools were not in themselves leisure, but there was a leisure side to them in their annual outings, and in Lancashire in the famous Whit walks; they were in addition in their weekly meetings keeping young people away from less respectable activities. The real problems arose after children left Sunday school, normally in the later nineteenth century at the same time as they left elementary school. It was partly to keep a hold on these children that William Smith established the Boys' Brigade in Glasgow in 1883. Thereafter uniformed youth movements, particularly for boys, were to attract a high proportion of the youth population. The Boys' Brigade had its denominational rivals, and from 1908 faced the much greater competition of the Boy Scouts. By 1914, at a very rough estimate, between one quarter and one third of the available youth population was enrolled in a youth movement – perhaps a lads' club (particularly prominent in Lancashire), or a local church or chapel club, as well as one of the national movements. By 1967 one adult in three had belonged to either the Boy Scouts or the Girl Guides, and three men in five had belonged to a uniformed youth movement.[86] All of them owed this experience to voluntary organisations. There were other initiatives to provide for holidays,

---

[85] *Manchester Guardian*, 21 May 1885, quoted in M. Harrison, 'Art and Philanthropy: T. C. Horsfall and the Manchester Art Museum', in A. J. Kidd and K. W. Roberts, eds., *City, Class and Culture: Studies of Social Policy and Cultural Production in Victorian Manchester* (Manchester, 1985), p. 121.

[86] J. Springhall, *Youth, Empire and Society* (1977).

for example the Cyclists' Touring Club (1878), the Manchester Young Men's Christian Association Rambling Club (1880), the Co-operative Holidays Association (1893), the Holiday Fellowship (1913) and the Workers' Travel Association (1921). Many of these were behind the formation in 1930 of the Youth Hostels Association which by 1939 had 83,417 members.

The provision of leisure by voluntary bodies probably served females less well than males, doubtless in part because the former were thought to pose less of a problem than the latter. The Girls' Friendly Society, formed in 1874, has a claim, however, to be the first national youth movement. It was predominantly rural and Anglican in its outlook, and many of its members were young domestic servants. Two further organisations came into being to meet their needs as they grew older, the Mothers' Union, founded in 1885 and with 7,000 branches by 1911, and the Women's Institutes, first established in Anglesey in 1915, and opening at the rate of five per week between the wars. In towns the Women's Co-operative Guild, with 1,700 branches and 60,000 members at the end of our period, existed 'to serve the interests of the working housewife'.

The Women's Co-operative Guild aimed to train women for democracy, and encouraged democratic practice; to the extent that it was successful the supply of leisure was in this case self-made. Nearly all voluntary organisations which recruited members, except those serving the very young, hoped that the local branches would increasingly sustain themselves and be run by the members. How far, we must ask, if they did so did they, consciously or otherwise, imbibe the ideology of the national organisation? Were such organisations, to adopt a contentious phrase, 'agencies of social control'? There can be little doubt that all the organisations aimed at youth, from the Mechanics' Institutes onwards, had as a fundamental purpose the moulding of youth in a basically conformist direction. This might not be their only purpose – the eclecticism that went into the making of the Boy Scouts has been rightly stressed[87] – but without a sense that youth was going astray they would not have come into being. But equally, if what they offered was unpopular, they did not survive, or at least not in their original form; that was the message of the history of the Mechanics' Institutes. The later youth organisations owed their success to the fact that what they offered was in demand.

[87] A. Warren, 'Sir Robert Baden-Powell, the Scout Movement and Citizen Training in Great Britain, 1900–1920', *English Historical Review*, 101 (1986), pp. 376–98.

Sometimes that demand, for example that of the early Girl Guides, was redirected into more acceptable, and in this case, feminine channels. But in general the leisure provided by voluntary organisations was shaped as much by the demands of the members as the ideologies of the suppliers; the maintenance of and competitiveness for members dictated this. It is evident, too, that some members might join in a calculating spirit – to extract from an organisation what they wanted and nothing else. This seems to have been the case with some of the early church- or chapel-based football teams, and of some recreational facilities set up by employers; people wanted to play football and were not fussy under whose auspices they played it. The Volunteer Force also offered forms of sport which were in demand, and then became dependent on them in order to maintain membership. Doubtless many members did absorb and internalise parts of the overt ideology of the organisations – they may well have been predisposed towards them – but it would be quite wrong to see the influences flowing in one direction only. There was a tension between the desire to propagate an ideology and the need to maintain membership, and every voluntary organisation on the supply side of leisure was fully aware of it; it was a necessary condition for their survival.

Most voluntary organisations saw themselves as in direct competition with commercial supply of leisure. Indeed they often established themselves as a deliberate counter-attraction to commercialised forms of leisure which they perceived as a juggernaut whose destructive progress they must endeavour to halt. Historians, in a less judgmental fashion, have shared this perspective; commercialised entertainment has been seen as playing a larger and larger role in the supply of leisure. The commercialisation of leisure for the well-to-do in the eighteenth century, it is argued, diffused itself to the working class in the mid-nineteenth century, and to the masses in the twentieth century. There are reasons for some scepticism. It is true, of course, that there was an increase in the scale of commercial organisation, but then there was an increase in the scale of everything in these two centuries; what is not so clear is that commercialised leisure, as a proportion of the total supply of leisure, was on the increase. It is unlikely that we will ever know the answer to this, and in any case, as we have seen, commercialised forms of supply cannot always be differentiated from other forms. If we confine ourselves to the more obvious ways in which people paid for leisure, as consumers of alcohol, print, entertainment (fairs, theatre, circus, music hall, cinema, dance halls) and sport, we can see shifts in the direction of that expenditure over time, but not with any definitiveness an increase as a proportion of income. Alcohol is a critical item of expenditure here. If it was excluded from leisure expenditure, and considered simply as an item of diet, then the case for an increasing commercialisation of leisure stands. But there are overwhelming reasons for not excluding alcohol. The pub, as we have seen, was a major space for leisure, and the publican a major organiser; his chief business, however, was the sale of alcohol, and drinking in the pub was the main way in which most men spent their leisure throughout these two centuries. What happened, of course, was a dramatic shift in the amount that they drank. In Scotland consumption of spirits (proof gallons) per head of population per year declined from 2.55 in the 1830s to 0.35 in the 1930s. In the United Kingdom as a whole between 1831 and 1931 per capita consumption of spirits fell from 1.11 proof gallons to 0.22, and of beer from 21.6 gallons to 13.3 gallons. It was by no means, however, a steady decline: the peak quinquennium for both spirit and beer consumption was 1875–9, and there was a further high point at the turn of the century; thereafter the trend was downwards, particularly from the First World War.[88] But until the 1930s expenditure on alcohol constituted over half of total expenditure on leisure goods and services.

The causes of this major shift were a relative increase in the price of alcohol, a tightening of licensing and the supply of alternative ways of spending leisure time and money. In particular, there emerged forms of commercialised entertainment, most notably the cinema, which were totally divorced from the sale of alcohol. In the eighteenth and nineteenth centuries the sale of alcohol was likely to be an integral part of commercialised entertainment; it was there in the fairs, in the bars of the theatres, in the music hall and as an accompaniment to professional sport. The 'caterers', that significant contemporary name for the early music hall proprietors, were always poised between their music hall initiatives and their dependence for part of their profit on the sale of alcohol. By the later nineteenth century they were confident enough to agree to the removal of alcohol from the auditorium, but they had not made the break-through to alcohol-free commercialised entertainment; attempts by temperance organisations to provide

---

[88] G. B. Wilson, *Alcohol and the Nation* (1940), esp. pp. 8, 335; G. P. Williams and G. T. Brake, *Drink in Great Britain 1900 to 1979* (1980).

it were not an encouraging precedent. The cinema was, therefore, in this respect of profound importance.

The cinema also went one step further than the music hall in the organisation and concentration of capital. From the very early days of music hall the proprietors had organised to defend their interests – which were considerable; in 1866 the thirty-three largest London halls had an average capitalisation of £10,000. Syndicates began to be established in the 1890s, both in London and in the provinces; the Moss Empire music hall syndicate of 1900 had a capitalisation of nearly £2 million. Initially in cinema there was a multitude of small exhibitors, though the capital invested is estimated to have been over £11 million in 1914. In the late 1920s the movement towards concentration took off: in 1927 Gaumont British Picture Corporation was registered with an initial circuit of 187 cinemas and in addition production and distribution facilities; Associated British Cinemas followed in 1928 and Odeon in 1933. By the end of the 1930s three main circuits owned 1,011 cinemas. The extent of domination by these circuits can, however, be exaggerated. As a proportion of all cinemas, they owned only 21 per cent; a further 15 per cent were owned by smaller circuits with ten or more cinemas, and the remaining 64 per cent were independent. It is true that the bigger and plusher cinemas were owned by the circuits, and that they had a higher proportion of seats and takings than of cinemas; in 1951 the large circuits had 25 per cent of all cinemas, 38 per cent of seats and 48 per cent of gross takings.[89] Nevertheless, the continued existence of independently owned cinemas is instructive. There is some evidence of a similar undergrowth of small music halls alongside the Empires, and, in the mid-nineteenth century, of small circuses existing profitably in the interstices left by Lord George Sanger.

The capital structure of the leisure industries cries out for more research. To what extent did brewers diversify into the entertainment industry? What was the source of capital? There is some evidence that investment was counter-cyclical, and that in the Lancashire seaside industry the major investment came from the cotton towns.[90] It is clear that there were spectacular failures as well as successes; the history of the Alexandra Palace, for example, is a story of overambitious investment in providing leisure for the masses. It seems, also,

---

[89]   Richards, *Age of the Dream Palace*, p. 38; Browning and Sorrell, 'Cinemas and Cinema-Going', p. 153.
[90]   Walton, *English Seaside Resort*, pp. 92–175, 220–1.

that in some forms of leisure investment there was a feeling that excess profitability was inappropriate; in football clubs dividends were limited to 5 per cent, and directors were more concerned that there should be utility maximisation than profit maximisation.

It was not only in football that there was a commercial morality different from that to be found in the wider capitalist world. The attempts by the voluntary organisations to raise the level of morality in leisure rubbed off on the commercial entrepreneurs. The state with its licensing powers had them under surveillance, and voluntary organisations were quick to remind the state of its duties; not surprisingly, therefore, capitalists with large investments in leisure took steps to ensure an acceptable level of morality in the entertainment which they offered. In horse racing the owners controlled on-course betting while the government stepped in to ban off-course betting in the Street Betting Act of 1906. In music hall the proprietors reduced the likelihood of an offence to morality by cutting down on exchanges between performer and audience, and by carefully monitoring the individual acts. And in cinema the industry formally established its own form of censorship in 1912 in the British Board of Film Censors, a body which had no hesitation in removing from the screen anything likely to offend not only moral but also political susceptibilities. The leisure industries presented themselves and acted as guardians of morality and upholders of national traditions. There was nothing new in this. Promoters of prizefighting in the late eighteenth and early nineteenth centuries had been equally assertive in proclaiming their virtue, and advertisers of the most unlikely shows in the same period had stressed the 'rational recreation' which they were offering.

Those employed in the entertainment industries may have had a different perspective. In football, music and theatre there were attempts to form unions and sporadic industrial action; it can be seen as part of the history of labour and of industrial relations in an increasingly capitalised society. Certainly there was a shift from the patron–client relationship which characterised the employment of professionals in cricket and music in the second half of the eighteenth century to an employment relationship more akin to that of the industrial world; indeed one feature of that industrial world, insecurity of employment, was particularly prevalent among those employed in the leisure industries. This was in part because of the seasonal nature of much of such employment, but also because of lack of control over entry to leisure jobs. The numbers employed, the inadequate statistics indicate, were growing, certainly in the late nineteenth and early twentieth centuries; between 1871 and 1911 the population of England and Wales rose on average 0.8 per cent per year and the number employed in arts and entertainment by 4.7 per cent per year. In Great Britain the number of actors and actresses peaked in 1911 at over 19,000, having quadrupled in the previous thirty years. In 1921 the total number professionally engaged in entertainments and sport was 103,455, rising to 124,181 in 1931, but then falling to 113,325 in 1951. Technological unemployment amongst musicians with the introduction of the talkies was the main cause of this decline; their numbers in England and Wales fell from 25,900 in 1931 to 14,800 in 1951. Another set of figures, for those employed in leisure services (as distinct from those who were professionals), showed a more positive trend: between 1928 and 1938 the numbers nearly doubled to reach 247,900 in the latter year.[91]

In nearly every section of the leisure industries there were attempts to raise the status of entertainers. The outcome was the achievement of status for a select few, the stars, who were raised above the rank and file; the latter had to be content with wages at roughly semi-skilled level. The promotion of stars certainly became more sophisticated, but it is difficult to deny that they existed from the beginning of our period; Paganini, Tom Cribb and Andrew Ducrow had the star quality as much as W. G. Grace, Marie Lloyd and Fred Archer. As the means of publicity grew, so did the salaries of the stars. The best actors and actresses were already getting up to £150 a week in the 1830s. In the late nineteenth century at least ten jockeys were earning £5,000 each season. But against the rags to riches stories – and often an early death – must be set those of the majority who achieved at best a modest competence. By the 1890s the better professional cricketers were earning about £275 a year. Between 1906 and 1914 the wages of performing musicians probably doubled to reach about £200 a year. Even the best football professionals could not earn high wages, for the Football Association set the maximum wage at £208 per year; only a minority got this amount. Most professional footballers were part-timers, dependent for their livelihood on other sources of income. On the whole, though, complaints about wages and conditions of service within the entertainments and sports world were muted. The lure of acceptance as a profession for the collectivity, the hope of

[91]   J. Lowerson and J. Myerscough, *Time to Spare in Victorian England* (Hassocks, 1977), p. 21; Jones, *Workers at Play*, p. 42.

stardom for the individual and the sense that to be in the entertainment world was unlike any other job, for the most part curtailed any open conflict.

IV CONCLUSION

The history of leisure within the past two decades has made the transition from something which was of interest mainly to those of an antiquarian cast of mind to full absorption within the mainstream of social and cultural history. We might compare its historiography to that of work or labour. The histories of particular trade unions and industries within labour history can be paralleled by histories of particular activities and forms of entertainment (cricket, melodrama and so on) within the history of leisure. Local histories flourish within both historiographies. But where labour history may be said to have the advantage is at the level of generalisation. The histories of different trade unions are more easily compared and brought within a common interpretative framework than the histories of different leisure activities whose variety is their main characteristic. Labour history has both a longer pedigree and a more homogeneous body of material out of which to generate a debate about work nationally rather than at the level of industry or locality.

Such debate as there has been about leisure within the mainstream of social and cultural history has had to do mainly with the extent to which leisure may have contributed to the stability and reproduction of society. In practice this has meant examining how far in leisure people were able to give expression to themselves as members of a class, or how far, on the contrary, they were manipulated in their leisure towards support of the status quo.[92] It is now widely recognised that to pose these as absolute alternatives is to distort the historical record; things, as ever, are more complicated than that. Few would now adhere to a crude social control interpretation of the history of leisure; rather, leisure is perceived as a field of contention and negotiation in which the outcome was neither the submission of subordinate groups to new standards nor an untrammelled celebration of class identity. This debate has now probably worked its way through to an agreed, if complex, conclusion, though it has recently been challenged by an interpretation which downplays the role of the reform

[92] G. S. Jones, 'Class Expression versus Social Control? A Critique of Recent Trends in the Social History of "Leisure"', *History Workshop*, 4 (1977), pp. 163–70.

tradition within leisure in favour of a populist emphasis on the supremacy of the market.[93] The entire discussion has been primarily concerned with working-class leisure, though it would be both possible and desirable to consider the middle classes in their relationship to the aristocracy within the same terms.

In the historiography of leisure there has also been debate about issues of continuity and change. There is no longer much support for the view that the industrial revolution was a cataclysmic force which destroyed in its entirety a self-contained world of pre-industrial leisure and replaced it with new recreations more suited to an urban and industrial society. The boundaries between the pre-industrial and industrial worlds, which were once considered fixed, are in all fields of history dissolving, and in the history of leisure the emphasis in recent years has been much more on continuity than on change. This stress on continuity can, of course, be taken too far. What is being asserted is that many leisure occasions, from the Lancashire wakes to Guy Fawkes night, survived the impact of industrialisation, urbanisation and legislation; they were neither destroyed, nor did they 'die away' in any natural way. They did not, however, survive unchanged; on the contrary, they were often transformed in the manner of their celebration and in their social function, and it is precisely the extent and character of that transformation which has engaged the attention of historians. Such an emphasis makes any attempt at periodising fraught with difficulties and necessarily hedged with qualifications, but few would doubt that a combination of more hours of leisure, greater disposable income, changes in technology and greater urbanisation opened up new opportunities to more and more people in the late nineteenth century; to that extent the two centuries divide into two parts, with the mid-Victorian period as a time of transition.

Underlying these debates, implicitly more than explicitly, has been a lingering doubt about the contribution of leisure to the emergence and maintenance of social structures. In other words, does leisure merit the attention which has been lavished on it? Should it perhaps have been left to the antiquarians? There are, in conclusion, two ways of looking at this fundamental question which deserve further attention.

The first concerns the contribution of leisure towards the making of particular national characters. Joseph Strutt opened his pioneer

---

[93]   J. M. Golby and A. W. Purdue, *The Civilisation of the Crowd: Popular Culture in England 1750–1900* (1984).

The Sports and Pastimes of the People of England (1801) with the claim that 'In order to form a just estimation of the character of any particular people, it is absolutely necessary to investigate the Sports and Pastimes most generally prevalent among them.' At the end of our period Seebohm Rowntree agreed: 'It is hardly an exaggeration', he wrote, 'to say that the way in which communities spend their leisure is a criterion of the national character.'[94] The study of 'national character' is now neither popular nor perhaps permissible, but it is worth noting that in common talk such national characters are widely assumed to exist, and that leisure behaviour is thought to exemplify them: consider, for example, the relationship of either cricket or football to the perception of what it is to be English. If, moreover, one moves beyond 'national character' to a now more acceptable phrase, 'national identity', the importance of leisure becomes apparent. In the current search for the defining features of Englishness, and for the chronology and formative influences in the making of Scottish and Welsh identities, leisure ought to be in the front rank. Many of the 'invented traditions' which, we now know, went into the formation of national identities were leisure traditions, the last night of the Proms, for example, and although the element of myth in the recording of these traditions needs to be differentiated from the way people actually experienced them, further exploration of these traditions will undoubtedly highlight the intermeshing of the histories of nationalism and leisure. In the Welsh case there are already some significant pointers. It is no accident that the first golden age of Welsh rugby in the Edwardian period coincided with a period of immense cultural, political and economic activity within Wales as a whole; nor is it an accident that Welsh rugby was in the doldrums in the interwar slump. These identities, moreover, formed and nourished in leisure, were not only national; they were also, if we keep with the Welsh rugby example, class identities; in this case, in contrast, say, to Scottish rugby, a working-class identity.[95]

The importance of leisure in giving people a sense of national and social identity may perhaps be matched by a greater significance placed on leisure in people's individual life-choices and priorities than has often been recognised. Leisure preference, the object of so much condemnation in the eighteenth century, is normally assumed to have

[94]   Strutt, *Sports and Pastimes*, p. xvii; Rowntree, *Poverty and Progress*, p. 329.
[95]   G. Williams, 'From Grand Slam to Great Slump: Economy, Society and Rugby Football in Wales during the Depression', *Welsh History Review*, 11 (1983), pp. 338–57.

been a feature of pre-industrial society which could not survive the greater emphasis on consumerism in an industrialised society. There is, though, as we have seen, much evidence that however much people might want higher wages, there came a point at which they would sacrifice them in favour of shorter hours. Moreover, as the hours of leisure grew longer, so leisure activities became a more central interest in people's lives. *The New Survey of London Life and Labour* in the 1930s, for example, found it necessary to devote a whole volume to leisure where Charles Booth had been able to dispose of it in a chapter, because 'all the forces at work are combining to shift the main centre of interest of a worker's life more and more from his daily work to his daily leisure'.[96] Most leisure, of course, required not only time but also money. The statistics on leisure expenditure, which might be thought to hold the key to the significance people placed on leisure, are unfortunately riddled with possible errors, and before the First World War are probably best ignored. For the interwar period, however, some calculations are possible (Table 6.2). The striking shifts were in the proportion of incomes spent on alcohol, betting and tobacco. Overall, the increase in the proportion of incomes spent on leisure was steady but not dramatic. These are figures for the whole population, and as the early family expenditure surveys showed,[97] the middle class certainly spent a higher proportion of income on leisure than did the working class. It would be wrong, however, to conclude from this that working-class families did not value leisure. Throughout the period 1900–50 expenditure on food remained the basic and essential item in the family economy, constituting one third of the total; leisure expenditure necessarily took a subordinate place.

Expenditure patterns, moreover, are not the only way of assessing the significance of leisure in people's lives. Any rounded analysis would need to take account of such factors as the separation of work and leisure with the concomitant sense, evident from the mid-nineteenth century, that people valued especially the time they could call their own; the residential patterns of the twentieth century which distanced people from their work and helped to make the home and family more of a centre for leisure activities; and the evidence that

---

[96]   H. Llewellyn Smith, *The New Survey of London Life and Labour*, 9 vols. (1930–5), vol. 9, p. 1.

[97]   R. Stone and D. A. Rowe, *The Measurement of Consumers' Expenditure and Behaviour in the United Kingdom 1920–1938* (Cambridge, 1966), p. 113; Department of Employment and Productivity, *British Labour Statistics*, pp. 381, 386.

Table 6.2 *Estimated expenditure on entertainment and recreation by final consumers in the United Kingdom as a percentage of total expenditure, 1920–38*

	1920–4	1925–9	1930–4	1935–8
Public entertainments	1.2	1.3	1.5	1.4
Hotels, restaurants, etc.	1.5	1.3	1.5	1.7
Reading matter	1.3	1.5	1.6	1.5
Toys, travel goods and sports equipment	0.7	0.5	0.5	0.6
Betting	2.0	2.9	3.9	4.5
Other	0.2	0.2	0.2	0.2
Total	6.9	7.7	9.3	9.9
Alcohol	8.9	8.0	7.1	6.3
Tobacco	2.7	3.1	3.7	3.9
Total, including alcohol and tobacco	18.5	18.8	20.1	20.1

Notes:
1. Expenditure on hotels includes only the earnings of employees and the gross profits of the proprietors. Gross expenditure would be about three times as large as the figures given here.
2. Figures for betting are for gross expenditure.
Source: Calculated from Stone and Rowe, *Measurement of Consumers' Expenditure.*

people increasingly found their identities both individually and collectively in their leisure activities rather than in, say, religion. In a society in which it has been plausibly argued that work has become of diminishing importance, and in which there is lively debate about what kind of work the future offers, it is of fundamental importance to assess the significance which people in the past have placed on their leisure time and leisure activities. The evidence suggests that it may have been greater than we have yet appreciated.

Bibliographies

Place of publication is London, unless otherwise stated.

1 THE SOCIAL IMPLICATIONS OF DEMOGRAPHIC CHANGE

Anderson, M., *Family Structure in Nineteenth-Century Lancashire* (Cambridge, 1971)
'Marriage Patterns in Victorian Britain: An Analysis Based on Registration District Data for England and Wales', *Journal of Family History*, 1 (1976)
Approaches to the History of the Western Family, 1500–1914 (1980)
'What Is New about the Modern Family: An Historical Perspective', Office of Population Censuses and Surveys, *Occasional Papers*, no. 31 (1983)
'The Social Position of the Spinster in Mid-Victorian Britain', *Journal of Family History*, 9 (1984)
'The Emergence of the Modern Life Cycle in Britain', *Social History*, 10 (1985)
'Urban Migration in Victorian Britain: Problems of Assimilation?', in E. François, ed., *Immigration et société urbaine en Europe occidentale: XVIe–XXe siècles*, Editions Recherches sur les Civilisations (Paris, 1985)
'Households, Families and Individuals: Some Preliminary Results from the National Sample from the 1851 Census', *Continuity and Change*, 3 (1988)
Population Change in North-Western Europe, 1750–1850 (1988)
Anderson, M., and Morse, D. J., 'The People', in W. H. Fraser and R. J. Morris, eds., *People and Society in Scotland*, vol. 2 (Edinburgh, 1989)
Ansell, C., *On the Rate of Mortality at Early Periods of Life* (1874)
Baines, D., *Migration in a Mature Economy: Emigration and Internal Migration in England and Wales, 1861–1900* (Cambridge, 1985)
Banks, J. A., *Victorian Values: Secularism and the Size of Families* (1981)
Booth, C., *Life and Labour of the People of London*, 1st ser., *Poverty*, vol. 3 (1889)
Buckatzsch, E. J., 'Places of Origin, of a Group of Immigrants into Sheffield, 1624–1799', *Economic History Review*, 2nd ser., 2 (1949–50)
Carrier, N. H., and Jeffery, J. R., 'External Migration: A Study of the Available Statistics', *Studies of Medical and Population Subjects*, 6 (1953)
Cash, R. A. M., et al., *The Chester-Beatty Research Institute Serial Abridged Life Tables, England and Wales, 1841–1960*, 2nd edn (1983)
Clark, P., 'Migration in England during the Late Seventeenth and Early Eighteenth Centuries', *Past & Present*, 83 (1979)
Coale, A. J., and Watkins, S. C., *The Decline of Fertility in Europe* (Princeton, 1986)
Corfield, P. J., *The Impact of English Towns, 1700–1800* (Oxford, 1982)
Crozier, D., 'Kinship and Occupational Succession', *Sociological Review*, new ser., 13 (1965)

Davidoff, L., 'Mastered for Life: Servant and Wife in Victorian and Edwardian Britain', *Journal of Social History*, 7 (1974)

Dennis, R., 'Intercensal Mobility in a Victorian City', *Transactions of the Institute of British Geographers*, new ser., 2 (1977)

Flinn, M., ed., *Scottish Population History from the Seventeenth Century to the 1930s* (Cambridge, 1977)

Frankenburg, R., *Communities in Britain* (1966)

Fussell, G. E., and Goodman, C., 'The Housing of the Rural Population in the Eighteenth Century', *Economic History*, 2 (1930)

Gittins, D., *Fair Sex: Family Size and Structure, 1900–39* (1982)

Glass, D. V., and Grebenik, E., 'The Trend and Pattern of Fertility in Great Britain', *Papers of the Royal Commission on Population*, 6 (1954)

Goldstone, J. A., 'The Demographic Revolution in England: A Re-Examination', *Population Studies*, 40 (1986)

Haines, M. R., *Fertility and Occupation: Population Patterns in Industrialization* (1979)

Hannah, L., *Inventing Retirement: The Development of Occupational Pensions in Britain* (Cambridge, 1986)

Hardy, T., *Tess of the d'Urbervilles* (1925 edn)

Haskey, R., 'The Proportion of Marriages Ending in Divorce', *Population Trends*, 27 (1982)

Holmans, A., 'Housing Careers of Recently Married Couples', *Population Trends*, 24 (1981)

Holmes, C., 'The Promised Land? Immigration into Britain 1870–1980', in D. A. Coleman, *Demography of Immigrants and Minority Groups in the United Kingdom* (1982)

Hopkin, W. A. B., and Hajnal, J., 'Analysis of the Births in England and Wales, 1939, by Fathers' Occupation', *Population Studies*, 1 (1947–8)

Houston, R. A., 'Mobility in Scotland 1652–1811: The Evidence of Testimonials', *Journal of Historical Geography*, 11 (1985)

Johansson, S. R., 'Sex and Death in Victorian England: An Examination of Age- and Sex-Specific Death Rates', in M. Vicinus, ed., *A Widening Sphere: Changing Roles of Victorian Women* (1977)

Kiernan, K., 'Teenage Marriage and Marital Breakdown: A Longitudinal Study', *Population Studies*, 40 (1986)

Kussmaul, A., *Servants in Husbandry in Early Modern England* (Cambridge, 1981)

'The Ambiguous Mobility of Farm Servants', *Economic History Review*, 2nd ser., 34 (1981)

Laslett, T. P. R., *Family Life and Illicit Love in Earlier Generations* (Cambridge, 1977)

Laslett, T. P. R., *et al.*, eds., *Bastardy and its Comparative History* (1980)

Laslett, T. P. R., and Wall, R., eds., *Household and Family in Past Time* (Cambridge, 1972)

Lawton, R., and Pooley, C. G., *The Social Geography of Merseyside in the Nineteenth Century*, Final Report to SSRC (1976)

Leneman, L., and Mitchison, R., 'Scottish Illegitimacy Ratios in the Early Modern Period', *Economic History Review*, 2nd ser., 40 (1987)

Lenman, B., *Integration, Enlightenment and Industrialisation: Scotland 1746–1832* (1981)

Lesthaeghe, R., and Wilson, C., 'Modes of Production, Secularization and the Pace of the Fertility Decline in Western Europe 1870–1930', in A.

J. Coale and S. C. Watkins, *The Decline of Fertility in Europe* (Princeton, 1986)

Levine, D., *Family Formation in an Age of Nascent Capitalism* (1977)
Reproducing Families (Cambridge, 1987)

Lindert, P. H., and Williamson, J. G., 'English Workers' Living Standards during the Industrial Revolution', *Economic History Review*, 2nd ser., 36 (1983)

McBride, T., *The Domestic Revolution* (1976)

McGregor, O. R., *Divorce in England* (1957)

McGregor, O. R., *et al.*, *Separated Spouses: A Study of the Matrimonial Jurisdiction of Magistrates Courts* (1970)

McLaren, A., *Birth Control in Nineteenth-Century England* (1978)

Mercer, A. J., 'Smallpox and Epidemiological-Demographic Change in Europe: The Role of Vaccination', *Population Studies*, 39 (1985)

Mitchell, B. R., and Deane, P., *Abstract of British Historical Statistics* (Cambridge, 1962)

Mitchell, B. R., and Jones, H. G., *Second Abstract of British Historical Statistics* (Cambridge, 1971)

Mitchison, R., *British Population Change since 1860* (1977)
'Webster Revisited: A Re-Examination of the 1755 "Census" of Scotland', in T. Devine, ed., *Themes in Scottish Social History* (Edinburgh, 1989)

O'Tuathaigh, M. A. G., 'The Irish in Britain: A Problem of Integration', *Transactions of the Royal Historical Society*, 31 (1981)

Pamuk, E. R., 'Social Class Inequality in Mortality from 1921 to 1972 in England and Wales', *Population Studies*, 39 (1985)

Peach, C., 'The Growth and Distribution of the Black Population in Britain, 1945–1980', in D. A. Coleman, *Demography of Immigrants and Minority Groups in the United Kingdom* (1982)

Pooley, C. G., 'Residential Mobility in the Victorian City', *Transactions of the Institute of British Geographers*, new ser., 4 (1979)

Pritchard, R. M., *Housing and the Spatial Structure of the City* (Cambridge, 1976)

Richards, E., *A History of the Highland Clearances*, 2 vols. (1982, 1985)

Robin, J., 'Illegitimacy in Colyton, 1851–1881', *Continuity and Change*, 2 (1982)

Rosser, C., and Harris, C. C., *The Family and Social Change: A Study of Family and Kinship in a South Wales Town* (1965)

Rowntree, G., and Carrier, N. H., 'The Resort to Divorce in England and Wales, 1858–1957', *Population Studies*, 11 (1958)

Saville, J., *Rural Depopulation in England and Wales, 1851–1951* (1957)

Schofield, R. S., 'English Marriage Patterns Revisited', *Journal of Family History*, 10 (1985)
'Did Mothers Really Die? Three Centuries of Maternal Mortality in "The World We Have Lost"', in L. Bonfield *et al.*, eds., *The World We Have Gained* (Oxford, 1986)

Shorter, E., *et al.*, 'The Decline in Non-Marital Fertility in Europe 1880–1940', *Population Studies*, 25 (1971)

Smith, R. M., 'The Structural Dependence of the Elderly as a Recent Development: Some Skeptical Historical Thoughts', *Ageing and Society*, 4 (1984)

Smout, T. C., *A History of the Scottish People, 1560–1830* (1969)
'Sexual Behaviour in Nineteenth Century Scotland', in T. P. R. Laslett *et al.*, eds., *Bastardy and its Comparative History* (1980)

Stevenson, T. H. C., 'The Fertility of Various Social Classes in England and Wales from the Middle of the Nineteenth Century to 1911', *Journal of the Royal Statistical Society*, 83 (1920)

Tabutin, D., 'La Surmortalité féminine en Europe avant 1940', *Population*, 33 (1978)

Teitelbaum, M. S., *The British Fertility Decline* (Princeton, 1984)

Thomson, D., 'I Am Not My Father's Keeper: Families and the Elderly in Nineteenth Century England', *Law and History Review*, 2 (1984)

Tranter, N. L., *Population and Society, 1750–1940* (1985)

Wachter, K. W., *et al.*, *Statistical Studies of Historical Social Structure* (1978)

Wall, R., 'Regional and Temporal Variations in English Household Structure from 1650', in J. Hobcraft and P. Rees, eds., *Regional Demographic Development* (1977)

Family Forms in Historic Europe (Cambridge, 1983)

Walvin, J., *Black and White: The Negro in English Society, 1555–1945* (1973)

Weber, A. F., *The Growth of Cities in the Nineteenth Century* (1899; reprinted 1967)

Winter, J. M., 'Some Demographic Consequences of the First World War in Britain', *Population Studies*, 30 (1976)

Woods, R. I., 'The Structure of Mortality in Mid-Nineteenth Century England and Wales', *Journal of Historical Geography*, 8 (1982)

'The Fertility Transition in Victorian England', *Population Studies*, 41 (1987)

Wrigley, E. A., 'Family Limitation in Preindustrial England', *Economic History Review*, 2nd ser., 19 (1966)

'Marriage, Fertility and Population Growth in Eighteenth Century England', in R. B. Outhwaite, ed., *Marriage and Society: Studies in the Social History of Marriage* (1981)

Wrigley, E. A., and Schofield, R. S., *The Population History of England, 1541–1871: A Reconstruction* (1981)

'English Population History from Family Reconstitution: Summary Results 1600–1799', *Population Studies*, 37 (1983)

Young, M., and Willmott, P., *Family and Kinship in East London* (1975)

2 THE FAMILY IN BRITAIN

Anderson, M., 'The Social Position of the Spinsters in mid-Victorian Britain', *Journal of Family History*, 9 (1984)

Banks, J., *Prosperity and Parenthood: A Study of Family Planning among the Victorian Middle Class* (1956)

Beattie, J. M., 'The Criminality of Women in 18th century England', *Journal of Social History*, 8 (1974–5)

Blomfield, R., 'Farmer's Boy', *Poems* (1845)

Brierly, W., *Means-Test Man*, 2nd edn (Nottingham, 1983)

Burnett, J., *Useful Toil: Autobiographies of Working People from the 1820s to the 1920s* (1974)

Church, R., *Over the Bridge* (1958)

Davidoff, L., 'The Separation of Home and Work? Landladies and Lodgers in Nineteenth and Twentieth Century England', in S. Burman, ed., *Fit Work for Women* (1979)

The Best Circles: Society, Etiquette and the Season (1973)

Davidoff, L., and Hall, C., *Family Fortunes: Men and Women of the English Middle Class, 1780–1850* (1987)

Gilbert, A., *Autobiography and Other Memorials of Mrs Gilbert*, ed. J. Gilbert, 2 vols. (1874)

Gillis, J., *For Better, For Worse: British Marriage 1600 to the Present* (Oxford, 1985)

Girouard, M., *Life in the English Country House: A Social and Architectural History* (1978)

The Return to Camelot: Chivalry and the English Gentleman (New Haven, 1981)

Gittins, D., *Fair Sex: Family Size and Structure in Britain, 1900–39* (1982)

'Marital Status, Work and Kinship, 1850–1930', in J. Lewis, ed., *Labour and Love: Women's Experience of Home and Family 1850–1940* (Oxford, 1986)

Golding, S., 'The Importance of Fairs in Essex, 1759–1850', *Essex Journal*, 10 (1975)

Heren, L., *Growing Up Poor in London* (1973)

Hett, F., *The Memoirs of Susan Sibbald, 1783–1812* (1926)

Jeffreys, S., *The Spinster and her Enemies: Feminism and Sexuality, 1880–1930* (1985)

Joyce, P., *Work, Society and Politics: The Culture of the Factory in Later Victorian England* (Brighton, 1980)

Lane, M., *The Tale of Beatrix Potter* (1971)

LaPorte, W., *Cursory Remarks on the Importance of Agriculture in its Connection with Manufacturing and Commerce* (1784)

Laslett, P., 'Long-Term Trends in Bastardy in England', in *Family Life and Illicit Love in Earlier Generations* (Cambridge, 1977)

Lawson, J., *Letters to the Young on Progress in Pudsey During the Last 60 Years* (Stannenglen, 1887)

Leonard, D., 'A Proper Wedding', in M. Corbin, ed., *The Couple* (Harmondsworth, 1978)

Lewis, J., *Women in England, 1870–1950* (Brighton, 1984)

Lutyens, M., *To Be Young: Some Chapters of Autobiography* (1959)

Minor, I., 'Working Class Women and Matrimonial Law Reform, 1890–1914', in D. Martin and D. Rubinstein, *Ideology and the Labour Movement* (1979)

More, H., *Coelebs in Search of a Wife* (1809)

Mundy, H. G., ed., *The Journal of Mary Frampton from the Year 1779 until the Year 1846* (1885)

Osterud, N., 'Gender Divisions and the Organization of Work in the Leicester Hosiery Industry', in Angela John, ed., *Unequal Opportunities: Women's Employment in England, 1800–1918* (Oxford, 1986)

Porter, R., *English Society in the 18th Century* (Harmondsworth, 1982)

Powis, J., *Aristocracy* (Oxford, 1984)

Roberts, E., *A Woman's Place: An Oral History of Working Class Women, 1890–1940* (Oxford, 1984)

RIBA, *Rooms Concise: Glimpses of the Small Domestic Interior*, Catalogue of RIBA Exhibition (1981)

Rose, S., '"Gender at Work": Sex, Class and Industrial Capitalism', *History Workshop Journal*, 21 (1986)

Ross, E., *In Time of Trouble: Motherhood and Survival among the London Poor, 1870–1918* (Oxford, forthcoming)

Scannell, D., *Mother Knew Best: An East End Childhood* (1974)

Shorter, E., *The Making of the Modern Family* (1977)

Taylor, B., '"The Men Are as Bad as Their Masters . . .": Socialism, Feminism, and Sexual Antagonism in the London Tailoring Trade in the 1830s', in J. Newton, M. Ryan and J. Walkowitz, eds., *Sex and Class in Women's History* (1983)

Thane, P., 'Women and the Poor Law in Victorian and Edwardian England',

History Workshop Journal, 6 (1978)
Thompson, P., 'The War with Adults', *Oral History*, 13 (1975)
    'Women in the Fishing: The Roots of Power between the Sexes', *Comparative Studies in Society and History*, 27 (1985)
Thompson, T., 'Thomas Morgan', *Edwardian Childhoods* (1982)
Trustram, M., *Women of the Regiment: Marriage and the Victorian Family* (Cambridge, 1984)
Vicinus, M., *Independent Women: Work and Community for Single Women, 1850–1920* (1985)
Vincent, D., *Bread, Knowledge and Freedom: A Study of 19th Century Working Class Autobiography* (1981)
Walkowitz, J., *Prostitution and Victorian Society: Women, Class and the State* (Cambridge, 1980)
Wall, R., 'Inferring Differential Neglect of Females from Mortality Data', *Démographie historique et condition feminine*, Annales de Démographique Historique (Paris, 1981)
Weeks, J., *Sex, Politics and Society: The Regulation of Sexuality since 1800* (1981)
Wolfram, S., *In-Laws and Outlaws: Kinship and Marriage in England* (1987)

3 WORK

Alexander, S., *et al.*, 'Labouring Women', *History Workshop Journal*, 8 (1979)
Anderson, M., *Family Structure in Nineteenth-Century Lancashire* (Cambridge, 1971)
    'Sociological History and the Working-Class Family: Smelser Revisited', *Social History*, 3 (1976)
Anderson, P., *Arguments within English Marxism* (1980)
Bailey, P., *Leisure and Class in Victorian England* (1978)
Behagg, C., 'Custom, Class and Change: The Trade Societies of Birmingham', *Social History*, 4 (1979)
    'Myths of Cohesion: Capital and Compromise in the Historiography of Nineteenth-Century Birmingham', *Social History*, 11 (1986)
Benson, J., *The Penny Capitalists: A Study of Nineteenth-Century Working-Class Entrepreneurs* (Dublin, 1983)
Benyon, H., *Perceptions of Work* (Cambridge, 1972)
    Working for Ford (1973)
Berg, M., *The Age of Manufactures 1700–1820* (1985)
Berg, M., Hudson, P., and Sonenscher, M., eds., *Manufacture in Town and Country before the Factory* (1983)
Booth, C., 'Occupations of the People of the United Kingdom 1801–1881', *Journal of the Statistical Society*, 49 (1886)
Braveman, H., *Labour and Monopoly Capital: The Degradation of Work in the Twentieth Century* (New York, 1977)
Burawoy, M., *Manufacturing Consent: Changes in the Labour Process under Monopoly Capitalism* (Chicago, 1979)
    The Politics of Production: Factory Regimes under Capitalism and Socialism (1985)
Burgess, K., *The Origins of British Industrial Relations* (1975)
    The Challenge of Labour (1980)
Burman, S., ed., *Fit Work for Women* (1979)
Burnett, J., *Useful Toil* (1974)
Bythell, D., *The Sweated Trades* (1978)
Campbell, A. B., *The Lanarkshire Miners: A Social History of their Trade Unions,*

1775–1874 (Edinburgh, 1979)

Campbell, R., *The London Tradesman* (1747)

Cannadine, D., 'The Past and the Present in the English Industrial Revolution 1880–1980', *Past & Present*, 103 (1984)

Clapham, J. H., *An Economic History of Modern Britain*, 3 vols. (Cambridge, 1926–38)

Cousins, J., and Brown, R., 'Patterns of Paradox: Shipbuilding Workers' Images of Society', in M. Bulmer, ed., *Working Class Images of Society* (1976)

Crossick, G., *The Lower Middle Class in Britain, 1870–1914* (1977)
  An Artisan Elite in Victorian Society: Kentish London, 1840–80 (1978)

Cunningham, H., *Leisure in the Industrial Revolution c. 1780–c. 1880* (1980)

Danson, J. T., and Welton, T. A., 'On the Population of Lancashire and Cheshire 1801–1851', *Transactions of the Historic Society of Lancashire and Cheshire*, 11 (1858–9)

Deane, P., and Cole, W. A., *British Economic Growth 1688–1959* (Cambridge, 1962)

Dickson, T., ed., *Capital and Class in Scotland* (Edinburgh, 1982)

Dobson, C. R., *Masters and Journeymen: A Pre-History of Industrial Relations 1717–1800* (1980)

Edwards, R., *Contested Terrain: The Transformation of the Workplace in the Twentieth Century* (1979)

Elbaum, B., Lazonick, W., Wilkinson, W., and Zeitlin, J., 'The Labour Process, Market Structure and Marxist Theory', *Cambridge Journal of Economics*, 3 (1979)

Eley, G., and Nield, K., 'Why Does Social History Ignore Politics?', *Social History*, 5 (1980)

Fisher, C., *Custom, Work and Market Capitalism* (1981)

Foster, J., *Class Struggle and the Industrial Revolution* (1974)

Foucault, M., *Discipline and Punish* (1977)

Freifeld, M., 'Technological Change and the "Self-Acting" Mule: A Study of Skill and the Sexual Division of Labour', *Social History*, 11 (1986)

Furbank, P. N., *Unholy Pleasure, or the Idea of Social Class* (Oxford, 1985)

Gallie, D., *In Search of the New Working Class* (Cambridge, 1978)

Gilbert, V. F., *Labour and Social History Theses* (1982)

Godelier, M., 'Work and its Representations: A Research Proposal', *History Workshop Journal*, 10 (1980)

Goodway, D., *London Chartism, 1838–1848* (Cambridge, 1982)

Gospel, H., 'Managerial Structure and Strategy: An Introduction', in H. Gospel and C. R. Littler, eds., *Managerial Strategies and Industrial Relations: An Historical and Comparative Study* (1983)

Gray, R., *The Labour Aristocracy in Victorian Edinburgh* (Oxford, 1976)
  The Aristocracy of Labour in Nineteenth-Century Britain, c. 1850–1900 (1981)
  'The Deconstruction of the English Working Class', *Social History*, 11 (1986)

Habakkuk, H. J., *American and British Technology in the Nineteenth Century* (Cambridge, 1967)

Hannah, L., *The Rise of the Corporate Economy* (1976)

Hareven, T., *Family Time and Industrial Time* (Cambridge, 1982)

Harrison, B., 'The Workplace Situation', *Times Literary Supplement*, 24 October 1980

Harrison, R., ed., *The Independent Collier* (Hassocks, 1978)

Harrison, R., and Zeitlin, J., eds., *Divisions of Labour: Skilled Workers and Techno-*

logical Change in Nineteenth Century England (Brighton, 1985)

Hartley, C. K., 'Skilled Labour and the Choice of Technique in Edwardian Industry', *Explorations in Economic History*, 11 (1973–4)

Hinton, J., *The First Shop Stewards' Movement* (1973)

History Workshop Journal, editorial, 3 (1977)

Hobsbawm, E. J., 'Custom, Wages and Work Load', and 'The Labour Aristocracy in Nineteenth-Century Britain', in *Labouring Men* (1964)

Industry and Empire, 2nd edn (1971)

Holbrook-Jones, M., *Supremacy and Subordination of Labour: The Hierarchy of Work in the Early Labour Movement* (1982)

Holcombe, L., *Victorian Ladies at Work* (Hamden, Conn., 1973)

Hopkins, E., 'Working Hours and Conditions during the Industrial Revolution: A Re-Appraisal', *Economic History Review*, 2nd ser., 35 (1982)

Hudson, P., 'Proto-Industrialisation: The Case of the West Riding', *History Workshop Journal*, 12 (1981)

Hunt, E. J., *British Labour History 1815–1914* (1981)

Johnson, C., 'The Problem of Reformism and Marx's Theory of Fetishism', *New Left Review*, 119 (1980)

Johnson, R., 'Thompson, Genovese and Socialist-Humanist History', *History Workshop Journal*, 6 (1978)

'Culture and the Historian', in J. Clarke, C. Critcher and R. Johnson, eds., *Working-Class Culture: Studies in History and Theory* (1979)

Jones, E. L., *Agriculture and the Industrial Revolution* (Oxford, 1974)

Joyce, P., *Work, Society and Politics: The Culture of the Factory in Later Victorian England* (Brighton, 1980)

'Labour, Capital and Compromise: A Response to Richard Price', *Social History*, 9 (1984)

'Languages of Reciprocity and Conflict: A Further Response to Richard Price', *Social History*, 9 (1984)

'In Pursuit of Class: Recent Studies in the History of Work and of Class', *History Workshop Journal*, 25 (1988)

Visions of the People: Conceptions of the Social Order in England before 1914 (Cambridge, 1990)

ed., *Historical Meanings of Work* (Cambridge, 1987)

Kanefsky, J. W., 'Motive Power in British Industry and the Accuracy of the 1870 Factory Returns', *Economic History Review*, 2nd ser., 32 (1979)

Kaplan, S. L., and Koepp, C. J., ed., *Work in France: Representations, Meaning, Organization and Practice* (Ithaca and London, 1986)

Kocka, J., 'The Study of Social Mobility and the Formation of the Working Class in the Nineteenth Century', *Le Mouvement Social*, 3 (1980)

'Problems of Working Class Formation in Germany: The Early Years, 1800–1875', in I. Katznelson and A. Zolberg, eds., *Working Class Formation: Nineteenth-Century Patterns in Western Europe and the United States* (1980)

Lawton, R., *The Census and Social Structure* (1978)

Lazonick, W., 'Industrial Relations and Technical Change: The Case of the Self-Acting Mule', *Cambridge Journal of Economics*, 3 (1979)

Lazonick, W., and Elbaum, B., *The Decline of the British Economy: An Institutional Perspective* (Cambridge, 1986)

Lee, C. H., *British Regional Employment Statistics 1841–1971* (Cambridge, 1979)

Lees, L. H., *Exiles of Erin: Irish migrants in Victorian London* (Manchester, 1979)

Leeson, R. A., *Travelling Brothers* (1979)

Littler, C. R., *The Development of the Labour Process in Capitalist Societies* (1982)

McBride, T., *The Modernization of Household Service in England and France 1820–1920* (New York, 1976)

McClelland, K., 'Shipbuilding Workers on Tyneside *c.* 1850–1880' and 'Time and Work, Time to Live: Some Aspects of Work and the Re-Formation of Class in Britain, 1850–1880', in P. Joyce, ed., *The Historical Meanings of Work* (Cambridge, 1987)

McClelland, K., and Reid, A., 'The Shipbuilding Workers 1840–1914', in R. Harrison and J. Zeitlin, eds., *Divisions of Labour: Skilled Workers and Technological Change in Nineteenth Century England* (Brighton, 1985)

McKenna, F., *The Railway Workers 1840–1920* (1980)

Mallet, S., *La Nouvelle Class ouvrière* (Paris, 1963)

Mann, M., *Consciousness and Action among the Western Working Class* (1973)

Mayer, A., *The Persistence of the Old Regime* (1981)

Medick, H., Kriedte, P., *et al.*, *Industrialisation before Industrialisation: Rural Industry in the Genesis of Capitalism* (Cambridge, 1981)

Melling, J., '"Non-Commissioned Officers": British Employers and their Supervisory Workers, 1880–1920', *Social History*, 5 (1980)

'The Foreman: A Forgotten Figure in the Social History of the Workplace?' (unpublished paper)

'Scottish Industrialists and the Changing Character of Class Relations in the Clyde Region, *c.* 1880–1918', in T. Dickson, ed., *Capital and Class in Scotland* (Edinburgh, 1982)

Messenger, B., *Picking up the Linen Threads: A Study in Industrial Folklore* (Austin, Texas, 1975)

Meyer, A., *The Persistence of the Old Regime* (1981)

Mingay, G., ed., *The Victorian Countryside*, 2 vols (1981)

Mitchell, B. R., *British Historical Statistics* (Cambridge, 1988)

Mitchell, B. R., and Deane, P., *Abstract of British Historical Statistics* (Cambridge, 1962)

Mitchell, J., and Oakley, A., eds., *The Rights and Wrongs of Women* (1976)

Moore, R., *Pitmen, Preachers and Politics* (Cambridge, 1974)

Moorehouse, H. F., 'The Marxist Theory of the Labour Aristocracy', *Social History*, 3 (1978)

'History, Sociology and the Quiescence of the British Working Class: A Reply to Reid', *Social History*, 4 (1979)

More, C., *Skill and the English Working Class, 1870–1914* (1980)

Musson, A. E., 'Industrial Motive Power in the United Kingdom, 1800–70', *Economic History Review*, 2nd ser., 29 (1976)

The Growth of British Industry (1978)

Neff, W., *Victorian Working Women* (1966)

Perrot, M., 'On the Formation of the French Working Class', in I. Katznelson and A. R. Zolberg, eds., *Working Class Formation: Nineteenth-Century Patterns in Western Europe and the United States* (1983)

Pickering, P. A., 'Class without Work: Symbolic Communication in the Chartist Movement', *Past & Present*, 112 (1986)

Pinchbeck, I., *Women Workers in the Industrial Revolution* (1977)

Pollard, S., *The Genesis of Modern Management* (1965)

Peaceful Conquest: The Industrialisation of Europe, 1760–1970 (Oxford, 1981)

Price, R., *Masters, Unions and Men: Work Control in Building and the Rise of Labour, 1830–1914* (Cambridge, 1980)

'The Labour Process and Labour History', *Social History*, 8 (1983)

'Conflict and Co-operation: A Reply to Patrick Joyce', *Social History*, 9 (1984)

'The Structure of Subordination in Nineteenth-Century Relations in Production', in G. Crossick, R. Floud, and P. Thane, eds., *The Power of the Past: Essays in Honour of E. J. Hobsbawm* (Cambridge, 1984)

Labour in British Society (1986)

Prothero, I., *Artisans and Politics in Early Nineteenth-Century London* (Folkestone, 1979)

Reddy, W. M., *The Rise of Market Culture: The Textile Trade and French Society, 1750–1900* (Cambridge, 1984)

Money and Liberty in Modern Europe: A Critique of Historical Understanding (Cambridge, 1987)

Reid, A., 'Politics and Economics in the Formation of the British Working Class: A Response to H. F. Moorhouse', *Social History*, 3 (1978)

'The Division of Labour and Politics in Britain, 1880–1920', in W. J. Mommsen and H.-G. Husung, eds., *The Development of Trade Unionism in Great Britain and Germany, 1880–1914* (1985)

Reid, D., 'The Decline of Saint Monday, 1766–1876', *Past & Present*, 71 (1976)

Roberts, B., Finnegan, R., and Gallie, D., eds., *New Approaches to Economic Life* (Manchester, 1985)

Rule, J., *The Experience of Labour in Eighteenth-Century Industry* (1981)

ed., *English Trade Unionism, 1750–1950: The Formative Years* (1988)

Sabel, C. F., *Work and Politics: The Division of Labour in Industry* (Cambridge, 1982)

Salaman, G., and Littler, C. R., *Class at Work* (1984)

Samuel, R., 'The Workshop of the World: Steam Power and Hand Technology in Mid-Victorian Britain', *History Workshop Journal*, 3 (1977)

'British Marxist Historians I', *New Left Review*, 120 (1980)

ed., *Village Life and Labour* (1975)

ed., *Mines, Quarrymen and Saltworkers* (1977)

ed., *People's History and Socialist Theory* (1981)

'Artisans and Workers in South-West Bethnal Green' (unpublished paper)

Saunders, C., *Seasonal Fluctuations* (1936)

Savage, M., *The Dynamics of Working Class Politics* (Cambridge, 1987)

Seed, J., 'Unitarianism, Political Economy and the Antinomies of Liberal Culture in Manchester, 1830–1850', *Social History*, 7 (1982)

Sewell, W., *Work and Revolution in France: The Language of Labour from the Old Regime to 1848* (Cambridge, 1980)

Smelser, N., *Social Change in the Industrial Revolution* (1959)

Snell, K., *Annals of the Labouring Poor: Social Change and Agrarian England 1660–1900* (Cambridge, 1985)

Stedman Jones, G., *Outcast London: A Study in the Relationship between Classes in Victorian Society* (Oxford, 1971)

'Working-Class Culture and Working-Class Politics in London: 1870–1900: Notes on the Remaking of a Working Class', *Journal of Social History*, 7 (1974)

'England's First Proletariat: "Class Struggle and the Industrial Revolution"', *New Left Review*, 90 (1975)

'The Language of Chartism', in D. Thompson and J. Epstein, eds., *The Experience of Chartism* (1982)

Storch, R. D., ed., *Popular Culture and Custom in Nineteenth-Century England* (1982)

Thompson, E. P., 'Time, Work-Discipline, and Industrial Capitalism', *Past & Present*, 38 (1967)

The Making of the English Working Class, 2nd edn (1968)

The Poverty of Theory (1978)

'Eighteenth-Century English Society: Class Struggle without Class?', *Social History*, 3 (1978)

Thompson, F., *Lark Rise to Candleford* (1973 edn)

Thompson, P., *The Nature of Work: An Introduction to Debates on the Labour Process* (1983)

Thompson, P., and Lummis, T., eds., *Living the Fishing* (1983)

Tilly, L., and Scott, J., *Women, Work and the Family* (New York, 1978)

Touraine, A., *The Post-Industrial Society* (1971)

Vincent, J., *The Formation of the Liberal Party, 1857–1868* (1966)

Wallman, S., ed., *The Social Anthropology of Work* (1979)

Webb, S., and Freeman, A., *The Seasonal Trades* (1912)

Webb, S. and B., *The History of Trade Unionism* (1920)

Wiener, M. J., *English Culture and the Decline of the Industrial Spirit, 1850–1980* (Cambridge, 1981)

Williams, A., *Life in a Railway Workshop* (1915)

Wood, S., *The Degradation of Work?* (1982)

Wrigley, C., ed., *A History of British Industrial Relations, 1880–1920* (Brighton, 1982)

Zeitlin, J., 'The Emergence of Shop Steward Organisation and Job Control in the British Car Industry: A Review Essay', *History Workshop Journal*, 10 (1980)

'Social Theory and the History of Work', *Social History*, 8 (1983)

'From Labour History to the History of Industrial Relations', *Economic History Review*, 2nd ser., 40 (1987)

Zeitlin, J., and Sabel, C., 'Historical Alternatives to Mass Production', *Past & Present*, 108 (1985)

4 HOUSING

Allan, C. M., 'The Genesis of British Urban Redevelopment with Special Reference to Glasgow', *Economic History Review*, 2nd ser., 18 (1965)

Ashmore, O., 'Low Moor, Clitheroe: A Nineteenth-Century Factory Community', *Transactions of the Lancashire and Cheshire Antiquarian Society*, 73–4 (1963–4)

Ashworth, W., 'British Industrial Villages in the 19th Century', *Economic History Review*, 2nd ser., 3 (1951)

The Genesis of Modern British Town Planning: A Study in Economic and Social History of the Nineteenth and Twentieth Centuries (1954)

Aslet, C., *The Last Country Houses* (New Haven and London, 1982)

Barnsby, G. J., *A History of Housing in Wolverhampton 1750–1975* (Wolverhampton, n.d.)

Berbiers, J. L., 'Back-to-Back Housing, Halifax', *Official Architecture and Planning*, 31 (1968)

'The Victorian Working-Class Houses of Halifax', *Municipal Review*, 457 (1968)

Beresford, M. W., 'The Back-to-Back House in Leeds, 1787–1937', in S. D. Chapman, ed., *The History of Working-Class Housing* (Newton Abbot, 1971)

'The Face of Leeds, 1780–1914', in D. Fraser, ed., *A History of Modern Leeds* (Manchester, 1980)

Boddy, M. J., 'The Structure of Mortgage Finance: Building Societies and the British Social Formation', *Transactions of the Institute of British Geographers*, new series, 1 (1976)

The Building Societies (1980)

Bogdanor, V., and Skidelsky, R., *The Age of Affluence* (1970)

Bowley, A. L., and Burnett-Hurst, A. R., *Livelihood and Poverty* (1915)

Bowley, M., *Housing and the State, 1919–44* (1945)

Boyson, R., *The Ashworth Cotton Enterprise: The Rise and Fall of a Family Firm, 1818–80* (Oxford, 1970)

Brayshay, M., 'The Duke of Bedford's Model Cottages in Tavistock, 1840–70', *Transactions of Devonshire Association for the Advancement of Science*, 114 (1982)

Bristow, E., 'The Liberty and Property Defence League and Individualism', *Historical Journal*, 8 (1975)

Burnett, J., *A Social History of Housing, 1815–1970* (Newton Abbot, 1978)

Butt, J., 'Working-Class Housing in Glasgow, 1851–1914', in S. D. Chapman, ed., *The History of Working-Class Housing* (Newton Abbot, 1971)

'Working-Class Housing in Glasgow, 1900–39', in I. MacDougall, ed., *Essays in Scottish Urban History* (Edinburgh, 1979)

'Working-Class Housing in the Scottish Cities, 1900–50', in G. Gordon and B. Dicks, eds., *Scottish Urban History* (Aberdeen, 1983)

Caffyn, L., *Workers' Housing in West Yorkshire, 1750–1920* (1986)

Cairncross, A. K., *Home and Foreign Investment, 1870–1913* (Cambridge, 1953)

Carrier, J., 'The Four Per Cent Industrial Dwellings Co. Ltd.: The Social Composition of the Shareholders of an East London Dwellings Company at the End of the 19th Century', *East London Papers*, 11 (1968)

Chalklin, C. W., 'Urban Housing Estates in the 18th Century', *Urban Studies*, 5 (1968)

The Provincial Towns of Georgian England: A Study of the Building Process, 1740–1820 (1974)

Chapman, S. D., 'Working-Class Housing in Nottingham during the Industrial Revolution', *Transactions of the Thoroton Society*, 67 (1963)

ed., *The History of Working-Class Housing* (Newton Abbot, 1971)

Checkland, S. G. and E. O., 'Housing Policy: The Formative Years: A Review Article', *Town Planning Review*, 46 (1975)

Cleary, E. J., *The Building Society Movement* (1965)

Cole, G. D. H. and M., *Rents, Rings and Houses* (1923)

Cooper, T. M., and Whyte, W. E., *The Law of Housing and Town Planning in Scotland* (Edinburgh, 1920)

Craig, P., 'The House that Jerry Built? Building Societies, the State, and the Politics of Owner-Occupation', *Housing Studies*, 1 (1986)

Cramond, R. D., *Housing Policy in Scotland, 1919–64* (Edinburgh, 1966)

Crossick, G. J., *An Artisan Elite in Victorian Society: Kentish London, 1840–80* (1978)

'Urban Society and the Petty Bourgeoisie in Nineteenth-Century Britain', in D. Fraser and A. Sutcliffe, eds., *The Pursuit of Urban History* (1983)

ed., *The Lower Middle Class in Britain, 1870–1914* (1977)

Cullingworth, J. B., *Housing and Local Government in England and Wales* (1966)

Daunton, M. J., *Coal Metropolis: Cardiff, 1870–1914* (Leicester, 1977)

'Miners' Houses: South Wales and the Great Northern Coalfield, 1880–1914', *International Review of Social History*, 25 (1980)

House and Home in the Victorian City: Working-Class Housing, 1850–1914 (1983)

'Public Place and Private Space: The Victorian City and the Working-Class

Household', in D. Fraser and A. Sutcliffe, eds., *The Pursuit of Urban History* (1983)

A Property-Owning Democracy? Housing in Britain (1987)

ed., *Councillors and Tenants: Local Authority Housing in English Cities, 1919–39* (Leicester, 1984)

Davidoff, L., *The Best Circles: Society, Etiquette and the Season* (1973)

'The Separation of Home and Work? Landladies and Lodgers in Nineteenth and Twentieth Century England', in S. Burman, ed., *Fit Work for Women* (1979)

Doe, V., 'Some Developments in Middle-Class Housing in Sheffield, 1830–75', in S. Pollard and C. Holmes, eds., *Essays in the Economic and Social History of South Yorkshire* (Barnsley, 1976)

Donnison, D. V., *The Government of Housing* (Harmondsworth, 1967)

Duclaud-Williams, R. H., *The Politics of Housing in Britain and France* (1978)

Dunleavy, P., *The Politics of Mass Housing in Britain, 1945–75: A Study of Corporate Power and Professional Influence in the Welfare State* (Oxford, 1981)

Durant, R., *Watling: A Survey of Social Life on a New Housing Estate* (1939)

Dyos, H. J., 'Railways and Housing in Victorian London', *Journal of Transport History*, 2 (1955)

'The Slums of Victorian London', *Victorian Studies*, 11 (1968)

Dyos, H. J., and Reeder, R., 'Slums and Suburbs', in H. J. Dyos and M. Wolff, eds., *The Victorian City: Images and Realities*, vol. 1 (1973)

Edwards, A. M., *The Design of Suburbia* (1981)

Engels, F., *The Condition of the Working Class in England* (Panther edn, 1969)

Englander, D., 'Landlord and Tenant in Urban Scotland: The Background to the Clyde Rent Strike, 1915', *Journal of Scottish Labour History*, 15 (1981)

Landlord and Tenant in Urban Britain, 1838–1918 (Oxford, 1983)

Errazurez, A., 'Some Types of Housing in Liverpool, 1785–1890', *Town Planning Review*, 19 (1943–7)

Feinstein, C. H., *Domestic Capital Formation in the United Kingdom, 1920–38* (Cambridge, 1965)

Ferguson, T., *Scottish Social Welfare, 1864–1914* (Edinburgh, 1958)

Forster, C. A., *Court Housing in Kingston-upon-Hull: An Example of Cyclic Processes in the Morphological Development of Nineteenth-Century Bye-Law Housing* (Hull, 1972)

Franklin, J., *The Gentleman's Country House and its Plan, 1835–1914* (1981)

Fraser, D., and Sutcliffe, A., eds., *The Pursuit of Urban History* (1983)

Gaskell, S. M., 'Yorkshire Estate Development and the Freehold Land Societies in the 19th Century', *Yorkshire Archaeological Journal*, 43 (1971)

'Housing and the Lower Middle Class, 1870–1914', in G. J. Crossick, ed., *The Lower Middle Class in Britain, 1870–1914* (1977)

Building Control: National Legislation and the Introduction of Local Bye-Laws in Victorian England (1983)

Model Housing: From the Great Exhibition to the Festival of Britain (1986)

Gauldie, E., *Cruel Habitations: A History of Working-Class Housing, 1780–1918* (1974)

George, M. D., *London Life in the Eighteenth Century* (1925)

Giles, C., *Rural Houses of West Yorkshire, 1400–1830* (1986)

Girouard, M., *Life in the English Country House: A Social and Architectural History* (1978)

The Victorian Country House (1979)

Gourvish, T. R., 'The Standard of Living, 1890–1914', in A. O'Day, ed., *The*

Edwardian Age: Conflict and Stability, 1900–14 (1979)

Grace, R., 'Tyneside Housing in the Nineteenth Century', in N. McCord, ed., *Essays in Tyneside Labour History* (Newcastle, 1977)

Hall, P. G., *et al.*, *The Containment of Urban England*, 2 vols. (1973)

Harper, R. H., 'The Conflict between English Building Regulations and Architectural Design, 1890–1918', *Journal of Architectural Research*, 6 (1977)

Victorian Building Regulations: Summary Tables of the Principal English Building Acts and Model Bye-laws, 1840–1914 (1985)

Hennock, E. P., 'Finance and Politics in Urban Local Government in England, 1835–1900', *Historical Journal*, 6 (1963)

Fit and Proper Persons: Ideal and Reality in Nineteenth-Century Urban Government (1973)

Hole, W. V., and Pountney, M. T., *Trends in Population, Housing and Occupancy Rates, 1861–1961* (1971)

Holmans, A. E., *Housing Policy in Britain: A History* (Beckenham, 1987)

Hunt, E. H., *Regional Wage Variations in Britain, 1850–1914* (Oxford, 1973)

Jackson, A. A., *Semi-Detached London: Suburban Development, Life and Transport, 1900–39* (1973)

Jackson, J. T., 'Nineteenth-Century Housing in Wigan and St Helens', *Transactions of the Historic Society of Lancashire and Cheshire*, 129 (1980)

Jarman, J. R., *Housing Subsidies and Rents: A Study of Local Authorities' Problems* (1948)

Jennings, J. H., 'Geographical Implications of the Municipal Housing Programme in England and Wales', *Urban Studies*, 8 (1971)

Jevons, R., and Madge, J., *Housing-Estates: A Study of Bristol Corporation Policy and Practice between the Wars* (Bristol, 1946)

Johnson, P. B., *Land Fit for Heroes: The Planning of British Reconstruction, 1916–1919* (Chicago, 1968)

Joyce, P., *Work, Society and Politics: The Culture of the Factory in Later Victorian England* (Brighton, 1980)

Kellett, J. R., 'Property Speculators and the Building of Glasgow, 1780–1830', *Scottish Journal of Political Economy*, 8 (1961)

The Impact of Railways on Victorian Cities (1969)

Kerr, R., *The Gentleman's House: Or How to Plan English Residences from the Parsonage to the Palace*, 3rd edn (1871)

Kirby, D. A., 'The Inter-War Council Dwelling', *Town Planning Review*, 32 (1971)

Slum Clearance and Residential Renewal: The Case in Urban Britain (1979)

Langley, K. M., 'An Analysis of the Asset Structure of Estates, 1900–49', *Bulletin of the Oxford University Institute of Statistics*, 13 (1951)

Lewis, J. P., *Building Cycles and Britain's Growth* (1968)

McHugh, J., 'The Clyde Rent Strike', *Journal of Scottish Labour History*, 12 (1978)

Maiwald, K., 'An Index of Building Costs in the United Kingdom, 1865–1938', *Economic History Review*, 2nd ser., 7 (1954)

Marriner, S., 'Cash and Concrete: Liquidity Problems in the Mass Production of Homes for Heroes', *Business History*, 21 (1979)

'Sir Alfred Mond's Octopus: A Nationalised House-Building Business', *Business History*, 21 (1979)

Melling, J., 'The Glasgow Rent Strike and Clydeside Labour', *Journal of Scottish Labour History Society*, 13 (1979)

'Employers, Industrial Housing and the Evolution of Company Welfare

Policies in Britain's Heavy Industry: West Scotland, 1870–1920', *International Review of Social History*, 26 (1981)

Rent Strikes: People's Struggle for Housing in West Scotland, 1890–1916 (Edinburgh, 1983)

ed., *Housing, Social Policy and the State* (1980)

Merrett, S., *State Housing in Britain* (1979)

Morgan, N. J., and Daunton, M. J., 'Landlords in Glasgow: A Study of 1900', *Business History*, 25 (1983)

Morris, R. J., 'The Middle Class and the Property Cycle during the Industrial Revolution', in T. C. Smout, ed., *The Search for Wealth and Stability* (1979)

'The Middle Class and British Towns and Cities of the Industrial Revolution, 1780–1870', in D. Fraser and A. Sutcliffe, eds., *The Pursuit of Urban History* (1983)

Muthesius, H., *The English House* (Berlin, 1904–5; English edn, 1979)

Muthesius, S., *The English Terraced House* (1982)

Nevitt, A. A., *Housing Taxation and Subsidies: A Study of Housing in the United Kingdom* (1966)

O'Brien, P., and Keyder, C., *Economic Growth in Britain and France, 1780–1914: Two Paths to the Twentieth Century* (Oxford, 1978)

Offer, A., *Property and Politics 1870–1914: Landownership, Law, Ideology and Urban Development in England* (Cambridge, 1981)

Olsen, D. J., *Town Planning in London in the Eighteenth and Nineteenth Centuries* (1964)

The Growth of Victorian London (1976)

The City as a Work of Art: London, Paris, Vienna (1986)

Orbach, L. F., *Homes for Heroes: A Study of the Evolution of British Public Housing, 1915–21* (1977)

Parish, F. W., 'The Economics of Rent Restriction', *Lloyds Bank Review* (1950)

Pollard, S., 'The Factory Village in the Industrial Revolution', *English Historical Review*, 79 (1964)

Powell, C. G., 'Fifty Years of Progress: The Influence of the Tudor Walters Report on British Public Authority Housing', *Built Environment* (1974)

An Economic History of the British Building Industry 1815–1979 (1980)

Price, S. J., *Building Societies: Their Origin and History* (1958)

Pritchard, R. M., *Housing and the Spatial Structure of the City* (Cambridge, 1976)

Ravetz, A., 'From Working-Class Tenement to Modern Flat: Local Authorities and Multi-Storey Housing between the Wars', in A. Sutcliffe, ed., *Multi-Storey Living: The British Working-Class Experience* (1974)

Model Estate: Planned Housing at Quarry Hill, Leeds (1974)

Reeder, D. A., 'The Politics of Urban Leaseholds in Late Victorian Britain', *International Review of Social History*, 6 (1962)

Richardson, H. W., and Aldcroft, D. H., *Building in the British Economy between the Wars* (1968)

Rimmer, W. G., 'Working-Men's Cottages in Leeds, 1770–1840', *Publications of the Thoresby Society*, 46 (1960)

Robb, J. G., 'Suburb and Slum in Gorbals: Social and Residential Change, 1800–1900', in G. Gordon and B. Dicks, eds., *Scottish Urban History* (Aberdeen, 1983)

Roberts, E., 'Working-Class Standards of Living in Barrow and Lancaster, 1890–1914', *Economic History Review*, 2nd ser., 30 (1977)

'Working-Class Housing in Barrow and Lancaster, 1880–1930', *Transactions of the Historic Society of Lancashire and Cheshire for 1977*, 127 (1978)

Rodger, R. G., 'The Law and Urban Change: Some Nineteenth-Century Scottish Evidence', *Urban History Yearbook 1979* (Leicester, 1979)

'Speculative Builders and the Structure of the Scottish Building Industry, 1860–1914', *Business History*, 21 (1979)

'Rents and Ground Rents: Housing and the Land Market in Nineteenth Century Britain', in J. H. Johnson and C. G. Pooley, eds., *The Structure of Nineteenth-Century Cities* (1982)

'The Evolution of Scottish Town Planning', in G. Gordon and B. Dicks, eds., *Scottish Urban History* (Aberdeen, 1983)

'The Invisible Hand: Market Forces, Housing and the Urban Form in Victorian Cities', in D. Fraser and A. Sutcliffe, eds., *The Pursuit of Urban History* (1983)

'The Victorian Building Industry and the Housing of the Scottish Working Class', in M. Doughty, ed., *Building the Industrial City* (Leicester, 1986)

Schifferes, S., 'Council Tenants and Housing Policy in the 1930s: The Contradiction of State Intervention', in Political Economy of Housing Workshop, *Housing and Class in Britain* (1976)

Simpson, M. A., and Lloyd, T. H., eds., *Middle-Class Housing in Britain* (Newton Abbot, 1977)

Singer, H. W., 'An Index of Urban Land Rents and House Rents in England and Wales, 1845–1913', *Econometrica*, 9 (1941)

Smith, R., 'Multi-Dwelling Building in Scotland, 1750–1970: A Study Based on Housing in the Clyde Valley', in A. Sutcliffe, ed., *Multi-Storey Living: The British Working-Class Experience* (1974)

Stedman Jones, G., *Outcast London: A Study in the Relationship between Classes in Victorian Society* (Oxford, 1971)

'Working-Class Culture and Working-Class Politics in London, 1870–1900: Notes on the Remaking of a Working Class', *Journal of Social History*, 7 (1974)

Steffel, R. V., 'The Boundary Street Estate: An Example of Urban Redevelopment by the London County Council, 1889–1914', *Town Planning Review*, 47 (1976)

Summerson, J., *Georgian London* (1945)

Sutcliffe, A., 'Working-Class Housing in Nineteenth-Century Britain', *Bulletin of the Society for the Study of Labour History*, 24 (1972)

ed., *Multi-Storey Living: The British Working-Class Experience* (1974)

Swenarton, M., *Homes Fit for Heroes: The Politics and Architecture of Early State Housing in Britain* (1981)

Swenarton, M., and Taylor, S., 'The Scale and Nature of the Growth of Owner–Occupation in Britain between the Wars', *Economic History Review*, 2nd ser., 38 (1985)

Tarn, J. N., 'The Peabody Donation Fund: The Role of a Housing Society in the Nineteenth Century', *Victorian Studies*, 10 (1966)

'Housing in Liverpool and Glasgow: The Growth of Civic Responsibility', *Town Planning Review*, 39 (1968–9)

Five Per Cent Philanthropy: An Account of Housing in Urban Areas between 1840 and 1914 (Cambridge, 1973)

Taylor, I. C., 'The Court and Cellar Dwelling: The Eighteenth Century Origin of the Liverpool Slum', *Transactions of the Historic Society of Lancashire and Cheshire*, 112 (1970)

'The Insanitary Housing Question and Tenement Dwellings in Nineteenth-Century Liverpool', in A. Sutcliffe, ed., *Multi-Storey Living: The British*

Working-Class Experience (1974)

Treble, J. H., 'Liverpool Working-Class Housing, 1801–51', in S. D. Chapman, ed., *The History of Working-Class Housing* (Newton Abbot, 1971)

Vance, J. E., 'Housing the Worker: The Employment Linkage as a Factor in Urban Structure', *Economic Geography*, 42 (1966)

'Housing the Worker: Determinative and Contingent Ties in 19th-Century Birmingham', *Economic Geography*, 43 (1967)

Weber, B., 'A New Index of House Rents for Great Britain 1874–1913', *Scottish Journal of Political Economy*, 7 (1960)

Wendt, P. F., *Housing Policy. The Search for Solutions: A Comparison of the United Kingdom, Sweden, West Germany and the United States since World War II* (Berkeley and Los Angeles, 1952)

White, J., *Rothschild Buildings: Life in an East End Tenement Block, 1887–1920* (1980)

Wilding, P. R., 'Towards Exchequer Subsidies for Housing, 1906–14', *Social and Economic Administration*, 6 (1972)

'The Administrative Aspects of the 1919 Housing Scheme', *Public Administration*, 51 (1973)

'The Housing and Town Planning Act, 1919: A Study in the Making of Social Policy', *Journal of Social Policy*, 2 (1973)

Wohl, A. S., 'The Housing of the Working-Classes in London, 1815–1914', in S. D. Chapman, ed., *The History of Working-Class Housing* (Newton Abbot, 1971)

The Eternal Slum: Housing and Social Policy in Victorian London (1977)

Worsdall, F., *The Tenement. A Way of Life: A Social, Historical and Architectural Study of Housing in Glasgow* (Glasgow, 1979)

Yelling, J. A., *Slums and Slum Clearance in Victorian London* (1986)

Young, T., *Becontree and Dagenham* (1934)

Youngson, A. J., *The Making of Classical Edinburgh, 1750–1840* (1966)

5 FOOD, DRINK AND NUTRITION

Ashton, T. S., *Economic Fluctuations in England, 1700–1800* (Oxford, 1959)

Barker, T. C., and Drake, M., eds., *Population and Society in Britain 1850–1980* (1982)

Barker, T. C., McKenzie, J. C., and Yudkin, J., eds., *Our Changing Fare* (1966)

Barnett, L. Margaret, *British Food Policy during the First World War* (1985)

Bell, A., *Sydney Smith: A Biography* (Oxford, 1982)

Beveridge, Sir W. H., *British Food Control* (1928)

Burnett, John, *Plenty and Want: A Social History of Diet from 1815 to the Present Day* (1966; revised edn, 1989)

Christian, G., ed., *James Hawker's Journal: A Victorian Poacher* (Oxford, 1978)

Cobbett, William, *Cottage Economy* (1821)

Crawford, William, *The People's Food* (1938)

Curtis-Bennett, Sir N., *The Food of the People: Being the History of Industrial Feeding* (1949)

Davies, David, *The Case of Labourers in Husbandry Stated and Considered* (1795)

Davies, Maud F., *Life in an English Country Village: An Economic and Historical Survey of the Parish of Corsley in Wiltshire* (1909)

Dingle, A. E., 'Drink and Working-Class Living Standards', *Economic History Review*, 2nd ser., 25 (1972)

Drummond, J. C., and Wilbraham, Anne, *The Englishman's Food*, revised edn, ed. Dorothy F. Hollingsworth (1957)

Eden, Frederic M., *The State of the Poor*, 3 vols. (1797)

Ensor, R. C. K., *England 1870–1914* (Oxford, 1936)

Gibson, D., ed., *A Parson in the Vale of White Horse* (Gloucester, 1982)

Hammond, R. J., *History of the Second World War: Food*, 3 vols. (1951–62)

Harrison, B., *Drink and the Victorians* (1971)

Hollingsworth, D. F., 'Rationing and Economic Constraints of Food Consumption since the Second World War', in D. J. Oddy and D. S. Miller, eds., *Diet and Health in Modern Britain* (1985)

Lancet, 'The Diet of Toil', 1 (1895)

McKeown, Thomas, *The Modern Rise of Population* (1976)

Mason, Charlotte, *The Ladies' Assistant*, 6th edn (1787)

Ministry of Education, *The Health of the School Child 1954–55* (1956)

Morris, J. N., 'Coronary Thrombosis: A Modern Epidemic', *Health Education Journal*, 14 (1956)

Oddy, D. J., 'Working-Class Diets in Late Nineteenth-Century Britain', *Economic History Review*, 2nd ser., 23 (1970)

'The Health of the People', in T. C. Barker and M. Drake, eds., *Population and Society in Britain 1850–1980* (1982)

'Urban Famine in Nineteenth-Century Britain: The Effects of the Lancashire Cotton Famine on Working-Class Diet and Health', *Economic History Review*, 2nd ser., 36 (1983)

Oddy, D. J., and Miller, D. S., eds., *The Making of the Modern British Diet* (1976)

Diet and Health in Modern Britain (1985)

Orr, J. B., *Food Health and Income*, 2nd edn (1937)

Pember Reeves, Magdalen S., *Round about a Pound a Week* (1913)

Perren, R., *The Meat Trade in Britain 1840–1914* (1978)

Rowntree, B. S., *Poverty: A Study of Town Life* (1901)

Stead, J., *Food and Cookery in 18th Century Britain: History and Recipes* (1985)

Steven, M., *The Good Scots Diet* (Aberdeen, 1985)

Turner, E. S., *Taking the Cure* (1967)

Woodforde, James, *The Diary of a Country Parson 1758–1802*, ed. John Beresford (Oxford, 1978)

Yudkin, J., ed., *Diet of Man: Needs and Wants* (1978)

6 LEISURE AND CULTURE

Altick, R. D., *The Shows of London* (1978)

Bailey, P., ' ''A Mingled Mass of Perfectly Legitimate Pleasures'': The Victorian Middle Class and the Problem of Leisure', *Victorian Studies*, 21 (1977)

Leisure and Class in Victorian England (1978)

Bailey, P., ed., *Music Hall: The Business of Pleasure* (Milton Keynes, 1986)

Baker, M., *The Rise of the Victorian Actor* (1978)

Bienefeld, M. A., *Working Hours in British Industry* (1972)

Bowen, R., *Cricket: A History of its Growth and Development throughout the World* (1970)

Bratton, J. S., ed., *Music Hall: Performance and Style* (Milton Keynes, 1986)

Briggs, A., *Mass Entertainment* (Adelaide, 1960)

The History of Broadcasting in the United Kingdom, 4 vols. (Oxford, 1961–79)

British Journal of Sports History (1984–   )

Browning, H. E., and Sorrell, A. A., 'Cinemas and Cinema-Going in Great

Britain', *Journal of the Royal Statistical Society*, ser. A, 117 (1954)

Burke, P., 'Popular Culture in Seventeenth-Century London', *London Journal*, 3 (1977)

Carr, R., *English Fox Hunting: A History* (1976)

Cashman, R., and McKernan, M., eds., *Sport: Money, Morality and the Media* (Kensington, N.S.W., n.d. [1980?])

Chalklin, C. W., 'Capital Expenditure on Building for Cultural Purposes in Provincial England, 1730–1830', *Business History*, 22 (1980)

Chorley, K., *Manchester Made Them* (1950)

Clark, P., *The English Alehouse: A Social History 1200–1830* (1983)

Clarke, J., and Critcher, C., *The Devil Makes Work: Leisure in Capitalist Britain* (1985)

Clarke, J., Critcher, C., and Johnson, R., eds., *Working-Class Culture: Studies in History and Theory* (1979)

Clayre, A., *Work and Play* (New York, 1974)

Cunningham, H., *Leisure in the Industrial Revolution c. 1780–1880* (1980)
  'Leisure', in J. Benson, ed., *The Working Class in England 1875–1914* (1985)

Darcy, C. P., *The Encouragement of the Fine Arts in Lancashire 1760–1860* (Manchester, 1976)

Davidoff, L., *The Best Circles: Society, Etiquette and the Season* (1973)

Davies, M. F., *Life in an English Country Village: An Economic and Historical Survey of the Parish of Corsley in Wiltshire* (1909)

Dennis, N., Henriques, F., and Slaughter, C., *Coal Is Our Life: An Analysis of a Yorkshire Mining Community* (1969)

Department of Employment and Productivity, *British Labour Statistics: Historical Abstract 1886–1968* (1971)

Dickens, C., *Sketches by Boz* (1836)

Dunning, E., and Sheard, K., *Barbarians, Gentlemen and Players: A Sociological Study of the Development of Rugby Football* (New York, 1979)

Ehrlich, C., *The Piano: A History* (1976)
  The Music Profession in Britain since the Eighteenth Century: A Social History (Oxford, 1985)

Fraser, W. H., *The Coming of the Mass Market 1850–1914* (1981)

Freeman, A., *Boy Life and Labour* (1914)

Gershuny, J., 'Technical Change and "Social Limits"', in A. Ellis and K. Kumar, eds., *Dilemmas of Liberal Democracies: Studies in Fred Hirsch's 'Social Limits to Growth'* (1983)

Gillis, J., 'The Evolution of Juvenile Delinquency in England 1890–1914', *Past & Present*, 67 (1975)

Giuseppi, J., *The Bank of England: A History from its Foundation in 1694* (1966)

Golby, J. M., and Purdue, A. W., *The Civilisation of the Crowd: Popular Culture in England 1750–1900* (1984)

Gray, R. Q., 'Styles of Life, the "Labour Aristocracy" and Class Relations in Later Nineteenth Century Edinburgh', *International Review of Social History*, 18 (1973)

Haley, B., *The Healthy Body and Victorian Culture* (1978)

Halsey, A. H., ed., *Trends in British Society since 1900* (1972)

Harrison, B., *Drink and the Victorians* (1971)
  Peaceable Kingdom: Stability and Change in Modern Britain (Oxford, 1982)

Harrison, M., 'Art and Philanthropy: T. C. Horsfall and the Manchester Art Museum', in A. J. Kidd and K. W. Roberts, eds., *City, Class and Culture: Studies in Social Policy and Cultural Production in Victorian Manchester* (Manchester, 1985)

Hausmann, W. J., and Hirsch, B. T., 'Wages, Leisure and Productivity in South Wales Coal Mining 1874-1914: An Economic Approach', *Llafur*, 3 (1982)

Hazlitt, W., *Selected Essays*, ed. G. Keynes (1948)

Higgs, E., 'Leisure and the State: The History of Popular Culture as Reflected in the Public Records', *History Workshop*, 15 (1983)

Hobsbawm, E. J., 'Artisan or Labour Aristocrat?', *Economic History Review*, 2nd ser., 37 (1984)

Hoggart, R., *The Uses of Literacy* (Harmondsworth, 1958)

Holt, R., *Sport and the British: A Modern History* (Oxford, 1989)

Hone, W., *The Every-Day Book*, 2 vols. (1878)

Howitt, W., *The Rural Life of England*, 3rd edn (1844)

Huizinga, J., *Homo Ludens: A Study of the Play Element in Culture* (1949)

Hutchison, S. C., *The History of the Royal Academy 1768-1986* (1986)

Itzkowitz, D. C., *Peculiar Privilege: A Social History of English Foxhunting 1753-1885* (Hassocks, 1977)

Jones, G. S., 'Class Expression versus Social Control? A Critique of Recent Trends in the Social History of "Leisure"', *History Workshop*, 4 (1977)

Jones, S. G., 'Trade-Union Policy between the Wars: The Case of Holidays with Pay in Britain', *International Review of Social History*, 31 (1986)

Workers at Play: A Social and Economic History of Leisure 1918-1939 (1986)

'State Intervention in Sport and Leisure in Britain between the Wars', *Journal of Contemporary History*, 22 (1987)

Kelly, T., *A History of Public Libraries in Great Britain 1845-1975* (1977)

Low, R., and Manvell, R., *The History of the British Film*, 5 vols. (1948-79)

Lowerson, J., and Myerscough, J., *Time to Spare in Victorian England* (Hassocks, 1977)

Mackerness, E. D., *A Social History of English Music* (1964)

McKibbin, R., 'Working-Class Gambling in Britain 1880-1939', *Past & Present*, 82 (1979)

'Work and Hobbies in Britain, 1880-1950', in J. Winter, ed., *The Working Class in Modern British History* (Cambridge, 1983)

Malcolmson, R. W., *Popular Recreations in English Society, 1700-1850* (1973)

Mangan, J. A., *Athleticism in the Victorian and Edwardian Public School* (Cambridge, 1981)

Mason, T., *Association Football and English Society, 1863-1915* (Hassocks, 1980)

Mathias, P., 'Leisure and Wages in Theory and Practice', in his *The Transformation of England: Essays in the Economic and Social History of England in the Eighteenth Century* (1979)

Mayhew, H., *London Labour and the London Poor*, 4 vols. (1861-2)

Meller, H. E., *Leisure and the Changing City, 1870-1914* (1976)

Metcalfe, A., 'Organized Sports in the Mining Communities of South Northumberland, 1800-1889', *Victorian Studies*, 25 (1982)

Minihan, J., *The Nationalization of Culture: The Development of State Subsidies to the Arts in Great Britain* (New York, 1977)

Money, J., *Experience and Identity: Birmingham and the West Midlands 1760-1800* (Manchester, 1977)

Munsche, P. B., *Gentlemen and Poachers: The English Game Laws 1671-1831* (Cambridge, 1981)

Myerscough, J., 'The Recent History of the Use of Leisure Time', in I. Appleton, ed., *Leisure Research and Policy* (Edinburgh, 1974)

New Survey of London Life and Labour, 9 (1935)

Pearson, G., *Hooligan: A History of Respectable Fears* (1983)

Pegg, M., *Broadcasting and Society 1918–1939* (1983)

Pimlott, J. A. R., *The Englishman's Holiday: A Social History* (1947)
  The Englishman's Christmas: A Social History (Hassocks, 1978)

Plumb, J. H., *The Commercialisation of Leisure in Eighteenth-Century England* (Reading, 1973)

Reay, B., ed., *Popular Culture in Seventeenth-Century England* (1985)

Reid, D., 'The Decline of Saint Monday, 1766–1876', *Past & Present*, 71 (1976)
  'Popular Theatre in Victorian Birmingham', in D. Bradby, L. James and B. Sharratt, eds., *Performance and Politics in Popular Drama* (Cambridge, 1980)

Revels History of Drama in English, vol. 6: *1750–1880* (1975); vol. 7: *1880 to the Present Day* (1978)

Richards, J., *The Age of the Dream Palace* (1984)

Roberts, R., *The Classic Slum* (Manchester, 1971)

Rosenfeld, S., *The Theatre of the London Fairs in the 18th Century* (Cambridge, 1960)
  Strolling Players and Drama in the Provinces 1660–1765 (New York, 1970)

Rosman, D. M., *Evangelicals and Culture* (1984)

Rowntree, B. S., *Poverty and Progress: A Second Social Survey of York* (1941)

Rowntree, B. S., and Kendall, M., *How the Labourer Lives: A Study of the Rural Labour Problem* (1913)

Rowntree, B. S., and Lavers, G. R., *English Life and Leisure: A Social Study* (1951)

Russell, D., *Popular Music in England, 1840–1914: A Social History* (Manchester, 1987)

Russell, J. F., and Elliot, J. H., *The Brass Band Movement* (1936)

Sanderson, M., *From Irving to Olivier: A Social History of the Acting Profession in England 1880–1983* (1984)

Saxon, A. H., *The Life and Art of Andrew Ducrow and the Romantic Age of the English Circus* (Hamden, Conn., 1978)

Schlicke, P., *Dickens and Popular Entertainment* (1985)

Simpson, A. W. B., *Cannibalism and the Common Law* (Harmondsworth, 1986)

Springhall, J., *Youth, Empire and Society* (1977)

Spring Rice, M., *Working-Class Wives: Their Health and Conditions* (1981)

Stone, R., and Rowe, D. A., *The Measurement of Consumers' Expenditure and Behaviour in the United Kingdom 1920–1938* (Cambridge, 1966)

Storch, R. D., ed., *Popular Culture and Custom in Nineteenth-Century England* (1982)

Strutt, J., *The Sports and Pastimes of the People of England* (1830 edn)

Temperley, N., ed., *The Athlone History of Music in Britain*, vol. 5: *The Romantic Age 1800–1914* (1981)

[Thom, W.], *Pedestrianism* (Aberdeen, 1813)

Thompson, E. P., 'Time, Work-Discipline, and Industrial Capitalism', *Past & Present*, 38 (1967)

Trollope, A., ed., *British Sports and Pastimes* (1868)

Vamplew, W., *The Turf: A Social and Economic History of Horse Racing* (1976)

Veblen, T., *The Theory of the Leisure Class* (New York, 1899)

Walker, H., 'The Popularisation of the Outdoor Movement, 1900–1940', *British Journal of Sports History*, 2 (1985)

Walton, J. K., 'The Demand for Working-Class Seaside Holidays in Victorian

England', *Economic History Review*, 2nd ser., 34 (1981)

The English Seaside Resort: A Social History, 1750–1914 (Leicester, 1983)

Walton, J. K., and Walvin, J., eds., *Leisure in Britain, 1780–1939* (Manchester, 1983)

Walvin, J., *Leisure and Society 1830–1950* (1978)

Ward, C., and Hardy, D., *Goodnight Campers! The History of the British Holiday Camp* (1986)

Warren, A., 'Sir Robert Baden-Powell, the Scout Movement and Citizen Training in Great Britain, 1900–1920', *English Historical Review*, 101 (1986)

Weber, W., *Music and the Middle Class: The Social Structure of Concert Life in London, Paris and Vienna* (1975)

Whitaker, W. B., *Victorian and Edwardian Shopworkers* (Newton Abbot, 1973)

Wild, P., 'Recreation in Rochdale, 1900–40', in J. Clarke, C. Critcher and R. Johnson, eds., *Working-Class Culture: Studies in History and Theory* (1979)

Williams, G., 'From Grand Slam to Great Slump: Economy, Society and Rugby Football in Wales during the Depression', *Welsh History Review*, 11 (1983)

Williams, G., *History of the Liverpool Privateers and Letters of Marque with an Account of the Liverpool Slave Trade* (1966)

Williams, G. A., *The Merthyr Rising* (1978)

Williams, G. P., and Brake, G. T., *Drink in Great Britain 1900 to 1979* (1980)

Wilson, G. B., *Alcohol and the Nation* (1940)

Yeo, E. and S., eds., *Popular Culture and Class Conflict, 1590–1914: Explorations in the History of Labour and Leisure* (Brighton, 1981)

Index